1848.

1848.

HISTORICAL REVELATIONS:

inscribed to LORD NORMANBY

by

LOUIS BLANC

NEW YORK:

HOWARD FERTIG

1971

First published in English in 1858
by Chapman and Hall, London

Howard Fertig, Inc. Edition 1971

Library of Congress Catalog Card Number: 71-85079

PRINTED IN THE UNITED STATES OF AMERICA
BY NOBLE OFFSET PRINTERS, INC.

233/77

PREFACE.*

IT will ever be to the glory of England, that, in the middle of the nineteenth century, she should have been the only impregnable asylum, in Europe, for the exile driven from his country by absolutism or usurpation. The indomitable energy with which the English people have maintained the right of asylum is the more honourable, as they do not espouse the opinions of those they harbour, nor think either of countenancing their views or encouraging their hopes. How imposing the spectacle of a nation, whose genius is so eminently practical, running the risk of war rather than condescend to the ignoble task of hunting down the homeless!

And not only is England a safe place of refuge for

---

* Since this preface was written, I grieve to say that the British Government has instituted, under manifest pressure, political prosecutions, which are looked upon with alarm by all enlightened friends of Liberty. Still, as I believe that these prosecutions will be condemned by juries and rebuked by public opinion in this country, I suffer what I have written to stand, and I confidently hope I shall have nothing hereafter to retract.

every foreigner who, in his native land, has fallen a victim to civil discords, but she is, in fact, the last sanctuary, in Europe, open to the human mind itself.

That Louis Bonaparte and other Continental despots should stand in fear of plots and conspiracies, is natural enough ; but it is not these that are their worst terrors. What really alarms and exasperates them, is the mere idea that there is in Europe a place where their adversaries are enabled to speak out. The conspiracy that makes them inwardly tremble is that of human thought. They know that all their armies and all their treasures are powerless against that unrelenting enemy of despotism—free speech.

The attempt by Louis Bonaparte to make political capital out of assassination, and to turn Italian vengeance into a pretext for tightening his deadly grasp upon France—the finishing blow struck at the press— the obliteration of the last remaining vestiges of personal liberty—the retrospective scheme of persecution aimed at men already persecuted—the mockery of compelling universal suffrage to swear fealty for ever to the Empire, by one who boasts of being emperor through universal suffrage *—the recent division of the whole

* Everyone knows that it has been recently proposed that no candidate for a seat in the legislative body should be permitted to offer himself to the electors without swearing allegiance to the Imperial dynasty, which is radically inconsistent with the principle of universal suffrage, and a satire upon the sovereignty of the people, from which the Empire professes to derive.

country into five great military districts — Belgium, Piedmont, and Switzerland, placed under coercion, and the savage crusade preached against a handful of exiles —are even more than the necessary development of that war to the knife which Louis Bonaparte is doomed to wage against unfettered thought; they are a demonstration never to be forgotten, and a desperate confession, of his impotence. He feels that some five or six harmless refugees having nothing left on earth but their pens, and freely writing in a London garret what they hold to be true, are more powerful than he is at the head of four hundred thousand soldiers; for he fears them, and they fear him not.

Nor is it possible for him to halt in his destined track. A sinister logic goads him unmercifully on, and he cannot help going all the lengths of tyranny— servant of the very soldiers he commands, and, while striking terror into others, struck with a worse terror himself.

England, therefore, cannot expect to be pardoned by Louis Bonaparte, whatever may be her policy towards the refugees, as long as she shares their guilt, by asserting the right of free speech.

Fortunately, she is strong enough to hold that sacred right against all comers.

Meanwhile, it is no small honour to her that her language should be, at this moment, the vernacular of

Liberty; the only language in which freemen of every
nation can interchange ideas, and print their thoughts
with any chance of finding a public allowed to read
them.

These are the reasons why I publish this book in
English and in England.

No period in history having been so deplorably
misrepresented as the Revolution of February, 1848,
more especially in this country, it was my intention to
avail myself of the earliest opportunity to dispel the
clouds which hang over that great event. The opportunity I was looking for, has just been afforded me
by Lord Normanby's book, A YEAR OF REVOLUTION
IN PARIS.

When the Revolution of February broke out, Lord
Normanby was in Paris, where he had been sent for
the special purpose of closely watching the movements
of French society. Under his eye did those prodigious
events take place, which made the heart of every oppressed nation throb with hope and joy. All around him
did the air reverberate with shouts of patriotic enthusiasm, which were re-echoed from one end of the world
to the other. No very strict investigation was required
to be apprised of what was thundered out in each
street, of what was done in the *Forum* by the whole
people. Yet, strange to say, Lord Normanby seems
to have seen nothing, to have heard nothing, to have

known nothing. The spectacle proved, evidently, too grand for the spectator.

The small talk and the second-hand calumnies which his lordship has given to the public in the shape of historical records, are by no means of a nature to call forth a minute or even a serious refutation. Can any reflecting mind lay stress upon a book which is a one-sided register of idle rumours and unsifted reports?

But, unluckily, it is no easy matter for the public at large to conceive how a man of high station, who was some time the representative of a great nation abroad, an ambassador of England, could have ventured to publish a work teeming with errors about events which he was so well situated to ascertain. From the very name of Lord Normanby, and also from the position he held in France, it is natural enough to infer that he must have known something of what he relates. Here is the danger.

I take it, therefore, to be necessary to show, by opposing undeniable testimonies and documents to unsupported assertions, how little Lord Normanby is to be trusted, either in his statement of facts or his delineation of characters.

Not that I intend to publish a merely polemical work, far from it! To point out in any other way than *en passant* the numerous and really amazing errors the noble marquis seems to have fondly cherished, would be to attach to his book a degree of importance it does not deserve. I will avail myself of its appearance, only as affording me an opportunity for sketching, in their historical connection and succession, the striking and unexampled scenes I was called upon to take part in; leaving others to expose, as far as they are individually concerned, his lordship's blunders and misrepresentations, but making it a point to repel, with the authority of one who was personally involved in the events, such false imputations as cast a blemish upon the cause I serve, or strike at the honour of my country.

ERRATA.

Page 290, *for* "working men" *read* "leading men."
Pages 20, 29, 30, 152, 189, *dele the notes* "See Appendix," &c.

CONTENTS.

CHAPTER I.

HOW THE PROVISIONAL GOVERNMENT WAS ESTABLISHED.

Page

CHAPTER II.

THE REPUBLIC PROCLAIMED.

CHAPTER III.

THE REPUBLIC UNIVERSALLY ACKNOWLEDGED.

CHAPTER IV.

GENEROUS CHARACTER OF THE REVOLUTION OF FEBRUARY.

CHAPTER V.

THE "DROIT AU TRAVAIL."

CHAPTER VI.

THE LUXEMBOURG—SOCIALISM IN THEORY.

CHAPTER VII.

THE LUXEMBOURG—SOCIALISM IN PRACTICE.

CHAPTER VIII.

CHAPTER IX.

CHAPTER X.

CHAPTER XI.

CHAPTER XII.

REVOLUTION IN TRAVAIL.

CHAPTER XIII.

SOLEMN MARCH THROUGH PARIS.

CHAPTER XIV.

THE ALARUM.

CHAPTER XV.

CALUMNIES.

CHAPTER XVI.

THE ELECTIONS.

CHAPTER XVII.

INVASION OF THE NATIONAL ASSEMBLY.

CHAPTER XVIII.

LOUIS BONAPARTE'S PROSCRIPTION CANCELLED.

CHAPTER XIX.

THE INSURRECTION OF HUNGER !

CHAPTER XX.

OSTRACISM.

CHAPTER XXI.

PERSONAL INTERCOURSE WITH LOUIS BONAPARTE. -

CONCLUSION.

1848.

HISTORICAL REVELATIONS.

CHAPTER I.

HOW THE PROVISIONAL GOVERNMENT WAS ESTABLISHED.

Louis Philippe was a prince gifted with many good qualities. His domestic virtues were such as to command respect. He was by no means wanting in enlightened perceptions. Both from a disposition naturally merciful, and from a philosophical notion of the value of human life, he was so averse to shedding blood, that his ministers were sure to meet with an almost desperate resistance on his part, whenever they asked him to affix his signature to a sentence of death. Upon the whole, he was a man of remarkably sober character. Nor did Liberty, under his reign, receive any mortal wound. In times of foreign and internal difficulties, he succeeded in warding off imminent dangers, and the middle classes were indebted to him for the repose they so dearly prized.

Still, when the hour of his doom struck, no wish was expressed for his crown's preservation; no helping hand was held out to him; the moneyed classes kept aloof; the soldiers either refused to fight or fought reluctantly; for the first time, the shopkeepers seemed to have forgotten that revolutions are bad for trade; the most active part of the National Guard actually countenanced the insurrection; the old King, looking around him, and seeing nothing but a dreary solitude, became disheartened, and a government which had lasted no less than seventeen years was overthrown by a touch.

How is such a phenomenon to be accounted for? In my " History of Ten Years," the reader will find the causes explained and the result foretold. Of these causes, the most effective lay in Louis Philippe's utter inability to comprehend all that there was of chivalrous and elevated in the genius of France. To the meaner principles of action he applied for support. Bribery was his principal engine of government. He fostered the blind fears of the *bourgeoisie*, and took pleasure in nursing selfishness. His policy was systematically inimical to anything like a generous hope or a noble impulse. Not only did he struggle against all efforts originating in the spirit of improvement, but it was his constant endeavour to make the nation, if possible, after his own image; that is, greedy of gain, true only to the debasing worship of the cash-box, heedless of the past, and faithless in the future. Even what happened to be good in his policy was done through objectionable means, and everyone knows that it was only by wounding beyond measure in the heart of the French the feeling of national self-importance, that he succeeded in averting the calamities of war. So completely had he stifled around him all promptings of devotedness and disinterested attachment, that these supreme resources proved wanting when needed; so that he may verily be said to have been the sole artificer of his own ruin.

The fact is, that, two months before the downfall of Louis Philippe, it had become quite certain that the Democratic party was about to appear, in its turn, on the public stage, and to take possession of it exclusively.

This was made obvious by the " *banquet de Dijon*," whose news spread all over France with the rapidity of lightning. There, in an immense hall, decorated with flags and devices symbolic of liberty, in the presence of thirteen hundred guests—operatives, manufacturers, tradesmen, magistrates—words reverberated; which M. de Lamartine, seized with short-sighted terror, termed the "tocsin of opinion." At Lille, M. Ledru Rollin had previously said:

" Sometimes, the stagnant pools of the dried-up Nile, and the detritus in a state of decomposition on its banks, engender epidemics; but let the flood return, the river, in its impetuous course, will sweep away all these impurities, and will deposit on its borders germs of fecundity and re-awakened life." *

These audacious allusions were repeated by MM. Ledru Rollin and Flocon at the " *banquet de Dijon* " without exciting surprise, so thoroughly was the idea of an impending revolution present to every mind. And, for the same reason, no one took exception to this passage of my speech—prophecy and menace:

* *Compte-rendu du banquet de Lille.*

" The power which but yesterday seemed so vigorous, sinks under its own weight, without even being pushed. An invisible will goes on its way through the highest regions of society, sowing degrading catastrophes. Unexpected acts of insanity, shameful disasters, unaccountable suicides, crimes to make the hair stand on end, come, one after another, stunning public opinion into stupor. Then, that Society, apparently so prosperous, becomes agitated ; it wonders at the mysterious virus which it feels running through its veins. ' *Corruption* ' is the cry of the day ; and everyone exclaims : ' That such things should last any longer, is impossible ; what will to-morrow bring ? ' Gentlemen, when the fruit is rotten, it only needs a breath of wind to shake it from the tree."

This was said towards the end of December ; and at the end of February, hardly two months after, the blast had come which blew down the monarchy.

The circumstances connected with the downfall of Louis Philippe being generally known, I will enter at once upon my subject by explaining how the Provisional Government was established.

At that period, the Republican party, numerically inferior in the provinces, was prevalent in Paris. Its accredited organs were the *National* and the *Réforme* ; the latter paper being more acceptable to the workmen, on account of its social tendencies, whilst the other, merely political, had a stronger hold on the middle classes. M. Marrast was the editor of the *National*. The *Réforme* was edited by M. Flocon, and superintended by a committee, the members of which were

MM. Ledru Rollin, Schælcher, Guinard, Pascal Duprat, Ribeyrolles, and myself.

My most dear and most lamented friend, Godefroy Cavaignac, had belonged to that committee, but he was dead when the Revolution of February broke out : a loss which was considered by us all as a national calamity. For he was a man of vast acquirements and sound parts, endowed with indomitable courage, and far superior in every respect to General Cavaignac, his brother. Had he lived longer, there is no doubt whatever that he would have been one of the Provisional Government, wherein his presence might have turned the scale in favour of a true Republic.

This loss, however, great as it was, did not so impair the republican party as to prevent its growing from day to day more powerful. Unfortunately, at the end of January, 1848, the disagreement between the *Réforme* and the *National* happened to swell into embittered polemics ; so that, on the break out of the Revolution, the republicans might have failed to remain masters of the field, had not the necessity of acting in common been felt on both sides. I was, therefore, appointed by the *Réforme*, on the 24th of February, to negotiate a reconciliation, M. Martin (de Strasbourg), a distinguished barrister, having been chosen by the *National* to the same effect.

The situation was one of extraordinary enthusiasm mingled with dangerous excitement. The passions let loose by the struggle were still burning. The aspect of Paris was terrible. Here and there infuriated groups were seen emerging from behind the barricades, boastful of the blood which stained their dress, flourishing muskets, swords, hatchets or pikes, and shouting fiercely: *À bas les Bourbons !* The palace of the Tuileries had just been invaded, amidst an unparalleled tempest formed by the threatening clamours of the combatants, the uproar of the rushing multitudes, the beating of drums, the shots incessantly fired, the fits of laughing and the loud jests in which, on any such occasion, the *gamins de Paris* are wont to indulge. As to the particulars which marked the invasion of the royal abode, I know nothing more than what any one could, at the time, pick up from flying reports. But it is a matter of public notoriety that some sat down at card-tables and began in joke to bet the millions of the Civil list; that many a jolly fellow delighted in putting on the rich velvet dressing gowns which had been worn by princely personages; that two insurgents whose firelocks lay beside them on the ground, were noticed playing at chess with a fixed look and uninterrupted attention, despite the deafening turmoil. "Marquis," asked a facetious companion to a youth who held in his hands a plan of Neuilly, "what are you about?" "Viscount," replied the lad, "I am examining the plan of my estates." By superficial minds, these apparently trifling incidents may be deemed to have no other import than to show the levity so complacently ascribed to the French. But those who do not judge of the inside by the outside will easily perceive through all this the deep-rooted love of equality which is the true characteristic of the French nation.

Under such circumstances, M. Martin (de Strasbourg)

and I concurred in thinking that this was not the proper time for handling the abstruse questions which the Revolution was likely to start. The main point was to insure the triumph of the Republic by baffling the intrigues of petty parliamentary coteries on one hand, and by preventing, on the other, the wild confusion into which the general rush towards the unknown could not fail to plunge everything, in the absence of all regular direction. Two great evils were to be averted : despotism and anarchy, for anarchy is nothing better than a tumultuous despotism. An immediate selection of united leaders was therefore required; and although the republicanism of M. de Lamartine, a new convert, seemed somewhat unsteady; although rumours had already become current about the support which M. Garnier Pagès might possibly be disposed to give to the Regency of the Duchess of Orléans, the influence of such men over the middle classes certainly deserved to be taken into serious consideration. Subsequent events have shown, indeed, that alliances of this kind are fraught with impediments and perils. But it must be borne in mind that the republican party, however strong in Paris, was far from being able to get the mastery in the provinces. The middle classes contained a considerable number of republicans, sincere though timid, whom it was impolitic to frighten out of our ranks. Moreover, the situation was dreadfully unsettled, and the morrow overcast with clouds. To bring a man like M. de Lamartine to commit himself irrevocably in the service of the Republic was considered a stroke of sound policy, and even now, I do not think the step we took would have proved a fatal one, had it not been made so by an astounding concurrence of unfavourable circumstances, which it was then impossible for any one to foresee.

So, it was determined that M. de Lamartine should rank with the republican leaders.

The exertions of M. Martin (de Strasbourg) and my own having been attended with full success, the two leading papers of the republican party came to an understanding, the result of which was the adoption in common of a list to be presented to the people.

It is singular—and this is one of the most peculiar features of the Parisians—how an intuitive perception of the necessity of order combines in their character with occasional outbursts of turbulence. One may think it wonderful, still it is perfectly true, that Paris never witnessed a rising in which the insurgents did not preserve, all through, a sense of discipline, and an almost uneasy preoccupation of the immediate consequences. In June, for instance, in those formidable days of June, the fact was ascertained that the insurgents, while fighting desperately, were busy writing down, on the very stones of the barricades stained with their blood, the names of a Provisional Government.

So, on the 24th of February, scarcely was the fight at an end, when the people flocked from every quarter to the offices of both Republican papers, in quest of a central direction.

An immense crowd surrounded the office of the *Réforme*, the smallest part of which was pent up to suffocation in the court of the Hôtel Bullion, while the rest overflowed the neighbouring streets, and more especially the street of Jean Jacques Rousseau. A sort of considerate anxiety was visible in everyone's countenance. The only shout sent forth was *Vive la République !*—a shout which grew tremendous, but gradually dwindled into solemn silence, when I made my appearance at a window, holding a paper in my hand. Then it was that I read the following list, which had been agreed to by the *Réforme* and the *National :*—

DUPONT (DE L'EURE).	ARMAND MARRAST.
FRANÇOIS ARAGO.	CRÉMIEUX.
LEDRU ROLLIN.	GARNIER PAGÈS.
FLOCON.	LAMARTINE.
MARIE.	LOUIS BLANC.

The utterance of these names was hailed with loud acclamations, quickly succeeded by a general cry: *Albert ! Albert !*

Albert had never been considered as a political leader. Still less had he ever entertained any hope or desire of being chosen as such. He was a mechanic. Amongst us, he was but little known personally. For my part, I had never seen him. But his uprightness, both of heart and mind, his unbounded devotion to the cause of the people, the disinterested fervour of his convictions, his unassuming manners, his courage, had endeared him to the workmen. To them the presence of a man of that stamp in the Provisional Government was a token that no measure would be taken without being anxiously scrutinised, and, if prejudicial to their interests, strenuously opposed. Moreover, what could be better calculated to mark the commencement of a new era—what could inaugurate in a more striking way the official acknowledgment of the rights of labour, than this previously unheard-of rising of a workman to a post of the highest eminence? I took up a pen; I wrote down the name of Albert with a feeling of deep emotion, and, hastening to the office of the *National,* I had there no difficulty in getting the name added to the list, which was immediately circulated all over Paris, and happened, as regards the other names, to agree with those which emanated from every other popular centre of action, save that on some the name of M. Recurt, afterwards Minister of the Interior, and very popular then in the Faubourg St. Antoine, figured in the place of the names of Crémieux or Garnier Pagès.

On my returning to the office of the *Réforme,* I found the same crowd still remaining, and quite in a fit of indignation, as intelligence had been brought that, in the Chamber of Deputies, the partisans of the Regency were claiming for the child of the Duchess of Orleans that throne which the flight of Louis Philippe had left empty, and which, carried away from the palace of the Tuileries, was, just at that moment, triumphantly paraded about by some of the insurgents.

They cried out, " The Chamber of Deputies has no longer any legal power. It belonged to that system of corruption and national debasement we have pulled to pieces. Must so much blood have been shed in vain? Are we to submit anew to the worn-out monarchical yoke? *À bas la Régence! À bas les Corrompus!* " *Les Corrompus!* Such was, under the rule of Louis Philippe, the popular designation of the Chamber of Deputies.

Whereupon, some made their way to the Palais Bourbon, with a view to put an end to any further discussion of the pretended rights of the Duchess of Orleans, whilst the other hurried away M. Flocon and myself to the Hôtel de Ville.

As I did not attend the sitting of the Chamber of Deputies on the 24th of February, I will not stop to give a circumstantial account of what took place there· But this much I will say, there being no discrepancy on these points between the various testimonies :—

That there was hardly a semblance of regular discussion at the Palais Bourbon ;

That the deputies soon showed themselves conscious of their disqualification for settling the nation, which M. de la Rochejaquelein stated in this most impressive manner : " *To-day, Gentlemen, you are nothing ;* "

That, despite the presence, and the dignified, touching attitude of the Duchess of Orleans, who stood there, holding her two children by the hand, the efforts of MM. Dupin, Sauzet, and Odilon Barrot in her favour, proved miserably abortive ;

That the true situation could not be more accurately described than in the words of M. Thiers, when rushing on a sudden into the house, his face pale, his coat all in rags, he exclaimed : " *Gentlemen, the tide is coming in ! The tide is coming in !* "

In fine, that the Chamber of Deputies, *as such,* arrived at no conclusion whatever.

For, the moment anything like a decision was taken, the Chamber of Deputies had ceased to exist, even materially, so to speak ; armed bands had tumultuously invaded the hall; M. Sauzet, the President, had disappeared like a phantom; most of the deputies, struck with terror, had stolen away; the Duchess of Orleans, no longer able to face the storm, had been respectfully compelled to retire; and the tribune was occupied by Captain Dunoyer, who, waving the tricolor flag with one handa nd brandishing his sabre with the other, had already proclaimed the sovereignty of the people. Well might then M. Ledru Rollin say: " What we want is a Provisional Government elected by the people—*not by the Chamber.*"

Now, let it be remembered, that M. de Lamartine had hitherto refrained from expressing any opinion whatever, as if on the look-out to ascertain the direction of the wind. He did not make up his mind to support the proposition of a Provisional Government before it became obvious that it was much more advisable to follow than to stem the torrent. Nor was it by him that the list was read, which contained the names of Dupont (de l'Eure), Lamartine, Ledru Rollin, Marie, Garnier Pagès, Crémieux.*

Here I will pause to point out one of the innumerable and really surprising misstatements of Lord Normanby. His lordship says:

"The names written down by Lamartine could not be heard when read from the President's chair by poor old Dupont (de l'Eure). He transferred the list to the

---

* See, about the sitting of the 24th of February, the *Moniteur*, the "History of the Revolution of February," by M. Robin, the "History of the Revolution of February," by M. Delvau, and the very clever work published on the same subject by Countess d'Agoult, under the name of Daniel Stern.

person standing next to him, who, having a weak voice, was equally inaudible. As it was important no time should be lost, these names were then given to M. Crémieux, who has the lungs of Stentor, and he added his own name, which was, amidst all the confusion, adopted with the others." *

Lord Normanby wrote this on the 26th of February, so it appears from his own book. Well, on the 26th of February, the account of the *Moniteur* was in the hands of every human being in Paris,—with the exception of Lord Normanby, it must be presumed—and there was not even a *concierge* in Paris who did not know what the ambassador of England was ignorant of, namely, that the list proposed at the Palais Bourbon on the 24th of February, had been read by Ledru Rollin, and not by M. Crémieux, who has by no means *the lungs of Stentor*, and was not, at all events, entitled on that score to serve as a speaking-trumpet.

True it is, however, that the names were read amidst such confusion as to render the adoption of them a matter of doubt. At any rate, the list met with a strong opposition, as far as the names of MM. Marie and Garnier Pagès were concerned.†

From these uncontradicted facts two consequences may be inferred.

First, the list of the Palais Bourbon was of no more value, in a parliamentary sense, than that which the people adopted at the offices of the *Réforme* and the *National*.

* " A Year of Revolution in Paris," vol. i., p. 129.
† See the *Moniteur* and the above-mentioned books.

In the second place, M. de Lamartine must have been under the impression of a strangely delusive dream, when he went so far as to write : " Lamartine had only to drop a word to get the Regency immediately proclaimed. He had only to say to the duchess and her sons, rise ! " * How prodigious the deceptions incident to self-admiring genius ! The truth is, that, in the triumphal pomp of the Republic, the poet who had burnt so much incense on the altars of kingship, was dragged among the vanquished, and it was for no other purpose than better to exhibit as a public spectacle that illustrious captive, that the Republic allowed him to sit behind her on the car of triumph.

The Hôtel de Ville having been made, in Paris, the appointed place for the consecration of all revolutionary powers, as Rheims was once the appointed town for the coronation of kings, MM. de Lamartine, Ledru Rollin, and the others did not fail to go thither, and they had already reached the traditional spot, when I arrived there with M. Flocon.

There was something fearful to behold in the display of the revolutionary power around the Hôtel de Ville. The Grêve was so overcrowded, that it would have been utterly impossible for us to get through, had not the general and spontaneous acceptance of the list emanating from the united republican papers invested our names with a sort of magical power. Not only did the crowd open as we went on, but it so happened that some robust workmen, fearing lest I should be crushed,

* Histoire de la Révolution de 1848, par A. de Lamartine, vol. i., p. 132. Brussels, 1849.

on account of my diminutive stature, lifted me up and
carried me on their shoulders to the Hôtel de Ville,
crying out, "Make room for a member of the Provisional Government to pass!" Thus I was enabled
to reach the staircase, which overflowed with rolling
waves of men, divided into two opposite streams. For
an uninterrupted communication had been established,
and was kept up between a great popular meeting held
in the Salle Saint Jean, and the multitude out of doors,
so that the decisions taken by the meeting could be
made instantly known to the whole mass of the people,
the only possible way of imparting to such decisions
some character of regularity.

A sense of decorum, hardly credible under such
circumstances, prevailed in the Salle Saint Jean,
despite occasional bursts of indignation or enthusiasm.
But outside, all along the lobbies and in the courts of
the Hôtel de Ville, there was, of course, a Babel of
uproar and conflicting clamours. Some shouted incessantly, *Vive la République!* Others, with a most
extraordinary mixture of candid enthusiasm and
menacing frenzy, chanted the *Marseillaise.* The
courts, encumbered with horses riderless, wounded
men lying on straw, half-distracted lookers-on ; wild
speakers, soldiers in rags, and workmen waving flags,
presented the threefold sight of a field hospital, a field
of battle, and a camp.

It was growing dark. I was shown into the Salle
Saint Jean, whither all the members of the Provisional
Government had to repair, in order to declare their
principles, and to have their election sanctioned by

popular suffrage, if found worthy of the trust committed to them.

On entering the hall, I learnt that the necessary trial had just been undergone by MM. Ledru Rollin, Garnier Pagès, Dupont (de l'Eure), Arago, and Lamartine.

M. Ledru Rollin, on being asked whether he thought he held his powers from the Chamber of Deputies, answered peremptorily in the negative, and his speech was hailed with repeated cheers.

M. Garnier Pagès met with a somewhat different reception, owing to the fact that he was supposed to lean to the side of the Regency.   Nevertheless, he was elected Mayor of Paris, but it remained doubtful whether his name ought to be struck out from the popular list as a member of the Provisional Government.

Out of regard for the advanced age of Dupont (de l'Eure), for his unequalled probity and his well-known adherence to republican principles, the meeting would relieve him from making any declaration of opinions.   The venerable old man insisted on doing so, through a lively perception of what he considered to be a duty.   But he could only utter a few words.   Overpowered by emotion, and physical fatigue, he turned pale, almost fainted, and was helped out amidst the most touching marks of universal concern.

The health of M. François Arago had been seriously impaired for months.   He had no speech to deliver and was allowed to withdraw, after a very short appearance.

It was now for M. de Lamartine to come to a decisive conclusion.   Strikingly cautious and involved was his

exordium. He said that the question to be solved was
one of paramount importance, one which the nation
would naturally be called upon to examine, and which
he, Lamartine, did not mean to prejudge. These words
gave rise to a violent tumult. A tremendous shout of
Vive la République! shook the walls of the building.
Laviron, the same undaunted man who afterwards was
killed on the walls of Rome, whilst fighting for the
Roman Republic, protested in a most spirited manner
against any attempt to cheat the people of what they had
so dearly paid for. The warning was clear enough.
M. de Lamartine resumed his speech, but he took great
care to deviate by degrees from the path he had got into,
and he concluded by declaring for the Republican form
of Government, whereupon he was warmly applauded.

Such are the circumstances with which I was made
acquainted by several members of the meeting, and
M. de Lamartine had just left the hall, when I came in.
I wore the uniform, once unpopular, of a National
Guard; but the National Guards having now, not only
refrained from resisting, but openly countenanced the
insurrection, their uniform was sure to be welcome.
Dusk had given way to night, and the armed Areopagus
stood haughty and stern in the mingled light of tapers
and torches reflected from a forest of guns.

It has always been my opinion that the Republican
form of Government is not the sole object to be aimed
at, even by the politicians of the Republican school, if
their love for the commonwealth be sincere and disinterested. For there is no form of government which
may not be used as a weapon against the interests of

the community.   How often did the name of REPUBLIC
serve only to mask oppression and to gild tyranny!
On the 24th of February, I could certainly not foresee
that, under the Republican form of Government, the
blood of the people would be poured forth in torrents;
that General Cavaignac, a republican, would order the
transportation sans jugement et en masse, and would
allow Paris to be a prey to all the horrors of a savage
resentment; that Louis Bonaparte, the president of the
French Republic, would send soldiers to Rome, there
to crush the Roman Republic. No such things could
be anticipated. But to me the history of the past was
a sufficient testimony. I believed then, as I do now,
that the chief object to be aimed at is to make him
that works enjoy the fruits of his work, to restore to
the dignity of human nature those whom the excess of
poverty degrades; to enlighten those whose intelligence,
from want of education, is but a dim vacillating lamp
in the midst of darkness; in one word to enfranchise
the people, by endeavouring to abolish this double
slavery;—ignorance and misery! A very arduous task,
indeed, whose accomplishment requires much study on
the part of the leaders, much wisdom and power of
endurance on the part of the people; a task which
cannot possibly be performed except by a slow, gradual
progress, but which it is the right and the lot of every
generous mind to contemplate.

These were the principles I laid down.   M. Flocon
made a speech to the same effect.   We said we were
confident that Albert, whom we had not yet seen,
would give us an effective support in the Provisional

Government. *Vive la République sociale!* shouted the Assembly. A workman rose, who in plain, straightforward language, congratulated us on having set the question in its proper light, and our election was confirmed by loud acclamations.

To avoid being disturbed by the still raging tempest, MM. Dupont (de l'Eure), Arago, Lamartine, and Ledru Rollin, had retired to a remote room, where MM. Marie, Garnier Pagès, Marrast and Crémieux, hastened to join them, and it was not without difficulty that we succeeded in finding them out, through the winding passages of the Hôtel de Ville. Some five or six pupils of the Polytechnic School, sword in hand, kept sentry at the door. They presented arms to us, and we entered the sanctuary.

The scene was one deserving of notice : M. de Lamartine looked radiant, M. Ledru Rollin resolute, M. Crémieux excited, M. Marie suspicious and gloomy. The face of M. Dupont (de l'Eure) betrayed a feeling of noble resignation. M. Marrast had on his lips his usual inquisitive smile. M. Garnier Pagès seemed rather out of countenance. As to M. Arago, how uneasy he was! How different from himself! Had not his declining health accounted for his depression of spirits, the change would have been inconceivable. He had been an intimate friend of mine for about six years; far from objecting to my political views, he was known to be one of my warmest eulogists ; more than once, before taking a decisive step, he had condescended to ask my advice, with a degree of confidence of a nature to put me to embarrassment, as I felt it was not for me to

counsel a man so much older than I was. How he
happened to alter his mind in the space of a few hours
is more than I can make out. Certain it is that, on
the 24th of February, as soon as he saw me, he became
disconcerted, and began to question the validity of those
elections which had not been carried at the Palais
Bourbon. I need not say that the matter dropt immediately. "Come! Come!" exclaimed M. Garnier
Pagès, "the Provisional Government must of necessity
be divided into various departments. It cannot do without good penmen;" and, pointing to MM. Marrast,
Flocon, and myself, he dropt in his familiar, easy way
the word *Secretaries*. We attached no importance
whatever to the designation, which seemed to refer only
to our professional habits. Nor was it the proper time
for clinging to petty personal pretensions and disputing
about trifles, when we had to look to public interests,
in a most formidable emergency. The main point was,
that our opinion should fall into the scale with its full
weight, and such was the case. From the very moment
anything came under deliberation, all of us were
called upon to decide, on a footing of perfect equality.
It must even be remarked, as will be seen in the subsequent chapter, that the three persons who, in the
evening of the 24th of February, set on the Council to
pledge themselves to the service of the Republic *officially
and irrevocably,* were M. Ledru Rollin, M. Flocon, and
myself.

Now, let the reader glance at the *Fac Simile* * of the
first proclamation signed by the Provisional Govern-

* See the Appendix No. 1.

ment; he will find that my signature, as affixed to the original document, is followed by no such designation as that of secretary, which was added, I know not by whom, in the printed copy of the *Moniteur*.

Be this as it may, the decrees which appeared in the *Moniteur* of the 25th of February, led the public naturally to think that the position of MM. Marrast, Flocon, Louis Blanc, and Albert, was one of a subordinate character. The fact was viewed in the light of a manœuvre by the most ardent Republicans. The workmen grew indignant at the supposition that their will, so clearly expressed, had been disregarded, and that underhand attempts were already made to weaken the influence of those by whom they thought their cause was more especially represented. The consequences might have been terrible. Everyone, in the Provisional Government, became sensible of the danger: so, "the adjunct of secretaries," the very moment it appeared in the *Moniteur*, that is, in the morning of the 25th, hardly a few hours after the Provisional Government had met for the first time, was put aside, without discussion, without even a word uttered on the subject, and quite as a matter of course. Nor was it ever again employed in any document or publication issued by the Provisional Government since their first hurried meeting.

This is my answer to the question put by Lord Normanby to M. de Lamartine, on the 13th of March: " How the original government of *seven* had become *eleven* ? "*

* " A Year of Revolution in Paris," vol. i., p. 223.

And what was, according to Lord Normanby's own statement, the answer of M. de Lamartine?

"M. de Lamartine said that was a question he could not answer precisely. The four others had been named secretaries, and as such had signed the decrees near the bottom of the page; that little by little they crept up and mixed themselves with the others; the adjunct of secretaries was then omitted, and they came to have a consultative voice with those first named." To which the Marquis of Normanby adds the reflection: "This certainly is a most original specimen of popular choice."

I beg your pardon, my Lord. This certainly is a most original specimen of gross misstatement, nothing more. That M. de Lamartine should have ventured to say, and Lord Normanby to repeat, that the "four others crept up little by little and mixed themselves with the others," is to me a matter of inexpressible astonishment. Should any one, among the readers of these pages, be anxious to know how boldly history can be falsified by official personages, I request him, the first time he goes to the British Museum, to ask for the *Moniteur* (Feb. 1848). There he will see that the decrees published in the *Moniteur* of the 26th, and consequently signed on the 25th, that is on the very morrow of the formation of the Provisional Government, which took place on the 24th, late in the evening, were all signed, not as secretaries but as members of the said government, by "the four others," whom it is, therefore, an inconceivable error to represent "creeping up little by little."

Nor is it less curious to observe that, *as early as the 27th*, the name of Albert, one of those who "*crept up little by little*," figured, for a special purpose, and—mark it well—at the very request of the "seven others," quite at the head of the list. *   .   .   .

Now, who could ever believe, were not the fact asserted by Lord Normanby himself, that, as late as March 13, he, the then ambassador of England, was totally ignorant of the manner in which the Provisional Government had been formed three weeks before? Who could believe that, as late as March 13, he had to ask M. de Lamartine how "the original government of *seven* had become *eleven?*"

What! On the 24th of February, five or six lists had been circulated all over Paris, placarded everywhere, spoken of by everyone, canvassed in every street; and Lord Normanby, as late as March 13, did not know that on those lists drawn up wherever there was a popular centre, in the faubourgs by the workmen, in the *École de Médecine*, and the *École de Droit* by the students, in the Republican newspaper offices by the journalists, the names of the *four* had been written down as members of the Provisional Government on the same footing with the names of the *seven!* Nor was Lord Normanby aware, as late as March 13, that in the evening of the 24th of February, an immense meeting composed of National Guards, artists, students,

---

* See the *Moniteur* of the 28th, in which appeared the decrees signed the day before.

The reason why Albert, on the 27th, was requested by the very members of the majority to put his name at the head of the list will be hereafter explained.

workmen, writers, citizens belonging to all classes and conditions, was held at the Hôtel de Ville, in the Salle Saint Jean, for the express purpose of giving the members of the new government the sanction of popular suffrage; that there the leaders whose names had figured on the lists were summoned to appear and to make a declaration of principles, before being invested with any authority at all, and that, in this Assembly of the people, the names of the *four* were proclaimed with the most fervid enthusiasm, whereas some among the names of the *seven* were objected to, and, almost reluctantly, admitted.

Had his lordship lived in the moon, he could not have remained a more perfect stranger to the events, of which, nevertheless, he gives us so confident an account.

As to the spirit that breathes in every page of his book, I will not stop to bring it under discussion. I leave to those more closely acquainted than I am with diplomatic usages and etiquette, to decide whether it be fit for an ambassador to speak in the following refined terms of a foreign government, whose members entertained with his country through his own medium the most amicable relations :

" It appears to be as easy to filch a share of a soi-disant popular dictatorship as to forge an acceptance, or to pick a pocket."*

This is simply an insult levelled at the French nation, and I trust every well-educated and true Englishman

---

* " A Year of Revolution in Paris," vol. i., p. 224.

will be ashamed to read any such lines in a book published by an ambassador of England.

Moreover, in my humble opinion, to be appointed ambassador by a Prime Minister, owing to high family connections, or, perhaps, to mere official intimacies, is something more easy than to become member of a Provisional Government, by attracting the eyes and winning the patriotic affection of about two hundred thousand men as clever and keen as the Parisians are known to be. At all events, the fact of coming forward in stormy hours, at the peril of one's life, and with a certainty to have deadly enmities to encounter, for no other purpose than to save a great nation, both from the grasp of despotism and the flood of anarchy, can hardly arise out of a low, vulgar ambition; and a man is really to be pitied who was not able to find in his own heart a motive, if not for sympathising with such as acted so, at least for doing them justice. I will not insist. Nor do I feel inclined to retort upon Lord Normanby the insulting expressions with which he has thought proper to adorn his style. Being neither a nobleman nor a diplomatist, I am sensible that it is no privilege of mine to use language unbecoming a gentleman.

CHAPTER II.

THE REPUBLIC PROCLAIMED.

THE first problem to be solved was this: Should the Republic be proclaimed or not?

MM. Ledru Rollin, Flocon, and myself, were decidedly of opinion that it should be. MM. Dupont (de l'Eure), Arago, and Marie, objected to this view. M. de Lamartine inclined to our side. MM. Garnier Pagès, Marrast, and Crémieux seemed to grope about for a middle course.

Even now, I am at a loss to comprehend how a discussion of this sort could spring up ; for almost all the members of the Provisional Government were Republicans, and they had certainly been elected *as such.*

Moreover, the people, both inside and outside the Hôtel de Ville, might be easily stirred to indignation by the delay, and some among the leaders had been heard to cry out " Treason ! "

It must be stated, in justice to the Provisional Government, that fear for their lives affected none of them. None of them felt chill and faltering at heart. In none of them was the sacred voice of duty stifled by a slavish sense of despondency. The uneasiness and the hesitation which some of them exhibited, had no other source than a more or less clear perception of the dangers that their country might incur.

MM. Dupont (de l'Eure), Arago, and Marie, opposed the immediate proclamation of the Republic, from a scruple of forestalling the will of the whole nation.

They said :

" Paris is not France. The very principle of the sovereignty of the people implies that we should have recourse to universal suffrage, before we take any decision on so momentous a subject as the proclamation of a new form of government. We must mind, also, not to feed anew that feeling of jealousy which the chief provincial cities and towns have been taught to entertain towards Paris. Should we proclaim the Republic, under the pressure of a population in a state of transitory excitement, the Royalists would be supplied with a pretext to represent the Republic as a mere accident— as the result of a surprise ; and its moral influence would be thus considerably weakened in the eyes of Europe."

These arguments were met in this way by M. Ledru Rollin, Flocon, and myself :

" It is not absolutely true that Paris is not France. Whether the irresistible preponderance imparted to Paris by the present system of centralisation be an evil or not, is not the question we have here to examine. The fact is, that as all enlightened and influential men flock incessantly to Paris from every part of France, Paris, in reality, is the point of confluence at which the various streams of provincial interest or intelligence

meet, there to combine, as it were, into a mighty basin.
France speaks through Paris, if by France we are to
understand that which expresses her true instincts, and
constitutes her genius.   A Republic being that form of
government which depends upon the national will, and
derives from the national will alone, regularly and
unmistakeably *expressed*, its legitimacy as well as its
existence,—contrary to a monarchy, which rests upon the
hereditary principle, and avails itself of the *tacit*, that
is, the *supposed*, consent of the people,—it is evident
that Sovereignty of the People and Republicanism are
convertible terms.   The whole nation assembled could
not possibly reject the Republican form of government
without forfeiting its own sovereignty—without com-
mitting suicide—nay, without encroaching in the most
iniquitous manner upon the rights of the generations
to come: whence the conclusion that, in proclaiming
the Republic, Paris does what France could not undo
by way of universal suffrage without destroying universal suffrage itself in its very essence.   So much for
the theory.   As to the practice, what more dangerous,
under the circumstances, than to leave the question
unsettled?   It would be to put all interests in sus-
pense, to let loose all anarchical passions, to encourage
all ambitious desires, and to give scope for action
to intriguers of every party.   Besides, is it in our
power to baffle the hopes and to counteract the will of
those who have made us what we are?   Do you not
hear the noise of horses, the clang of arms, and the
clamours upon every side of us?   The Republic is now
a fact, which we have not to create, but simply to

declare. If we shrink from the task, men are not wanting by whom it will be accomplished. Let the enemies of the Republic put upon our conduct such construction as may gratify their malignity, what matters it to us? Any attempt to disarm their censure cannot fail to be abortive. From our conscience alone we must draw our inspirations. To subdue the tempest is impossible; to fly from it would be dishonourable; but we may and must direct it."

At length, M. de Lamartine drew up the sketch of a proclamation, which contained these words, evidently intended by him as a compromise:—" Although the Provisional Government act only in the name of the people, and prefer a Republican form of government, neither the people of Paris nor the Provisional Government pretend to substitute their opinion for that of the whole nation, which must be called upon to decide about the definitive form of government to be proclaimed by the Sovereignty of the People." *

A declaration of this kind was strangely equivocal; it left the question unsettled; it actually implied that, if by any chance the majority of the provincial electors were for a monarchy, the people of Paris would have shed their blood for a Republic's sake to no purpose; it meant that universal suffrage had a right to suppress the only form of government consistent with universal suffrage; the words *"prefer a Republican form of government"* were ominously indecisive, and, upon the whole, the declaration was one not unlikely to turn the suspicions of the people into alarm.

* See Appendix, No. 1.

MM. Ledru Rollin and Flocon declined to affix their signatures to the document, and so, at first, I did. But seeing that our opponents appeared determined to go no further, and strongly impressed with the idea of the dark confusion into which everything was about to be plunged, I considered how I could remedy the evil, at least partially. I blotted out the words "though they *prefer*," &c., for which I substituted this much more emphatic and decisive affirmation, "though they *stand by*," and the document, thus modified, was sent to the *Moniteur*.*

May I beg of Lord Normanby to turn to the Appendix, and glance at the *fac-simile* of this document, which was the first issued by the Provisional Government, and to which my signature is affixed without the adjunct of secretary! And may I entertain any hope that his lordship will henceforth remain convinced that I, for one, did not creep up *little by little*, and mix myself with the others, and that I did not come, *little by little*, to have a consultative voice with such as had been less regularly and directly elected by the people than M. Ledru Rollin, Flocon, Albert, and myself?

Meanwhile, the patience of the people, in the Place de Grève, as night advanced, was nearly exhausted. They could not understand how so much time was required to solve so simple a question. A popular orator proposed to go and watch over the deliberations of the Provisional Government, a proposition to which every one agreed. Presently, a group of armed men forced themselves into the Council-chamber, in spite of

* For this *fac-simile*, see Appendix No. 1.

the efforts of those that kept sentry at the door.
The meeting held in the Salle Saint Jean, had not yet
broken up. M. de Lamartine repaired thither, and succeeded in calming the effervescence by his soothing
language.

On my side, I went out, and ordering some pupils of
the Polytechnic School, whose uniform I was sure
would make a favourable impression on the people, to
follow me, I descended towards the Place de Grêve. A
table had been placed at the foot of the staircase. I
stood on it, and cried out:—"The Provisional Government *will* the Republic." The grim faces I had before
me, made still more terrible by the glare of numberless
torches, expressed on a sudden a feeling of indescribable satisfaction, and this feeling burst out into a
triumphant roar.

As this was going on, some workmen having found in
a corner of the Hôtel de Ville a large piece of linen, took
a bit of charcoal and traced on it in colossal letters :
La République une et indivisible est proclamée en France.
Shortly after, they climbed up to the sill of one of the
windows of the Hôtel de Ville ; and, standing there,
unfolded the enormous scroll lit up by the blaze of
the torches they held. Redoubled shouts were thundered out from below, soon followed by a cry of alarm,
as one of the bearers of the scroll lost his footing, fell
into the square, and was carried away bathed in his
blood.

Under the influence of so many exciting emotions,
the aspect of the people had become such, that when
the proclamation drawn up by M. de Lamartine was

sent back from the *Moniteur* to the Provisional Government, a feeling, general now, prevailed that any equivocal phrase would be dangerous. I availed myself of the opportunity, to return to the charge; but M. Crémieux cut short any further discussion by taking up the pen, and, in the place of the objectionable phrase, inserting this one : *Le gouvernement veut la République, sauf ratification par le peuple, qui sera immediatement consulté.* The proclamation, amended in this way, was copied hurriedly on some hundred sheets of paper, which were showered down from the windows of the Hôtel de Ville.

It has been said that M. Bixio, in consequence of a secret understanding with M. Marrast, went to the *Moniteur,* for the express purpose of preventing the proclamation being printed, in which he could not succeed. But personally I know nothing about the circumstance.

The next step was to organise the Government. This was done in a manner which nobody is ignorant of, M. Ledru Rollin having been named home minister, M. de Lamartine minister for foreign affairs, M. Marie minister of public works, and so on.

In a passage of his diary, dated February 27th, Lord Normanby says :—

" The ascendancy of M. de Lamartine has been confirmed, and whilst his efforts have been all exerted in the most laudable direction, the effect of his eloquence, and the success of his energy, have been shown in his nomination to the Presidency of the Provisional Government, the age and infirmity of M. Dupont (de l'Eure) having induced him to resign that which from the first was only nominal on his part." *

Decidedly, his lordship has been misinformed on every point. Never was M. de Lamartine named to the Presidency of the Provisional Government. From the first day to the last, the Council had no other President than the venerable Dupont (de l'Eure), who received the title of the office, and actually discharged the duties attached to it, with a zeal and exactness which would have been praiseworthy in a man of any age, and were really admirable in a man of eighty. A reference to the *Moniteur* shows that our names were appended to the various decrees in no particular order, save that of Dupont (de l'Eure), which almost always and indeed always, except for some special purpose of the day, figured at the head of the list.

The exertions of the Provisional Government in that eventful night may be said to have been prodigious. We had to meet innumerable demands, we had to look to all sorts of exigencies which admitted of no delay; in fact, chaos was to be reduced to order. Among the decrees dated February 24, one is more especially worth being mentioned, as its very laconism gives a curious specimen of the omnipotence with which we found ourselves invested. To abolish the Chamber of Peers, these words were traced in haste: *Il est interdit à la Chambre des Pairs de se réunir,* and that was all.

But, after so much toil, nature began to claim her due, for I think none of us had breakfasted yet. Unfortunately, nothing was to be got. By dint of

* "A Year of Revolution," vol. 1., p. 127.

searching, the starving dictators of France were so befriended by fortune as to procure some black bread which the soldiers had left, a bottle of wine, a bit of cheese, and a pail of water just brought in by a good-natured workman. There being no vessel, the next difficulty for them was how to get at their drink. By another lucky chance, a cracked sugar-basin was discovered, which passed round, like the cup filled with more generous contents, in an ancient banquet. The operation was merrily conducted, and M. de Lamartine, smiling, said : *Voici qui est de bon augure pour un gouvernement à bon marché.*

I must not omit a particular which illustrates a striking feature in the character of the Parisian workmen. As I felt exceedingly fatigued and wanted to put off my national guard uniform, I tried to make my way home, accompanied by my brother and a friend of ours, through the dark narrow streets which went winding on from the Hôtel de Ville to the Maison Tortony, where I then lived. The barricades stood still erected, and were guarded by the people with anxious watchfulness, on account of a rumour that an attack was to be dreaded from the troops stationed at Vincennes. The pass-word, *havresac, liberté, réforme,* was rigorously exacted. At one of the barricades I was stopped, being neither known to the commander, nor aware of the pass-word, and put under arrest with my brother and my friend, till our case could be inquired into. In that predicament, it occurred to me to say that some of the workmen employed in guarding the barricade could not fail to recognise me, and I requested they should be summoned to my presence. Accordingly they came in, and, seeing me, shouted, "Vive Louis Blanc!" Of course, I was released, and given an escort home. I shall never forget with what feeling of extraordinary respect those terrible combatants received—the Republic being now proclaimed—the announcement that a member of the Provisional Government was passing, and with what mixture of military discipline and civic pride they presented arms. My reason for stating this, is to show that the Parisian workmen, so jealously attached to the principle of equality, and prompt as they are to overthrow any government inconsistent with it, are nevertheless just as ready as other people to do homage to a power of their own choice.

It was not long before I returned to the Hôtel de Ville. The people bivouacked in the streets as in a camp. Great fires were here and there burning, which cast their lurid light on groups of faces wonderfully expressive, while now and then was heard, in the stillness of the night, the sinister cry of the distant sentinel, as he challenged, *Sentinelles, prenez-garde à vous !*

CHAPTER III.

THE REPUBLIC UNIVERSALLY ACKNOWLEDGED.

Was the Government of Louis Bonaparte, after the 2nd of December, spontaneously acknowledged? No. Its sole supporters were the very agents of the conspiracy from which it had sprung. With hardly two or three exceptions, all men whether of intellectual or social eminence, the most renowned generals of France, its most illustrious poets, its greatest writers, its first-rate politicians, turned away from the new power. The Republican party was decimated but no way subdued. The Orleanists and the Legitimists were terrified, but did not cease to stand in silent revolt.

From the first day, great care had been taken to give out (no one being permitted even to whisper a contradictory word) that Paris streaming with blood— the prisons crowded with prisoners—so many persons of high standing persecuted or banished—France kept in awe by half-a-million of bayonets—the capital of the civilised world swarming with police spies—the press muzzled—an unexampled series of delations, proscriptions, confiscations and deportations, were facts unavoidably connected " with the sacred duty of saving society from utter destruction." But all this was in

vain. No men of independent position availed themselves of this specious pretence to cloak an act of
apostasy; no men were willing to undergo the new
government, except those whom their poverty compelled,
and their obscurity allowed, to do so.

Under the influence of a ruthless system of despotism,
at a moment when the stillness of terror was everywhere appalling, and the sabre was suspended over every
head, the electors were commanded to vote for an
emperor. So they did; and, as there was no real
scrutiny, no means of control, no publicity, no possibility whatever either of checking the returns or showing that, under the circumstances, a vote was a lie, the
Empire boldly termed itself the legitimate offspring of
universal suffrage, and was acknowledged in this capacity by foreign governments. A new pretext was thus
offered to any worshippers of the rising sun to screen
themselves behind the so-called national will. But
even then, neither the Republicans, nor the Orleanists,
nor the Legitimists, thought for a moment of rallying
round Louis Bonaparte. M. de Montalembert, who,
on hearing that the Panthéon was to be made a church,
had declared for the usurper, hastened to retrace
his steps. It soon became known that M. de Pastoret
had abandoned his party because he was about to be
repudiated by it, on account of some particular circumstances of a serious nature. M. de la Rochejaquelein
felt inwardly so ashamed of having suffered himself to
be made a senator, that, without being the object of
any public attack, he considered it necessary to publish
a pamphlet for his justification. As to M. de Cormenin,

that he had always been regarded by the Legitimists as a Republican, and by the Republicans as a Legitimist, is a fact which no person acquainted with the affairs of France can possibly deny. At all events, this solitary exception serves only to bring into stronger relief the indomitable firmness of the Republican leaders, none of whom hesitated to lead, in exile, a life full of suffering, rather than submit to violence and injustice.

Now, let us contrast this faithful picture of what occurred after the 2nd of December 1851, with those effusions of heart and that genuine flow of sympathy which impart to the advent of the Republic of February 1848, an indelible character of grandeur.

There was in Paris not a soldier left; nay, not a *serjeant de ville*. The Provisional Government were destitute of all means of enforcing obedience; they had no artillery, no bayonets at their disposal; they had no guards, not even any organised body of adherents; the armed crowds which, at intervals, filled the streets and the public squares, did by no means constitute a permanent, still less a disposable, force to be made use of against any individual act whether of resistance or protest. Besides, the unlimited liberty of the press was, from the first moment, sanctioned, and every one was allowed to speak out his mind.*

Such being the case, and in the absence of all compulsory power, declarations of adherence arrived from every quarter. Deputations sent by the constituted bodies, by every corporation of operatives, by every class

---

* To what extent this was carried out will be seen in a subsequent chapter.

of tradesmen, by public functionaries of every degree, by the magistracy, and by the clergy, flocked without interruption to the Hôtel de Ville. Numberless were the congratulatory addresses we received. A stream of bannered processions was constantly to be seen in the Place de Grève. Gifts of money were brought in, every minute. Never were the taxes paid so eagerly as during the first days of the Revolution of February. Ladies of rank, the Comtesse de Lamoignon, the Comtesse de Chastenay, the Comtesse de Biencourt, the Marquise de Lagrange, the Duchesse de Maillé, and so forth, made a point to inscribe their names on the lists of subscription opened in favour of the wounded combatants.

As early as the 24th of February, in the evening, Monseigneur Affre, Archbishop of Paris, manifested his allegiance to the Republic, in the name of the clergy, by directing the curates of his diocese to chant, at the church service, *Domine salvum fac populum*, instead of *Domine salvum fac regem*. His mandamus began with these words:

"On witnessing the great event that has just taken place, our first impulse was to weep over such as were so unexpectedly mown down. We weep over them all, because they are our brethren, and also because we have been taught once more how disinterested, how generous, how mindful of the right of property, are the people of Paris." *

* Wherefrom it may be inferred that the Archbishop of Paris did not exactly agree with Lord Normanby, who in his book calls these same men *ruffians*.

But a few days after, Father Lacordaire, alluding to the workmen who, in the very excitement of the struggle, had respectfully carried to the church of Saint Rock the crucifix which belonged to the chapel of the Tuileries, exclaimed from the pulpit of Notre Dame :

" Need I demonstrate the existence of God ? Should I attempt to do so, the gates of this cathedral would fly open, to give you the sight of a people adoring Christ, and, while in a state of sublime anger, carrying God to His altar ! "

The following was the declaration of the Ultramontane paper, the *Univers :*

" Through the last event, God speaks. The Revolution of 1848 is a notification of Divine Providence. No conspiracy could have turned society upside down, in such a manner, and in so short a time. Who thinks to-day of defending monarchy ? France fancied she was still royalist, whilst she was already republican. Monarchy, at present, has not a partisan left. There will be no more sincere Republicans than the French Catholics."

The members of the *Conseil d'État* appointed M. de Cormenin to give utterance to their feelings of admiration for what he termed " *cette grande et sublime révolution.*"

M. Gerusez, in the name of the University of Paris, bowed to a Revolution which he said had been accomplished for the sake of the human race, and was to be baptised " *Impérissable République !* "

All the judicial bodies came, one after the other, to

the Hôtel de Ville, there to strengthen their oaths by voluntary and enthusiastic affirmations.

It was by myself that the act of adhesion of the *Cour des Comptes* was received, on the 29th of February; nor have I forgotten with what bursts of almost juvenile sympathy the old magistrates hailed this sentence of my brief reply:

" The motto of the Republic will no longer be *Liberté, Ordre public;* these two things are inseparable.   What we must henceforth enjoy is *L'Ordre dans la Liberté.*"*

In their turn, the members of the *Cour de Cassation,* on the 3rd of March, repaired to the Hôtel de Ville, where, by the mouth of their first president, M. Portalis, they made a solemn declaration that " the Provisional Government was the centre around which it was the duty of all to rally."   The speech of M. Portalis ended with these words:

" We have confidence in your wisdom, in your patriotism, and in your firmness.   What you are capable of doing is shown by what you have already done.   The nation will sustain you."

The heads of the army vied with each other in offering their services to the Republic, namely, Marshal Soult, Marshal Sebastiani, Marshal Gérard, General Oudinot, General Lahitte, General Baraguay d'Hilliers, &c.

It would take a large volume to register all the letters in which important military personages swore to be true to the Republic.   I will content myself with quoting the following ones, the selection of which needs no commentary :—

* See the *Moniteur,* 1st of March, 1848.

"TO THE MINISTER OF WAR.

" Monsieur le Ministre,—

"Taking into consideration the events which have just been accomplished, and the necessity of securing, by union, both order at home and independence abroad, I think it a duty incumbent on me to put my sword at the disposal of the government newly instituted. I have always considered as the most sacred of duties that of defending one's country.

"Duc d'Isly."

This letter has a peculiar significance; it was written by that very Marshal Bugeaud who, in the days of Louis Philippe, had so deeply imbrued his hands in the blood of the Republicans !

Shortly after came a letter from General Changarnier. It ran as follows :—

"TO THE MINISTER OF WAR.

" Monsieur le Ministre,—

"I request the Republican Government to make use of my devotedness to France. I solicit the command of the troops on the frontier most threatened with war. My experience in managing soldiers, the confidence which the army reposes in me, an impassioned love of glory, *la volonté et l'habitude de vaincre*,* will, I trust, enable me successfully to perform my duties. What I venture to say regarding myself is not

---

* I leave this phrase in the original, for I confess myself unable to render it into English.

to be considered as the expression of a childish vanity, but as the outpouring of my ardent desire to devote all my faculties to the service of my country.

" CHANGARNIER."

In reference to the attitude assumed by General Changarnier, I remember a fact which I think is worth mentioning. He had in the Council a very warm supporter, who was M. Marrast, and a decided adversary, who was myself. Not that I felt disposed to underrate his military deeds ; no one having ever sounded his praises, in this particular respect, as much as I had done in the " History of Ten Years." But it had been my impression, that he always showed himself inimical to the Republic; and I was confirmed in this belief on hearing that, when apprised of the proclamation of the Republican Government, he broke out into a military ejaculation expressive of rough repugnance. I had it from good authority, as a friend of mine was present when the thing occurred. Accordingly, the moment M. Marrast mentioned, in the Council, the name of General Changarnier, I objected to his being invested with a power he might make use of to turn the scale in favour of the opposite side, should an opportunity offer. I have every reason to think that M. Marrast did not feel himself bound to keep what had been observed secret; for General Changarnier, without losing time, called upon me at the Luxembourg, and, protesting he had been painted in wrong colours, he left nothing unsaid that might convince me of his readiness faithfully to serve the Republic.

At the same period, and at the same place, M. de la Rochejaquelein paid me a visit, which a singular circumstance stamped on my memory. The very instant this gentleman's name was brought in, a numerous deputation of workmen stood at the door. I desired M. de la Rochejaquelein to be ushered in, for no other purpose than to express to him by word of mouth how sorry I was to be obliged to put off the interview he asked for. He was in a real state of rapture, which I believe was perfectly sincere. " Never mind; never mind ; " he exclaimed, in a somewhat hurried manner, " I have nothing particular to tell you. I only wished to let you know what feelings such marvels as these awaken in my heart. *Ah! que c'est beau! que c'est beau !* " Then he clasped me in his arms, and went out.

I will not dwell upon the public declarations of M. Dupin and M. Baroche. The mode of proceeding of these gentlemen, in any such emergency, is a matter of course. But it may not be uninteresting to English readers to know what was, at the time, the language held by such men as M. de Montalembert and M. de Falloux, two of the heads of the Legitimist party.

M. de Montalembert, addressing the constituency of the Département du Doubs, thus lamented that he had not earlier been initiated into the science of Socialism :

" In the political sphere, I have had only one standard, liberty in all and for all. I have demanded the liberty of teaching, and the liberty of association, as the basis and the guarantee of liberty in all its forms. I have, perhaps, to reproach myself with having shared—I will

not say the indifference—but the ignorance of most
politicians respecting several of the social and economical questions which fill, to-day, so vast and so fitting
a place in the thoughts and feelings of the country.
Were the way to a political career thrown open to me
by the suffrage of my fellow-citizens, I should in good
faith, and without the least *arrière pensée*, assist in
laying the foundations of the Republic."

Lord Normanby's *ruffians* were described as follows by
M. de Falloux, in a letter expressing his intimate feelings:

" I cannot end this scribbling without consigning
here—and this will astonish no one except those that
are distant from the theatre of the events—my *admiration* (I underline the word) for the people of Paris.
Their courage had something of heroism in it ; their
instincts were of a generosity and delicacy which sur-
pass by far anything like it exhibited by the political
bodies which governed France for sixty years.   It may
be said that the combatants, arms in hand, in the
double intoxication of danger and triumph, have set an
example on which all cool-headed men have hereafter
nothing better to do than to model their conduct.
They have imparted to their victory a sacred character:
let us unite ourselves with them, in order that this
character may remain unimpaired."

Louis Bonaparte was in Paris on the 28th.   He proceeded to pay his respects to the Provisional Government, in this manner:

" GENTLEMEN,

        " The people of Paris having destroyed by its

heroism the last vestige of foreign invasion, I hastened from the land of exile to enlist myself under the banners of the Republic, which has just been proclaimed. With no other ambition than that of serving my country, I beg to make the members of the Provisional Government aware of my arrival, and I request them to be assured, both of my devotion to the cause they represent, and of my personal sympathy for them.

" NAPOLEON LOUIS BONAPARTE."

At that time, the sentence of banishment against the Emperor's family had not yet been annulled. But the policy of the Provisional Government was too generous to take advantage, against any one, of so unjust a law. Whether, as has been said, some of the members of the government caused it to be intimated to Louis Bonaparte, that they feared his presence might possibly lead to tumults, is a circumstance I am ignorant of; but I have no recollection that any such step was the subject of a decision taken in the Council, or even of discussion. Nor was there any occasion for it; as the presence of Louis Bonaparte in Paris, at that moment, was scarcely noticed. He soon perceived that it was better for him to withdraw, and he returned to London. But his letter will remain a lasting testimony to that irresistible moral power which compelled all parties, each in its turn, to bow down before the Republic.

Will it be contended that the professions of service and fidelity made by so many individuals, from so many quarters, were all equally insincere? Supposing this to be true, what stronger proof could be adduced of the prodigious moral force of the new government? If the idea of its durability had not been deeply impressed on every mind, would all men of note have consented to crawl into its favour? Would they have thought it worth while to plunge into perjury and hypocrisy, for the sake of ingratiating themselves with a still-born power? I will not deny that there are in France men to whom *might* is *right*, and who, like M. Dupin, like M. Baroche, never swore allegiance but to their places and emoluments; but the persons of this stamp would be the very last whom a faltering government might expect to bring over. Consequently, whatever construction the maligners of the Republic may choose to put upon the outbursts of sympathy which the Revolution of February called forth everywhere, these outbursts would be utterly unaccountable, had not the Republic been viewed generally in the light of an institution full of vitality.

Now, is the supposition I have just examined, to be admitted to any considerable extent? In justice to my country, I do not hesitate to answer: No. That even then, success had its worshippers, is certain; but I feel bound in duty to deny that such a voluntary flow of good-will as made its way to the Hôtel de Ville, was but a swelling tide of falsehood. The truth is, that the general impulse was genuine, much more so than some, to-day, would be able to perceive, or willing to confess. The magnanimity of the people, in February, 1848, morally subdued many of the most determined adversaries of its cause. On seeing how disinterested and generous those men were, who had so

often been depicted as barbarians ready to overwhelm
the civilised world, many, like M. de Falloux and
the Archbishop of Paris, felt their hearts greatly
affected, and could not help expressing their admiration. More than one politician became a Republican all on a sudden, whose sole reason for not
having been so before, was, that he considered the
advent of the Republic to be impossible. More than
one haughty personage perceived, for the first time, that
nobleness and poverty are not irreconcileable. There
was a happy revival of the sense of public honour,
and the tone of public life was prodigiously raised.

The elevation of mind which, in those unparalleled
days, may be said to have pervaded all classes, shone
forth on the 27th of February, when the Republic
was in a solemn manner inaugurated at the Place de
la Bastille, amid the unbought and tremendous
plaudits of all Paris, and still more strikingly on the
4th of March, at the celebration of the funeral of
such as had been killed during the struggle. The
ceremony was performed in the Church of La Madeleine, full of, and surrounded by, a vast concourse
of people, whose touching attitude will never be forgotten by those who were present. The church was
hung in mourning, and lighted by fifteen funeral
torches. An immense *catafalque* had been erected
between the nave and the choir, on each side of which
these words were inscribed: *Morts pour la patrie!*
There stood, wearing crape on the arm, and with no
other characteristic badge than a tri-coloured scarf, the
members of the Provisional Government. There were

assembled the members of the municipality of Paris, the mayors of the twelve districts, the relatives of the victims, a great number of general officers both of the Army and Navy, the pupils of the Polytechnic School, the students belonging to the law-schools, and to the Medical College; deputations from all the educational, literary, or scientific institutes; from all the corporations of workmen; from the Cour de Cassation, the Cour d'Appel, the Cour des Comptes, the Conseil d'État, and the tribunals. In fact, all that constitutes French society was there.*

At half-past one, the funeral service being over, the cortège left the church, and took the way to the Place de la Bastille, between a double row of National Guards, which extended from the Place de la Madeleine to the Colonne de Juillet. No vain display was there to be seen, no splendid equipage, no crowd of lackeys, no troop of horse caracoling, sword in hand, round a gilt carriage of state. The members of the Provisional Government walked among their fellow-citizens, with no other guard around them than public respect and love. At half-past four, the coffins were lowered into the vaults beneath the Column of July, from the top of which a long crape, powdered with silver tears, was flowing down. Appropriate speeches were delivered by MM. Crémieux and Garnier Pagès, whereupon the people retired in solemn silence.

The following passage of the *Moniteur* gives a faithful picture of the moral aspect of this most impressive ceremony:

* See the *Moniteur* of the 5th of March.

"Yesterday, the prevalent feeling was the intoxication of triumph; to-day, it is the calmness of force. A multitude which can only be counted by hundreds of thousands attended the funeral. All Paris was in the streets, or at the windows. Numberless labourers had come to range themselves, no longer under the banner of superstition, as in the middle ages, but under the intelligent banner of Republican fraternity, waiting for the Provisional Government, which, as it walked behind the natural families of the victims, seemed to represent their adoptive family, the whole of France. Any one unacquainted with the habits of the marvellously sagacious population of Paris, may wonder how three or four hundred thousand men could be found to obey, without direction, the same feeling, and to preserve the same aspect. But they did so, and it is most remarkable that, in so vast a multitude, there was not a man prepared to hear those clamours with which all victorious powers are wont to be hailed. The Parisians, with that exquisite perception of propriety which is in them a natural instinct, felt that, in the presence of so many coffins, the calmness of an indomitable conviction was to take the place of the triumphal excitement of victory. At every window, on every balcony, along the Boulevards, women were waving their handkerchiefs and their hands; every one respectfully took off his hat, as the members of the Provisional Government passed; but the people, at this particular juncture, had a grave countenance, and the general feeling was one of repressed emotion. The fasces were not, this time, surmounted by the consular axe; the terrible symbol had disappeared, in consequence of the sublime decree for the abolition of capital punishment, and the lance, which should be reserved for the foe only, had been substituted for the axe of civil war; so that the remembrance even of the heroic ages was effaced by that revolution which surpasses all others, by superadding modern generosity to antique grandeur. To the French Republic solely it belonged to give rise to that regulated, formidable, and grave enthusiasm which was never known to the courtiers of ancient monarchies. Silence—the lesson of kings—was to-day, for the first time, the eloquent form of the sympathy of a whole people." *

Can one word more be wanting to prove that it is sheer madness to term the Republic of 1848 "the Republic of surprise!" A government "of surprise" was the Empire, for it was the offspring of a conspiracy long hatched in the dark and of a night ambush which took Paris unawares; nor did Louis Bonaparte find it very difficult to keep the field, once conquered through an unexampled piece of treachery, since he proved capable of having recourse to appropriate means, that is, an unbounded military tyranny, the gagging of the press, donatives showered upon the men of the Second of December out of the public purse, and, above all, a permanent system of terror, which naturally resulted in sham elections and a mockery of universal suffrage. But the members of the Provisional Government did not possess, nor were they the men to use, any such means. Had their dictatorship, or a part of it, been "*filched*," as Lord Normanby was not ashamed to say,

* See the *Moniteur* of the 5th of March, 1848.

France would deserve to occupy the lowest rank in the scale of nations, for not having chastised an attempt both so monstrous and so silly, while the most eminent personages of France ought to be branded with ever-lasting infamy, for having bent the knee before usurpers whom they could have blown away with a puff.

On the other hand, had the French people been so violently and universally averse to the Republic, as asserted by politicians of Lord Normanby's school, those would have been above the level of humanity, who, without treasures, without soldiers, without police, without anything like an organised force, were able to maintain their power as long as they thought fit, estab-lishing a new form of government, proclaiming new principles, installing new functionaries, pacifying the people, keeping the army in awe, adjusting the forms of law to their will, issuing decrees never disobeyed, and eliciting, after their voluntary abdication, from a National Assembly called upon to judge their conduct, an acknowledgment thus worded: " L'ASSEMBLÉE NATIONALE DÉCRÈTE : LE GOUVERNEMENT PROVISOIRE A BIEN MÉRITÉ DE LA PATRIE ! "

That the Republic of 1848 was "the Republic of surprise," is therefore an assumption, not only at vari-ance with the established facts and with the well-known pride of the French people, but also utterly inconsistent with all the laws of probability.

This brings me to controvert an opinion not unlikely, if persisted in, to weaken, in future, those bonds of amity which it is so desirable should remain unrelaxed between England and France.

That Republican institutions are not suited to the French nation, has almost become a proverbial expression in this country; and, although I believe it to be a mistake, I must candidly confess that the view the English take of the subject is grounded on circumstances which, if not carefully analysed, may seem to justify such a conclusion.

In the first place, most people in England have been taught that the French Republic of 1792 and 1793 was but a wild rush towards despotism through anarchy.

In the second place, it may be contended, with much show of reason, that the Republican Government from 1848 to 1852 turned out to be a failure.

Thirdly, foreigners who have a superficial insight into the manners of the French people, and the lurking causes of the historical vicissitudes of France, can hardly be expected to ascribe strong Republican propensities to a nation which they see, at this very hour, lying prostrate at the feet of a despot.

But these facts require to be examined in their true light.

First, the French Revolution of 1792 and 1793 having been a gigantic struggle between the old world and a thoroughly new one, the very magnitude of the contest, while it exhausted the nation into fainting in the arms of a military despot, made it impossible, as long as it lasted, to establish any definitive form of government whatever. Let the reader be remembered that the Constitution of 1793 was never carried out, its framers having decreed that it should not be put in practice till after the close of the war; which shows that the violent *régime* forced upon the Republicans of that period was not regarded by themselves as a regular Republican form of government.

Respecting the Republic proclaimed in February 1848, it crumbled away, because those whom it entrusted with the power, happened to be its most deadly enemies: a circumstance which was by no means the result of any fundamental defect in the new institutions, as applied to the French people, but sprung from a merely accidental combination of treacherous manœuvres and repeated blunders which I will hereafter explain. Who does not know that the majority of the late Legislative Assembly rose in opposition against their own constituencies, and made it their constant study to undermine the Republic, railing on every occasion at Republican principles, hunting down every sincere Republican, consigning to beggary the Republican primary teachers, goading the workmen into self-destructive fits of wrath, disarming the people, trampling on that very principle of universal suffrage of which they were born, and, out of hatred to the Republic, foolishly investing Louis Bonaparte with the monstrous power that enabled him, on the second of December, to crush both the Republic and themselves?

Now, that, in consequence of an unexpected stroke of military violence, a nation should be momentarily manacled, and that France herself should be kept in awe by four hundred thousand bayonets incessantly levelled at her, is conceivable enough. But it is obvious that, as regards her natural tendencies, nothing is to be inferred, either from her immobility, since Paris disarmed lies surrounded with artillery and soldiers, or from her silence, since a lynx-eyed police is everywhere and freedom nowhere.

If the Empire, as its supporters are not ashamed to boast, rests on eight millions of *real* suffrages, and the sympathy of the nation, why does not Louis Bonaparte set France at *liberty* to give full scope to her enthusiasm? Why, better to prove the legitimacy of his power, does he not hasten to unmuzzle the press, to allow free meetings, to respect electoral independence, to unfetter public opinion, to abolish his arbitrary police, and to send his soldiers to the frontiers, there to defend their country, if needful? Granted that there exist some elements of internal disturbance, is not the will of a great nation, operating through law, sufficient irresistibly to suppress them! Let Louis Bonaparte try, only for a month! But no. He is perfectly aware that the very moment the French felt themselves free from the overwhelming weight of four hundred thousand bayonets, his reign would be at an end. So thoroughly is he alive to the precarious and unsafe character of his position, that, after having made it a danger for France to speak, nay, to whisper, he grows feverish at the bare idea that she is still permitted to breathe. What a conclusion, then, may be fairly drawn, as regards the true feelings of France, from a situation so artificial and so transitory!

The English opinion to which I object, rests, therefore, on no really historical grounds; and still less can this opinion be maintained from a philosophical point of view.

For my part, I am ready to admit that one of the
chief merits of political institutions lies in their adaptive-
ness to the character of the nation for which they are
intended; and this is the very reason why I think
Republican institutions suited to the French people.

The English are impressed with the idea that their
friends on the other side of the Channel are exceedingly
fond of pageantry. I will not deny the fact. But
when the Parisians swarm in the streets, to catch a
glimpse of some pompous train of high personages
riding on horseback or in gilt carriages, (which, by the
bye, is more or less the case in every country,) their
desire to have their curiosity gratified blends always
with a lively proneness to laugh at livery-men of every
kind, and to ridicule any show which does not cor-
respond to a lofty feeling, or is at variance with their
sense of equality. Moreover, no French Republican
dreams of a Republic cast in the Lacedæmonian mould ;
no French Republican is blind to the necessity of
adjusting political institutions to the manners of the
French, so as to satisfy their relish for grand spectacles,
and to keep pace with the progress of civilisation in its
most brilliant aspects. In the essence of a Republic
there is nothing irreconcileable with pomp; nor is it
obvious why, in a country where the *prestige* of kingship
has been destroyed by so many revolutions, the people
would prefer the gorgeous display of one man's power
to the imposing manifestation of its own.

Let us now examine another and more comprehensive
side of the question.

A deep thinker, Mr. John Stuart Mill, says, in a

most admirable paper written by him in reply to Lord
Brougham, concerning the Revolution of February :

" The general habit and practice of the English
mind is compromise. . . . The English never feel
themselves safe unless they are living under the
shadow of some conventional fiction. Now, constitutional royalty is precisely an arrangement of
this description. The very essence of it is, that the
so-called sovereign does not govern, ought not to govern,
is not intended to govern; but yet must be held up to
the nation, be addressed by the nation, as if he or she
did govern. This, which was originally a compromise
between the friends of popular liberty and those of
absolute monarchy, has established itself as a sincere
feeling in the mind of the nation—who would be
offended, and think their liberties endangered, if a king
or queen meddle any further in the government than to
give a formal sanction to all acts of Parliament, and to
appoint as ministry, or rather as minister, the person
whom the majority in Parliament pointed out; and yet
would be unaffectedly shocked, if every considerable act
of government did not profess and pretend to be the
act and mandate of the person on the throne." *

Not so with the French people; and, in thus expressing myself, I mean no disparagement to the
habit of the English mind; far from it! The relish
of the English for compromise arises out of that
practical and patient genius, to which they are indebted for the calm of their political life. But all
comparisons unfavourable to either of these two great

* " Westminster and Foreign Quarterly Review," for April, 1849.

nations being put aside, I may be allowed to say that the general habit and practice of the French mind is logical directness. They would submit to no system purporting to be something else than the very thing intended to be acted upon. The tone of thought and feeling congenial to them leads them irresistibly to think, that if the part of royalty be restricted to the mechanical act of registering the laws, a cipher would do as well, and be less expensive. Hence, the utter impossibility to implant on the other side of the channel this subtle distinction : *Le roi règne et ne gouverne pas.* Should a king be willing to comply with a maxim of the sort, he would sink rapidly in public estimation. But could possibly any such king be found in France ? I doubt it very much. Need I remind the reader with what crafty perseverance Louis Philippe strove to break the fetters of the constitutional theory, although he seemed to be the very man to feel satisfied with a position which requires moderate talents, little pride, a very confined ambition, no intellectual longings, and a sufficient amount of good sense ?

It is a common English saying that the French are a fickle people. This is a misconception, too; but as it derives sanction from appearances of a really delusive nature, to detect it requires close examination. The fact is, that directness is mistaken for fickleness. The French have a marked tendency to act upon this principle, which, true as it is in mathematics, is dangerous in politics—that the straightest line is the shortest. Accordingly, the premises once admitted, they go straight to the logical conclusion, ready to crush any obstacle that may lie in the way, if there be no better means to avoid it than to go round. The consequence is, that, whenever the new idea they contend for, is opposed with momentary success by the interests of long standing or the inveterate prejudices it has to encounter, the struggle ends in a retreat not of purpose but of fact, which make all superficial minds believe that the previously advancing nation has abandoned its tenets, and lost sight of its aim. But not so. It clings to both more tenaciously than ever, and regains its ground through an undermining process, till at last the obstacle is exploded, which, being done, it starts with renewed vigour from the point just reached, and goes on, always straightly, to the next stage. An illustration of this will be found in the history of our successive revolutions during the last century; for none of them has failed to be the immediate and logical consequence of the preceding one, although the interval between the two had been filled, almost invariably, by an apparent surrender of the antecedent conquests. It is obvious that the political institutions best suited to such a people are Republican institutions, on account of their elasticity, which allows public opinion to wend its way quietly, whilst the existence of an unyielding barrier would have for its natural effect, sooner or later, to swell the stream into a devastating torrent.

It will, perhaps, be objected that the same peaceful result may be attained, under constitutional monarchy, combined with liberty of the press and a fair scope for public discussion. I have partly disposed of this objection, as far as the French are concerned, by stating how uncongenial it is to them to submit to anything like a fiction or a compromise. I will complete the demonstration by adding to the philosophical considerations suggested by their character, such political arguments as are to be drawn from the very nature of things.

When, under the French Monarch, Henry III., the Duc de Guise was told that the king wished him dead, he answered: "*No one will dare to do it.*" But the king did dare, for the duke was treacherously murdered. Was this a proof of force on the part of the monarch? Just the reverse, the sense of his impotence having made him a coward and an assassin. Now, what was Queen Anne's conduct, when she came to the resolution of getting rid of Marlborough! She simply wrote to him that he was dismissed. The bringing these two facts together shows that monarchy, in England, has, within its constitutional limits, a degree of power of which monarchy, in France, was actually in want, even at a time when, in theory, it was supreme. English monarchy, as Delolme says, "*is a good ship, which Parliament can lay high and dry when it will.*" But what matters it? Never was royalty, in England, as would be the case in France, a power standing solitary at the summit of a society tormented with the love of equality. The queen, in this country, borrows her strength, as well as her splendour, from the aristocracy which surrounds the throne, and is, above all things, interested in preserving the established hierarchy, because the whole chain would vibrate throughout its length, the moment its first link was touched.

Besides, royalty, in England, is propped up by respect

for class distinctions, a feeling so deeply rooted in the hearts. And, indeed, a foreigner cannot look into the manners of the English without being amazed at finding them so proud and so humble, so independent and so submissive, so fond of the forms of liberty and so attached to the distinctions of aristocracy. In this remarkable country, the language of the press is aggressive, bold and unrestrained; nevertheless, ranks are, so to speak, labelled in the most symmetrical order. Personal pride is, among the English, highly developed; nevertheless, they strictly obey the law of precedency. The queen, to pass the gates of the city, must obtain the Lord Mayor's permission; nevertheless, the observance of distinctions of ranks finds its way from the drawing-room to the servants' hall.

Thus, two feelings govern the English nation: an indomitable love of liberty, and a respect for class distinctions; a phenomenon the causes of which may be traced in history; for, of the two races, Saxon and Norman, brought face to face by conquest, neither having been able to absorb the other, the result was a compromise between two principles equally balanced. The vanquished nation was obliged, in self defence, to establish a vigorous system of guarantees, while the conquerors were led closely to watch, for their preservation, over the inviolability of a system of privileges.

It is otherwise in France; so much so, that no one of all the conditions Montesquieu declares requisite for the maintenance of Monarchy, could possibly be found there. Montesquieu says, for instance, that this is a political axiom: *No monarch, no nobility; no nobility, no monarch.*

Well, has there been any nobility in France, since 1789; or, could anything be more foolish than an attempt to revive it? According to Montesquieu, a monarchical government is simply impossible, if not combined with the law of primogeniture. Now, is this law existing in France, or likely to be re-established?

I conclude:

In England, royalty blends its roots with those of the nation, with which it has developed itself in a normal way, under the influence of nearly identical necessities.

In France, on the contrary, any old tradition on which royalty might rest has been destroyed.

In England, a strong aristocracy lends both its power and its lustre to the throne.

In France, nobility no longer exists,—is no longer possible.

In England, the hereditary descent of the crown is in perfect harmony with the principle of entails.

In France, the principle which goes on dividing property so far as to pulverise the soil, leaves political hereditary power without social foundations.

In England, royalty is an institution perfectly consistent with an almost universal leaning to class-distinctions.

In France, the sense of equality is developed to the utmost.

It would be, therefore, at variance both with the acknowledged facts and the most obvious deductions of logic, to assume that constitutional monarchy is of a nature to be adapted to France, because it works well in England.

Nor are the seventeen years of the reign of Louis Philippe of any weight, in this discussion. Constitutional monarchy, under Louis Philippe, was tolerated as a provisional expedient, but never viewed by the nation at large in the light of an accepted principle. Not for a moment did the ruler of France himself mistake his position; he knew he could have no other engine of government than the terror of the shopkeepers at the idea of a new revolution; that is of some hindrance to the selling of their brittle wares; and by constantly holding out to them the prospect of pillage as the unavoidable consequence of any future outbreak, he succeeded in securing their support, till even that artificial support gave way under him. So that, in France, constitutional monarchy, as long as it lasted, was nothing better than a scarecrow placed in a field to prevent birds from devouring the corn. But when the Revolution of February broke out, there were no rapacious birds to be found, there was no corn devoured; and the throne of Louis Philippe, it was manifest, had rested, for seventeen years, on a mere calumny!

As to absolute monarchy, how could it be possible in France, with anything like the consent of the people? Or how could it be compatible with the natural growth of the principles proclaimed in 1789?

It would be a power of an aristocratic character, born of the *bourgeoisie*, which has broken the chain of hereditary distinctions.

It would be a power exclusively conservative, born of the *bourgeoisie*, which has opened up an unlimited career to human ambition.

It would be a traditional power, born of the *bourgeoisie*, by which all ancient traditions have been effaced.

It would be an omnipotent power, born of the *bourgeoisie*, which suffered the omnipotence of Louis XVI. to sink in blood, and which chastised by an eternal exile the omnipotence of Charles X.

It would be, in one word, the strangest, the most inexplicable, and the most monstrous of all institutions; as its nature would at every point give the lie to its origin, and its origin would at every point give the lie to its nature.

On these terms, the King would be like a protestant made a Pope.

Consequently, when the members of the Provisional Government, on the 24th of February, assumed the responsibility of a change of government, they did not act under the impulse of a juvenile enthusiasm, but from a mature and practical consideration of the wants and the tendencies of French society : and the best proof that they were right is that the Republic had no sooner been proclaimed than it was universally and spontaneously acknowledged.

CHAPTER IV.

GENEROUS CHARACTER OF THE REVOLUTION OF
FEBRUARY.

NEVER was perhaps in History anything equal to the magnanimity displayed on the morrow of the Revolution of February, both by the people and the government sprung from their spontaneous suffrage. Even before the excitement of the struggle had subsided, all past offences were forgotten. No cry for vengeance was heard; not a Royalist fell a victim to public or private resentment; not a Republican thought of evoking the manes of his brothers slaughtered in the Rue Transnonain, or seemed to remember how unmercifully the Republicans had been hunted down. Not only were their bitterest enemies left unharmed, but they met with the most generous protection.

Well might have Louis Philippe spared himself the trouble of overhasty flight and the humiliating annoyance of a disguise, as neither the people nor their chosen rulers took the slightest notice of him. His name was not even mentioned in the first deliberations of the Provisional Government, and it was only some six or seven days after the establishment of the Republic, that one of us, I do not recollect who, said: " *A propos,*

Messieurs, qu'est devenu Louis Philippe?" a question
which gave rise to no other feeling than one of kind
solicitude. M. Marrast was therefore appointed to go
in quest of the fugitive king, in order to escort and, if
needed, to shield him. M. Marrast was to be attended
by MM. Ferdinand Lasteyrie and Oscar Lafayette.
He declined to be the Odilon Barrot of another
Charles X.; but he despatched agents to Havre de
Grace, with special directions to watch over the fallen
monarch and to facilitate his embarking.

The Duchesse de Montpensier had found a refuge at
M. Lasteyrie's. After a short stay in the house of this
gentleman, she left Paris, and crossed France, perfectly
safe.

The Duc de Nemours remained in Paris two days,
without molestation of any kind. Being informed that
he was hidden in a house close to the Luxembourg, we
made it a point to wink at it.

Lord Normanby did not think, of course, that such
facts as these deserved being noticed. His lordship
was not the man to be moved at the adoption by a set
of revolutionists of a policy which, for its merciful and
self-reliant character, has no parallel in the history of
nations. All he could do was to admit that, among
the members of the Provisional Government, one at
least, M. de Lamartine, may have been susceptible of
some good feelings. Well, let the noble marquess be
apprised of a circumstance which I trust will teach
him the danger of confining within two narrow limits
one's acknowledgment of the truth. A false rumour
having become current that the Duchesse d'Orléans

had been arrested at Mantes, M. Ferdinand Lasteyrie got extremely alarmed, and hastening to the Hôtel de Ville, besought us to order that the princess should be released. All the members of the Provisional Government complied with the request, except M. de Lamartine. To the entreaties of M. Ferdinand de Lasteyrie, his answer was : "*Le salut public repose sur ma popularité; je ne veux pas la risquer.*" Whereupon, one of the members came forward, and so warmly opposed anything like a petty persecution against a woman and a mother, that M. de Lamartine was obliged to desist. The person to whose chivalrous interference I here allude, was M. Albert.

The abolition of the punishment of death for political offences is a fact which Lord Normanby could not decently pass over in silence. The following is his statement of the case :

" . . . M. de Lamartine announced to the people, amidst universal cheers,—that which was not accepted the day before—the abolition of the punishment of death for all political offences. This most virtuous act is the greater *personal* triumph to him, when we consider what were the details of the day before. The great contest between the two parties was upon the question of the change of flag, from tricoloured to red. M. Lamartine said, with great energy, that the tricoloured flag had been waved in victory from one end of Europe to the other, whilst the red was only known to the Champ de Mars, as having taken its colour from the blood of Frenchmen."*

* "A Year of Revolution," vol. i. pp. 127, 128.

Nothing could be more unjust and more contrary to the truth than to give credit to M. de Lamartine exclusively for what Lord Normanby condescends to term "a most virtuous act;" and, on the other hand, nothing could be more calumnious than to contrast, by way of insinuation, the conduct of those who insisted on the punishment of death being abolished, with the opinion of those who were for the change of flag, from tricoloured to red. Lord Normanby will probably be amazed at hearing that the Provisional Government was urged to change the flag, and prevailed upon to abolish the punishment of death, by *the same person*, and that that person was—myself! The fact may seem strange to Lord Normanby, who is evidently impressed with the ludicrous idea that, red being the colour of blood, those only are likely to wish for a red flag who delight in bloodshed. But, I am sorry to say, his lordship has yet much to learn.

The truth is this :

On the 25th of February, M. de Lamartine started the question whether it would not be expedient to abolish capital punishment for political offences. The principle involved in the measure was unanimously adopted; but the practical side of the question, in all its bearings, was considered by some to be of a nature to open a wide field of difficult discussion, and the proposition was rejected, to my great disappointment, there being no book of mine in which the inviolability of human life is not proclaimed.

It so happened that, the very next day, an article appeared in the most important of the royalist newspapers, hinting that France might expect to see the axe of the executioner become once more the sole engine of government. On reading this, I felt indignant, and I repaired to the Cabinet Council, holding in my hand the slanderous paper. Then, from the abundance of my heart, my mouth spoke. I said, that to take life from a man, except in case of actual self-defence, is to usurp a power which belongs to God; that a judge must be *infallible* who dares to inflict an *irrevocable* punishment; that this sanguinary counterfeit of justice is more especially monstrous in time of social convulsions, when a conscientious error of opinion is so easily mistaken for a crime, when to be vanquished is to be guilty. I called upon my colleagues to remember how many illustrious personages were put to death within the last fifty years, whose heads dropped pell-mell with those of the most abandoned criminals into the same fatal basket. Even in a merely practical point of view, could any doubt be entertained about the necessity of disconnecting the new Republic from the dismal remembrance of the policy which, under different circumstances, was forced upon the old? The still lasting terror created by the events of 1793 and 1794 being the most serious obstacle we had to contend with, the best way of removing it was to fling down the guillotine. Moreover, any generous display of self-reliance on the part of the Provisional Government, was sure to make a favourable impression abroad, and to win the heart of the French nation, always ready to applaud whatever implies some idea of grandeur.

Whilst I was speaking, M. de Lamartine stood motionless at the other end of the room. He ran up to me, seized me by both hands with rapture, and exclaimed, "Ah! there you have accomplished a noble act!" A scene ensued of half-suppressed enthusiasm, at which crafty politicians will sneer perhaps. Be it so. We lay no claim to that sort of statemanship which consists in a systematic and vile disregard of every elevated principle of action. Old Dupont (de l'Eure) thanked God for having permitted him to live long enough to witness the thing that was done; and we passed, with a feeling of religious emotion, the following decree, the second part of which was drawn up by M. de Lamartine, and the first by myself:—

"The Provisional Government, convinced that grandeur of soul is the supreme policy, and that every revolution accomplished by the French people owes to the world the consecration of a philosophical truth;

"Considering that there is no sublimer principle than the inviolability of human life;

"Considering that, in the memorable days we have just gone through, the Provisional Government has, with pride, taken note that not a single cry for vengeance has issued from the lips of the people;

"Declare,

"That, in their judgment, the penalty of death for political motives has been abolished, and that they will present this their desire for ratification to the National Assembly.

"The Provisional Government has so firm a conviction of the truth they proclaim, in the name of the

French people, that if the guilty men who have caused
the blood of France to flow were in the hands of the
people, it would be in their eyes a more signal punishment to degrade than to strike them." *

Now, may I be allowed to call the attention of the
reader to the fact that the man who prevailed upon the
Provisional Government to adopt this decree, and who
drew up its preamble, was precisely that one, by whom,
on *the same day*,† the change of flag, from tricoloured
to red, was demanded! a decisive proof that such a
demand had not the slightest reference to terrorism
and bloodshed!

To complete this statement, let me recal the words
I uttered, on the 10th of March, from the tribune of the
Luxembourg:—

"The men who were *impossible* are suddenly become
the men who are *necessary*. They were denounced as
the apostles of the Reign of Terror. Well, their first
act, when the Revolution swept them into power, was to
abolish the punishment of death, and their most fondly
cherished hope is to be enabled one day to lead you to
some public square, and there, in all the splendour of a
national fête, to set fire to the last remains of the scaffold." ‡   It must be added, to the credit of the people
of Paris, that they hailed with tremendous cheers this
appeal to the noblest part of human nature.

As to the preference they gave to the red flag, it
originated in a feeling as honourable as it was sound.
That any stress should have been laid on a change of

* See the *Moniteur*, 27th February, 1848.   † *Ibid.*
‡ See the *Moniteur*, 11th March, 1848.

flag, may appear singular to Englishmen. Yet nothing is more congenial to the character and habits of the French than to attach a particular importance to what is meant to tell upon the imagination and to speak to the eye.

What was the national colour in the remotest and most obscure ages of French history, is a point of no great importance. But if we refer to a more recent period, we find that the red flag, called *oriflamme*, was, from the reign of Henry I. to the time of Charles VII., the national standard; whilst the white banner marked with fleurs-de-lys was what Froissart terms " *bannière souveraine du roy*." The white flag began to be substituted for the red one under the reign of Charles VII., that is, at the very period when the baneful system of standing armies was established in France, for the sake of propping despotism. In 1789, the middle classes having raised themselves, over the ruins of the feudal *régime*, to the highest pitch of political power, Lafayette, on the 13th of July, moved, at the Hôtel de Ville, the adoption of a new flag to be formed by the association of white, which was considered the colour of royalty, with red and blue, which were the colours of the *Tiers État Parisien*.

The tricoloured flag was, therefore, the result and the symbol of a compromise between the king and the people. Kings having been done away with, there was no reason why their past power should continue to be symbolised. The workmen of Paris could not, of course, be expected to act from any subtle historical knowledge; but they knew—and this was enough—that white meant

kingly power, and that red had long been the national
colour. In their eyes the prestige of the tricoloured
flag had been irrevocably broken by its having become,
under the reign of Louis Philippe, the dishonoured flag
of *La paix à tout prix*. To give it up was to repudiate
seventeen years of corrupt policy, in the manner best
suited to the tone of thought and feeling characteristic
of the French people. So strongly were the people of
Paris impressed with this idea, that no other flag was
hoisted during the struggle than the red flag. Whence
a natural desire to keep, after the victory, the standard
under which the battle had been fought.

Moreover, it was generally understood that to new
institutions new emblems should be adapted. The
royalists were suspected of fraud and artifice ; hatching
plots were spoken of in every quarter; even the Provisional Government was far from inspiring the people
with an unlimited confidence, as it comprised new
converts like M. de Lamartine, and more than one man
whose conduct had betrayed an alarming disposition to
accept the Regency of the Duchesse d'Orléans. Decep-
tion was vaguely, still strongly dreaded, and the people
wanted to be shown a token that the Republic would
not be a brief halt on the road from a rotten monarchical form of government to another not better or
perhaps worse.

The consequence was that, on the morrow of the
Revolution, men wearing red ribands were to be found
in every street, in every public square, in every public
garden, and all along the quays. Lord Normanby tells
us that he himself "saw some few of his countrymen

walking about the streets with bits of red riband in their button-hole."*   The red flag was spontaneously clamoured for; and the excitement grew so intense that we had to take it into serious consideration.   Numbers of people stood on the *Place de Grève,* with red armlets and red cockades, whilst red flags were seen waving at the windows of the neighbouring houses, many on the roofs.   A Cabinet Council was held.   I urged the expediency of expressing by the very choice of a new symbol that royalty had been abolished for ever, that the old distinction between classes had ceased to exist, and that, above or apart the sovereign power of the nation, there was nothing henceforth to be represented, in the shape of a standard.   On this occasion, my sole opponent, as far as I remember, was M. de Lamartine, who showed himself reluctant to break off with the past by any such decisive step.   However, the discussion was very calm on both sides, and M. de Lamartine began to give way, when, on a sudden, M. Goudchaux, the minister of finances, who happened to have been sent for, entered the room, protesting with vehemence against a display of popular force which he thought intended to intimidate the Provisional Government.   This supplied M. de Lamartine with an argument all the more pressing, as I felt my own pride deeply wounded at the bare idea of a decision which might be imputed to want of energy. It was then suggested that the best way of solving the problem would be to pass the following decree, which wss done, in consequence of the vote of the majority :—

"The Provisional Government declare :

---

* "A Year of Revolution in Paris," vol. i. p. 114.

"The national flag is the tri-coloured flag, whose colours shall be re-established in the order which was adopted by the French Republic. On the flag will be inscribed these words: FRENCH REPUBLIC—*Liberty, Equality, Fraternity,*—three words in which the whole substance of democratic principles is embodied. The tri-coloured flag is the symbol of those principles, while its colours are meant to express their traditional character.

"As a rallying sign and grateful recognition of this last revolutionary act, the members of the Provisional Government and all the public functionaries shall wear a *red* rosette, and a *red* rosette shall be fastened round the staff of the flag."*

From this text, which M. de Lamartine took great care not to mention in his book, but which any one may read in the *Moniteur* of the 27th February, 1848, it follows that the discussion ended in a sort of treaty of peace between the two contending parties. Far from being rejected, the red colour was solemnly selected to represent the revolutionary power, and, according to the very terms of the decree, as a *rallying point*.

It remained to make known the decision to the crowd gathered on the Place de Grève, a task for whose accomplishment M. de Lamartine was the fit person, since the question now was to bring the people to acquiesce in the conditional maintenance of the tri-coloured flag.

To describe and analyse M. de Lamartine's nature, I could do nothing better than to apply to him what the author of "Jane Eyre" puts in the mouth of the heroine

* See the *Moniteur* of the 27th February, 1848.

of that most beautiful novel: "My sole relief was to allow my mind's eye to dwell on whatever bright visions rose before it; and certainly they were many and glowing; to let my heart be heaved by the exultant movement, which, while it swelled it into trouble, expanded it with life; and, best of all, to open my inward ear to a tale that was never ended,—a tale my imagination created and narrated continuously, quickened with all of incident, life, fire, feeling, that I desired and had not in my actual existence." Such is M. de Lamartine. He is incessantly labouring under a self-exalting hallucination. He dreams about himself marvellous dreams, and believes in them. He sees what is not visible; he opens his inward ear to impossible sounds, and takes delight in narrating to others any tale his imagination narrates to him. Honest and sincere as he is, he would never deceive you, were he not himself deceived by the familiar demon who sweetly torments him. His eminent qualities I do acknowledge; but in his narratives I cannot find anything else than the confessions of a *haschisch* eater.

Accordingly, I will not stop to refute the innumerable and glittering fancies with which he has spangled the recital of his triumph over the stormy multitudes. Nor will I complain of the fantastic part he assigns to me, when he says I appeared to him like a pallid phantom, "*à travers cette espèce de nuage que l'improvisation jette sur les yeux de l'improvisateur.*" To discuss from an historical point of view mere optical illusions would be perfectly childish. Stripped of all exaggerations, the account of what fell out amounts to this (and my testimony is worthy of belief, since in that emer-

gency I stood constantly near M. de Lamartine, and
witnessed all that was going on) :

M. de Lamartine presented himself before an armed
crowd with praiseworthy courage, as did all his colleagues on many a similar occasion, and on this very
occasion, those among them who happened to be at the
Hôtel de Ville. There were in the throng a certain
number of over-excited persons, as was the case daily
for more than two months on the Place de Grève, at the
Luxembourg, at the Préfecture de Police, everywhere.
But the people at large did not seem disposed to any act
of wild violence. That a shot might have possibly been
fired by some unknown and unseen hand is not to be denied ; but I am bound in duty to state that the accounts
of the transaction, all more or less copied from the
fanciful recital of M. de Lamartine, have magnified the
peril beyond measure. In reality, the prevalent feeling
was a marked tendency to suspicion, nothing more.
M. de Lamartine had a clear satisfactory explanation to
give, but no general hostility to surmount. As for
me, I was in a position of extreme perplexity, as I
could neither speak contrary to my conviction against
the red flag, nor make a public appeal in its favour ; a
step sure to be attended with the overthrow of the
Provisional Government, at the risk of an immense
and irretrievable confusion. Under such circumstances, if anything fatal had occurred, it would have
been my lot to suffer for an opinion which was not my
own. But, I must repeat it, this was not very
probable, as it is by no means congenial to the
generous people of Paris to strike at men who, not

being in a condition to defend themselves, come confidently forward.

M. de Lamartine harangued the crowd in a strain of impressive eloquence, and succeeded in removing their suspicions, by affirming that the maintenance of the tri-coloured flag did not imply in any degree whatever retrogression to the past; that the Provisional Government were resolved upon preserving the Republic, and that the tri-coloured flag was henceforth intended to be a Republican symbol. In that way he went so far as to say that the reason why the tri-coloured flag ought to be preferred to the red one was, that the former had been carried round the world by our victorious armies, whilst the latter had only been dragged round the Champ de Mars in THE BLOOD OF THE PEOPLE.

How curious! This argument, which made great impression at the time, and has been, ever since, so often re-echoed, rests upon a most extraordinary historical blunder. It is absolutely untrue that the red flag, on the 17th of July, 1791, was dragged, at the Champ de Mars, in the blood of the people. Far from it! In violation of what was strictly prescribed by law, it was not even unfurled; and the unhappy Bailly was afterwards sentenced to death on that very ground, because they urged against him that the unfurling of the red flag, in case of popular disturbance, had for its object to warn the rabble, and to induce them to disperse, so as to prevent bloodshed. The fact is that if, on the 17th of July, 1791, the legal formalities had been observed, the most important of which was the unfurling of the red flag, *the blood of the people* would not have been shed at all; as those gathered at the Champ de Mars were unarmed, actuated by no seditious feelings or warlike intentions, and quite disposed to withdraw, if warned in time.*

I have another remark to make, and a singular remark too. That the red flag should be deprecated by the enemies of the Republic, on account of its having been erected over the barricades during the last struggle, was natural enough. But no such objection was set forth, because no one dared to whisper a word against the Republic. The popular emblem was therefore denounced as being the portentous symbol of sanguinary and anarchical passions, which was indeed the height of impudence, if we consider that, till the Revolution of February, the red flag, according to the rules of "Martial Law," had never been displayed except in stormy times, by the appointed agents of the constituted authorities, and for the sake of preserving order! So, a flag which, from the legal point of view, was the *drapeau de l'ordre,* was on a sudden baptised the *drapeau de l'anarchie* by those very men who pretended to be *les hommes d'ordre!*

Who does not remember what followed? M. de Lamartine was extolled to the skies, for having got a signal victory over this most formidable enemy of humankind . . . . the red colour; and it escaped the attention of everybody, it escaped the attention of Lord

* Such as are anxious to become acquainted with the details of that terrible event, will find them stated, at full length, either in the trial of Bailly, "Hist. Parl.," vol. xxxi., or in my "History of the French Revolution," vol. v., at the chapter entitled *Massacre du Champ de Mars.*

Normanby himself, who was in constant communication with M. de Lamartine, that the conqueror of *the red colour* was obliged to wear and actually wore a *red* rosette in his button-hole, in obedience to a decree to which he had appended his own signature !

Of course, it was given out by those hardened in their hatred to the Republic, that society had been seen for a moment verging to its utter destruction; that fortunately a few words issuing from the magical lips of M. de Lamartine had wrought a miracle ; and that, contrary to all human calculations, a Republic had actually been installed, without everything being put to fire and sword.

Meanwhile, in Paris, where there was not a *sergent de ville,* not a soldier left, a hundred thousand famished workmen, armed to the teeth, were making themselves a voluntary police ; not a drop of blood was shed, owing to the conduct of the sanguinary partisans of the red flag, then in complete possession of the street ; the houses of the rich were guarded by the poor, and men in rags stood as sentinels at the gates of their calumniators.

CHAPTER V.

THE " DROIT AU TRAVAIL."

THE bands which carried the red flag had left the
Place de Grêve hardly an hour when it again began to
be thronged with a highly excited crowd. Masses of
people, urged by some new impulse, rushed into it,
filling it with their clamours, which reached us, while
engaged in organising the *mairies*. Suddenly, the
council-door was flung open, and a man appeared,
spectre-like. His face, savage in its look at the moment,
but noble, expressive, and handsome, was of a deadly
paleness. He had a gun in his hand, and his blue eye
kindled, as he fixed his glance intently upon us. But
whence came he, and what could be his object? He
presented himself in the name of the people, pointed
with an imperious gesture to the Place de Grêve, and
making the butt of his musket ring upon the floor,
demanded the recognition of the " *Droit au Travail.*"
I must confess that the bullying form of the summons,
for a moment, roused in me a feeling of defiance; but I
instantly suppressed this inward protest, so unjust
towards one who, after all, was only demanding his
due. M. de Lamartine, who is as little versed in political economy as can be, and who fears any new idea of

this class as children do ghosts, advanced to the stranger, and placing one hand upon his arm in a familiar, carressing way, addressed him, and went on evidently luxuriating in the copiousness of his own eloquence, the object of which was to puzzle the man into losing sight of his demand. Marche—such was the name of the workman—looked at the orator for a while with great earnestness, as though bent on penetrating into the real meaning concealed by this haze of words. But soon discovering that there was little there, he became impatient, rang his musket on the ground, and roughly broke in with the popular form of interruption : *Assez de phrases comme ça !*

It was now time for me to interfere. I drew Marche aside, and showed him a paper on which, while M. de Lamartine was speaking, I had written the following decree :—

"The Provisional Government engage themselves to guarantee the existence of the workmen by means of labour.

"They engage themselves to guarantee labour to every citizen.

"They take it to be necessary for the workmen to associate with one another, in order to reap the legitimate reward of their toil."

Marche, the deputy of that mighty crowd which stood, in the Place de Grêve, awaiting his return with grim impatience, seemed satisfied with the nature of the engagement, but rather uneasy as to the prospect of its being executed. Perceiving this, I strongly impressed upon him the difficulties which lay in the way of accomplishing such a project, and urged the absolute necessity of patience and trust in the good will of the Government, on the part of the people; whereupon he approached M. de Lamartine, and addressed to him these memorable words: "*Eh bien, Monsieur, le peuple attendra ; il met trois mois de misère au service de la République.*"

The decree, in the form which I had drawn up, having been adopted by my colleagues, M. Ledru Rollin then proposing this additional clause, to which no one objected, though I internally felt that it was not a thing calculated to be agreeable to those for whom it was intended:

"The Provisional Government restore to the workmen, who are its real owners, the million belonging to the late civil list, which will be soon due."

As the above-mentioned decree has been made the subject not only of the severest but of the most abusive criticism, more especially in this country, it is natural that I should leave my defence in the hands of one whose authority the English people have long since learned to respect,—a man highly distinguished for his qualities both of head and heart, and incontestably the first political economist of our day, Mr. John Stuart Mill.

"To one class of thinkers, the acknowledgment of the '*Droit au Travail*' may very naturally appear a portentous blunder; but it is curious to see who those are that most loudly profess this opinion. It is singular that this act of the Provisional Government should find its bitterest critics in the journalists who dilate on the excellence of the Poor-law of Elizabeth; and that the same thing should be so bad for France, which is perfectly right, in the opinion of the same persons, for England and Ireland. For the '*Droit au Travail*' is the Poor-law of Elizabeth, and nothing more. Aid guaranteed to those who cannot work, employment to those who can; this is the act of Elizabeth, and this the promise, which it is so inexcusable in the Provisional Government to have made to France.

"The Provisional Government not only offered no more than the promise made by the act of Elizabeth, but offered it in a manner, and on conditions, far less objectionable. On the English parochial system, the law gives to every pauper a right to demand work, or support without work, for himself individually. The French Government contemplated no such right. It contemplated action on the general labour market, not alms to the individual. Its scheme was, that when there was notoriously a deficiency of employment, the State should disburse sufficient funds to create the amount of productive employment which was wanting. But it gave no pledge that the State should find work for A or B. It reserved in its own hands the choice of its work-people. It relieved no individual from the responsibility of finding an employer, and proving his willingness to exert himself. What it undertook was, that there should always be employment to be found. It is needless to enlarge on the incomparably less injurious influence of this intervention of the government in favour of the labourers collectively, than of the intervention of the parish to find employment individually for every able-bodied man who has not honesty or activity to seek and find it for himself.

"The '*Droit au Travail*,' as intended by the Provisional Government, is not amenable to the commoner objections against a Poor-law, it is amenable to the most fundamental of the objections, that which is grounded on the principle of population. Except on this ground, no one is entitled to find fault with it. From the point of view of every one who disregards the principle of population, the '*Droit au Travail*' is the most manifest of moral truths, the most imperative of political obligations.

"It appeared to the Provisional Government, as it must appear to every unselfish and open-minded person, that the earth belongs, first of all, to the inhabitants of it; that every person alive ought to have a subsistence before anyone has more; that whosoever works at any useful thing, ought to be properly fed and clothed before anyone able to work is allowed to receive the bread of idleness. These are moral axioms. But it is impossible to steer by the light of any single principle without taking into account other principles by which it is hemmed in. The Provisional Government did not consider, what hardly any of their critics have considered—that although every one of the living brotherhood of human kind has no moral claim to a place at the table provided by the collective exertions of the race, no one of them has a right to invite additional strangers thither without the consent of the rest. If they do, what is consumed by these strangers should be substracted from their own share. There is enough and to spare for all who *are* born; but there is not and cannot be enough for all who *might* be born; and if

every person born is to have a first claim to a subsistence from the common fund, there will presently be
no more than a bare subsistence for everybody, and a
little later there will not be even that.   The ' Droit au
Travail,' therefore, carried out according to the meaning of the promise, would be a fatal gift even to those
for whose special benefit it is intended, unless some
new restraint were placed upon the capacity of increase,
equivalent to that which would be taken away.

"The Provisional Government then were in the
right; but those are also in the right who condemn
this act of the Provisional Government.   Both have
truth on their side.   A time will come when these two
portions of truth will meet together in harmony.   The
practical result of the whole truth might possibly
be, that all persons living should guarantee to each
other, through their organ the State, the ability to earn
by labour an adequate subsistence, but that they should
abdicate the right of propagating the species at their
own discretion and without limit; that all classes alike,
and not the poor alone, should consent to exercise that
power in such measure only, and under such regulations, as society might prescribe with a view to the
common good.   But before this solution of the problem
can cease to be visionary, an almost complete renovation must take place in some of the most rooted
opinions and feelings of the present race of mankind." *

This is the light in which the subject has been viewed

* Defence of the French Revolution of 1848, in reply to Lord Brougham
and others.   From the *Westminster and Quarterly Review* for April,
1849, pp. 31—33.

by one of the most eminent philosophers and writers of
this country. It must be observed that he finds no
fault with the solemn acknowledgment of the " *Droit
au Travail*," except in reference to the principle of
population.   His only objection is grounded on the
supposition that society cannot endeavour to secure
employment for all its members, without encouraging
the increase of population, which should, on the contrary, be kept within certain limits.   With all due
deference for the opinion of Mr. Mill, I beg to say,
that even this objection loses much of its weight, as
regards the constant practice of family-life in France.
In France, there is no need of social restrictions or
prohibitive regulations to prevent an ominous increase
in the number of additional strangers in quest of " a
place at the table provided by the collective exertions
of the race."   The check on over-population lies in the
good sense and the foresight of each father of a family
in good circumstances, who takes great care not to give
existence to more children than his means allow him
to support, and to put into a condition, when grown up,
to support themselves.   A statistical description of
France has shown, of late, that the population there,
far from increasing at any alarming rate, is rather
stationary ; nor must we overlook the most striking
fact that, if any excessive increase of population is to
be noticed in France, it is precisely in the class of the
poor and of the *unemployed* ; whence our French word
prolétaires. And why so? Because those have little
business to trouble themselves with the future, who
have no hold on the present ; because poverty and

foresight are contradictory terms; because brutish sensuality is incident to a condition which affords no other sources of enjoyment; because he who lives from hand to mouth, is naturally led to adopt for his children, as he does for himself, the proverb, " sufficient for the day is the evil thereof." How heart-rending, and still how unavoidable, the well-known French saying: *À la grace de Dieu !* The consequence is, that a great falling-off of employment, by increasing poverty, increases the very number of improvident husbands, while the principle of the " *Droit au Travail*," wisely carried out, would have for its effect to check that overgrowth of population, which accrues from the combined action of ignorance, carelessness, and forced leisure.

However this may be, such as have indulged in so many abusive outpourings against the " *Droit au Travail*," will do well to meditate upon the comparison drawn by Mr. John Stuart Mill between this most vituperated measure and the poor-law of Elizabeth. Let them not forget these remarkable words: " From the point of view of every one who disregards the principle of population, THE ' DROIT AU TRAVAIL ' IS THE MOST MANIFEST OF MORAL TRUTHS, THE MOSP IMPERATIVE OF POLITICAL OBLIGATIONS."

Whatever may be the opinion of the reader about the scientific value of the acknowledgment of the " *Droit au Travail*," it cannot, at any rate, be denied that there was a singular elevation of thought and purpose in the demand itself. The people, at that moment, let it be remembered, were absolute and uncontrolled masters. Well, in this plenitude of their power, on the very morrow of a revolution, what did they exact? *Panem et Circences?* No: *Bread through Labour!* Was that too much? The difference of character in these two demands brings into strong relief the progress of our age, and that nobleness of feeling so conspicuous in the people of Paris.

When I drew up the decree acknowledging the "*Droit au Travail*," I was perfectly alive to the vast difficulties of the task; but what I aimed at was to involve the government in an obligation to adopt such practical measures as were indispensable. Of these, the principal, of course, was the immediate creation of a special public department fully provided with all the means of carrying out the object. And this my purpose was quite in harmony with the construction which the people put on the decree.

Accordingly, on the 28th of February, the Council having again assembled, we unexpectedly saw the people spreading over the Place de Grêve, and ranged, as it were, in order of battle. Over them waved numerous banners, bearing these words: *Ministère du Progrés; Organisation du Travail.* Almost immediately after, a deputation from the people was announced. Instant decision was required, and, without hesitation, I proposed that the popular request should be complied with. Since the Revolution had a social direction, why not present it at once in its true light? I argued that it would have been either childish or fraudulent to write on a scrap of paper the acknowledgment of the "*Droit au Travail*," if, when the time for action came, we did not proceed to use all available means of carrying the principle into practice.

To this view M. de Lamartine vehemently objected. He contended that we were not a constituent power; that we had no right, in a matter of such importance, to forestall the decisions of the National Assembly about to be elected; that he did not see the necessity of the proposed department, and that, with respect to the *Organisation of labour,* it was a thing he could not comprehend nor ever would.

The majority of the Council went with him, upon which I on the spot tendered my resignation; as, according to my feeling, to assist in working a govern- ment on any other principle than one's own, is to stoop to the most degrading of humiliations, and he deserves to be ranked with the lowest of men who covets power for power's sake only.

They shrank from accepting my resignation; but as I persisted in pressing it, they offered me the presidency of a Commission, wherein, until the National Assembly was constituted, all social questions should be discussed and elaborated.

Thus, in fact, instead of a department having at its disposal offices, agents, funds, administrative machinery, effective power, means of application, resources for action, it was proposed to have—what? A stormy school established, in which it would be my task to deliver a course of lectures upon hunger to hungry people! Need I say how warmly I declined the offer?

Then it was that M. Arago, his voice broken by emotion, adjured me not to persist in a refusal that would involve the rising of the people of Paris. Pointing to his grey hair, he appealed to me, in the name of his age. He stirred up in my heart all the powerful influences of an old and unswerving attachment. He reminded me that he had been to me a father. He declared his readiness to sit in the Commission, and there to give me his assistance, in the capacity of a vice-president. I loved M. Arago, and I respected him as much as I loved him. Never for an instant had his sincerity been a matter of doubt to me. His self-denial in thus proposing to fill a subordinate position, and to discharge by my side perilous duties, embarrassed while it touched me.

Cruel alternative !—

If I gave way, to me, to me alone, the multitude was sure to rush for relief, a multitude famished, restless, imperious, masterful: how little probable that I could either constrain them, with no means of enforcing obedience, or persuade them to postpone their demands, and to stand in silent revolt against their destiny! What could be more insane than to incur the overwhelming responsibility of a situation which I was denied all practical means to control! Are fair words a sufficient balm to the wounded hearts of men whose wives and children gasp for life? Should I not be accused of artfully cajoling the people into foregoing their most legitimate claims? Should I not expose ideas which I believed to be true, to the discredit into which they would certainly fall, from want of application? If I gave way, I should find myself on the brink of an abyss.

But if, on the contrary, I persisted in my determination to resign, what might be the consequence? Was not a popular insurrection likely to arise from a schism in the government under such circumstances and for such a motive? In the midst of a civil war, would not the Republic run the risk of either getting furious or perishing? And since, by a strange fatality, I happened to be placed between two sorts of responsibility equally frightful, was it not my duty to accept in preference that which appeared to me bloodless?

These were the conflicting thoughts which distracted my mind, during such moments as will never fade away from my memory!

On the other hand, I said to myself that *Mens agitat molem;* that I was called upon to ascend a tribune from which I might advocate, so as to be heard by the whole world, those principles of eternal justice whose triumph had been the aim and the intellectual stimulus of my life; that the diffusion of a noble idea, by the aid of a great moral power, was not a result to be disdained; that it was not, after all, an unimportant privilege to bring under discussion, before an almost limitless auditory, the despotism of evil. Possibly I might be crushed in the struggle, but what of that? The work would survive—the furrow be traced.

These last considerations seemed to me powerful, if not absolutely conclusive, and I made up my mind to act accordingly. It was therefore agreed that a "Government Labour Commission" should be instituted at the Luxembourg. The deputation of workmen was introduced.

A mechanic, completely bald-headed, of an iron mould and stern expression, came forward, holding a paper in his hand. With a monotonous but firm voice, that sounded like the beating of a hammer, he read a petition to the effect that a new ministerial department should be created, the *Ministère du Travail*. M. de Lamartine, hastening to sweeten the lip of the bitter cup with his most honeyed words, enlarged upon the expediency of a " GOVERNMENT LABOUR COMMISSION," which he affirmed would answer the purpose, by framing plans afterwards to be adopted by the National Assembly. There is in the Parisian workman a singular acuteness of intellect. The members of the deputation perceived at once that mere speeches could not make up for action; that the largest part of France being still plunged in darkness, those to be elected by peasants under the influence of their landlords, were not fit persons to solve the social problem, and that the surest way to make the *Organisation of Labour* appear impracticable, was to deny me all practical means of realisation. They cast at M. de Lamartine a scrutinising look, and then turned to me, as if anxious to hear me give utterance to their own thoughts. But I could not do it, without bringing the State to a chaos of confusion, by an aggressive disclosure of our internal dissensions. They guessed probably what I felt—what I suffered; for they had the generosity not to insist, and, after a moment of gloomy hesitation, they retired in silence.

I drew up the following decree, which was published, the next day, in the *Moniteur*, with the signatures of all the members of the Provisional Government :—

" Considering that the Revolution accomplished by the people must be intended for the people;

" That it is high time to put an end to the unjust and protracted sufferings of labourers;

" That the question of labour is one of paramount importance;

" That there is no problem more deserving of attention on the part of a Republican government;

" That it is a duty more especially incumbent on France to look into, and to endeavour to settle, a question started in all the manufacturing countries of Europe;

" That it is advisable to think, without delay, of making him that works enjoy the legitimate reward of his work;

" The Provisional Government decree:

" A permanent Commission shall be formed for the express purpose of inquiring into the social condition of the operatives.

" In order to show how great is the importance the Provisional Government attach to the solution of such a problem, they place at the head of the ' GOVERNMENT LABOUR COMMISSION ' two of their colleagues, MM. Louis Blanc and Albert, the former in capacity of president, the latter, a workman himself, in that of vice-president.

" Workmen will be called upon to be members of the said Commission, the seat of which will be the Luxembourg."

This decree was dated February 28; its publication in the *Moniteur* of the 29th, could not be expected to answer the sanguine expectations to which the Revolution had given rise.

Consequently, a new attempt was made by the most ardent among the working classes, and the agitation, this time, exhibited so threatening a character, that my presence was deemed necessary to calm the popular effervescence. I repaired in haste to the Place de Grêve, whither M. Arago, prompted by a noble feeling, would accompany me.

Here is the *Moniteur's* account of what took place on this occasion:

"To day, at about three o'clock in the afternoon, nearly 6000 workmen belonging to various trades have made their appearance on the Place de l'Hôtel de Ville, waving flags and demanding that a *Ministère du Travail et du Progrès* should be instituted. After receiving several deputations in the Council-Chamber, MM. Arago, Louis Blanc, Marie, Bethmont, as representing the Provisional Government, descended from the Hôtel de Ville and made their way through the crowd. M. Arago went on from one group to another, haranguing them, and was hailed everywhere by the warmest acclamations. M. Louis Blanc, addressing the people, said that the ' GOVERNMENT LABOUR COMMISSION,' already formed, would meet to-morrow at the Luxembourg, there to set to work immediately, with the assistance of all competent judges, and mainly of mechanics elected by their fellow-workmen."

It was added by M. Louis Blanc that the power of the Provisional Government lay in the confidence of the people, and the strength of the people in their very moderation. He urged the necessity of their being firm, to keep in awe any ill-disposed persons, and calm, to allow the Provisional Government that freedom or mind requisite for deliberation.

" The speech of the honourable member was earnestly cheered; and as M. Louis Blanc, owing to his small stature, had entirely vanished in the crowd, two workmen, lifting him up, carried him on their shoulders round the Place de Grêve, amidst loud acclamations." *

Alas! At the sight of this burst of candid and affectionate enthusiasm, I felt my heart rending, as it had now become doubtful to me whether I should be enabled to requite the popular sympathies by any efficient service. My mind kept wandering in a waste of dark conjectures and portentous uncertainty. Ominous was the fear evinced by almost all my colleagues at the bare idea of anything like a social renovation. Would it be possible for us all to act in common? If not, how fatal the consequences!

* See the *Moniteur* of the 1st of March, 1848.

CHAPTER VI.

THE LUXEMBOURG—SOCIALISM IN THEORY.

WHEN I left school, I was scarcely of an age to look for employment. Still I found myself obliged to do so, on account of family circumstances which admitted of no delay. Among the friends of my family was a man of great merit, who had been vice-president of the Legislative Body during the *Cent Jours,* in which capacity he uttered, when the intelligence of the defeat of Waterloo reached the Assembly, these memorable words: " *Du calme ! Messieurs, après la bataille de Cannes, l'agitation était dans Rome et la tranquillité dans le Sénat.*" The gentleman I allude to was M. Flaugergues. He had not much influence at that period, owing to his liberal views and independent character; but I knew he was acquainted with M. le duc Decazes, then grand referendary of the House of Peers, and I applied to him. Of what took place, I have preserved a vivid recollection. One fine morning, M. Flaugergues took me to the palace of the Luxembourg, where we were ushered into the duke's bedroom. He was sitting up in bed, and reading the *Constitutionnel.* M. Flaugergues, after the usual formalities of introduction, requested him to exercise his influence on my behalf.   M. Decazes turned round to me, and, tapping my cheek with his hand, in a lofty patronising way, said, "We'll see what can be done for the lad." We parted, nor did we meet again.   Well, strange to say, on the First of March, 1848, it was the lot of this lad to sleep in that very bed on which, many years ago, he had seen the duke sitting, and which the duke had just been obliged to vacate for his use.*

This was singular enough; but how much more extraordinary, in the way of contrast, the spectacle of an assembly of workmen in their *blouses,* opening their session in the gorgeous palace of Marie de Medicis, and in the very hall where the peers of France were wont to meet!

When I went to take possession of the Luxembourg, which had been assigned to me as a residence, I was accompanied by Albert, the vice-president of the "Government Labour Commission."   I have not yet spoken of Albert.   On the 29th of February, at the Cabinet Council held at the Hôtel de Ville, there stood among my new colleagues one person only whom I had never seen, a man of middle stature, with a pale, regular-featured face, rather stern, but remarkable by its straightforward and yet watchful expression.   This was Albert.   Up to this time, a poor mechanic, unknown to all save to his fellow-workmen of the faubourg St. Antoine, he had never moved in any other class than his own.   What struck me, therefore,

---

* This visit to the Duc Decazes was probably the occasion of the ridiculous story which has found its way in some so-called biographies, respecting my introduction by Pozzo-di-Borgo to the Duchesse   Dino, whom I never saw in my life.

was the composure of his countenance, exhibiting
neither pride, conceit, nor rudeness, and evincing, by a
mixture of self-respect and modesty, that, though
thrown so suddenly into the society of men like Arago
and Lamartine, the latter especially conspicuous for
his elegance of manner, he felt quite at home. While
business was going on, he preserved an unbroken
silence, and listened with great earnestness to everything that was said, at the same time casting at each of
us in turn a calm but scrutinising glance. At the
close of the Council, he rose, walked up to me, and
said: " I see you really love the people." Then, with
much warmth and frankness, he gave me his hand; and
from this moment we were friends.

Albert was a man of no ordinary stamp. Employed
as he had been from his early youth in manual labour,
the culture of his mind could not fail to be neglected;
but he had a great quickness of perception and a clear
intellect, never to be dazzled by brilliant appearances
or fascinated by artful eloquence. He spoke little, but
sensibly and home to the point. His self-denying
attachment to me may be said to have been heroic.
How assiduously he contrived to keep in the back
ground, to show me off to greater advantage! How
actively, when called upon to deal with his fellow-
workmen, he exercised his influence in my behalf,
always ready, in my absence, either to ascribe to me
alone the merit of any welcome measure, or to assume
the exclusive responsibility of any step open to misrepresentation or blame! And this was the more
admirable, since his feelings towards me could only

have their source in his unbounded devotion to the cause I advocated, which he believed to be just. I say, therefore, without affectation, and as a tribute strictly due to him, that the noblest part performed at the Luxembourg was his.

I think I may repeat here, as recorded at an earlier period, the impression I received on entering the deserted palace of the Luxembourg. Dreary and silent were those spacious halls which a white-haired aristocracy had just left, to make room for a ragged people; and, while traversing them, for the first time, in the dead of night, I felt as if my thoughts, like pallid phantoms, stood up around me. I at once perceived that in the dark, trackless waste I was about to cross, I was exposed to tread upon many a serpent sleeping in the shade. All the calumnies I should have to face, assumed a sort of corporeal form, and became, so to speak, visible. My heart could not have throbbed with greater agitation, had Faust himself been there, whispering these terrible words to me : " Ever has he been trampled upon, who, having a profound conviction, was not wise enough to keep it secret, and conceal his views from the knowledge of the world."

Nor was anything better calculated to realise the threat, than the views I had to proclaim. To trace a new road, higher, much higher than the sphere of party-spirit, to bring upon my head the blind enmity of the upholders of old things, by showing that poverty is slavery; to contrast the manifold advantages of the principle of association, gradually carried out, with the evils of that system of competition which makes the domain of industry a field of battle, and to set against me all those whose prosperity had been derived from the downfall of their neighbours ; to defy the *littera scripta*, the abiding words of the wealthy lords of the press, with no other shield than the evanescent shouts of the poor subsiding into long-lived, but unlettered, and, in so far, ineffectual sympathies ; and, what was still more difficult, to guard against all purposeless agitation those predisposed by suffering to combat—living weapons so often thrown away after being made instruments of massacre, blood-stained dice in the game of false tribunes and ambitious leaders. . . . Such was the task that had to be accomplished, a hard one, indeed, full of bitterness and perils. I call God to witness that when I resolved to act, solely under the impulse of my conscience, I was the sport of no illusion. I knew that a society grown old in corruption and injustice is not easily to be shaken ; I knew that if a sick man, unconscious of his disease, be told of it, he becomes irritated at the unwelcome warning. But he indeed would be a poor creature, who, having been raised to the highest station by the suffrage of his fellow men, should for a moment hesitate to fulfil his duties, whatever the consequences to himself. I, therefore, made up my mind, and, my resolution once formed, I clung to it all the more strongly, since I was prepared for the worst; so that fortune, though it overwhelmed, neither surprised nor troubled me.

Before I come to the proceedings of the Luxembourg, I think it necessary to give a brief exposition of the circumstances which made it imperative to institute, on the morrow of the Revolution, with a view to practical and prompt results, a solemn inquiry into that department of social science, bearing especially on the question of labour.

Long before the Revolution of February, a deep-seated evil was exhausting the French industrial world, and demanded extensive social reforms. Competition, —whose worst dangers England had warded off by her daring, her perseverance and genius, that is, by her dominion of the sea, by laying hold of the most distant markets, and accomplishing, through commerce, what Rome had done by the sword, the conquest of the world;—in France was confined within a circle too narrow and too restricted, not to terminate, sooner or later, in the most fearful calamities. Thus, the industrial world was transformed into an armed camp, and industry became a deadly warfare; production was governed by no foresight, the blindest chance directing its feverish activity; merchants were compelled to live a precarious life and to play a terrible game, panting after the stake, between stoppage one day and bankruptcy the next; all interests were opposed to each other; and to complete the confusion, crowds of labourers were there, eager to sell themselves at the lowest price, every day increasing in number, and every day more hungry and furious. Who does not remember the social insurrection which broke out at Lyons, in the reign of Louis Philippe, and the ominous motto which the workmen inscribed on their flag : *" Let us live by working, or die fighting ? "*

I have in my possession a collection of letters addressed to me by different manufacturers, after my installation at the Luxembourg.   Nothing can be more conclusive, and at the same time more melancholy than the testimony they offer.   Some volunteer to make us a present of their establishments as being unable to continue them; others, in placing at the disposal of the government their buildings, raw material, and machinery, ask no better remuneration than to be appointed superintendents of establishments remodelled according to a new system; and all loudly demand the intervention of the State for the protection of industry, which they prove must be utterly ruined if assistance were not speedily rendered.   One thing which is not generally known is, that the expediency of framing a plan of social reform was suggested by vehement and repeated solicitations proceeding, not only from the workmen, but from many a large manufacturer, who had been reduced to unutterable distress, arising out of causes of long duration.*

The Revolution of February, then, did not produce the commercial crisis; it merely showed it in all its intensity.   It is the height of ignorance and childishness to attribute the convulsions of trade to the promulgation of the very reforms intended to prevent them. Moreover, the Revolution was not the originating principle of those contemplated reforms, but served only to bring them more prominently into sight.   For a long time, an under-current of opinion had been

---

* To publish all the letters confirmatory of this would, of course, be impossible.   A specimen of them will be found in the Appendix No. 2.

spreading among the people, which found no echo in
the parliamentary tribune, and was but feebly heard
in the daily press or other publications. While vulgar
great men were endeavouring to satisfy their ambition
in the ballot-box, and filled the world with empty
noise, poor operatives, in the close atmosphere of their
factories, supposed to be absorbed in the cares of their
daily labour, were elevating their minds to considerations of vast import, living in the highest regions of
thought, and studying the causes of the misery under
which they groaned. Their hopes conceived a radiant
future that would succeed the present diseased and
enervated system. They inquired into the law of past
social changes, to ascertain if civilisation had not yet
another step to take; and observing that the lower
classes had first ceased to be *slaves*, and afterwards
to be *serfs*, stimulated by noble aspirations, they
asked themselves if they should not now cease to be
paupers, this being but a new form of slavery. But
where could they find the means of enfranchising
themselves? It had already been pointed out to our
generation by this motto, the eternal glory of our
fathers—LIBERTY, EQUALITY, FRATERNITY; it only
required to have a clear practical insight into the sense
of the three terms of this sacred device : and here the
natural instinct of the people of the great towns of
France, especially of the people of Paris, did not
deceive them.

They understood :

That LIBERTY is not only the *right*, but also the
power, granted to every man to develop his faculties

under the dominion of justice and the safeguard of the law ;

That a diversity of talents and capabilities being a necessary condition for the existence of society, EQUALITY consists in all having an *equal* scope for the development of their *unequal* faculties ;

That, lastly, FRATERNITY is but the poetical expression of that state of mutual dependence and harmony which will eventually make Society one great family.

Therefore, they said :

We must have done with the system of *Laissez-faire*, because it is the abandonment of the poor, the weak and the ignorant; and for thousands of human beings, to *let them alone* is to *let them die*.

Anarchical competition must be, by a series of gradual and practical measures, put an end to, because anarchy is nothing else than despotism run mad, and the contest between the strong and the weak cannot but terminate in oppression.

There must be no more motives derived from the fierce antagonism of interests, because, where the success of one necessarily depends on the ruin of others, society is filled with hatred and verging on civil war.

Such are the ideas that, for many years, were silently forming in the people's mind,—I do not speak, of course, of the French peasants, plunged as they are in deep intellectual darkness ;—I speak of the workmen of Paris and of all our principal manufacturing towns. But those who live in the upper circles of society, were utterly ignorant of the movement going on among the lower classes. The *soi-disant* statesmen of the monarchy, seemingly so wise in politics and legislation—your clever financialists—your celebrated manufacturers, had no idea that a new world was growing up beneath them. But the hour had to come, when they would be all of a sudden aroused, as it were, by a thunder-clap. That hour did come at last, and will ever remain in History as the *Democratic and Social Revolution of February.*

It is absolutely beyond doubt that to the working classes a republican revolution, with no attempt at social reforms involving the question of labour, would have been a bitter disappointment; and the scenes already described show into what formidable extremities a disappointment of this kind might have hurried them.

Under such circumstances a Government Labour Commission having been instituted, did the leading members of it put forth any pretension of changing society in a day by the application of some new system, sprung full-grown from their heads, as Minerva sprang armed from the brain of Jupiter? Or did they show they had any intention of violating the principle of liberty by an abrupt and compulsory obtrusion of their views? Here is the answer.

Scarcely were Albert and myself installed at the Luxembourg, when we addressed to the workmen the following proclamation :—

" Citizen Workmen, the Commission appointed to prepare the solution of the great problems in which you are interested is bent on its task. But however legiti-

mate may be your impatience, we adjure you not to
allow your exigencies to outspeed our researches. All
the questions relating to the organisation of labour are
complex; they embrace a number of interests opposed
to one another, if not in reality, at least in appearance ;
they require then to be approached with calmness and
examined with ripeness of judgment. Too great impatience on your side, too great precipitation on ours,
would only end in injury to both. The National
Assembly will be convoked. We shall present to its
deliberations the draft of laws we are now working out,
with the firm resolution to ameliorate your condition,
morally and materially ; and on these schemes your
own delegates are to be summoned to express their
opinion." *

Thus, to cast a prudent glance at the questions
having reference to the moral and the material improvement of the working classes; to expose frankly
the results discovered or partially detected ; to accept
discussion for a weapon, and public opinion for a judge ;
to call upon that public opinion to pronounce itself
pacifically by universal suffrage and through a National
Assembly, such was the course which, from the first,
we pledged ourselves to pursue, by a solemn and
voluntary declaration.

How we redeemed this pledge will be seen presently.
In fact we did not go further than proposing a series of
temporary measures, adapted to the existing order of
things, and susceptible of immediate application. For

---

* The proclamation here referred to appeared in the *Moniteur* of
March 9, 1848, signed by Albert and myself.

we knew very well that, in the slow and painful journey of mankind towards a reign of justice, there are many stages to pass through, and that it is wise, nay indispensable, to proceed by gradual reforms. Who but a madman would dream of immediately transporting an ignorant and corrupt society into such high regions as lofty intellects may imagine or righteous hearts conceive? But if he is a fool who thinks he can reach the end by destroying the road, no less fool is he who starts, not knowing whither he goes. When a mechanician is about to construct a machine, he certainly does not think of striking it off in an instant; still he designs his plan. When a poet composes a drama he puts one act after another most assuredly; still he does not neglect to trace beforehand the general framework of his plot. The earnest pioneers of social progress can have no other method of proceeding.

A broad distinction must, therefore, be made between the principles which were regarded at the Luxembourg as the ultimate consequence of social science when fully developed, and the suggestions of a merely practical character which were propounded for immediate application.

The former may be summed up as follows:

Men have received from God certain faculties—the faculty of love, of knowledge, of action. But these faculties were not given us to employ in solitary isolation, since they essentially suppose a society in the midst of which they may be exercised. They are, consequently, the supreme indication of what each of us owes to the society of which he is a member; and that indication God himself seems to have written with his own hand, in shining characters, in our organisation. If your strength is twice as great as mine, it is a proof that God has destined you to bear a burden twice as heavy as mine. If you are more intelligent, God has destined you to diffuse around you more light. Weakness is the creditor of strength, ignorance of instruction. The more a man *can* do, the more he *ought* to do; and that is the sense in which we read the immortal saying of Christ: " Let the first among you be the servant of all." Hence, then: FROM EVERY MAN, ACCORDING TO HIS FACULTIES. Such is DUTY.

But, together with our faculties, we have been endowed by God with certain wants, intellectual, moral, physical: wants of the heart, of the mind, of the imagination. How can each of us fulfil his providential function, and accomplish his destiny, so long as social institutions do not lend themselves, in each of us, to the free development of our entire being, by the satisfaction of those wants which the organisation of each induces? Hence, then, taking the word *wants* in its broadest and noblest sense: TO EVERY MAN—WITHIN THE LIMITS OF THE RESOURCES OF THE COMMUNITY—ACCORDING TO HIS WANTS. Such is RIGHT.

To superficial minds, of course, but also to minds unaccustomed to deal with this class of subjects, these views will seem Utopian. Yet, if we take the trouble of analysing the matter a little, we shall find that they are not quite as visionary as they may appear.

Respecting this question of wants, the very first

objection that meets us at the threshold is the impossibility to apply to them any standard of measurement. The truth is, on the contrary, that nothing can be more easily measured, since the measurement of a want is the force of the want itself. We cease to eat when we have no longer appetite, to drink when we have no longer pleasure in drinking, to walk when we feel tired, to read when the mind is weary, to sit at any kind of play when the enjoyment goes off, in fact to persist in any want whatever, physical or moral, when it has received full satisfaction. We are speaking, of course, of wants that are healthy, not morbid, in a normal, not in an exceptional state. And even in these last, there is a natural limit which cannot be passed. The difficulty is not, therefore, to find a measure for our wants, but to contrive such social arrangements as might secure to them their healthy development. But is this possible? Can any state of society be imagined in which the rule: " To each according to his wants," can be realised to the contentment of all? Well, it may be seen in operation daily. In the pivot institution of society, the family, it is not the member who produces most that necessarily takes most—often, exactly the reverse. Illustrations would be superfluous. But here, it may be said, the natural tie of affection accounts for the general contentment. This does not at all signify; moreover, instances which are not explicable by any such influence, are innumerable. Take a club. Here, a man, for a fixed sum, common to the members, has the use of its library, its billiard-room, its smoking-room, and so on. But he does not habitually make use

of all, nor does he think it a hardship that any of his
fellow-members should be taking advantage of a greater
number of these comforts than he does, or can do.
Consequently, the principle : " To each according to
his wants," is there in full operation, not from any
feeling of moral sympathy, but simply for the sake of
personal gratification.   A club, therefore, is, on a small
scale, the practical working out of the great object of
Socialism, which aims at securing gradually to all the
members of society the *equal* satisfaction of their
unequal wants.

But both justice and the interest of society require
that every man should give as well as receive, and when
receiving to the extent of his wants, that he should give
to the extent of his faculties.   Whence the corresponding duty : " From each according to his faculties."

At this point arises the practical question : Can such
a state of society be conceived wherein every man
would be naturally induced to contribute according to
his faculties ?   Let us inquire into it.

It is a truism that a man will do that most agreeably
and effectively which he is by his nature best qualified
to do.   Now, in the present state of society, this capital
fact is practically ignored, the adjustment of employ-
ments depending, for the most part, on casual combina-
tions, hereditary positions in life, and so forth.   The
labourer can only be by chance suited to his labour,
which, in many cases, therefore, must be and is necessarily repugnant to him.   Hence idleness, which is
a violation of man's nature, a pure social creation.
For nature has not given us faculties to remain

unemployed : and to induce us to employ them, she has made the exercise of them, when voluntary, a pleasure. It is the satisfaction we derive from seeing, that disposes us to observe; it is the satisfaction we derive from hearing, that disposes us to listen. Accordingly, if there were a state of society in which this principle of congruity, this adaptation of man's faculties to the ends most gratifying to them, obtained, then labour would be carried to the highest amount of development in each, without any other stimulus than the gratification of a natural want.

To show that this is not, in itself, an unattainable result, and also to what an extent education can mould the character, and supply us with new standards of opinion and feeling, I will give the following remarkable illustration.

In May 1848, I received a visit from a gentleman named Allier, the director of an industrial school for pauper children at Petit Bourg. He came to invite me to see his institution with Monsieur and Madame Victor Hugo and their daughter. We all went. On our arrival, M. Allier at once took us into the workshops, where a number of children were being taught a variety of handicrafts. The cheerful eagerness with which they applied themselves to their tasks was extremely striking. One might really have thought them a group of boys, not working, but playing at work. This became still more remarkable when we entered the smithy, where the first thing we noticed, amid the smut and din, was a child merrily hammering away at a piece of iron, with a look joyous, and bright as the sparks that were flying about him—and this before a hot fire, in a hot spring day. We were then conducted to the garden, and there found a host of tiny gardeners busily engaged; some cultivating flowers, some watering borders, others tending vegetables. The glowing faces of the children, the brilliancy of the day, the beauty of the spot, on very high ground, commanding a splendid view, of which I was reminded, on my first visit to the Crystal Palace, presented a delicious scene. As I gazed upon it, I could not help thinking that the young Vulcans in the pandemonium we had just left, must have some slight envy of the more fortunate tenants of this little Eden. On my making the remark, " Well," triumphantly exclaimed M. Allier, " this is a mere matter of choice. All these children are doing precisely what they prefer, and therefore that air of cheerful ardour which has so much struck you." Seeing us look surprised, he proceeded to explain that, after the opening of the institution, it had been the practice to assign the occupations according to some arbitrary preconceptions of fitness, which proved to be a failure, as the children soon got tired of their work, grew weary and listless, and were constantly soliciting a change of employment. " Then," added M. Allier, " we hit upon a new plan. Whenever a child comes to us, we give him the free range of the workshops for a month, allowing him to try his hand at anything he likes. At the end of the time, he is required to fix upon some one occupation, with a clear understanding that he is to keep to it. The result is what has so much astonished you."

This needs not a word of comment. But now came something still more astonishing, which I particularly recommend to the attention of those ready to declare beforehand impossible what, within their own experience, is new and untried.

As we went through the building of Petit Bourg, our attention was directed to what we were informed was the place of punishment. There we saw a poor little fellow sitting; in fact, a prisoner. Moved at the contrast between him and his fellow-pupils, we asked for his pardon—a request with which M. Allier good-naturedly complied, as a compliment to us. He set the boy at liberty, saying to him in a tone of admonition, " Tell your friend not to do it again." One may well imagine that a scolding of the sort was a perfect mystery to us, until M. Allier solved it in this unexpected way : " It is now," he said, " the custom of the school that every new comer must, after a certain time, publicly choose some one of his fellow-pupils as his *friend;* and the aim is to instil into them, in their relations with each other, a sense of reciprocal obligation, of kindness, and self-sacrifice. This is turned to account in a singular manner. When a boy has committed a fault—now, pray keep your countenance—it is not he who is punished, but his friend." In spite of the recommendation, we could not keep our countenance, but alluded to the story of certain little princes who, whenever they got into a scrape, were vicariously flogged in the person of their plebeian friends. " Aye," replied M. Allier, laughing; " but there was no reciprocity there." The fact is, that since this experiment has been in operation, the number of faults committed has wonderfully diminished. The most obdurate boy, who would have been made sullen by punishment, shrinks from the idea of exposing an innocent companion to the penalty of his offence, whilst the sufferer converts a punishment, unattended with shame, into a positive honour, by submitting to it with fortitude; so that, in point of fact, the whole moral retribution falls upon the offender."

Of course, I do not mention this curious proceeding with a view of recommending its adoption, but only to illustrate the amazing power of education in supplying unexpected motives to action, and making that appear natural and just which previously had been considered contrary to nature and unjust. But to return.

That men are unequal in strength, in talents, in wants, is self-evident, but society has been formed precisely in order to prevent this natural inequality from becoming a source either of oppression or suffering. Unfortunately, the social aim has not been reached as yet, and while no man physically stronger than another is suffered to crush him, the existing order of things affords us, under the deceitful name of free competition, the sad spectacle of a permanent struggle where the ignorant and the poor are left unprotected against any such persons as may be tempted to abuse the power of intelligence or that of money.

Were society constituted according to the laws of reason and justice, all its members, without exception, would have their place at the banquet of life, after having been equally invited, when children, to take their place at the grand sources of human knowledge, that is after having been enabled, from their earlier age, to manifest and to develop their different capacities and their unequal aptitudes. The speciality of vocations beiug thus asserted, every man, instead of being bent down, by poverty coupled with ignorance, under the yoke of a kind of labonr reluctantly uudertaken, often foreign to his natural dispositions, would be called to fulfil his vocation and to occupy that post in society, for which God himself, when he created him with certain peculiar qualities and predominating tastes, had in some sort designed him.

Such speculations as these are, of course, merely philosophical. No political man, no member of the Provisional Government, having to deal with the situation, could have laid them before the people, as susceptible of even a remote application, without justly incurring the accusation of encouraging an idle dream. But to declare that they are contrary to the very nature of things, or that the end descried in the far distance is necessarily and absolutely unattainable, would be to risk an assertion neither philosophical nor practical. It is, indeed, a truism that it has always been the fate of a new idea to be reputed impossible, till it had received application; it has become almost trite to remind one's audience that the precursor of Watt was thrown into a lunatic asylum, by way of recognition of his sublime discovery; that Galileo was forced to demand pardon on his knees for having professed the *impious error* of the earth's rotation, and that in the history of knowledge, every accepted fact has been at its birth

Utopian. The question is, therefore, to examine if the principles above stated are in themselves rational and calculated to prove beneficial to the community, it being understood that even though viewed in this light, we are nevertheless to proceed to their realisation with much caution, slowly, and to pause at each intermediate station as long as may be requisite.

Were this realisation to be declared for ever impossible, what would be the consequence ?—That, for most of the members of society, social liberty itself would be hopelessly impossible; inasmuch as social liberty, according to the very definition given of it by the upholders of the existing order of things, " consists in following that occupation which is best suited to one's talents, and in choosing one's own profession." *

Now, it would require an unusual amount of boldness to affirm that, in society as constituted at present, such is the case. Are those poor children free to enter the career of the law, to devote themselves to literature, to aspire after the lucrative offices of finance, who, in order to increase a parent's wages by the fruit of their infantine labour, are sent at the age of seven or eight to a factory, where the germ of their intellect is blighted, their soul's health ruined, and all their faculties engaged in watching a wheel? Are those youths, the poor man's sons, free to follow the bent of their inclination for agriculture or commerce, whom their helpless position devotes to military functions, turning death into a means of livelihood ? And are those frail

* Thus did M. Thiers express himself in the National Assembly on the 13th of September, 1848, when the *Right to Labour* was controverted.

women free to become honest matrons, who, according to the melancholy account of Parent Duchâtelet, are irresistibly driven into a life of prostitution by the depth of their misery? Who can deny that, under the present system, it is, in most cases, chance and not the natural law of talents and vocations, that decides the choice of a man's career? Who can deny that the fundamental vice of this system, is to disorganise and destroy all arrangements for the harmonious adaptation of pursuits to talents? Exceptions may be cited: but how few those are who, gifted with extraordinary energy, and aided by peculiar circumstances, have succeeded in overcoming the obstacles that surround the poor man's cradle! The poor man free, indeed! In France, we do not even leave him the liberty of enjoying the roadside causeway or the pavement of our streets; for if, from want of work, he asks our charity, we punish him as a beggar; or, if being without a better shelter, he sleeps upon our palace-steps, we imprison him as a vagabond. No, the poor man has not that social liberty without which it is hardly worth while living—scarcely, indeed, does the rich man himself enjoy it, enslaved as he is by social prejudices and despotic follies. Louis XVI., who, being passionately fond of locksmith's work, would have made a happy and respectable locksmith, owing to the accident of his birth, was compelled to leave his crown on the scaffold; and many a man has died on a mattrass, after having lived in a garret, who had in him the germs of an intellect that might have governed empires. If a proof of this be needed, it will be found in revolutions, which, by agitating society, and tearing off the surface, have so often dragged from their depths talents that have astonished mankind. To any impartial observer of facts, it is obvious that the present state of society, as far as scientific social arrangements are concerned, is but a practical negation of the, now inexorable, maxim : *" The right man in the right place."*

The evil is undeniable, and it originates in the fact that, in virtue of pre-existing social systems, all the roads to intellectual or moral improvement, all the means of education as well of subsistence, all the implements of labour, lands, and raw materials of every kind, are in the possession of a comparatively small portion of society : a state of things, the consequence of which is that a great part of the community are denied, from the very threshold of life, the necessary means of developing their natural powers, and must, accordingly, live, not as they ought and choose, but as they can.

Nor is this all. To those who would encourage them to labour, in the hope of becoming possessors, how many poor creatures might, with good reason, reply :

You call us to work ! But we have neither ground to till, nor wood to build with, nor iron to forge, nor wool, silk or cotton to make clothes withal. Nay, are we not forbidden to pluck that fruit, to drink of that fountain, to hunt those animals, to take shelter under that tree ? We stand in need of life itself as of labour : because, when we came into the world we found all around us invaded; because laws, that were made without our sanction, and before our birth, have left to chance the care of our destiny; because, in virtue of those laws, the *means of labour*, which the earth seemed to have granted for the use of all her children, have become the exclusive property of a few.   Theirs it is to dispose of us, for we have not the power to dispose of ourselves. We are quite ready to work—but does that depend upon our will alone?   And, when you cannot, or dare not, ensure us employment for our hands, how could you ensure us the fruits of our labour?   Is there any chance that the product of our toil will be for us or for our children?   Alas! our helplessness places us at the mercy of others, who offer us, in exchange for the results of our teeming activity, not that which we have created, but a pittance just enough to prevent us perishing in the act of producing,—a pittance which the stress of competition constantly tends to grind down to the lowest level of the bare necessities of life, and which, if even it left room for saving, must be swallowed up the first idle day that occurs from bad times or illness. How is it that the reapers should hunger for a loaf, that the weavers of precious silks should be clothed in rags, and that the builders of palaces should be sometimes at a loss to find where to lay their heads?

Such was the complaint which, on the morrow of the Revolution of February, was raised by hundreds of thousands of operatives, not only in Paris, but in all the principal towns of France; and, as far as I am concerned, I could not deny the evil, without ceasing to be true to myself.   On the other hand, far from complacently nursing chimeras, or aiming at abrupt violent changes, which, in my opinion, would have been detrimental to the people themselves, I made it my study to propose such a plan as could be carried out by a series of partial, progressive measures, expressly intended to prevent any individual from suffering injury.

It struck me that society was making, every day, through its representatives, trial of all sorts of destructive engines, and spending much time, as well as much money, in all sorts of petty experiments, while nothing was tried to ascertain what mode of social relations was most likely to be conducive to the happiness of the different members of the community. I thought that a question so vital to the welfare of a nation, was worthy of calling forth the exertions of real statesmen.

Then came the consideration, in what manner they could advantageously interfere?

Here I will just observe that, in England, the principle of advancing public money in aid of private enterprises is not unpractised. The grant of money by the Privy Council to individuals associated for the purpose of erecting and conducting schools, under certain stipulated conditions, and subject to a certain control, is a remarkable instance. These grants, moreover, it must be remarked, were so entirely the act of the executive as to give rise, on that account, to great opposition, especially from the late Sir Robert Peel, when they were first brought under the notice of the Legislature in 1849, his objection being directed against the issue of any public money, without the previous sanction and vote of parliament. Nevertheless, the practice has been maintained up to a late period, when it received some modification.

Well, the scheme I proposed, at the Luxembourg,

was based on the same principle, free, in its working, from the objections of Sir Robert Peel. For the difference between my industrial plan and the educational practice of England, was: First, that, in my own, the grant would have been a loan secured by mortgage on the establishment to which it was advanced, and not a mere donation; Secondly, that no such grant could have been made by government, except under stipulations, not prescribed by the executive, but resulting from the deliberations and vote of a National Assembly born of universal suffrage.

In short, the plan propounded, at the Luxembourg, amounted to this:

The State—by which I mean the nation acting as a whole—would have called upon a determinate number of effective labourers, belonging to both agricultural and industrial pursuits, to volunteer to form associations working on the co-operative principle, under stipulations meant to secure the accurate application of that principle, that is the combined action of individual efforts for a common end and joint benefit. The workmen, thus selected, if willing to offer themselves, would have received from the State such a loan to be repaid with interest, as might be required to enable them, after a reasonable time, to become self-supporting. In this manner would a great national experiment have been accomplished.

Nor was the principle of co-operation to be confined to the members of each association, but it was to be established between the various associations, through the agency of a general relief fund contributed by all of them, so that, when any one branch of trade was momentarily embarrassed, it would be assisted by those in a more prosperous condition.

That, in suggesting a scheme of this kind, we were not doing anything to shock the sober and practical intelligence of the English people, may, I presume, be justly inferred from the view which has been taken of it by one whom the " Economist "—a paper least of all likely to have any sympathy with my views—recently spoke of as the first political economist of the day, Mr. John Stuart Mill. He says :

" This is Socialism ; and it is not obvious what there is in this system of thought, to account for the frantic terror with which everything bearing that ominous name is usually received on both sides of the British Channel.

" It really seems a perfectly just demand that the government should aid with its funds, to a reasonable extent, in bringing into operation industrial communities on the Socialist principle. It ought to do so, even if it could be certain beforehand that the attempt would fail; because the operatives themselves cannot possibly be persuaded of this except by trial; because they will not be persuaded of it until everything possible has been done to make the trial successful; and because a national experiment of the kind, by the high moral qualities that would be elicited in the endeavour to make it succeed, and by the instruction that would radiate from its failure, would be an equivalent for the expenditure of many millions on any of the things which are commonly called popular education." *

---

* "Westminster and Foreign Quarterly Review," April 1849.

Such was the plan which has been made the subject of so many misrepresentations; it simply consisted in laying, in the midst of the present social system, left untouched, the foundations of another system, that of co-operative production, the latter being established as a vast national experiment, with the assistance, and under the control of the State.

As a consequence, two great modes of Industrial action, an old and a new one, would have been placed face to face:

The one, based on the principle of antagonism; the other, on the principle of co-operation:

The one, stimulating individuals to an eager pursuit of their own purposes, irrespective of the interests of others, or even in absolute hostility to them; the other, necessarily leading each individual to identify his own interest with that of the whole:

The one, therefore, sowing discords, jealousies, hatreds; the other, enforcing concord as the *sine quâ non* of success:

The one, resembling a duel, in which the safety of one too often demands the destruction of the other, and is not unfrequently attended with the destruction of both; the other, a really emulative movement, wherein the principle of action is also a personal interest, but requiring, for its satisfaction, that sense of duty which proceeds from an habitual sympathy with, and a necessary fidelity to, the prosperity of all:

The one, fostering a production which gambles away its substance on a blind computation of chances; the other, creating a production proportioned to the foreseen wants and exigencies of the market:

The one, consequently, making success the uncertain result of lucky sagacity; the other, the certain reward of scientific knowledge.

At any rate, experience being called upon to determine which was the best of the two, the best would gain ground little by little, without violence, without commotion, on account of its attractive power, while the worst would gradually disappear, from the very fact of its inferiority being practically proved and generally acknowledged.

These were the famous theories of the Luxembourg, these were the speculations addressed to an excited and victorious multitude, not—mark it well—as ideas susceptible of a full immediate application, but serving as land-marks to direct the march of society towards a more prosperous condition, which only their posterity would have any chance of enjoying. Nor have I attempted here to soften down the bold character of these views, my object being to bring out in strong relief the spectacle, unique in history, of a great population deriving from abstract doctrines inducements to enlightened resignation. On this extraordinary fact, an able writer, whose social opinions do not exactly coincide with my own, has thus expressed himself:

" Was it nothing to have changed a population armed to the teeth into a deliberative body; to have turned cries of disorder into peaceful harangues, and the anguish of hunger into patient hopes? What other people was ever known to forget its wretchedness while listening to philosophic theories, or to take off the edge of its hunger by intellectual food? What other government ever yet dared to present itself as a subject for discussion, to challenge the spirit of inquiry, and the subtlety of paradoxical views? What greater evidence of its force, its morality, its profound consciousness of being in the right, could be afforded than this appeal to a popular council composed of the people, and commissioned to elaborate the articles of a new faith? When were ever civil wars brought to a similar conclusion?" *

* *Histoire du Gouvernement Provisoire, par M. Elias Regnault*, p. 127.

CHAPTER VII.

THE LUXEMBOURG—SOCIALISM IN PRACTICE.

THE first sitting of the GOVERNMENT LABOUR COM-
MISSION took place at the palace of the Luxembourg,
on the 1st of March, 1848.

At nine in the morning, about two hundred workmen, sent as deputies by the various trades-unions of
Paris, having taken their seats in the places formerly
occupied by the peers of France, I entered the room
accompanied by Albert. As we made our appearance,
an enthusiastic cry of " *Vive la République!* " shook the
walls, immediately followed by a solemn silence; and,
after a few remarks on the novelty and greatness of the
scene before me, I proceeded to explain the object of
the GOVERNMENT LABOUR COMMISSION, which was to
inquire into all social questions, to embody in a bill,
to be laid before the National Assembly, the results of
their deliberations, and, meanwhile, to listen to the
most urgent appeals of the working classes, with a
view to doing all that was possible and just.

Thereupon, a workman rose, and, in the name of
his comrades, made two demands, which, he said,
required immediate attention. They were as follows:
the shortening of the hours of labour; abolition of

Marchandage, that is to say, the employment of work-men by middle-men, or sweaters.

But I observed that the first step to be taken was to organise the representation of the working classes at the Luxembourg, for which purpose I suggested that every craft should elect three delegates, one of whom should take part in the daily labours of the GOVERN-MENT LABOUR COMMISSION, and the two others in general meetings, to receive reports submitted to them for their deliberation and discussion. In other words, I proposed to instal at the Luxembourg, in a regular way, a LABOUR-PARLIAMENT—a proposition which was carried amid rapturous acclamations.

Now came the hour of trial. The two demands previously addressed to me were resumed and insisted upon with an almost threatening vehemence. So de-termined were the workmen to gain their point, that they would not allow delay; and, I am bound to declare, in justice to them, that nothing could be nobler than the considerations they urged: "We insist," they said, "on the shortening of the hours of labour, that there may be more employment at the disposal of our fellow workmen who stand in need of it, and that every one of us may have, at least, one hour to live the life of intelligence, the life of heart and home. Again we ask for the abolition of *Marchandage,* because it is odious that there should be between the head manufacturers and the working men rapacious interlopers who reap their profits out of the skill, strength, and earnings of the men, and, however generous may be the head manufacturer, cause wages to decline so as to reduce us to starvation."

These representations were in full accordance with my own feelings and views, as developed in my writings. Still, I did not permit them to weigh with me so far as to induce me to act upon them, without having previously appealed to the employers for their advice on so delicate a subject. This I did not hesitate to express in frank, energetic language, and then to call their attention to various objections that had been made, more especially as regards the shortening of the hours of labour. Would not this, it had been asked, be to diminish production, to raise the price of produce, to restrict consumption, to run the risk of being under-sold on our market by foreigners,— a circumstance too well calculated to be prejudicial to the workman himself? I proceeded to say that these were objections deserving of serious consideration; that it was the interest of the working classes to keep their demands within moderate limits, and to reflect that, in the actual form of our economical organisation, every step forward, however small, could not fail to be attended with risk and perplexity.

My address, on this occasion, was not, I must confess, as warmly received as it would have been a little later, when we became better acquainted with each other. There was a gloomy silence, forerunner of some coming struggle, and indeed, scarcely had a minute elapsed, when a great number of workmen, rising altogether and talking loud, declared that no kind of labour should be resumed until the two demands had been

conceded. Painful in the extreme was my position.
My personal opinion, nay my heart, were undoubtedly
on the side of the workmen; but it seemed to me
neither prudent nor just to decide out of hand so
delicate a question, without hearing both parties; and,
as this was our first meeting, I at once resolved to
show, from the beginning, that I would not allow myself
to be made instrumental in accomplishing anything
which I did not think strictly right. I, therefore, persisted in saying that, before any further step was taken,
every class of interests should be consulted, so that
justice might be done to all.

At this moment, M. Arago unexpectedly entered.
He had heard what was going on, and, in fulfilment of
the promise he had made, at the Hôtel de Ville, to aid
me in my difficult task, he now came manfully to give
them his support.

Whoever has seen the man, with his tall figure, his
noble and handsome face, still more interesting from
the pallor left by recent illness, and his keen, flashing
eyes, shaded by shaggy eye-brows—all this heightened by
his world-wide reputation, may well imagine the instant
and deep impression he produced on the assembly.

Soothing and persuasive were the few words he
addressed to the workmen; and I took advantage
of their effect to make a pressing appeal to their
patriotism and to claim their confidence. "To risk
one's life on a barricade or in a battle," I said,
"requires no doubt great resolution; but, believe me,
it requires a still greater energy of will to make oneself
responsible for the lives of others. Do you think we

would have undertaken so formidable a responsibility, had not our determination to discharge it been indomitable? But, for the successful performance of our duty, we need your assistance; our force is derived from you, and this force is the confidence you repose in us, which we demand in exchange for our devotion to your case."

That men who had erected barricades, overthrown a government, and displayed a courage worthy of veteran soldiers, should have permitted themselves to be conquered by fair words alone, is certainly one of the most marvellous proofs of the intelligence and the generosity of the people of Paris. Well, such was, then, the case ; no further resistance was made or even thought of; no murmuring was heard ; and the assembly separated with joyful cries of *Vive la République !*

Immediately afterwards, I dispatched several active citizens on horseback to invite the employers of every description of labour to a general meeting. This was held, on the following day, at eight o'clock in the morning, at the Luxembourg, and attended by a great number of employers. The question being brought under their consideration, was calmly discussed; and the majority of the master-workmen having yielded of their own accord to the workmen's requests, from a conviction either, of the propriety of concession, or the peril of refusal, the consequence was the issue by the Provisional Government of a decree abolishing the objectionable kinds of *Marchandage,* and shortening the hours of labour from eleven to ten in Paris, and from twelve to eleven in the provinces. Need I add that this news was received with loud acclamations by the deputation of workmen who, throughout the day, thronged around the palace?

I have dwelt upon the particulars of this first transaction, to show how little we were open to the reproach of mob-sycophancy. As to my having inflamed the people, and instilled into them dangerous and chimerical hopes, the reader will be soon enabled to judge how unjust this accusation is, which has so often and so complacently been levelled at me. To the bold and false assertions of Lord Normanby I will oppose decisive proofs; although I might dispense with them, having to quote in my favour the following passage of Mr. John Stuart Mill, whose approbation, confined within three lines, is to me more than a sufficient compensation for a large volume of misrepresentations and calumnies. Referring to my speeches at the Luxembourg, Mr. Mill says: "Nothing could be less inflammatory and provocative than his tone, nor more sober and reasonable than every suggestion which he propounded for immediate adoption."*

The LABOUR PARLIAMENT was formed in the way I had proposed; that is, by the popular election, in every craft, of three delegates called upon to represent, at the Luxembourg, the whole body of the workmen belonging to that craft. So, a powerful engine was put at the disposal of the GOVERNMENT LABOUR COMMISSION, and the people of Paris were enabled to act as a single man, through the agency of a permanent meeting composed of their most clever and influential leaders.

As to the "Government Labour Commission," the

* "Westminster and Foreign Quarterly Review" for April 1849.

most competent men of every shade of opinion were invited to contribute their opinions and their criticisms. Amongst our fellow-labourers, we had MM. Charles Duveyrier, Cazeaux, Victor Considerant, and Jean Reynaud, all of them eminent representations of the various forms of social science, M. Wolowski representing the Political Economy in vogue. If some distinguished thinkers were absent from amongst us, it was either because they happened not to be then in Paris, as M. Pierre Leroux; or because they declined to join, as M. Emile de Girardin; or because their ideas found their way to us through other persons present, as those of M. Enfantin through MM. Duveyrier and Cazeaux.

I must not omit that I was most powerfully assisted by M. Vidal, Secretary-General of the "Government Labour Commission," and by M. Pecqueur, both men of high merit, of vast knowledge, and deeply versed in matters of political economy.

After a thorough discussion of the general principles by the members of the commission, the two gentlemen last-mentioned and myself framed a plan for the establishment of agricultural colonies on the co-operative principles; of certain institutions of credit on a large scale, calculated to give facilities to commercial transactions; of a national insurance office comprising every variety of insurance, and of a national central bank, with branches throughout France,—all this constituting a group of measures intended for immediate application.

The nature and the limits of this book preclude me from entering into the details of a plan so compre-

hensive, exposed, of course, to so many objections, and
requiring a lengthy explanation. I must content
myself with referring any one desirous of fuller information to a report drawn up with great clearness and
precision by the Secretary-General, M. Vidal,—a report
published in several numbers of the *Moniteur,* and
afterwards in a collective form, in a book entitled
" La Revolution de Février au Luxembourg, 1849."

The opening of the LABOUR PARLIAMENT took place
on the 10th of March, and I delivered, on this occasion,
a speech of which I think it not unnecessary to give
some extracts. I began as follows : —

" Seeing you assembled in this hall, which has been
hitherto the sanctuary of privilege, in which so many
laws have been made without you, in spite of you, and
against you, I feel an emotion which I can with difficulty repress. On these same seats, once glittering
with embroidered coats, what do I now see? Garments
threadbare with honourable toil, some perhaps bearing
the marks of recent conflict. You will remember it
was from the very place where I am speaking, that a
tribune of the aristocracy, not long since, evoked against
the mere idea of a Republic all the darkest recollections
of the past; that at his voice the peers of France rose
to their feet in an indescribable transport of delight,
and that grey-haired legislators gave way to a display
of passion which time it might have been thought had
for ever benumbed. Here, too, the Republic of our
fathers was cursed; here the Republic was expressly
prohibited to our children, and hand after hand was
raised to swear hatred against the future.

"But a few days passed away; and where is now the accuser? Where, at this moment, are they who heard him? No one knows. But what we do know is, that where they sat, you sit, representatives of labour. So replies the future.

"Of the republicans it was said they were factious men, impossible men, mere dreamers; and it turns out—thanks to the victory of the people and their courage—that those who were called factious are now charged with the responsibility of preserving order, that those who were called dreamers have now upon their hands the task of remodelling society, and that the *impossible men* have, all at once, become the *indispensable men*. They were denounced as the carefully-drilled apostles of terror; but when a Revolution lifted them to power, what did they do? They abolished capital punishment, and their dearest hope is to be soon able to lead you to some vast public square, and there, amid the pomp of a great national festival, to ask you to sweep away every remaining vestige of the scaffold."

After some further remarks, in which I did but justice to the calmness and heroic self-restraint they had displayed, I went on to say :

"The questions we have to resolve unhappily are not easy of solution. If we touch but one single abuse we menace them all. So completely has the chain of evil intertwined itself with society through all its parts, that it is impossible to shake a single link without causing a general vibration. This is the difficulty of the position, and not a slight one . . .

" How injurious, for instance, would be any attempt

at restricting the use of machinery, connected as it is
with the progress of the industrial world! Still, you
are well aware of the cruel and immoral competition
which machinery has often maintained against human
labour, and how often, in the hands of some one employer, it has enabled him to empty the workshop of
those whose bread depends upon their work. Nevertheless, the use of machinery is a great progress.
Whence then this inauspicious anomaly? It springs
from the fact that, in the midst of the industrial
anarchy now prevailing, and by consequence of the
division of interests, everything is inevitably transformed into an element of contest. Subsitute association for conflict, and, from that moment, machinery
becomes an immense boon, because it then works to
the profit of all, and supplements work without suppressing the workman.

"The questions, therefore, that engage us require
to be investigated as a whole. What we have to
look for now, to-morrow, the day after, is the endeavour to make association possible, and to establish an
intimate union of interests between all classes of
society. Why should we not strive to transfer to
things that are good that connexion of mutual de-
pendency which certainly exists in things that are evil?
Society, in this, is like the human frame, in which one
leg being defective, the action of the other must be
impeded. An invisible, but real and fatal tie binds
the oppressor to the misery of the oppressed. Sooner or
later the moment must come when this reciprocal responsibility will give rise to the most terrible retribution

. . . So, to plead the cause of the poor is, it cannot be too often repeated, to plead the cause of the rich. Hence, we are the men of no faction; it is as a whole that we love our country, that we are devoted to it, and are resolved to serve it, irrespective of any distinction arising from party-spirit.

" Under the influence of these feelings was the GOVERNMENT LABOUR COMMISSION constituted. We thought the time had come when men bold enough to dictate to their fellow-men, must find their justification in the fact of being useful; we thought that, henceforth, power should act upon this definition: Governing is self-devotion. . .

" Now, how august will be an assembly which has to deliberate upon the most important interests that can move the hearts and minds of men! For that which must occupy it will be no less a matter than the abolition of slavery: the slavery of poverty, of ignorance, of evil; the slavery of the working man, who has no refuge for his aged father; of the poor man's daughter, who, at sixteen, is compelled to get her bread by infamy; of the poor man's child who, at ten, is buried alive in the pestilential atmosphere of a factory. Is all this so inevitable to the nature of things, as to make it a folly to believe that it can be one day changed? Who will dare to affirm it, and to utter such a blasphemy against progress? If society requires mending, mend it. Abolish slavery.

" But, mark, nothing is more difficult than the settlement of such high questions. Precipitation would be fatal; and to arrive at a happy solution of problems so great as these it is necessary, not only to combine every possible effort with every amount and variety of information, but, moreover, to supplement them with the most sincere good will . . . In the first Revolution our fathers were great, even to heroism. On them fell all the bitterness of the work which we have only to follow up by means of inquiry and science. We will not, depend upon it, fail either in tenacity or patience; by God's good help and the people's, we will go at your head, deterred by no difficulties, fatigued by no resistance, utterly fearless of the enemies of our commonwealth. With such confidence in the triumph of a resolute conviction, with such trust in justice as to feel assured that her reign will one day inevitably come, we must succeed in placing on a firm, unshakeable basis our great and beloved Republic."

At this point of the proceedings, being summoned to attend the meeting of the council, I concluded abruptly, saying: "I must leave you now; but to meet again, that is the first moment any grave problem has to be solved, any patriotic act to be accomplished. Here be our rendezvous!"

"Then," states the *Moniteur*, "all the assembly rose, some of the workmen being so overpowered by their emotion as to shed tears."

I must also mention, in order to bring out into full relief the good feeling of the Parisian workmen, that my language, although intended as a check upon their too forward impatience, was, in the very words of the *Moniteur*, "listened to with the deepest silence, only broken by repeated bursts of applause."

An Englishman may be struck, at first, by the warm colouring of this speech, so different from the more sober tints of English elocution; but the reader must remember that I was addressing a French popular audience, and not suffer himself to be diverted from attending to the sobriety of the matter and the constant appeal to the good sense, moderation, and self-control of the hearers.

Some may think that I am too sanguine in supposing the day will come when, by better arangements, the present partial distribution of social advantages may be modified and expanded, to the signal benefit of the whole community. But that was not the question then; the question was to prevent the suffering classes from giving way to a movement of hostility against the more fortunate ones; and this was the import of these words, " to plead the cause of the poor, is to plead the cause of the rich," showing that progress must be effected, not by the antagonism, but by the concord, of classes. Now, what could be more creditable to the working men of Paris and more strikingly indicative of their feelings, than that such language should have been so enthusiastically received by them, at a moment when they were starving and exasperated at what they believed to be the abuse of capital !

As I say this, I feel it all but impossible not to do the delegates of the Luxembourg the justice of conveying to the reader a clear apprehension of what they really were.

First, it must be borne in mind that their services were perfectly gratuitous. Neither from any special subscription, nor from myself, who had not a farthing of public money or any funds whatever at my disposal, did they receive compensation for their loss of time. More than that, they could not accept and perform the duty of advocating the general cause of their fellow-workmen, without incurring the underhand persecution of the least liberal of the employers, the consequence of which was, that most of them were, under one pretext or another, either discharged, or exceedingly hampered in their attempts to obtain employment. Hence, many of them, some with families, were subjected to the severest privatious. Yet, no murmur, no complaint, no evidence of being disheartened, no symptom of a desire to retreat from their onerous position, ever betrayed in them any wavering in their cause, or any disposition to relax in their efforts to uphold the interests of their comrades, whatever might be the amount of self-sacrifice required.

No less remarkable was their personal attachment to such men as Albert and myself, who were utterly destitute of all means of giving them immediate relief, and whose seemingly unwelcome task it was to prescribe to them that most difficult of all virtues under the circumstances—patience.

Here is an illustration of this attachment, which was touching as it was disinterested :—

Albert and myself used to go on foot, except when we were compelled by pressing business to take a carriage, which by the bye, was a hired one, and not at all one of those princely vehicles which have so ludicrously figured in some calumnious libels in connection with our usual means of conveyance. One evening, as we made our way to the Hotel of the Minister of the Interior through the dark crooked streets that run in the neighbourhood of the church of Saint Sulpice, Albert perceived that we were tracked by an armed man who seemed anxiously to watch all our movements. To ascertain the fact, we changed our direction in various ways; but the man would not lose sight of us. At last, thinking he had some sinister intention, we turned round abruptly, and went straight up to him. To the question what he was about, he at first replied nothing, looked very much confused, and then made evasive answers, calculated to confirm our suspicions. At length, on being pressed with questions, he held out to us a card which showed he was one of the delegates of the Luxembourg, adding: "I am on duty to-night." What he meant we were at a loss to comprehend, when he proceeded to say, that his comrades, fearful lest we might be in danger, while going about unarmed, had formed among themselves a sort of voluntary and secret body-guard, of the existence of which we were then made aware for the first time. So do the people love!

I must mention another fact equally illustrative of that exquisite delicacy and refinement of feeling for which the Parisian workmen are so remarkable. After the fatal month of June, but a few days before my departure from Paris, I was taking a walk in a lonely part of the outer boulevards, when an old female mendicant approached me, asking charity. I examined my pocket, and it so happened that, that day, I had gone out without money. The old woman, looked wretched in the extreme, insisted in the most lamentable way, and my annoyance at having nothing to give her probably became visible in my countenance, for at this moment, a man in a *blouse* ran up to me, and with an embarrassment of manner and in a tone of voice so exceedingly affecting that the sole remembrance of it brings tears to my eyes, he said: "Citizen, I was one of the delegates of the Luxembourg. I cannot bear the idea of a suffering person begging your assistance in vain. Pray, do me the favour to accept this, so that the poor woman may bless you." And he respectfully offered me a few pence out of his hard earned wages. What I experienced, words can scarcely express. I squeezed his hand, held out to me, and I felt that I had nothing to regret in all the miseries I had drawn upon myself, in defending the cause of such men.

On the fifth of March, the GOVERNMENT LABOUR COMMISSION having met, I reminded it that our business was, not only to prepare laws bearing upon the labour-question, for the approval of the National Assembly, but also to take measures to effect such improvements as the most urgent exigencies of the moment required.

Accordingly, I submitted a proposition, capable, I thought, of producing much good without endangering any interest. It had been suggested that in each of the four most populous districts of Paris, a model lodging-house should be formed large enough to lodge about four hundred families of working men, with a separate apartment for each family; so as to secure to each of them, by means of a consumption on a great scale, the advantage of a considerable saving in rent, fuel, food lighting, &c., a saving which would be equivalent to an increase of wages, without interfering with employers. It was also proposed to annex to it a reading-room, a room for children at nurse, a school, court, garden, and baths.

According to the estimates presented to me by two distinguished architects, Messrs. Nott and Daly, the cost of each establishment would have been about a million of francs. To meet this expense, the government was to open a loan. It was part of the scheme, that the generous assistance of women should be made use of to procure subscriptions, and that all ranks of society should be called upon to furnish zealous agents for carrying out a financial negociation so entirely novel.

As to the scheme itself, similar establishments, I remarked, had been long in existence in various countries; so that we proposed nothing impracticable.

Still, the idea was open to objections.

For instance, from the very fact of these establish- ments offering such great advantages, it was argued that the number of demands for admission would be too numerous to be satisfied. To meet this objection, various expedients might be suggested. First, it was proposed as an indispensable condition that none but lawfully married men should be admitted, bachelors being declared ineligible. Secondly, the preference was to be given to working men with the largest families, or, in case of two families equally large, to that in which the children were the youngest.

The question having been examined in all its bearings

by MM. Vidal, Dupoty, Dussard, Duveyrier, and Malarmet, the last a worker in bronze, of high intelligence, and thoroughly acquainted with the subject, I undertook, in conclusion, to draw up a bill embodying the views and opinions that had been approved by the meeting, and to submit it to the deliberation of the Provisional Government.

This plan, which I felt, and still feel, would have been in the highest degree beneficial to the working classes of Paris, might have been immediately put in execution. had the public department for labour I asked for been instituted. Unfortunately, as the matter stood, all I could do was to suggest, and, from the rapid succession of events, the tide having turned, the suggestion, with many others of a practical nature, fell to the ground.

I particularly notice this, because the impression has been diligently spread in England that, having every command of means, I failed in carrying out my views owing to their impracticability, combined with my administrative deficiency. For instance, a lively writer, Mr. Saint John, speaking of me amongst others, in his "Louis Napoleon," etc., says, " . . . But, upon the establishment of the Republic, having been elevated into an official situation, his remarkable abilities as a writer only served to bring out into stronger relief his deficiency in administrative talent." * Another author observes it was made too convincingly evident in 1848 that my administrative capacity, even in the

* "Louis Napoleon : a Biography." By Augustus Saint-John. p. 268. 1857.

execution, with ample means, of my own projects, was of no very high order.*

How singular that I should have been taunted with inefficiently *administering*, where there was nothing to *administer !* How strange that authors who pretend to be well informed should have ventured to speak of the *ample means* I had at my disposal, when the fact of my having been placed at the Luxembourg without funds or any other *administrative* resources, is so notorious and so absolutely undeniable !

I will say more.

It may be remembered that, when at the Hôtel de Ville, I was offered the presidency of a GOVERNMENT LABOUR COMMISSION, in place of a "public department of labour," I expressly declined to accept a position in which the responsibility to be incurred would be immense, and the *means* of discharging it *nil ;* it may be also remembered that, if I at last consented to confront it, it was only in order to prevent civil war, and in compliance with the earnest entreaties of M. Arago.† Well, this was nothing less than a conspiracy concocted against me, not by M. Arago, who was made, I am sure, the *unconscious* instrument of it, but by some other of my colleagues ; and what I, at that time suspected, turned out to be the case. My most decided opponent in the Council was the Minister of Public Works. Now, here are, as revealed by himself to M. Emile Thomas, his confidant,

---

* " Napoleon the Third. Review of his Life, Character, and Policy, &c."
By a British Officer, p. 141. 1857.

† See chapter IXth, The "*Droit au Travail.*"

the secret motives which induced him to insist upon my being placed at the head of a " Government Labour Commission," destitute of all administrative resources.

" M. Marie told me " (these are the words of M. Emile Thomas, whose statement has never been contradicted), " that it was the determined intention of the Government to allow that experiment (of the Luxembourg) to have its run ; that in itself it would have the good result of convincing the workmen of the emptiness of Louis Blanc's inapplicable theories " (they had begun, mark it well, by depriving me of the means of application) ; " that, in this manner, the working classes would be disabused by experience ; that their idolatry of Louis Blanc would of itself crumble to pieces, and that he would lose for ever all his influence, all his prestige, and cease to be a danger." *

It is true that, as far as my popularity was concerned, these respectable anticipations were frustrated. Not only did the confidence of the delegates of the Luxembourg in me remain unshaken, but it assumed a particular character of generosity amounting to grandeur. With that instinct which baulks the petty manœuvres of the would-be-adepts in politics, the people had recognised their own.

After all, intentionally beggared as I was of all efficient powers, I contrived to extract from my unpromising position practical results of value, the most important of which was the energetic impulse given to the establishment of the self-supporting co-operative societies. But this result, on account of its great importance, requires

* *Histoire des Atéliers Nationaux, par M. Emile Thomas,* p. 47.

to be treated of in a separate chapter. The others I shall notice here briefly.

A pressing evil was the difficulty for men out of work to discover without delay the employers who stood in need of hands. In order to bring the supply and the demand within the reach of each other as instantaneously as possible, I obtained the sanction of the Provisional Government to a decree establishing, at the cost of the State, a "Labour Registration Office" in every municipal district of Paris, where the requisite information could be had gratuitously.

Another cause of mischief, bitterly complained of, was the ruinous competition the operatives had to sustain against the low-priced produce of criminals, fed, in prisons, at the expense of the State. The "GOVERNMENT LABOUR COMMISSION" urged that prison labour should be suspended, and that the contractors should receive from the State such an indemnification as might be, either amicably settled, or else fixed by a court of law, after valuations given in by competent judges. This provision, applying also to the work executed in barracks, was made the object of a decree to which all the members of the Provisional Government affixed their signatures.*

Besides this, in a great number of conventual establishments, women, well cared for, were enabled to undersell and forestall a mass of poor houseless creatures, either employed upon starvation wages, or actually perishing for want of employment. I caused a decree to be issued, enacting that, henceforth, no work would be allowed in

* *Moniteur* of the 25th of March, 1848.

religious communities, except under regulations so adjusted as to prevent any unfair competition.*

It would carry me too far to enumerate all the measures that were taken by the " Government Labour Commission " to meet the exigencies of the moment; but I cannot pass over in silence a document which shows that, while bent on alleviating as much as in our power lay the sufferings of the people, nothing could induce us to go, even for this purpose, beyond what we considered to be just.

The English public has learnt through a profusion of bitter reports, bitterly commented upon, and from Lord Normanby,† that, after the Revolution of 1848, a cry was got up in France against the foreign working men, whose competition, in fact, had become extremely injurious to a not inconsiderable number of natives. It is my painful duty to acknowledge the fact. But, in connection with it, there are important circumstances which Lord Normanby has carelessly withheld from the English people, and which, for this very reason, I am bound to relate.

As soon as I was apprised, at the Luxembourg, of the agitation that pervaded the working classes, I resolved to resist it instantly. Nor did the attempt require much courage on my part; for I knew enough of the character of the people of Paris, to feel assured beforehand that any lofty appeal to their sense of honour would produce a decisive effect. I, therefore, drew up the following declaration, which was signed by all my

---

* *Moniteur* of the 25th of March, 1848.

† A Year of Revolution in Paris, vol. i. p. 178.

colleagues of the *Provisional Government,* and appeared
in the *Moniteur* of the 9th of April, 1848 :

"In conformity with the proposal of the 'Government Labour Commission,'

"Considering :

" That Fraternity is the principle which the Republic
proclaimed on the morrow of its victory ;

" That the recent battle was fought in the name, and
won for the sake, of humankind ;

" That all countries, however dissimilar, ought, in
the person of a foreigner, to protect and respect man ;

" That France must be true to her own genius, and
accomplish her duty, by rendering her triumphs, nay
her sufferings, beneficial to other nations ;

" That, if she feeds, at this moment, a great number
of foreigners, a number far greater still of Frenchmen
live by their labour in England, in Germany, in Switzerland, in America, and on the most distant shores ;

" That to drive back our alien brothers would be to
call forth retaliatory measures—a retribution no less
calamitous than humiliating ;

" The Provisional Government place foreign labourers
under the special protection and safe-guard of French
operatives, their fellow-men, and, full of confidence in
the generosity of the people, make them responsible
for the honour of the country."[*]

Our expectations were not disappointed ; the agitation
subsided, as if by magic, and there was an end of the
matter.

The truth is that, to influence those really noble

* See the *Moniteur* of the 9th of April, 1848.

men, the surest way was to address their feelings.
Nor was even this in most cases necessary. To their
genuine disposition to follow the lead of any elevated
idea springing up spontaneously from among themselves, I might adduce numerous testimonies. Suffice
it to say, that those employed, reduced as they were
to the utmost straits, volunteered to contribute, out of
their low wages, and did actually contribute, a comparatively large sum of money to be spent by the Provisional
Government in procuring work for those unemployed.*

But still more praiseworthy was the moderation of
their demands and language, at a time they were
all-powerful. Let the reader who remembers the circumstances pay attention to the following declaration
which was addressed by a set of workmen to the
" Government Labour Commission," and posted on all
the walls of Paris :—

" We, whose names are under-written, do declare
that we are satisfied with the decree issued by the
Provisional Government for the shortening of the hours
of labour from eleven to ten, and that we hold it to be
unjust to bring forward any further demand that might
lead to the ruin of our employers, and to a stoppage.
We adjure our brethren to exact nothing beyond what
is reasonable and just ; we adjure them to guard against
any counsel arising from a factious disposition."†

It was this amount of moderation and good sense in

---

* The example was set by the mechanics employed in the workshops of
M. Henry Leclerc. See the *Moniteur* of the 11th of March, 1848.

† See this declaration, with the signatures appended to it, in the
Moniteur of the 11th of March, 1848.

the working classes that made it possible for the "GOVERNMENT LABOUR COMMISSION" effectually to interfere as arbitrator between operatives and masters, whenever the necessity arose either of preventing or adjusting a dispute—which, it must be remarked, was never done, except at the united request of both parties.

Need I observe that, sober as the popular feeling may have been upon the whole, it was not to be expected that the tempest of February should pass away, without any stirring up of interests and passions? The legitimate hopes awakened in many hearts broke out here and there into complaints,—sometimes into protests. Whenever the social arrangements were so oppressive as to be insufferable, the oppressed could not always abstain from attempting to shake off the yoke at once. But it so happened, that, had some of the demands that were made been fully admitted, the result would have proved fatal to the complainants themselves; whilst, on the other hand, men were found, in the moneyed class, who, clinging to obvious abuses, and regardless of the danger, would not give way, even when circumstances allowed them to be just. Now, any one who looks back to the glorious but stormy days of the Revolution of February, will easily conceive what disturbances would have taken place, had not public confidence invested some high tribunal with the power of removing all causes of conflict by means of friendly arbitration. Well, owing to the very nature of things, the GOVERNMENT LABOUR COMMISSION became the tribunal required; and the services which the Luxembourg rendered, in this capacity, may be said to have been invaluable.

Many a disastrous stoppage was brought to a close, as in the case of the factory of Derosne et Caille; numberless disputes were settled, to the satisfaction of both contending parties—namely, those between the pavement-contractors and the paviours—the paper-makers and their workmen—the lightermen and the wood merchants—the coach-masters and the coachmen—the blacksmiths and the journeymen-smiths—the stone contractors and the stone-cutters, &c. &c.*

There was no, for instance, compulsory power by which the paviours could have been made to replace the paving-stones, dug up during the struggle to form barricades; but to the conciliatory decision of the Luxembourg they did not hesitate to submit. For a moment, vehicles of all kinds ceased to roll in Paris; but no sooner had the Luxembourg interfered, than the coachmen readily consented to resume their work, on reasonable terms.

On one of these arbitrations I beg to dwell, inasmuch as it saved Paris from an imminent danger.

Little did the Parisians dream that, on the 29th of March, 1848, they were within an ace of being left without a supply of bread. Yet, such was the case. On the 25th, the following letter was addressed to me from the delegates of the syndicate of bakers :—

"Citizen,—two delegates from the syndicate of Paris are commissioned to communicate to you that there are very serious apprehensions entertained respecting the course that will be taken by the journeyman bakers this evening. They beg to inform you they had yes-

* See the Appendix, No. 2.

terday two interviews with the prefect of police, and
that they will have another with him to-day, at half-
past one. Perhaps you will have the kindness to be
present. It is so important you should be, that we ask
your attention to this communication, in the name of
the tranquillity of the city of Paris.—Part.Ch. Pécourt."

The *Moniteur* of the 28th of March alluding to this
letter, says :

"The official intervention of the GOVERNMENT LABOUR
COMMISSION has to-day been again solicited, and under
very peculiar circumstances. The subject was the state
of the bakehouses of Paris, in which the slightest
disturbance might have seriously endangered the subsistence of the capital. Among the working classes,
there is no set of men whose position demands a more
immediate improvement than that of the journeymen
bakers. The oppressive arrangements to which they
had been obliged to submit, having, at last, inclined
them to violent measures, Paris might have suffered
from a total failure of the supply of bread, had not a
complete and satisfactory compromise been effected
through the intervention of the Luxembourg.

"The delegates from the employers and the journeymen bakers have, this day, submitted their differences
to the president and vice-president of the GOVERN-
MENT LABOUR COMMISSION, and after a short, friendly
discussion, a new scale of wages having been proposed,
met with the warm acceptance of both parties. Meantime, a great crowd of journeymen bakers overflowed
the court of the palace, awaiting the issue of the
appeal with impatience and agitation. On M. Louis

Blanc's appearing and reading the decision, the most enthusiastic acclamations were uttered; and the sincere expressions of gratitude both from the delegates of the employers and those of the workmen amply recompensed the COMMISSION for the anxiety it had undergone. Before they parted, a workman, sent by his comrades, rushed up to M. Louis Blanc, and warmly shaking his hand, offered, in their name, a contribution of two francs a head, to be deducted from the first day's wages of each of them,—the collective amount to be placed at the disposal of the Provisional Government.

"These facts are very significant, especially as they do not stand alone. For, without recalling the many difficult cases which have been successfully submitted to the arbitration of the 'Government Labour Commission,' we may just observe that, as late as yesterday, the Commission was able, by well-timed negociations with the Railway Company of Lyons, to smoothe down the difficulty which threatened to prolong the lamentable stoppage of the establishment of Farcot, at St. Ouen." *

Is it not strange that Lord Normanby, with these documents under his eyes, as they must have been, should have expressed himself in this way? "There was no flour in the town, and the bakers had ceased to distribute bread. Lamartine's timely exertions, therefore, in causing the barricades to be removed, saved us from dangers quite as serious, though of a less ostensible description than massacre." †

---

* *Moniteur* of the 28th of March, 1848.
† A Year of Revolution in Paris, vol. i. p. 145.

My statement, resting on official documents, and explaining whence the danger of the starvation, why the streets were not repaved, and what put an end to these difficulties, exhibits in a ludicrous light the historical accuracy of Lord Normanby's compliments to M. de Lamartine.

To form a right notion of the burden M. Albert and myself had on our shoulders, the reader should know that all the things just mentioned were accomplished, with the efficient and zealous assistance of M. Vidal, in the short space of two months, during which we had, in addition to these duties, to attend every Cabinet-Council held at the Hôtel de Ville by the Provisional Government. I do not remember having ever worked, at that period, less than fourteen hours a day. Albert, who was made of iron, could stand any fatigue : not so with me, and my health was severely impaired.

Such were our crimes.

And now M. Albert is lingering in a prison; whilst I am reduced to write these lines in a foreign land, and in a foreign language, because some of these moneyed men I protected, have driven me from my country, bereft me of all I held dear, after showering upon me all manner of calumnies, and, as will be seen hereafter, twice attempting to murder me in broad day-light. But let that pass. No soldier is allowed to complain of being wounded in battle; and what were we doing, if not fighting for the sake of justice ?

CHAPTER VIII.

CO-OPERATIVE ASSOCIATIONS, ESTABLISHED BY THE LUXEMBOURG.

In the subsequent chapter, I shall call attention to the establishment of those famous *National Workshops,* which, through a really inconceivable misimpression, all Europe has been induced to attribute to me, although, as will hereafter be proved, they were founded and organised, not by me, but against me, or, more properly to speak, against that social science of which circumstances made me the official exponent.

In the present chapter, I propose to give an account of a very different kind of establishments; I mean, those co-operative associations, which were so rich in practical and permanent results. This subject will be found novel, and, I am confident, highly interesting; for it illustrates an effort at realising a new principle, which, to use the language of the Countess d'Agoult, in her remarkable history of the Revolution of 1848, was, in this our age, " the starting point of a system of organisation of the working classes, not less important to them than was the formation of burghs to the trading classes of the middle ages." *

* *Histoire de la Revolution de* 1848, *par Daniel Stern,* Vol. ii., ch. 8.

I have already said that, in my opinion, the State should take the initiative in setting up co-operative associations; and this would have been easy enough to effect, had the Provisional Government consented to create for such a purpose a public department, with funds, administrative machinery, and so forth. My earnest negociations at the Hôtel de Ville to this effect, the great lengths the workmen were prepared to go in support of my demand, the objections raised by my colleagues, and the motives of public safety which led me reluctantly to give way, are within the knowledge of the reader.*

So far, I found myself paralysed. Fortunately, two circumstances occurred, which gave me a hope of being able, despite this deprivation of means, to do something towards partially putting the co-operative system into a practical form.

In the first place, the Provisional Government had passed a decree incorporating citizens of every class into the National Guard, and providing that uniforms should be furnished at the public expense to all persons too poor to buy them for themselves.†

In the second place, the Government, while acknowledging that the rights of creditors should be protected by law, were nevertheless of opinion that the nature of the protection should not be revolting to reason and humanity; and that, fraud of all kinds being within

Daniel Stern is the pseudonym of Madame la Comtesse d'Agoult, and I quote her all the more willingly, as her views, although liberal, differ from my own in more than one respect.

    * Chapter v. pp. 89—93.
    † See the *Moniteur* of the 16th of March, 1848.

the reach of the criminal law, it was a gratuitous outrage to human dignity to treat the personal liberty of
a citizen as a proper equivalent for a pecuniary debt.
Accordingly, they had abolished imprisonment for
debt ; * and the consequence was, that the Prison de
Clichy, which had hitherto been the debtor's prison,
was now vacated. †

These two circumstances suggested to me the idea
that the order for the uniforms of the National Guard
might be intrusted to a co-operative association of
tailors, and that the Prison de Clichy might be handed
over to them for their use.

About this time, I was told that there was among
the delegates of the tailors at the Luxembourg, a man
possessed of rare and commanding qualities, and who
stood very high in the estimation of his comrades. I
requested him to wait upon me, which he did most
readily ; nor have I forgotten how strongly the first
glance I had of him, as he entered, prepossessed me in
his favour. He was a middle-aged man, of ordinary
size, with a slender figure, pallid hollow cheeks, and a
smooth marble forehead, scantily shaded by thin light
hair—all which conveyed the impression of a man who
had suffered much and was not likely to live long. But
the signal repose of his countenance, and the benignant
expression of his sunken blue eyes, showed that he had
borne the brunt of life's troubles with unconquered
serenity. His name was Bérard.

"My object," said I, " in sending for you, was to ask

---

* See the *Moniteur* of the 16th of March, 1848.
† See the *Moniteur* of the 10th of March, 1848.

your opinion about the practicability of forming a co-operative society in your trade."

"Before I answer the question," he replied, "allow me to ask, in my turn, if I am to infer that the Provisional Government is willing to appropriate money for this purpose?"

"No. This was precisely what I wanted the Provisional Government to do, when I pressed for the formation of a 'public department of labour and progress;' but you are aware that my demand was refused."

"Yes, I know it; and my fellow-workmen know it, too." Here, a bitter smile curled his lips, and he stopped, as though he strove to suppress a rising thought.

"Well?"

"Well, I cannot conceal from you that the workmen of Paris felt painfully surprised at your not maintaining your ground, when, sure, they would have supported you to the death."

"The time," I replied, "is not yet come for the just appreciation of my motives, but it is not far off.—Now, to the point. Is a co-operative association in your trade possible, without the aid of the State?"

After a moment's hesitation, "The great difficulty," he said, "in founding co-operative associations, is the acquisition of such implements of labour as are required, and the outlay which the purchase of raw material necessitates. There are in Paris, at present, nearly two thousand men belonging to my trade, who, I have no doubt, would be quite ready to form among

themselves such an association; but how could they be
expected to raise out of their savings the amount of
money requisite, almost all of them being unemployed,
on account of the commercial crisis, and in a state of
utter destitution?"

On my inquiring whether this were the only difficulty, "There is another," he observed, "which must
not be lost sight of, in all trades like my own. Mind,
Sir, that there are merchants who are constantly on
the look-out for ruin and bankruptcies, and who profit
by the misfortunes of their fellow-tradesmen, to obtain
at fabulous prices goods sold afterwards below the
market price, with an enormous profit. Could fraternal
associations of workmen tread in the foot-marks of such
people, without being untrue to their own principle?
Could they speculate on slackness of labour and upon
misery? Again, how difficult it would be for a co-operative association of workmen, prompted by a desire of
contributing to the affranchisement of labour, to stand
out the competition of those slop-shops which employ
women to do the sewing, to whom they are not ashamed
to give the miserable pittance of fifteen sous for a waist-
coat, knowing very well that it takes them two days to
make one? Ah! Citizen, I would rather die of hunger,
than march towards fortune through such wrong ways;
and this is a general feeling amongst us, for we know
that a woman, to live in a becoming manner, must have
at least one franc and a half a day; and we consider it
to be a most cruel evil, that poor young girls should
be compelled to sit up long nights, to the destruction
of their health, without reaping any fruit from an

exhausting toil, or, perhaps, should be dragged down through suffering to prostitution."

While thus speaking, the honest workman had gradually grown excited; his cheeks were no longer bloodless, and the involuntary emotion of his heart glowed in the liquid lustre of his eyes.

I resumed : " Suppose you were to be found in raw material and premises ? "

" Oh," replied he, cheerfully, " this would be a somewhat different case, especially if we could obtain good terms.   There is now in Paris, as I already told you, a great number of journeymen tailors almost starving : they would be too happy to join ; and, for my part, I should feel still happier in assisting to carry out a principle which I believe to be necessary and just."

" But," I remarked, " I have been told that you are a first-rate workman, in the habit of receiving high wages. This will be bad work for you."

" Oh, don't mention it.   I have had tougher jobs than this."

In consequence of this interview, a co-operative association of journeymen tailors having been formed, at the head of which Bérard and his two fellow-delegates were placed, I procured for them from the city of Paris an order for a hundred thousand military frocks intended for the National Guard, and also the use of the Prison de Clichy.*

There, about two thousand journeymen tailors, then out of employment, were installed and set at work immediately.

* See the *Moniteur* of the 17th of March, 1848.

This co-operative association was founded upon the principles I had eight years before propounded in my book entitled " Organisation of Labour." *   The associates showed themselves, from the beginning, impressed with the idea that it was their duty to contribute as much as possible to the gradual emancipation of the working classes, by giving their fellow-men a practical proof of the advantages of the co-operative system, when carried out as a work of mutual responsibility † and devotedness.   The conditions of admission into their family were: first, the possibility of employing additional hands ; secondly, on the part of the candidate, a character for good conduct, good will, and a proper knowledge of the business.   They recognised amongst themselves no other authority than that of the whole, represented by elective managers and foremen —real public servants, sure to be, in this capacity, loved, respected, and obeyed.   Being thoroughly con· vinced that the weak, in an association of Christians, ought never to be sacrificed to the strong; that an unequal partition of the fruits of their collective labour would, in all probability, foster in those best remunerated a feeling of selfishness, and awaken in the others a feeling of envy, likely to loosen the tie of their fraternal union, and to bring it to a close through internal discord ; considering, moreover, that men who work togther, in the sight of one another, with a view

---

* The first edition of this book appeared in 1840 ; the ninth appeared in 1850.

† I use "mutual responsibility" for our French word "solidarité," which cannot be expressed by any single word in English, and which implies identity of interests combined with identity of feelings.

to a joint benefit, cannot fail to be spurred on by that self-same sense of honour which actuates men who fight side by side, with a view to a common victory— this being once admitted, that it is no less shameful for operatives to shrink from the assigned task than it is for soldiers to fly from the enemy,—the journeymen tailors at Clichy adopted the system of equal wages and equal profits. Besides, it was agreed that a fund should be set apart for the relief of the widows, orphans, or invalided associates, and that the profits should be divided into two parts—one to be distributed amongst the members, and the other to be reserved for the gradual accumulation of a permanent capital, or labour fund, intended to perpetuate the association, by supplying it with implements of labour successive generations of workmen.

It is rather surprising, that those who have raised a hue and cry against the system of equal wages adopted in the establishment of Clichy, and ever since in so many co-operative associations, should have over- looked the fact, that this is precisely the system which is carried out in a great number of handicrafts, in the army, in the navy, and in every class of public functions. Strange enough! In the French Constituent Assembly, whose members had a salary of twenty-five francs a day, and where, consequently, the least clever and efficient amongst them had been, in point of remuneration, placed on the same footing with first-rate orators and politicians, I have heard the system of equal wages criticised by the former as wrongful to talent; the critics being utterly heedless of the consequences of their logic as applied to themselves.

But the same inconsistencies between objections and facts run through the whole of the adverse criticisms.

Are all soldiers, though serving for the same pay, equally brave, active and zealous? Are all judges, receiving the same salary, equally learned and intelligent? Still, this contribution of unequal work for equal pay seems natural to every one.

True, it may be replied; but, in these cases, there is the stimulus of personal advancement, that is a calculation on the contingency of future advantages.

Granting, for the case of argument, this to be invariably the fact, which it is not, the same stimulus, in another form, will be found powerfully operating amongst the members of an industrial association, where every member has an increased share in the increase of the general profits. In point of fact, the stimulus of personal interest is here all the stronger from the reward being more certain, more immediate, and from every one knowing that he cannot possibly work for the benefit of others, without receiving a fair share of the benefit for himself. But this certainty of being recompensed for his exertions, is precisely what is absent in the case of the soldier. How shadowy his hope of advancement! How dependent on opportunity! How susceptible of being baffled by circumstances over which he has no kind of control! How subject to the caprice or injustice of superiors! And what is true of the soldier, is true of every class of public officers.

Then again, it must be remembered that there is in a co-operative society, as in a nation or an army, that great moving force which on a large scale is called public spirit, and on a small scale *esprit de corps.* Another incentive common to all is the "point of honour," or the obligation in each individual to do that utmost which cannot be always outwardly measured, and the open neglect of which will be visited with dishonour. Amongst soldiers, this "point of honour" prevents that shirking work, in the act of killing, which is stigmatised as *cowardice*: why, amongst associated workmen, should not the "point of honour" prevent that shirking work, in the act of creating, which might very properly be stigmatised as theft; for theft it is ?

The system of equal wages, in the case of a co-operative association as in the other mentioned cases, is certainly amenable to the objection that it gives no more to the father of a family than to the bachelor. But how much stronger still is the objection against the payment by piece-work, in which a poor workman with four children may be reduced, if weak, to a salary of two or three francs, whilst a robust bachelor will have the double ?

Besides, never did, either the journeymen tailors at Clichy, or the workmen who trod afterwards in their foot-steps, adopt the system of equal wages as the best possible. No. The reason why they submitted to it momentarily, was that the existing order of things did not allow the practical realisation of a far superior one, that which is embodied in the maxim: " *From* each according to his faculties. *To* each according to his wants." The system of equal wages was viewed by the workmen in no other light than that of a provisional proceeding, which, though imperfect, came nearest to the doctrine of fraternity, as it implied, at least, the so eminently Christian principle, " *He does what he ought, who does what he can.*"

As to the results, they may be said to have been in every respect remarkable.

I remember having received, at the Luxembourg, a visit from Mr. Moffatt, M.P., and Mr. Wilson. These gentlemen having expressed a desire to have a letter of introduction to the manager of the Clichy association, I readily complied with their request; and I trust they have not forgotten the courteous reception they met with there, and the impression made upon them, not only by the discipline, good order, and active industry of the establishment, but also by the gentlemanly air and manners of the workmen who conducted them round.

Certain it is, that all the engagements the journeymen tailors composing the Clichy association had contracted, were scrupulously fulfilled; the order they had received was completed in due time; a sum of eleven thousand francs they had borrowed from the master-tailors, was promptly repaid, and when, the agreement with the city of Paris being at an end, the association broke up, to be reconstituted on a smaller scale, far from winding up with a loss, they had a balance in their favour.*

---

* See in the *Nouveau Monde* a letter addressed by Bérard, the chief manager of the association, to the *Constitutionnel*, on the 11th of July, 1849.

And what deserves special notice, is the example they set to their brethren, as men and as citizens. Among them, the rule was to take into account the good will of every individual, however humble and destitute of intellectual advantages he might be, and to encourage, to guide him, to render to him as easy as possible the performance of his task. Among them, there was no favouritism. Each man's place was assigned to him by election. Every employment carried greater obligations with it, and every dignity was a burden; so that one of the most touching and profound maxims of the Gospel found there its application, the first among them being really the servant of all!

A few facts will be enough to give an insight into the spirit which pervaded this association.

One day, a great number of women occupied in embroidery presented themselves at Clichy, making an offer to work for it at a certain price, comparatively high. Immediately after, the men engaged in the same trade, not aware of the step taken by the women, came and proposed to furnish similar work on lower terms. The Clichy association, knowing how injurious to morality were the results of extreme poverty and want of employment amongst women, did not hesitate for a moment to decline the more advantageous of the two offers, in order to secure occupation to the weaker sex.*

* See *Le Nouveau Monde, Journal historique et politique, for a letter signed by fifty-nine workmen, addressed to the Voix du Peuple*, in January, 1850. The *Voix du Peuple* was edited by M. Proudhon, and the letter of the workmen had reference to some slanderous remarks which had appeared in that journal.

Here is another instance of generous sacrifice. There were, at that time, thousands of needlewomen out of work, and the various mayors of Paris to whom they applied for relief, used to send them to Clichy, where it was supposed they would find employment. Nor was it ever refused, though many of the applicants were so unfit for the work required, that it was sometimes necessary to undo what they had done. But the members of the association preferred bearing such a loss, great as it was, to exposing poor girls to the risk of starving, and went even so far as to pay them the same wages they themselves received.*

When the agreement with the city of Paris was broken, there was no longer sufficient employment for all those who were willing to stand by the co-operative principle, and few only of them could find full work. Well, these, all skilled workmen, voluntarily submitted to hard privations, and thought it their duty to hand over to the general fund the whole amount of their share of it, in order to enable the association to establish on its own premises a kitchen, where food was prepared for three hundred of their brethren, at the cost per head of six pence a day, during several months.†

I might give numerous instances of the same sort; but this would be to write a history of the associations, which is not the object of my book.

The second association established by the Luxembourg, was that of the saddlers.

It will be remembered I prevailed upon the Provi-

---

* See note on previous page.   † *Ibid.*

sional Government to prohibit all persons fed and lodged at the expense of the State by charitable donations, from bringing their produce into the market to compete with that of the working classes. Following up this policy, I caused the orders for saddlery which used to be executed at the military establishment of Saumur, to be partially transferred to a number of saddlers in Paris, who were thus enabled to form a co-operative association.

Of course, I met with some obstruction from military quarters, in reference to which I will mention a circumstance not inappropriate, in these days when French colonels dictate through the *Moniteur* proscriptions to a great people.

It so happened that the delegates of the saddlers one day came to me, very much excited, saying that General Oudinot—the same that afterwards commanded the French expedition to Rome—was at that moment haranguing a large meeting of workmen, in opposition to the transfer alluded to, and requested me to interfere. I instantly got into a cab with them, and proceeded to the place of meeting, which was the salle Valentino in the Rue St. Honoré. There I found the hall crowded to excess, and the General speaking. My entrance was hailed by a burst of cheers, which continued as I walked up to the platform, and until I found myself face to face with General Oudinot. Immediately addressing him, I said: "Is it true, General, you are here to obstruct the views of the Provisional Government?" Whereupon, with a profusion of courtesies, he protested that he was only expressing a personal opinion, but that in this as in all other things, he was quite disposed to conform to the views of the Government. He then retired, amid loud demonstrations of satisfaction on the part of the working men at his departure, which I at once repressed.

So was the saddlers association formed. Their principle of action was exactly the same as that of Clichy, and when I left Paris, in August, 1848, they were getting on most prosperously.

Of the third association established by the Luxembourg, that of the spinners, the following letter from their delegates (December, 1849) will give a sufficient notion :—

"Scarcely are we separated by an interval of two years from the Revolution of February, and yet there are some persons who seem to have already forgotten its history. Surely, the establishment of the co-operative societies, in consequence of February, 1848, is a fact of some importance in the eyes of the people! Yet are there reactionist journals, as the *Constitutionnel*, for instance, which systematically strive to depreciate and to misrepresent them. And why? We think it better not to inquire too closely. As far as our association is concerned, we shall give the real facts of the case. There were three co-operative associations founded by the Luxembourg — those of the tailors, saddlers, and spinners. The order for the clothing of the National Guard gave rise to the spinners association. Citizen Louis Blanc made several applications to the mayor of Paris to obtain for us an order for a hundred thousand pairs of epaulettes. Citizen Marrast, then mayor, did not think proper to confide the execution of so large an order to persons without a plant or capital of any kind, offering, indeed, no other security but their honesty. Through Louis Blanc's intervention, however, the contract was made, on the 26th, between the city of Paris and the association, which, without the help of this order, would have found it impossible to begin business, considering the large sum indispensable for setting up spinning machinery, and the impossibility at that moment to get a market for their produce. Louis Blanc's next step was to put us in communication with the delegates of the gold-lace makers, who had amongst themselves a society *en commandite*, that is, with limited liability, with which we entered into a contract for the supply of epaulettes. Thus, owing to the impulse given by the Luxembourg, several hundreds of workmen were enabled, in the very first days of the Revolution, to carry into practice that principle of co-operation which is, at present, being so extensively developed. Now came a new difficulty. In spite of the securities for our solvency provided for by the terms of our contract, no trader was willing to trust us with raw material on credit, and no capitalist would make us advances. We, therefore, addressed ourselves to the President of the GOVERNMENT LABOUR COMMISSION. But he had no funds at his command; that is, the very man who had undertaken to organise the associations, had not a single farthing at his disposal. Nevertheless, thanks to his efforts, we obtained, on the

10th of April, from the Public Discount Office, established by the Government to lend money on good securities, a loan of twelve thousand francs, which enabled us to get to work. When the counter-Revolution got the upper hand, our contract was suspended, and afterwards brutally quashed by the Right of Might. They even refused to make us an indemnity for the fifteen thousand epaulettes we had in hand. ' Bring an action, if you like,' was the only answer we could get, ' your suit will last a year. Meanwhile, not a farthing shall you touch. Compromise, and we will pay up what we owe you already for goods delivered.' The matter was cut short in favour of the city agents by— hunger.

(Signed)   " BOULARD AND LEFRANC,
                " Ex-delegates of the Spinners." *

Such were the exertions that gave rise to a sudden up-growth of kindred institutions, whose number, after a few months, amounted to more than a hundred, belonging to all kinds of trades. It is true, that long before 1848, writings and tracts on the subject of co-operative association had been circulated amongst the workmen. I had myself treated the question at full length, as early as August, 1840 ;† and the co-operative system had been practically carried out by a little band of working jewellers, as early as 1843. This association, however, which never numbered more

---

* See this letter in the *Nouveau Monde, Journal historique et politique*, for December, 1849.

† See the " Organization of Labour," first edition, 1840.

than seventeen members, made no proselytes, though soundly constituted. The new principle had been germinating for years ; but it was only after the Revolution of February, and under its animating influence, that this principle began to put forth blossoms.

God knows by what labours, at the cost of what sacrifices, simple labourers succeeded in managing great enterprises of industry. From what they achieved in the way of self-organised societies, one may judge how wonderful would have been the result of their efforts, had the State held out to them, according to my views, a helping hand. It did just the reverse. No sooner did the re-actionists find themselves in possession of power, than they declared war against the co-operative system. Those associations which originated from the interference of the Luxembourg, were not even allowed to reap the fruit of the important orders I had procured for them from the city of Paris ; they were abruptly refused the execution of agreements passed with all the forms that render a contract binding and sacred ; when an indemnity was talked of, the agents of authority interposed delays, in the hope that those associations, now so cruelly dealt with, would perish before the time of payment ; and it even happened, on one occasion, that indemnity was flatly refused.*

On the other hand, how many obstacles had not self-organised co-operative societies, exclusively composed of workmen, to encounter and surmount ; to

* See the letter, above quoted, from the delegates of Spinners.

give motion and life to noble ideas ; to overpower routine, and to maintain themselves against the pressure of the old world, against a formidable display of means at the disposal of passions hostile to them against the coalition of all monopolies : monopoly of power, monopoly of riches, monopoly of science !

With such impediments thrown in their way, even had they failed, no conclusion could have been fairly drawn in condemnation of their principle. Moreover, who knows not the difficulties of a first *début ?* In the stormy seas of the New World, how many vessels were lost on the yet unexplored breakers before the art of navigation had taught men to follow a safe and certain course !

But here, the experiment, far from being a failure, was attended with an extraordinary success. To the detractors of association, the working men of Paris made a practical answer, like that of the ancient philosopher in whose presence motion was denied : they did the thing. They associated ; all actuated by the same spirit, governed by almost identical rules, and aiming at the same general result, that is, at protecting the labourer by a kind of social insurance, and gradually raising him, by means of fraternal co-operation, to the dignity of a self-dependent man.

So great was the success of the associations in Paris, that in some quarters of the town, their pay-tickets, which were cashed at the end of every month, used to pass current among the trades people, thus serving the double purpose of currency and advertisement.*

* This fact was ascertained by Mr. William Coningham, M.P., in

The following statement I extract from a public lecture delivered on the 28th of July, 1851, by Mr. William Coningham, now member for Brighton :

"On the 24th of April, I started for the capital of France. . . . As the principle of co-operative labour had always appeared to me an eminently practicable one, it was not without surprise, tempered however by distrust, that I read in the columns of the daily press, accounts of the successive downfall of the Paris associations, with the secret memoirs of the last of the co-operative cooks. If my surprise were great, it was marvellously increased, when, on my arrival in Paris, I discovered that, like Mr. Landor's conversations of other celebrated personages, the memoirs were purely imaginary, and that, far from the cooks being on their last legs, and the fraternal fires extinguished, co-operative broils of the most peaceful character still saluted the nostrils of the weary pedestrian with a social and savoury odour quite peculiar to themselves. In short, I found that there were in Paris upwards of forty associations of cooks. I moreover discovered that the much-abused fraternal association of tailors, first established in the old debtor's prison of Clichy by M. Louis Blanc himself, far from being defunct, had realised a fund of 70,000 francs, and opened a range of large, well lighted and ventilated shops and workrooms in the Faubourg St. Denis, and, instead of being at the mercy of either sweaters or middlemen, their business skilfully managed by functionaries elected by the association from among

April, 1851, and stated by him, three months after, in a public lecture which he delivered at Brighton on the 28th of July, 1851.

their own members—their original statutes greatly modified however, and the system of piece-work adopted.*
Indeed, so far from the co-operative principle being extinct, I found it rapidly spreading through the provinces, and the most skilful and intelligent of the workmen actively engaged in forming associations, and doing so with a sincerity of purpose and devotion to the cause, which is beyond praise, and with that self-denial without which all fraternal co-operation is impossible. The practical success of the self-organised co-operative associations in France has thus raised the question from the domain of theory to that of fact, and forced it upon the attention of her legislators."†

When the Clichy association was established, it was confidently asserted in high quarters, that nothing could be more absurd than an experiment of this sort; that simple labourers could not have sufficient zeal, intellect, spirit of order and discipline to do without a master. The result has shown how void of foundation were these so roundly asserted affirmations. Numberless are the testimonies I might adduce to the competency of operatives to work for themselves, had I to trace the history of the co-operative system in France.

At the Exhibition of Industry in Paris, the association of file-cutters obtained a silver medal for the unrivalled excellence of their work. Immediately after the establishment of this association in 1848, such was

---

* The circumstance of their statutes being then *greatly modified*, is a mistake. As to the adoption of the system of piece-work, the reasons of this change will be seen presently to have had nothing to do with its intrinsical merit.

† See the lecture above mentioned.

the increase of business, that they were obliged to set up in the Faubourg St. Germain a first supplemental workshop; to which it may be added that they were able to supply files equal, in every respect, to those of the best English manufacture at 25 per cent, less cost.*

In reference to the associations of cooks, the general poverty of the people in this occupation was so great, that the founders of one of these establishments were obliged in order to purchase the provisions necessary for the day of opening, to pledge at the *Mont de Piété* their watches, their trinkets, and even their clothes. Still, at the end of 1849, there were more than forty cooking establishments in a flourishing condition, and they were doing business to the amount of two million five hundred thousand francs a year. These culinary associations are particularly worth mentioning, for the effect they had in improving the food of the people. In the place of filthy eating-houses, where they were rather poisoned than fed, were substituted clean, spacious, convenient rooms in which the working classes, instead of aliments only fit for the gutter, found at all times varied and healthy nourishment.†

Again, among the' readers of this book, there may possibly be some who remember the superb book-case which attracted so much attention in the French department of the great exhibition at the Crystal Palace in 1851. This master-piece, which obtained a silver medal, was sent by the co-operative association of cabinet-makers. Nor is it perhaps uninteresting to

---

* See the *Nouveau Monde* for December 15, 1849. † *Ibid.*

remark that the design of this beautiful work of art was not furnished by any one person, but was developed out of the successive practical suggestions of all the members.*

Now, that among so many associations which were seen to rise and prosper, some should have perished at their very birth, whilst others, after a brilliant beginning, happened to fall or languish, is a fact undeniable; but it is elsewhere than in any defect in the principle on which they rested that the causes of such failures are to be found.

In the first place, let us remember that all the associations had not the same origin. Seeing that wherever the magic word ASSOCIATION was written, the people ran in crowds, and that some of the new establishments had obtained a colossal extension after a month's existence, certain masters, on the verge of bankruptcy, pulled down their signs, decorated their shops with the triangle, or symbol of equality, which was used as an emblem by all the associations, and under a mask, continued, in their old ways, so contriving at once to shear their workmen and gull the public. Nothing fraternal was there, but a deceptive semblance, the consequence of which was, that the fraud being discovered, customers disappeared, and the tricky speculators were ruined. In such bankruptcies, the fate of the workmen, suddenly deprived of employment, would have been the only thing to be lamented, had not the detractors of the co-operative system artfully laid on the principle the conse-

---

* See the *Nouveau Monde* for December 15, 1849.

quences of its dishonest simulation by its worst
enemies.

In the second place, the Government, instead of
lending assistance to the working associations, made it
a point to undermine them by every possible means.

It is true that, in 1848, under the influence of the
ideas proclaimed at the Luxembourg, the majority of
the Constituent Assembly, although opposed to my
views, was morally compelled to facilitate their first step
towards a practical result, by opening a credit of three
millions of francs in favour of the associations. But
neither in the majority, chiefly Orléanists, nor in
the Government, composed of Republicans belonging
to the old school of political economy, was there any
real desire of promoting social reforms; and the grant
of money was systematically misapplied, the prospect
of a share in the national bounty being held out to
each association as an inducement to change its
original statutes, and to sacrifice the general aim to
confined and selfish purposes.

Meantime, all such as, from various motives, longed
for the ruin of the new principle, were busily engaged
in luring the workmen out of the right path. Affecting great concern in their material welfare, they were
striving to break or to loosen the link it had been
my endeavour to form between the associated operatives. Imperfect and objectionable as it was, from a
merely economical point of view, the system of equal
wages had the advantage of instituting among the
working classes a sort of a highly moralising alliance
between the strong and the weak, and of causing the

individual efforts of everyone to converge to this grand end—the gradual enfranchisement of all. In fact, the principle of fraternity was intended, not only as a moral duty to be performed by the people, but also as a power-ful engine to be made use of by them, with a view to the ultimate conquest of their self-dependence. Nor were my adversaries blind to the import of my views; and, for this very reason, they did their best to set at variance the members of the great working family. They left nothing untried to detach the most skilful workmen from the common cause, appealing to their meaner impulses; diverting them from the considera-tion of their true self-interest, by the prospect of a more immediate satisfaction of their false self-interest, and expatiating on the injustice done to them in the offer of wages inadequate to their comparative strength and talent; as though an adequate remuneration of talent were the principal feature of the existing order of things, where intelligence is in so many cases brought into bondage by money or crushed by chance, and where we constantly meet with millionnaires in the cradle, men who roll in wealth simply because they happened to be born with a silver spoon in their mouth, or, as Beaumarchais says, because they took the trouble to come into the world!

A fact worth noticing is, that the writer who figured at the head of the counter-movement I speak of, was M. Proudhon, who, being the theorist of anarchy, felt naturally averse to anything likely to be conducive to industrial order. That he began his career by publishing a book entitled *" Property*

is robbery—la propriété, c'est le vol," is generally
known ; but what I suspect to be not so well known
in this country, is that never was there a more
unrelenting assailant, either of the Socialist leaders, or
of all the principles on which Socialism rests, than
M. Proudhon. Before the Revolution of February, he
had openly attacked the new ideas,* which were rapidly
spreading through France ; but the Revolution having
exhibited their force, he bethought him of assuming
the name, better to decry the thing, and whilst professing to be Socialist, he set upon Socialism with un-
relaxing rancour. By no paper in France, except the
Constitutionnel, were the co-operative societies of workmen so much abused and calumniated as by the " *Voix
du Peuple,"* whose editor was M. Proudhon.†

In spite of all this, the co-operative principle remained
for a long while unbroken in certain trades, and was
modified, in others, with respect to details of application only. But by the side of fervent apostles of a
doctrine; by the side of courageous initiators, who had
not concealed from themselves the difficulties of the
enterprise and stood ready for sacrifices; there were
weak-minded men, who thought they should find in a
new formula of labour the immediate gratification of
their desires, and a spontaneous welfare. To these I
had said, over and over again : " Remember that, in
forming yourselves into associations, you cannot march
towards the land of promise, except through rugged

---

* See his work, entitled *Contradictions économiques.*

† See in the *Nouveau Monde,* January, 1850, the letter addressed to
the *Voix du Peuple* by fifty-nine operatives.

paths. Let not your expectations be too sanguine,
lest they might lead you to bitter disappointments.
Every conquest requires patience and courage; remember that you have not to *accept* happiness, but to
conquer it."* Such language was not of a nature to be
listened to by everyone. Some were seen wavering,
after a long struggle; some even allowed themselves to
be made elements of disorder; but the greater part of
the associated operatives displayed the most admirable
firmness.

Unfortunately, the reactionists having decidedly got
the mastery, to the influence of underhand manœuvres
was added that of a savage persecution. The working
associations were subjected to the incessant interference
of the police. They were harassed in every imaginable
way, under pretext that they served only as a mask for
the formation of political societies. The reactionary
papers did not shrink from the shameful trick of falsely
announcing the downfal of even the most prosperous
of them, in order to ruin their credit and to shake the
confidence of their customers. The Clichy association,
that eldest daughter of the Luxembourg, was the point
more especially aimed at. How often had poor Bérard
to repel the slanderous attacks launched from opposite
quarters, now from Proudhon's *Voix du Peuple,* now
from the *Constitutionnel.* In what civilised country, I
ask, are not such nefarious attempts at ruining an
industrial enterprise visited with a severe penalty ?

---

* This was the language I held at the Luxembourg, as may be seen in
the *Moniteur*; and this was the language I held when addressing the
workmen from London, as may be seen in the *Nouveau Monde,* August,
1849.

Well, in France, during the presidency of Louis Bonaparte, they were not only left unpunished, but encouraged by the Government.

Long before this, I had been driven out of my country; I lived, an exile, in London; and all I could do, when applied to by the workmen, was to send them advice. In August 1849, some of them having consulted me about the best course to be pursued, I answered:

"Be careful, my friends, not to draw around your associations an insuperable circle, or even to render them difficult of access. This would be reviving the odious system of *Jurandes* and *Maitrises*.* If associations, instead of being opened to all—whenever there is work for additional hands—were only societies of a fixed and determinate number, united by no other nobler motive than the common desire of getting rich at the expense of their brethren, they would no longer have anything to distinguish them from certain commercial societies which abound around us, and would simply constitute fresh gangs of speculators.

"There is another point to which I cannot too earnestly call your attention. You have suffered competition to be introduced amongst your co-operative bodies. What has been the consequence? More than once, three associations, for want of a sufficient number of customers, have failed, where one alone would have prospered. This result would not have occurred, if the distribution and the management of associations had

---

* By *jurandes* and *maîtrises* is meant institutions like the ancient guilds in this country, that is, trade monopolies.

been entrusted to careful hands, instead of being abandoned to caprice and hazard; if a methodical plan had been adopted—a plan fixed upon beforehand by a competent committee. Remember this : working associations can only live by a mutual and close connection. There must be established between them the same bond which exists between the divers members of each of them. Isolated from one another, they would most assuredly fail in their struggle against the owners of privileges. Well united, resting upon one another, and giving each other a reciprocal help, they will form a compact mass, and will be enabled to resist the crisis of politics as well as those of industry, until the day when the State shall reckon amongst its first duties that of attending to the welfare of the labouring classes.

" To attain this object, here I suggest the means that might be employed :

" There should be established, under the denomination of *Committee of Associated Operatives*, a Council, in which should be represented all associations based upon the principle of fraternity.

" This Council would have for its object:

" To concentrate all individual efforts ;

" To investigate the great questions of production and distribution.

" To help in the formation of nascent associations, and the development of those that are in existence;

" To control the mutual intercourse between associations, for the exchange of produce, the loans, advances of money, tenders, bills of exchange, and circulation, &c.

"The *Committee of Associated Operatives* would direct their attention to those institutions which are the complement of association; such as stores, bazaars, labourers' homes, provident funds, asylums.

" They would exercise upon all associations a fraternal watchfulness, and would impart to them that uniformity of movement which is so desirable.

" Some associations exist in the provinces and in foreign countries ; the Committee would take it upon themselves to establish relations between these and the Parisian associations.

" Finally, they would occupy themselves with opening outlets to their produce by means of exportation—that commercial act so indispensable to the continual prosperity of great factories.

" Independent of the Committee, the associations would preserve their special direction, as well as the disposal and management of their capital.

" Such is, my friends, the plan I bring under your consideration." *

These suggestions were far from being fruitless. A committee was formed, which took the title of UNION OF ASSOCIATIONS, composed of twenty-three members, who began to act as a central body, and in a short time acquired a considerable influence. It would carry me too far to enter into a detail of their industrial operations ; suffice it to say, that they presented the aspect of a vast institution devoted to the interests of the working classes, and doing itself, for them and by their aid,

* This letter will be found *in extenso* in the *Nouveau Monde*, where it was published in August, 1849.

that which the State had refused, and was actually opposing. This being the germ of operative self-government on an imposing scale, soon gave umbrage to the Government, which, in default of any lawful means of crushing it, had recourse to a miserable pretext for interference. A letter of mine, found amongst the Committee's papers, referring exclusively to industrial matters, furnished the opportunity of charging them with being directors of a political society. A more indecent proceeding can scarcely be conceived. People in this country will have difficulty in believing that men should be prosecuted and found guilty on such flimsy evidence as this; nevertheless, such was the case, and though Mr. Delbrouck, one of the most active and able managers of the Committee, clearly set forth what had been done, and what had been proposed to do, in a sober, impressive, and admirably reasoned speech, he was sentenced to the monstrous punishment of fifteen months' imprisonment, five hundred francs fine, and five years' deprivation of civil rights. "But this defence," says a writer by no means partial to Social experiments on a large scale and of comprehensive import, "was certainly not wasted on behalf of practical Socialism; showing, as it did, once for all, how much there is of moderation, and of elevation of views, in those who are devoted to it." *

The association of Clichy, it will be remembered, was the principal target at which the enemies of the Luxembourg directed their arrows. The reason of

---

* *L'Association Ouvrière, industrielle et agricole*, par M. Feugeray, p. 126, Paris, 1851.

their animosity was, that principle of fraternity on which its statutes were based, and which received a practical, although imperfect, application in the equal partition of wages. Obstructed in their operations, and worried out by these repeated attacks, some of the members suggested such a modification of their statutes as might stay the violence of this persecution. The proposition, though necessitated by circumstances, being rejected, out of a feeling of delicacy to me, it was agreed that I should be written to, with a view of obtaining my consent. This Bérard undertook to do. He accordingly wrote to me, setting forth the difficulties of the position, and biassing me, with evident hesitation and reluctance, to consent to the adoption of the proposed measure.

In reply, I stated I knew of no reason why the decision should be made to depend on me; but, since it was their pleasure to make it so, I could not withhold my sanction to a policy thought expedient by them, and of which they, in actual presence of the difficulties, must be the best judges. But, at the same time, I thought it my duty to warn them, that I did not think this modification of their rules would afford them any relief from implacable attacks, which were directed against the very existence of the association itself, as tainted with the original sin of having first been set on foot by the Luxembourg.

Unhappily, my anticipations were not void of foundation. The systematic obstructions, thrown in the way of the association often exhibiting themselves in infamous and mendacious attacks upon its credit, such as in England would have been severely punished, and such as no trader, however solvent, could withstand, finally proved insurmountable. After courageously struggling for some time, the association was compelled to stop; and its moving spirit, poor Bérard, soon after died, his feeble constitution completely broken up by the severity of his exertions.

But, though an association had fallen, association still survived. "They had scotch'd the snake, not killed it." The principal offender was destroyed; but around it other associations had sprung up, which, in spite of the long struggle they had to go through, survive to this hour, and are prosperous.

From a statement, for whose accuracy I am able personally to vouch, I can give the particulars of about twenty of those associations now in existence; those, namely, of the cabinet-makers, arm-chair makers, masons, turners, last-makers, tailors, file-makers, walking-stick makers, spectacle-makers, tinmen, blacksmiths, lanthorn-makers, brush-makers, wheelwrights, engravers, machine-makers, piano-makers, &c. &c.

Not only are all these, with one or two exceptions, in a most thriving condition, but their success is in curious disproportion to the bareness of means with which they started.

Who could, for instance, have expected that the association of masons, which, on the 10th of August, 1848, began business with a loan of 38 francs, advanced by an architect, M. Delbrouck, would have acquired a working capital of 237,000 francs, with which they were doing business to the amount of 1,200,000 francs in 1856, and of 1,000,000 francs in 1857 ?   There are 95 members, and, what is more extraordinary, they have never received anything from the State, out of the three millions voted in 1848 by the Constituent Assembly.

A singular case is that of the co-operative association of last-makers, who, having begun with four members and a *capital* of two francs, are, at present, doing a business of from 70,000 to 79,000 francs, with a net profit of from 3,000 to 4,000 francs.   It is said to be the largest last-making concern in or out of Paris.

The association of file-makers, also founded in 1848, was, last year, doing business to the amount of 101,176 francs, and has realised a capital of 47,638 francs 3 centimes, after having repaid, on the 4th of September, 1856, a loan of 10,000 francs it had received from the State.   The number of members—at the beginning, 13—is now 17.*

Lord Normanby, of course, had no eyes for this great social movement which passed before him ; unless, indeed, having said much he ought not to have said, he thought it right, by way of equipoise, to omit much he ought not to have omitted.   The omission is all the more striking, since his lordship should have known that this question of industrial co-operation has attracted the favourable attention of eminent minds in England.   I am sorry that Lord Normanby, through a sense of modesty, should not have aspired to a place in

---

* For further details, see the Appendix, No. 4.

this distinguished company, at the risk of being ranked with those prejudiced and superficial observers described in the following passage :

A writer of great influence in his day,—and a Tory writer, too,—Southey, alluding to certain co-operative experiments suggested in England, says: "The political economists will, of course, point their glasses at the distance, and calculate the result with unfailing certainty; but we have no faith in the reports of these political star-gazers. We leave them to prophesy, contenting ourselves with the humbler task of watching the progress and awaiting the issue of the experiment. It is, at present, in its infancy—a cloud no bigger than a man's hand. Whether it is to disappear in heat, or gradually spread over the land, and send down refreshing showers on this parched and withered portion of society, God only knows—time only can reveal." *

Since this was written, time has begun its revelations, and the cloud is becoming visible to the naked eye.

Moreover, in justice, I must say, amongst the " star-gazers," as Southey calls them, there are some real and great astronomers; but they are precisely those who have not overlooked the importance of the co-operative

* "Quarterly Review," No. 98, Art. "On the Co-Operatives," pp. 359—371.

I have no difficulty in ascribing this paper to Southey, on its internal evidence, and from the fact that, in his well-known work, "Colloquies with Sir Thomas Moore, or, Prospects and Progress of Society," he has expressed himself still more positively on the practicability of the co-operative system. Vol. i., p. 137.

system. In his "Principles of Political Economy," Mr. John Stuart Mill observes :

"It is most desirable that all these schemes should have opportunity and encouragement to test their capabilities by actual experiment. There are in almost all of them many features in themselves well worth submitting to that test; whilst, on the other hand, the exaggerated expectations entertained by large and growing multitudes in all the principal nations of the world, concerning what it is possible in the present state of human improvement to effect by such means, have no chance of being corrected, except by a fair trial in practice. The French Revolution of February, 1848, at first seemed to have opened a fair field for the trial of such experiments on a perfectly safe scale, and with every advantage that could be derived from the countenance of a government which sincerely desired their success.* It is much to be regretted these projects have been frustrated, and that the re-action of the middle class against anti-property doctrines has engendered for the present an unreasoning and indiscriminating antipathy to all ideas, however harmless or however just, which have the smallest savour of Socialism. This is a disposition of mind of which the influential classes, both in France and elsewhere, will find it necessary to divest themselves. Socialism has now become irrevocably one of the leading elements in

* If Mr. Mill be here alluding to those members of the Government who were the authors of these experiments, he is quite right; but if he mean the whole Government, a want of unity of action on this point, as is now unfortunately known, was a principal reason why the associations did not succeed as well as they might have done.

European politics. The questions raised by it will not be set at rest by merely refusing to listen to it, but only by a more and more complete realisation of the ends which Socialism aims at, not neglecting its means so far as they can be employed with advantage."*

What enhances the value of this most remarkable passage is, that, far from these prospects being frustrated, as might well appear to Mr. Mill in 1849, the co-operative experiments, in spite of the immense obstructions opposed to them, have been attended with a success which could hardly, under the circumstances, be anticipated.

* " Principles of Political Economy, by John Stuart Mill," vol. ii., chap. 7, p. 326.   1849.

CHAPTER IX.

M. MARIE'S "ATELIERS NATIONAUX," ESTABLISHED
AGAINST THE LUXEMBOURG.

THAT public opinion in Europe should have fastened
upon me the charge of being the founder and the
organiser of the national workshops; a charge, the
falsity of which was made so undisguisedly patent—by
my writings, my speeches, and my acts—by a series of
official documents inserted in the *Moniteur*—by the
evidence adduced before the solemn Commission of
Inquiry which the National Assembly appointed in
1848—by the *Histoire des Ateliers nationaux*, a special
and complete statement, for which we are indebted to
their very director, M. Emile Thomas—by the public
declarations of MM. Arago, de Lamartine, and Garnier
Pagès, all members of the Provisional Government—
by my public and repeated denials, never contradicted,
of any connection whatever with those national workshops—in fine, by the confessions of their real con-
trivers—is certainly one of the most extraordinary
illustrations on record of the power of calumny, when
used as the common weapon of divers hatreds conspiring for the destruction of an idea, in the person
of a man.

I proceed to give the details of the evidence here alluded to. On the twenty-seventh of February, 1848, in the first days of the Revolution, before the experiment of the Luxembourg was thought of, the *Moniteur* published the following decree: "The Provisional Government decrees the establishment of National Workshops. The Minister of Public Works is charged with the execution of the present decree."

The Minister of Public Works at that time was M. Marie.

The situation of Paris immediately after the great shock of February is well known. The immediate consequences of so violent and unforeseen a crisis, were, of course, a disturbance of industrial operations, a panic among capitalists, and a considerable multitude of working men thrown upon the streets, starving for want of work, and armed. Such a state of things could not but cause uneasiness to the Government, and hence the decree above mentioned.

But what were these *Ateliers Nationaux* to be? A mere ruinous empirical expedient, or a noble and vigorous experiment of the organisation of labour? A temporary resource against the rigour of circumstances, or a starting point of social regeneration? The *Moniteur* had pronounced the *name ;* how was the *thing* to be understood?

M. Marie knew my opinions better than any one; for only a few days before the Revolution of February, in a rather numerous gathering of deputies and journalists in his own house, I had clearly explained them; and I may add, they had encountered no more decided

opponent than M. Marie.   And yet, it was to him, who
totally misunderstood and dreaded Socialism, who had
sworn in his heart to resist it *à l'outrance,* that an
organisation of the national workshops was to be
abandoned; it was by him, as Minister of Public Works,
that it was naturally demanded; it was to him and to
him only, that the majority of the Council, of which
he was a member, was willing to see it entrusted.

If on the 28th of February, when the people
swarmed in vast masses on the Place de Grêve, to
demand the creation of a Ministry of Labour and
Progress, their demand had been complied with, I
should doubtless have commenced at once the application of those very ideas which M. Marie, so deter-
minedly repelled, and to which I had devoted my
whole life.   I have elsewhere related the violent resistance I encountered to any such proposals ; how my
resignation was warmly offered and refused; and how
the bleeding image of civil war was cast into the
discussion, and how I was made responsible for the disaster beforehand ; how, in fine, instead of a Ministry
of Labour and Progress, a simple Commission of Inquiry was instituted, without administrative resources
of any kind, without official agents, without any means
of action save the use of speech.

It was thus that the national workshops remained in
the sole charge of M. Marie, one of the fiercest adversaries of Socialism, and the decree of March 6, 1848,
which bears his signature, and his only, attests the fact.*

It is important to observe, that this decree was

* See the *Moniteur* of March 7, 1848.

framed after a deliberation held, not in the Council, as it ought to have been, but independently of the Council. MM. Buchez, Flottard, Barbier, Tremisot, Robin, Marie, Michel, Baude, Ouffroy de Bréville, these were the persons who were summoned to decide that terrible question which, as the event proved, bore the seeds of the insurrection of June. M. Marie was there, of course, and M. Garnier Pagès, mayor of Paris, presided. As for myself, I had neither been consulted, nor even informed of the meeting; * it was too well known how opposed I was in principle to the ideas which they sought to carry out.

Nay, not only was the direction of the national workshops entrusted to a person with whom I was unacquainted even by sight; but one of the claims which recommended that person, M. Emile Thomas, to the selection of M. Marie, was his ardent, indefatigable opposition to my doctrines. The declarations of M. Emile Thomas himself before the Commission of Inquiry leave no doubt upon this point:

First, in his deposition of July 28, 1848, M. Emile Thomas says: " I have never spoken to M. Louis Blanc in my life; I don't know him." Again: " While I was at the head of the workshops, I saw M. Marie daily, sometimes twice a day; MM. Buchez, Recurt, and Marrast almost every day. Never once M. Ledru Rollin, nor M. Louis Blanc, nor M. Flocon, nor M. Albert." †

* See l'Histoire des Ateliers nationaux, par M. Emile Thomas, pp. 47—57.

† Report of the Commission of Inquiry by the National Assembly, vol. i., pp. 352—358.

Secondly, on July 28, 1848, he deposes: "I always went along with the mayoralty of Paris, in opposition to MM. Ledru Rollin, Flocon, and the others. I was in open hostility to the Luxembourg. I openly contested the influence of M. Louis Blanc." *

Nor let it be objected, that though these national workshops were not organised with my concurrence, they were, at all events, in conformity with my principles. The truth is precisely the reverse. We see by M. Marie's own words, how much he was opposed to my doctrines, and with what earnestness of purpose he endeavoured secretly to undermine them. How then is it possible to suppose that, from mere wantonness, he would have applied the public money to an experimental trial of them?

In point of fact, it is monstrous to confound the industrial system developed in my ORGANISATION OF LABOUR with the system, so justly stigmatised, of the national workshops managed by M. Emile Thomas, under the sanction of M. Marie.

The *social workshops*, such as I had suggested, were each of them to consist of workmen belonging to the same trade.

The *national workshops*, as put in operation by M. Marie, exhibited a collection of workmen got together pell-mell, and—prodigious absurdity!—all put to the same kind of work.

In the *social workshops*, as suggested by me, the workmen were to pursue their business, the State

* Report of the *Commission of Inquiry* by the National Assembly, vol. i., p. 352.

lending them capital, to be repaid according to certain stipulations; they, working exclusively for their own profit, with a view to a joint benefit, that is to say, with all the stimulus of personal interest, combined with the influence exercised by the pursuit of a common object, and that point of honour which belongs to *esprit de corps.*

In the *national workshops,* as managed by M. Marie, the State interfered simply as a contractor; the operatives worked only as paid instruments. Now, as the kind of labour in these workshops was utterly unproductive and absurd, besides being such as the greater part of them were unaccustomed to, the action of the State was simply squandering the public funds; its money, a premium upon idleness; its wages, alms in disguise.

The *social workshops,* as suggested by me, consisted of families of working men, united by the most intimate ties and identity of interest; families, therefore, seriously concerned in being industrious and in the highest degree productive.

The *national workshops,* as managed by M. Marie, were nothing more than a rabble of paupers, whom it was enough to feed, from the want of knowing how to employ them, and who had to live together without any other ties than a military organisation, and under chiefs who bore the name, at once so strange and yet so characteristic, of serjeant-majors—*brigadiers.*

I might stop here, but I must go farther. I must prove that these workshops were organised in hostility to me, as the official representative of Socialism.

It will be remembered, that M. Emile Thomas, in

his deposition, already alluded to, extracted from the
"Report of the Commission of Inquiry," says : " I was
in open hostility to the Luxembourg. I openly contested the influence of M. Louis Blanc." To this
avowal, at once so naïve and so precise, the ex-director
of the national workshops has added some very curious
particulars, which ought to be made known.

In the first place, he formally declares, that if my
system remained in the state of theory, it was entirely
due to the resistance it received from the mayoralty of
Paris ; * that is to say, from the power in concert with
which, according to his own confession, M. Emile
Thomas was managing the national workshops.

The real truth is, that they were created for no other
purpose than of placing at the orders of the official
adversaries of Socialism, an army which, if needs were,
they might oppose to it.

The delegates of the Luxembourg did not receive a
single farthing ; the workmen of the national workshops were, on the contrary, paid. As a reward for the
duties which they discharged with so much zeal, the
former found themselves exposed to persecutions, which
went so far as to deprive some of them of their daily
subsistence ; the latter, on the other hand, depended
for their own subsistence and their families' on the
Minister of Public Works.

But the working men were not to be caught with
baits like these ; and the enemies of Socialism should
have known better the men with whom they had to
deal. As it was, they were not satisfied with having

* See l'Histoire des Ateliers nationaux, par M. Emile Thomas, p. 200.

embodied, *regimentally*, thousands of workmen of different trades, aggregated pell-mell, and set upon a labour equally ruinous and ridiculous; they were not content with having divided that vast crowd into *brigades*, as an army ready to be hurled, at need, against the Luxembourg; but they did worse: they inflicted upon this *army* of the national workshops the insult to suppose them purchaseable by an increase of pay.

Let us listen to the precious confessions of M. Emile Thomas:

"M. Marie sent for me to the Hôtel de Ville after the sitting of the Council. I went there, and was informed that a credit of five millions of francs was granted to the *Ateliers Nationaux*, and that the financial service would be more regular henceforth. M. Marie afterwards took me aside, and asked me, *in a low tone*, whether I thought I could count upon the working men.—'I think so,' I replied; 'but their number increases so considerably, that I find it very difficult to possess so direct an influence over them as I could wish.'—'Don't be uneasy about the number,' the minister rejoined; 'if you hold them in hand, the number can never be too large; but find some means of attaching them to you sincerely. *Don't spare money: if necessary, you may be supplied with secret service funds.*'—'I don't think this will be wanted: indeed, it might be the source of rather serious difficulties. But for what other purpose than the preservation of the public tranquillity, do you make these recommendations?'—'For public safety. Do you think

you will be able to master these men completely?
*The day is, perhaps, not far distant, when it may be
necessary to march them into the street.'* " *

Thus was I without a farthing, at the Luxembourg,
while the ex-director of the national workshops, in
order to create a power the object of which was hostility to me, received the under-hand offer of a share of
the secret service money.

Thus, to the exclusively moral influence which Albert
and I exercised through the unlimited confidence placed
in us by the delegates of the Luxembourg, the most
insidious pains were taken to oppose an influence
working through corruption, and at the public cost !

Thus, while in the Luxembourg, we were only uttering
words of peace, exhortations to union and tranquillity,
the covert instructions to the manager of the workshops
were : " Don't spare money . . . . do you think you
can succeed in getting *your men* well in hand? The
day perhaps is not far off when it may be necessary to
march them into the street ! "

But this is not all. To provide a permanent
means of influence over the working population of the
national workshops, M. Marie and M. Emile Thomas,
attempted to form a club.

"The idea suggested by one of the delegates of
founding a club," says M. Emile Thomas, " very much
struck the minister, who, when the delegates were gone,
revived the subject, and asked me what I thought of it.
I replied, that something good might come of it. . . .

---

* See *l'Histoire des Ateliers nationaux, par M. Emile Thomas.*

I saw in it a splendid opportunity of setting up an altar opposed to that of the Luxembourg." *

But the new altar had no worshippers. Popularity is gained, not bought. This failing, nothing was omitted that could draw off the delegates of the Luxembourg.

Well! was said to them, what good can come of all these delusive theories? they talk to you of the organisation of labour! they vaunt the benefits of association! they point out to you the extinction of pauperism in the far distance! Mere rhapsody all this! Utopian dreams, brilliant phantoms by which they lead you naked and hungry into the region of chimeras! Come to your senses, you unhappy men; leave to themselves these tribunes with their gaudy but barren words. Remember that poverty is the inevitable lot of the majority. Were your sufferings ever so keen as they are now? Come to a clearer comprehension of what is meant by the cries of your children, address your inquiries to the pallid cheeks of their mothers.

Yes, this was the language of men who, for a horrible purpose, were scattering capital to the winds, ruining credit by loud wailings at its ruin, interrupting labour begun, and labour offered. They kept up or augmented the evil, in order to prove the impossibility of destroying it; eager to show that the new ideas were incapable of realisation, they availed themselves of the results of manœuvres employed by themselves for the express purpose of preventing their being realised.

But the people were not deceived by all this. Menaces, promises, insidious counsels, distress prolonged almost

* See *l'Histoire des Ateliers nationaux, par M. Emile Thomas,* p. 157.

beyond bearing, could not shake the representatives of
the trades; nothing disturbed the deep calm with which
they held, at the Luxembourg, their great Inquest.

And for us—witnesses of this heroism hour after
hour, of this unpretending and unremitting devotedness, of virtues whose only recompense was the satisfaction springing from an enthusiasm, in some sort,
sacred—how would it have been possible for us to
remain untouched by feelings of regard and respect ?
Receive, ye magnanimous though vilified men, the
testimony here rendered you, from the depths of exile,
by a heart whose every throb has been known to you.
Amid all the ills which have befallen me, and in the
bitter solitude which surrounds me, one solace remains,
which it is beyond the power either of my enemies or
of fortune to deprive me, this is the happiness, the
glory to be loved by men like you.

But to resume and to exhaust this matter, I will
first observe that M. Garnier Pagès has vindicated
me from having participated any way, from first to
last, in the direction of these workshops.* Now listen
to the confessions, on the subject of these national
workshops, which M. de Lamartine has found it necessary to make in his *History of the Revolution of
February* in which he has exhibited an ill-will towards
me that is sufficiently out of his usual habit, and
sufficiently dexterous, to put his testimony in this
matter beyond all suspicion:

" M. Marie was temporising with the public works, at

* See *Un Episode de la Révolution de Février, par M. Garnier Pagès*,
p 48.

that moment in a state of great neglect. One of the
political and social solutions of the crisis would, according to some members of the Government, have been a
large enlistment of men out of work to be employed in
some productive agricultural labour on a great scale.
Lamartine was of this opinion. Some socialists, at
that time moderate and prudent, afterwards angry and
factious, were desirous that the Government should
originate a movement of this kind. A grand campaign
in the interior, with implements for arms, like those
campaigns of the Romans or Egyptians, for digging
canals, or draining Pontine marshes, appeared the
expedient best adapted to a Republic which desired to
remain at peace, and to save property by protecting
and elevating the labourer. It was the thought of the
hour. *A great department of public works would have
marked the era of the policy which the moment required.
It was one of the great faults of the Government to have
lost too much time before attempting to realise this view.*
While it was inactive, the national workshops, more
and more crowded by misery and idleness, became
day by day more unmanageable, more sterile, and
more menacing to public order.

"But as yet, they had not reached this point; they
were merely an expedient for preserving order, a rude
auxiliary summoned on the morrow of the Revolution
by the necessity of feeding the people, and not feeding
them idle, in order to avoid the disorders of idleness.
M. Marie organised them with skill, without any useful
result as respected productive labours. He formed them
into brigades, he gave them chiefs, he communicated to

them a spirit of discipline and order. Instead of being a force at the mercy of socialists and insurrectionists, he for the space of four months made of them a *prætorian band,* inactive indeed, but at the disposal of power. Commanded, directed, sustained by chiefs *who were in secret concert with the anti-socialist part of the Government,* the workshops served until the appearance of the National Assembly, as a counterpoise to the sectarian operatives of the Luxembourg, and the seditious operatives of the clubs. They scandalised Paris by their numbers and the inutility of their labour; they more than once protected and saved Paris without its being conscious of it. *So far from being in the pay of Louis Blanc, as has been said, they were the device of his adversaries."* *

It is remarkable that, in this passage, M. de Lamartine imputes it as a fault, attended with fatal consequences, to the Provisional Government, not to have instituted that public department of labour, which, suggested by me, was refused by the majority, and more especially by him.

As to the origin of the workshops, their military organisation for a purpose already revealed by another, and their SECRET CONNECTION with the majority of the Government, amounting to a conspiracy, the passage, unhappily, speaks for itself !

So, the calumny of which I have been made a victim is obvious; but the reason of it is obvious, too.

The national workshops emptied the exchequer with a dead loss; they humiliated the working man, who

* "History of the Revolution of February," by M. de Lamartine, vol. ii.

was reduced to *accept* the bread which he desired
to *earn;* they discredited State interference in
industrial matters. In the place of associations of
workmen, they set up battalions of paid idlers—a
strange army, sooner or later to be disbanded at the
risk of civil war! The routed logicians of the doctrine
of *Laissez-faire,* its vaunting advocates, now in their
extremity, had, of course, an immense interest in
fixing upon us the responsibility of all this mischief.
What a lucky chance for the disciples of the old
political economy, could they succeed in playing a trick
upon opinion; could they contrive to pass off as the
highest practical form of the organisation of labour,
those national workshops, which were nothing more
than its ignoble travesties! There was no mistake in
the object of this imposture; it furnished our adversaries, driven to their wits' end for arguments, with the
opportunity of saying, "Of what use so much reason-
ing? to all your theories we oppose a *fact.*" *

* This is the *fact* alluded to in the following passage of a biographical
work entitled "Men of the Time," &c., which I give as a sample of the
sort of information which has been conveyed to the English public respecting these important events :—"The experiment was made ; a number of
the most inefficient workmen sauntered about the *ateliers* in the day, and
listened to the glowing declamation of Louis Blanc in the evening ; but the
certain ruin delayed not; immense sums were sunk in the experiment,
which ended in recrimination and general disgust."

The author has certainly not overdone the bad results of the *fact,* for he
might have added, that it ended in insurrection and bloodshed too. The
trifling objection I have to make to the statement is, that I am rendered responsible for an experiment to which I was opposed, and represented as addressing my "glowing declamation" in the evening, to
persons with whom I had nothing to do, and in places where I never set
my foot.

The same well-informed writer favours his readers with a philosophical

But the associations originated by the Luxembourg —those, for instance, of the tailors, spinners, gold-lace workers, and saddlers—differing so radically as they did from the national workshops, were they not a sufficient and exterminating answer to this most impudent of all calumnies ? So, it seems to me, it should have been ; but the agents of this conspiracy of falsehood applied themselves with so much terrible zeal and audacity to mystify the facts, that at this very day many people confound the national workshops, which no longer exist, with those co-operative associations which still survive and prosper.

It is really enough to make one shudder, when one thinks how much of hatred, injustice, and atrocity, can be compressed into a lie.

It is as the organiser of the national workshops, organised against me, that I have had and have legions of enemies.

It is as the organiser of the national workshops, organised against me, that, in the opinion of the immense crowd of the ignorant, I have become accountable for the convulsions of industry and the calamities of the time.

It is as the organiser of the national workshops, organised against me, that I have been accused by every one who felt that his affairs were in a slippery state.

It is as the organiser of the national workshops,

view of the direful influence exercised over my career and writings by a slight I once received from the Duchesse de Dino, whom it has never been my good fortune to see in my life.

organised against me, that I have narrowly escaped two cowardly attempts at assassination; the first, on the very threshold of the Assembly; the second, in midday, on the crowded *boulevard*.

Do you want a synonym for calumniator? Here it is: Assassin.

CHAPTER X.

FOREIGN POLICY OF THE PROVISIONAL GOVERNMENT.

ALLIANCES between States are matters, of course, of the highest moment. But in order that such alliances should be permanent and secure, they must be formed between governments of a nature similar and congenial. Otherwise, the advantages may be one-sided, and there will be an absence of that equality of conditions indispensable to the duration of a good understanding. Consider, for instance, the relation of constitutional England to France, as supposed to be represented by the Imperial Government. How disadvantageous to the former, from the very nature of things! All being open as the day in England, and every motive, feeling, and view easily ascertainable, the Imperial Government is enabled to regulate its course by an accurate estimate of facts. On the contrary, everything being veiled in France, England is obliged to proceed by guesses or on trust. This is, indeed, an alliance between light and darkness.

Every national act being in England the result of slow public deliberation and of exhaustive discussion between various political parties, each throb of the nation can be felt, every step be foreseen and the

French Imperial Government is made aware, not only of what is doing, but of everything likely to be done, and can guard at leisure, if needs be, against any probable contingency. On the contrary, all being mystery in France, each coming hour an enigma impossible to solve, and the policy entirely dependent upon the caprice of a single man, England must be at every moment in the dark, and may at any moment be taken unawares.

As, at present, all alliances are, more or less, games of skill, it is obvious that, in one between an autocratic government and a constitutional monarchy, the despot is a player who overlooks both hands.

Something more lamentable still in this case is, that there is risk either from the wisdom or the folly of the despot.

For, if he be wise, foresight is easy to him, whilst it is impossible to you.

If he be a fool, you are exposed to being the victim of any rashness or frenzy that may seize him; and what, with you, only a parliamentary decision could effect, will be, perhaps, with him, the consequence of an extra glass of champagne.

The alliance of England with Louis Bonaparte is, therefore, as unsafe as it is unnatural; and the extraordinary efforts of Lord Palmerston to make such an alliance the pivot of the English policy, shows that there is little of a statesman in him.

Not that I think it would have been advisable, on the part of England, to declare war against the Empire, or to provoke it in any way. Great as my conviction is that Louis Bonaparte represents nothing else in France than brute force trampling on intelligence; that his accession to supreme power was a bloody usurpation; that the alleged consecration of the 2nd of December by universal suffrage was a sham; and that it is bitter mockery to call the " choice of France," as Lord Palmerston did of late in Parliament, a man who, in order to maintain himself, has avowedly no other resource than to hold France crouching, motionless and breathless, beneath the sabre; still, I cannot blame England for having shrunk from the dangers of a breach. But, to preserve peace, was it absolutely necessary to jeopardise the cause of freedom, and to abandon the cause of justice? Could not the calamities of a struggle be warded off, without converting a dignified prudent reserve into an unconditional alliance, and an unconditional alliance into a system of boundless adulation? How fatal to the principle of Liberty in Europe, the spectacle of a despot, one day reprobated and cursed as such by the whole English people, and the very next day crossing London in triumphant march, amid rapturous acclamations!

To what extent all this was consistent with morality, I will not stop here to inquire; but was it consistent with the real and permanent interests of England? Certainly not. The real and permanent interests of England consist in winning the sympathies of France, and nothing could be better calculated to alienate them than to fawn on him by whom she is enslaved.

To mistake an alliance with Louis Bonaparte for an alliance with France is an error likely, if not corrected, to give rise, at the next turn of the wheel, to the most sinister complications; and I do not hesitate to assert that the closer the connection between the two governments, the greater the difficulty of maintaining, in future, the amity of the two nations.

Nor is the price to be paid for this friendship between the two governments a matter of slight consideration to England. The "Conspiracy Bill," exacted by the imperial diplomacy, and backed by military threats, was but the commencement of a blockade against the principles of the English nation, and, as a means of weakening its power, a first aggression upon its honour. It may be very well for Lord Palmerston to affect about the matter a tone of supercilious levity. But, when two men stand face to face, who does not know that the retreat of one is to the other an irresistible inducement to march on? More than temerity itself, fear invites danger, and every step is, indeed, the descent from one humiliating concession to another.

Had the leading politicians of this country had a clear insight into their own situation as compared with that of Louis Bonaparte, they might have kept him in awe, instead of being kept in awe by him. They had only to let him *infer* that, although determined to refrain from any offensive measure, if respectfully dealt with, they were ready, in case of disagreement, to bestow on the liberal party in France an effective support. Such a policy would have been consonant both with the principles and the interests of a free country; the sympathies of an oppressed nation would have supplied England with a powerful lever; Louis

Bonaparte would have been brought by the sense of his perils to have a due regard for her; and so, peace, far from being endangered, would have been secured.

Unfortunately, the policy adopted has been just the reverse. Whilst these short-sighted politicians were caressing Louis Bonaparte—calling him, through sheer flattery, the Saviour of Europe; congratulating him, in the name of a *free* people, on his having made a successful attempt against *freedom*, and thus putting his pride to the utmost stretch—they seemed to take delight in estranging from England the most enlightened, liberal, and generous portion of the French people.

The results are what every one can see and appreciate at this very moment. England has been summoned to alter her laws by those very soldiers through whose exertions Louis Bonaparte became " the Saviour of Europe ! "

If I mistake not, the reason why the English people have suffered their political leaders to pursue a course so dangerous and so absurd, lies in certain prejudices sedulously spread and fostered in this country, respecting the Republican party—*the only one fated to rule France.* The English people were taught that, should the Republicans get the mastery, their foreign policy would be one of restless encroachment and military conquest. It is, therefore, important to relate the events that have reference to the foreign policy proclaimed in 1848 by the Provisional Government.

I will not try to exonerate the French Republicans from the glorious charge of claiming for France the right to assist any nation trampled on by foreign conquerors. I openly confess that the party to which I belong, regards the force of France as appertaining, not to herself only, but to humanity, and considers it her duty to put, when possible, the vindication of other "oppressed nationalities" on a level with the defence of her own. One of the grounds on which the French Republicans object to a monarchical form of government certainly is, that it involves a necessary dereliction from this high duty, by making national policy subservient to merely dynastic interests. Seeing that no despotic government has ever scrupled to aid another despotic government, whenever its aid was asked for, they cannot conceive why a free nation should be bound to forbear aiding another kindred nation, when unjustly assailed, or brought into bondage; and, as stated in my "History of Ten Years," it was with a feeling of genuine indignation, that, during the reign of Louis Philippe, they heard M. Casimir Perrier say, from the parliamentary tribune: "*Le sang français n'appartient qu'à la France.*"

But as much as the French Republicans are inclined to assist "oppressed nationalities," by mediation, by money, even by arms, if needed, so much are they averse to any war intended for the selfish purposes of ambition, military glory, and territorial conquests. The necessity of war, on certain occasions, is, in their eyes, one of the saddest proofs of the unsound condition of the world; they hold standing armies to be inconsistent with liberty, and they feel acutely enough how easily a victorious warrior is changed into a tyrant.

Never was war so strongly deprecated as by Robespierre in 1792 ; it was in spite of his resistance, seconded by that of the Jacobins, that France was brought to unsheath her sword against Austria; and it is a well-established, although not universally known, fact, that, in 1793, the war against England was *forced upon* the Convention by the systematic and repeated provocations of Mr. Pitt.* Nor must it be forgotten, that the CONSTITUTION OF 1793, drawn up by the most determined Montagnards, contains this clause : " The French people does not interfere with the government of other nations, and allows no other nation to interfere with its own." †

But, while laying down this general principle as the foundation of their foreign policy in ordinary circumstances, Robespierre and the Montagnards meant by no means to disclaim the right, or to neglect the duty, of interference, whenever there was an act of tyrannical violence perpetrated, *obviously* involving consequences contrary to the eternal laws of humanity and justice. For this is another clause of the CONSTITUTION OF 1793 : " The French people are the natural allies of all free nations ; " and as to Robespierre, he went so far as to say, in his DECLARATION OF THE RIGHTS OF MAN: " He who oppresses one single nation declares himself the enemy of all nations."

Such were the ideas of the Republican party in France about foreign politics, when, on the 2nd of

---

* Those who are desirous to get closely acquainted with all the particulars, will find them stated at full length in my " History of the French Revolution," vol. ix., p. 33.   † *Ibid*, vol. ix., p. 29.

March, 1848, the Provisional Government were called upon to discuss M. de Lamartine's Circular Manifesto to the European powers.

Three questions were to be solved :

Should a right be asserted, in the name of the French people, to afford military aid to nations attempting to shake off a foreign yoke?

Should the treaties of 1815 be repudiated?

Should a desire to maintain peace be expressed ?

Upon the first point there could be no difficulty ; and the following passage of M. de Lamartine's Manifesto met with unreserved approbation :—

" We avow openly, that if the hour of reconstruction for certain oppressed nationalities in Europe appeared to us to have struck in the decrees of Providence; if Switzerland, our faithful ally since Francis I., were constrained or menaced in that growing disposition developing within her to lend one prop more to the group of democratic governments ; if the independent states of Italy were invaded; if the attempt were made to impose limits or obstacles to their internal transformations, or to contest by force of arms their right of allying themselves with each other to consolidate a common country; the French Republic would consider itself at liberty to take up arms for the protection of these legitimate movements of growth and nationality." *

It must be observed, that the matter in hand was a very ticklish one. Cases of national usurpation being generally of a more or less relative character, and

* See the *Moniteur* of the 5th of March, 1848.

consequently, more or less open to dispute, it is very difficult, if not impossible, to trace beforehand an invariable and rigid line of demarcation between the duty of interference and the rule of non-interference. It was, therefore, a judicious policy to reserve to France the appreciation of the hour, the moment, the justice, the cause, and the means by which it would be fitting for her to intervene.

But the assertion of the right alluded to, even confined within these limits, has been made the occasion of the most extraordinary attacks on the Provisional Government. We have been charged with a breach of received principles, with a bold defiance of the law of nations, by the very men who admire Pitt for having, previous to any declaration of war, stirred up the French Royalists to rebellion against a French national assembly issued from universal suffrage ! We have been insultingly assailed by Lord Brougham * for professing the very doctrine to which England, a few months ago, had recourse, in her attempt to free the Neapolitans, not from the yoke of foreign conquerors, but—a much bolder encroachment !—from the despotism of their native ruler ! If the principle of interference is inviolable, why did the great powers of Europe agree, in three instances, to violate it, by interfering, as was remarked by Mr. Mill, between Greece and Turkey at Navarino, between Holland and Belgium at Antwerp, and between Turkey and Egypt at St. Jean d'Acre ? Again, if any meddling with the

* In the pamphlet which called forth the admirable and overwhelming reply of Mr. John Stuart Mill.

affairs of another nation is absolutely contrary to the law of nations, as understood by Lord Brougham, why was Russia suffered to march an army to crush the Hungarians? and why is Louis Bonaparte suffered to maintain in Rome a garrison of French soldiers, for the purpose of enforcing the obedience of the Italians to the degrading despotism of the priests and the Pope? How scandalous that, in certain quarters, the same principle should be held most wicked when proclaimed in behalf of the oppressed, and perfectly sound when carried out in behalf of the oppressors!

Respecting the treaties of 1815, the draught submitted to the Provisional Government for examination was by no means explicit. M. de Lamartine had evidently been fearful lest his Manifesto should sound all over Europe like the blast of a trumpet. To so much caution I did not hesitate to object; and I urged the danger of leaving so important a question undecided. It may be said, without exaggeration, of every Frenchman, that there is not a fibre in him which does not thrill at the bare remembrance of the treaties of 1815. They were imposed by conquest; they were agreed to by an intrusive government, under circumstances of humiliation never to be forgotten; they were signed before the territory had ceased to be occupied by foreign armies; they were avowedly intended, not only to bring France as low as possible, but to imprison her between insurmountable barriers; and "whereas, within the last half century, England, Russia, and Prussia had been aggrandised by important acquisitions, the French dominions were actually less extensive than they had been under Louis XV." * Were engagements of this sort of a nature to bind France for ever? Nothing, indeed, could have been more absurd than such a pretension on the part of the other parties, who, although interested in the maintenance of the said treaties, had never scrupled to violate them at their pleasure. After what had been seen at Cracow, in Italy, in Hungary, and in Germany, could any one deny that the treaties of 1815 had become waste paper, a bit of which was torn away by each party in turn? I, therefore, proposed that they should be peremptorily declared no longer binding on France. I need not add that the feeling of all the members of the Provisional Government was equally strong against them. Only, the minority, to which I belonged, was, perhaps, less open than the majority to the fear of displeasing foreign courts, and thus endangering peace. To remove the difficulty, a middle course was proposed, consisting in the solemn repudiation of the treaties of 1815 as obligatory, on the one hand, and, on the other, in accepting their territorial arrangements as existing facts, to be modified through diplomatic negotiations or any other proceedings which circumstances might suggest.

The following is, in reference to this point, the passage adopted:

" The treaties of 1815 no longer exist as obligatory,

---

* These are the very words used by an English writer, as illustrating the truth of this remark :—" There is nothing surprising in the fact that the treaties of 1815 should be distasteful to France." See "Edinburgh Review," vol. lxxxvii., p. 585.

in the opinion of the French Republic; but the territorial boundaries fixed by those treaties are an existing fact, which the Republic admits as a basis and a starting point in its relations with other countries. But, while the treaties of 1815 no longer exist except as a fact, to be modified by common agreement, and while the Republic openly declares that it has a right and a mission to arrive regularly and pacifically at such modifications—the good sense, the moderation, the conscience, the prudence of the Republic exist, and are for Europe a better and more honourable guarantee than the letter of those treaties, which she herself has so often violated or modified." *

I read in Lord Normanby's book :

"March 3. Lamartine stated to me to-day that he wished to mention to me the substance of his Circular Manifesto to the European powers, which had been discussed in the Provisional Council yesterday, and which would be issued in two or three days. He said that I was aware of the feeling which had existed for the last thirty years in France upon the subject of the treaties of 1815, the humiliation of which they had been considering as the constant record. *He should have wished to have said nothing whatever about them, but this seemed impossible. He should be obliged* to allude to the manner in which they had been violated, &c."†

I hope, for M. de Lamartine's sake, that his lordship's memory has played him false; but, unhappily, I am not entitled to contradict this statement, as I could

* *Moniteur* of the 9th of March, 1848.
† "A Year of Revolution in Paris," vol. i., pp. 164, 165.

not by any possibility be present at the interview. At all events, from this specimen of thoughtless indiscretion, M. de Lamartine will learn how little prudent it is, for a minister of foreign affairs, to make a foreign diplomatist his confidant.

The question whether the French Republic should declare its intention to remain at peace, gave rise to no discussion. I think, however, that the terms used by M. de Lamartine in his manifesto did not completely answer the views or gratify the feelings of the minority of the Council. For my part, I should have preferred on this point, a language less warm and more sober. To say, for instance : " The French Republic desires to enter into the family of instituted governments—La République française désire entrer dans la famille des gouvernements institués," * was, in my opinion, to overshoot the mark. Nor were such words quite consistent with these, far more to my taste : " To exist, the French Republic needs not be acknowledged.—La République française n'a pas besoin d'être reconnue, pour exister." † But, the modification referring to the treaties of 1815 once adopted, none of us could deny that, upon the whole, M. de Lamartine's manifesto was the eloquent expression of the only policy then possible.

Nevertheless, this policy has been assaulted by two parties, from opposite points of view, the one charging us with letting loose the spirit of disorder and anarchy throughout Europe, the other accusing us of want of

* See this manifesto in the *Moniteur* of the 9th of March, 1848.
† *Ibid.*

determination towards foreign powers, and of an attempt to pursue a trimming policy between two irreconcileable principles.

The passages just cited are a sufficient answer to the first count of this indictment. As to the second, it may be very briefly disposed of.

What was the position? In 1792, all Europe had combined to take the offensive against France: in 1848, no such result was to be apprehended; no military coalition could possibly threaten the cradle of the Republic; whether taught by experience, or paralysed by internal difficulties, even the governments the most hostile to it gave no sign of a disposition to attack, if not attacked.

Besides, England, which had been the soul of former coalitions against us, might, in the event of our remaining at peace, be relied upon as an ally, whereas any violent attempt to excite a universal conflagration in Europe, would probably have made her our enemy.

Was there, at all events, any certainty that the military protection of France, prematurely pressed upon nationalities still unprepared for a decisive struggle, would not have aroused their jealousies rather than their sympathies? The Germans had preserved a bitter recollection of the revolutionary occupation of Mayence and Frankfort by the French, and the famous song of the Rhine was not forgotten in Germany, even by the democrats. We knew it was among the Italian patriots a generally accepted idea that a nation is unworthy of being independent, which is not ready to work out its independence for itself. The crossing of the Alps by a French army would have been viewed, all over Italy, with a mingled feeling of suspicion and wounded pride. Could any warning be more clear than this Italian watch-word : *Italia fara da se?*

Nor was the question less deserving of serious consideration, as regards our internal affairs. The Republic before stretching abroad, had to be consolidated at home. Its opponents, in the provinces, were numerous and influential. The monarchical parties, stunned by the thunder-bolt of February, but not extinguished, were on the watch for the next favourable opportunity, and could not have failed to take advantage of the confusion likely to attend any military outbreak. The middle classes were most decidedly averse to war, while the ruling idea of the working classes was that of their social emancipation. Under such circumstances, would it have been wise to put to the venture the fate of the new Republic, and, perhaps, to bring upon France the horrors of a third invasion ?

At any rate, we could not be expected to run headlong into so many dangers, without soldiers and without money.

Now, with reference to these indispensable conditions of success, let us expose, in a few words, how matters stood.

The army, such as Louis Philippe had made and left it, was by no means able to take the field. Almost on the morrow of the Revolution, the most distinguished military chiefs having been summoned to the Council, and asked questions concerning the forces at our disposal, I remember their answer was that the state of things did not allow France to wage war, at the moment, with any reasonable chance of success. A " DEFENCE COMMITTEE "—" COMITÉ DE DÉFENSE " was instituted with a view to a special inquiry into the military resources of the country. Well, this committee, composed of General Oudinot, General Pelet, General Pailloux, General Vaillant, General Bedeau, General Lamoricière, M. Deniée, one of the heads of the Commissariat, and Major Charras, made a report, stating that, in the infantry, no regiment could supply more than two effective battalions of 500 men each, nor, in the cavalry, more than four effective squadrons, amounting in all to 525 men.* In fact, according to the estimates of the committee, the total number of men disposable did not exceed 101,000, whilst the number requisite, in the event of monarchical coalition, to line the frontiers, without unfurnishing Algeria, could not be less than 514,000 !

Soldiers, of course, might have been levied ; but what was wanting, as will be seen in the subsequent chapter, was, besides time to drill, money to maintain, them. For the monarchy of Louis Philippe had bequeathed to the Republic finances actually verging on bankruptcy, and, in consequence of the social commotion of February, commercial credit was at the very lowest ebb. What should have been done, in my opinion, to meet this emergency, I will say presently ; but no financial scheme, however well devised, could have made it possible for us, at that moment, to force war upon Europe,

* Rapport de M. Arago à l'Assemblée Nationale, séance du 8 mai, 1848.

without running the risk of drowning in blood, both the French nation and the Republic.

The best proof that the moral force of example and the prospect of an effective assistance, if required by circumstances, were sufficient to cheer on "oppressed nationalities" to a successful vindication of their independence—is that very series of spontaneous insurrections which broke out in 1848; nor were they suppressed during the Provisional Government, but afterwards, not in pursuance of its policy, but in utter opposition to it. Had the principles laid down in the manifesto been in force, and *all* the men who had proclaimed them been in power a few months longer, the Roman Republic would never have been assailed by any foreign troops, still less by French soldiers, and Russia would never have been suffered to march an army against the Hungarians. The Provisional Government resigned their power too soon, that is before the provinces had been intellectually put on a level with Paris by an incessant and wide diffusion of republican principles. This was the irretrievable blunder of the Provisional Government; and for this, those cannot be held responsible, who, like myself, did their best to obtain the postponement of the elections.

One word more. Let England remember that, in 1848, the Republicans held out a friendly hand to her, and then reflect that, on their sympathies with her rests the only chance of a real and lasting amity between the two countries.

CHAPTER XI.

THE FINANCIAL CRISIS.

FROM the first day of their installation, the Provisional Government found themselves on the brink of an immense financial abyss.

The budget of 1848—the *last* of the monarchy, and not at all, as some persons have been led to believe, the *first* of the Republic—presented a deficit of 245 millions of francs. *

Louis Philippe's ministers having, in the short space of seven peaceful years, added a sum of 800 millions to the principal of the public debt, this principal, which did not exceed 4,267 millions on the 1st January, 1841, amounted, on the 1st January, 1848, to no less than 5,067 millions.

Such were the strides of the monarchical government towards bankruptcy, that, during the 268 last days of its existence, it was spending, beyond the ordinary revenue, as much as 294 millions, that is more than one million of francs a-day ! †

The treasury bonds had increased to the amount,

---

* See *Rapport sur les comptes du Gouvernement Provisoire, Moniteur du 26 Avril,* 1849.

† *Un épisode de la Révolution de* 1848, par M. Garnier Pagès, p. 54.

hitherto unknown, of 318 millions, and the floating debt to the fabulous amount of 960 millions.

Now, what was there in the coffers of the State, on the morning of the 24th of February?

A sum of 57 millions of francs, in securities, available at successive periods of the financial year, and whose payment had become very doubtful — also 135 millions in specie, of which the Bank owed 45 millions to government. But from this sum of 135 millions was to be deducted that of 73 millions, destined to the payment of the half-year's interest of the five per cent stock.

Thus — for re-organising our military and naval forces, then in a state of decay—for completing the public works which had been commenced in the reign of Louis Philippe, and could not possibly be interrupted—for saving industry and commerce from the calamitous results of a crisis—for covering the current expenses, amounting to about 129 millions a month—for meeting the payments constantly coming due on account of an enormous floating debt of 960 millions —the only means at hand were . . . . a sum of 72 millions ! *

Such being the frightful situation bequeathed by the monarchy to the Republic, the ministry of finances was, in the first instance, intrusted to M. Goudchaux, a man of integrity and courage, but the very type of the *merely formal* Republican, resolute in action, while

* *Un épisode de la Révolution de* 1848, par M. Garnier Pagès, p. 54. It must be remarked that M. Garnier Pagès was minister of finances in 1848, and that the figures I extract from his book rest on official documents, undeniable and undenied.

over-timid in thought, opposing with boldness every
bold idea, and resisting with energy every energetic
advance. The Republic, in his eyes, was but one king
the fewer. Had this been the correct idea of a Republic, he would have been well qualified for the office
of minister of finances of the Provisional Government;
for, to high probity he superadded a large financial
experience, derived from his occupation as a banker of
old standing. But, at the outbreak of a revolution like
that of February, when every thing was in expectancy,
and so much progress in untried ways required, no one
could have been less fit for the office. Fettered, as a
banker, by the habit of routine, and never called upon by
the nature of his business to take comprehensive views
of social wants, he got alarmed the moment he heard
that there were to be conferences at the Luxembourg,
and his alarm, increased by proposals to abolish such
taxes as had become absolutely insufferable, was converted into panic, when the journalists urged their
demand for the suppression of the stamp-duty, as
materially hampering the liberty of the press. This
he opposed, upon the grand old obstructive principle
of refusing to give an inch, lest an ell should be
required, not perceiving that the Revolution had
brought with it many obligations not to be eluded,
and that the obnoxious duty was *de facto* abrogated by
the daily appearance of new journals, set up in defiance
of it.

On the 3rd of March, at a meeting of the Provisional Government, attended by all the members,
except M. Flocon, who was ill, M. Goudchaux pre-

sented a most doleful picture of the financial position. His broken voice, and the depressing character of the details he gave, so dismayed the majority of the council, that M. de Lamartine, leaning over towards M. Garnier Pagès, said, with visible anxiety, "*How is it, Garnier Pagès? Are we really gone?*"—"*Est-ce donc vrai, Garnier Pagès, sommes-nous perdus?*" *

After much perplexed deliberation, it was agreed to face the peril manfully. But, on the 9th of March, M. Goudchaux tendered his resignation, and on the majority declining to accept it, declared that, if they persisted, he would, within two hours, put an end to himself. Whereupon they gave way, convinced, from the character of the man, he would carry his threat into execution.

It has been given out by M. Goudchaux's friends, and I believe stated by himself in his evidence before the Commission of Inquiry in 1848 — but for this I cannot vouch, not having the report at hand—that one of the causes of his resignation was the fears everywhere spread by the audacious promulgation of the doctrines of the Luxembourg. The hollowness of such an allegation may be demonstrated by a simple approximation of two dates.

M. Goudchaux's resignation took place on the 5th of March. †

My first speech at the Luxembourg was on the 10th.‡

---

* This will be found confirmed in M. Garnier Pagès's pamphlet, *Un épisode de la Révolution de* 1848, p. 69.

† See the *Moniteur* of the 7th of March, 1848.

‡ *Ibid.*, 11th of March, 1848.

It is difficult to conceive how the latter could have influenced the former.

If M. Goudchaux was startled, which was never stated, by the shortening of the hours of labour, and the suppression of *Marchandage* — the only steps taken by the Luxembourg previous to the 5th of March, not only were these unconnected with any peculiar doctrines uttered there, but the principal feature of the meeting held on this occasion was my refusal to yield to any such demands of the operatives, without consulting their employers. And it may be remembered that it was not until a friendly arrangement had been made between both parties, that we recommended the above-mentioned measures to the Provisional Government — a conduct certainly little calculated to spread alarm. *

The truth is, that the crowning reason of M. Goudchaux's resignation was the failure of an expedient which he had, with the best intentions, suggested, but the effect of which disappointed his anticipations. In order to dispel financial uneasiness, and to veil from the public the difficulties of the moment, he had, as minister of finances, announced in the *Moniteur* † that the government was in a condition to pay, and would pay, in Paris on the 6th of March, and in the depart-

---

* So imperiously was the shortening of time required by circumstances, that, before the opening of the Luxembourg, the proprietors of the Northern Railway had, of their own accord, reduced the hours, not only to ten, but to nine. This fact is stated by Lord Normanby himself. See "A Year of Revolution in Paris," vol. i. p. 212.

† *Moniteur* of the 4th of March, 1848.

ments on the 15th, the half-year's interest upon stock, due only on the 22nd. But this affectation of readiness to pay what was not asked for, rendered the people all the more suspicious, and instead of calming, aggravated the public apprehensions. *

The Ministry of Finances being offered to M. Garnier Pagès, he accepted it, with that self-confidence which is one of the features of his character, but to which the moral courage required on this occasion imparted something really noble.

Like General Cavaignac, M. Garnier Pagès was in great part indebted for his political position to the prominent part a brother, then dead, had taken in the struggles of the Republican party, during the reign of Louis Philippe. Although a report was at the time current that, on the 24th of February, he showed himself disposed to support the Regency of the Duchess of Orleans—a report invariably contradicted by him—that he was a sincere Republican, cannot be doubted. But he belonged to that class of Republicans, who, mistaking the means for the end, do not see that the true and ultimate object to be accomplished through a Republic is Social Reform. This blindness to the object to be aimed at, could not fail to have a mischievous influence upon the course he pursued. But whoever noticed the physical characteristics of the man, the sickly appearance of his face, in contrast with the juvenile style of his locks, curling to his shoulders; his frail lank figure, his jerking movements, indicative of a highly excitable

* *Un épisode de la Révolution, &c.*, p. 65 ; Countess d'Agoult's *Histoire de la Révolution de* 1848, vol. ii. p. 113.

temperament, would never have anticipated the earnestness of purpose, and the steady activity which, in
carrying out what he undertook, he actually displayed.
He was ably seconded by M. Duclerc, a man of high
merit.

His first financial measure was one of relief to the
middle classes, and would have been still more so, had
it been made to assume a more comprehensive form,
and had the intervention of the state been admitted in
a larger degree.

In the midst of the crisis brought on by circumstances antecedent to the Revolution, but, of course,
increased by it, failures were spoken of everywhere as
imminent; the most respectable firms were reported
to be on the point of stoppage; some banking houses,
such as those of Gouin and Garmeron had already
stopped; the house of Baudin had also gone; others
were struggling against the torrent, with great difficulty;
and manufacturers, merchants, tradesmen, all of them
suddenly bewildered, turned to the Provisional Government for assistance.

As the most pressing evil to be remedied arose from
an excessive contraction of credit, the Bank of France
discounting no bills which did not bear three good
indorsements, a number of commercial people were
brought to a stand still. As a measure of relief, it
was proposed to establish throughout France offices of
discount, where merchants and others, on presenting
bills with two indorsements only, could get them
cashed. These offices were not to be permitted to issue
notes of their own, which would make it necessary for

them to have the bills discounted by them, re-discounted by the Bank of France.

This suggestion being approved, a decree instituting these discount offices appeared on the 8th of March.*

"In every manufacturing and commercial town there shall be established an office of discount, with a view to facilitate credit, in favour of all branches of production.

"These offices shall have a capital varying according to the wants of the places in which they are situated.

"This capital to be procured in the following way :—

"One third in money by shareholders.

"One third in town bonds.

"One third in treasury bonds."

As regards the city of Paris, the capital was fixed at 20 millions.†

It must be understood that the treasury and town bonds were merely securities, available only for the purpose of covering a deficit, should any arise. Consequently, the working capital was expected to be supplied by the very class which it was our object to relieve ; and so far the measure may appear, at first sight, to have been inconsistent. But the aim was to hold out safe inducements to those of the class that were not suffering to advance their money in aid of those that were.

Whilst the Provisional Government was thus bent on finding means of relief for the middle classes, influential men belonging to that class were busily

---

* *Moniteur* of that day.   † *Ibid.* of the 9th of March.

employed in getting up a financial riot, the object of which was of unparalleled absurdity. They had resolved to force upon the Provisional Government a decree to the effect that no holder of any bill or obligation should be permitted to exact payment until three months after its being due. Had such an extraordinary decree been issued, what would have been the consequences? How could the manufacturer have purchased raw material or paid his workmen, when deprived, for three months, of the money due to him on which he relied? The circulation of money, not less necessary to the life of society than the circulation of the blood is to the life of man, would have been stopped at once; our foreign commerce would have been destroyed by its becoming impossible to execute any further orders on the security of French bills; so that, in reality, we were asked to decree——What? Universal bankruptcy!

Strange to say, a demand, but too well calculated to ruin the very men who made it, was urged with a degree of earnestness amounting to fury. On the 10th of March, about three thousand gentlemen, who had chosen the Bourse for their place of meeting, repaired to the Hôtel de Ville, exhibiting such angry looks and bursting out into such wild threats, that the report of an attack upon the Hôtel de Ville spread through Paris, and the students swarming from every corner of the Quartier Latin, ran to the assistance of the Provisional Government.

The self-elected representatives of the " bourgeoisie " met with a firm and dignified reception, on the part of M. Garnier Pagès, energetically seconded by M. Paguerre

—a circumstance of which I was apprised in the evening, as I happened not to be at the Hôtel de Ville when the occurrence took place. Long was the struggle. Some of the traders got violent, even to outrage. On their selfish impatience being reproachfully contrasted by a member of the Provisional Government with the heroic power of endurance evinced by the working classes, a manufacturer exclaimed, in a fit of wrath: " Well! we will show you what those people are. To-morrow we will shut up our workshops and shops; we will lock the working men out, telling them to whom they are indebted for their distress. You will see, then, how far they are manageable, and if they want nothing more than praise for their patriotism!" But all this was in vain. A delay of ten days had been previously decreed, under the pressure of over-whelming difficulties; but no imperious summons, no threats, could extort from the Provisional Government any further concession; and the assailants retired grumbling.*

The picture of these facts, which were a matter of public notoriety when Lord Normanby was writing his diary, is softened down by him in his most honied language:

" March 11th. Two days ago the Government had a very serious determination to take: they received a *deputation* from men engaged in various business transactions in Paris, *requesting* that a further delay of

---

* See Countess d'Agoult's *Histoire de la Révolution de* 1848, vol. ii. p. 116 ; and *Un épisode de la Révolution de* 1848, par M. Garnier Pagès, p. 72.

ten days in the payment of the *écheances* should be decreed." *

It is true that the working-men of Paris had nothing to do with this unruly demonstration, which probably accounts for the lenient form of his lordship's inaccuracies on this occasion.

Meanwhile, the commercial crisis, increasing in violence, called for a prompt remedy. Of the three kinds of circulating medium which composed the currency before the Revolution of February—specie—notes of the Bank of France—private paper-money (bills of exchange, promissory notes, etc.),—the first hid itself, the second was imperilled, and the third had disappeared in the whirlwind.

Not that the Revolution created the evil; all it did was, as I have already said, to bring it to light. It was now long, very long, since a bill of exchange put into circulation had ceased to betoken that a *bonâ fide* seller had really handed over to a *solvent* buyer a product of the value represented by the bill. It was also very long since a crowd of speculators, without probity or solvency, blindly rushing into the general scramble, had forced into circulation a mass of paper which, in fact, corresponded to nothing. The Revolution breaking out, the alarm was given. As the distrust extended, it became easier and easier to see to the bottom of many manœuvres, which until then had escaped the scrutiny of the parties interested. It was discovered that a great number of commercial houses had had, for a long time, only a

---

* "A Year of Revolution in Paris," vol. i. p. 213.

factitious existence; that a considerable mass of bills of exchange and promissory notes reposed on no base whatever, representing merely an imaginary capital; and, consequently, all commercial transactions sustained by this species of currency came on a sudden to an end. A circumstance in high degree fatal, if we consider that, before the Revolution of February, the paper currency thus so suddenly discredited, constituted not less than 12,000 millions of francs out of the 15,000 millions which then made up the whole currency, including 2000 millions and a half in specie, and 400 millions in notes of the Bank of France.

It will not be difficult to understand that the working capital of manufacture and commerce consisting of a small quantity of specie, compared with the large amount of paper securities, there followed, of course, a general break up. Having to meet their old standing engagements with an inconvertible paper, and an amount of specie of no avail, many houses were ruined.

Is it necessary to say that the establishment of offices of discount, such as we have described above, was but a feeble remedy for so great an evil? The question, moreover, was to know if the shareholders would come forward? And they, it must be confessed, did not show themselves in a hurry to do so. The amount of shares taken in the Paris discount office, the gross amount of which, we have seen, was fixed at 6,666,000 francs, did not, on the 8th of August, reach a higher sum than 4,051,804 fr. 23 c.

And that which rendered the aspect of the crisis still

more alarming was the conduct of many of the rich, whose pride, prejudices, or egotism, were wounded by the Revolution. Resorting again to the unworthy manœuvre which the Faubourg Saint Germain had employed against Louis Philippe, they cut down all but their necessary expenses to the lowest point, disposing of their carriages and horses, turning off their servants, and practising that severity of domestic economy which they knew would starve numbers of working-people, and was intended to affect all the branches of industry, such as jewellery, dress-making, millinery, painting, sculpture, and objects of art of every kind.

Lord Normanby has taken care, as we have seen, not to forget whatever could deepen the shades of the Revolution. Why has he abstained from assigning the true causes of the evil he describes? And why does he not add, by way of contrast, what it is impossible he could be ignorant of—and what is so touching—namely, that while the more favoured classes of society were engaged in this house-keeping conspiracy, the people displayed a patriotism never to be forgotten? For then, as in the days of the first Revolution, when the country was in danger, poor workmen were to be seen running to the Hôtel de Ville, carrying a part of their hard-earned wages.* Their wives also made offerings to the Provisional Government of their chains and rings. Young girls, on the eve of their marriage, presented their wedding gifts. Numerous were the offerings of this kind, imparting a dignity to the

---

* I will give a very remarkable example of this, by narrating the events of the 16th of April.

enthusiasm which prompted them ; and, when brighter
days shall return, history will not recall without emotion
that it was for the purpose of receiving the gifts of the
poor, in a rough and trying moment, that the Commission was instituted which held its sittings at the palace
of the Elysée, presided over by two such men as
Beranger and Lamennais.

The value of these presents was not, of course, in
proportion to their abundance : nor could it be otherwise, since they came from the workshop or the garret;
but though of no value financially, they indicated something much more valuable, and that is the greatness of
soul of which a people is susceptible when animated by
a love of liberty. A trait would be wanting to this
picture should I omit to mention what occurred with
respect to the savings-banks.

Of the 960 millions of francs constituting the public
floating debt, 355 millions belonged to those establishments. Now, their deposits being locked up by the
late Government in public stock and canal shares, there
remained in them only a few millions. The crisis
breaking out, the depositors in a fright made a run for
their deposits. What was to be done ? Money there
was none ; the minister of finances was at his last gasp.
In this extremity it occurred to M. Garnier Pagès
to propose to pay in cash to the depositors a sum not
exceeding 100 francs, obliging those who insisted on
having their deposits entirely returned, to receive them,
one half in five per cent. stock, the other half in
Treasury bonds. But what was the state of things?
The five per cent. stock stood, at that time, at 77 francs,

and Treasury bonds were at a considerable discount. The position, therefore, in which the depositors were placed by this measure was one of great hardship, and the most angry opposition might naturally have been expected from them.

That M. Garnier Pagès thought he was acting for the best, under the circumstances, is quite certain; and those who have blamed him in this matter with so much violence, have not taken sufficiently into account the weight of the burden he had to bear. Nevertheless, it is not less true that the depositors had a right to say to him, "How! you put us off, us petty capitalists, us who live from hand to mouth, us, who by long and patient self-denial, have scraped together the savings thus confided to the good faith of the Government; and when we come to claim restitution of a sacred deposit, you impose heavy conditions on this restitution which is our right; you, who have paid up in full to the very minute to the fundholders, their half year's interest, many of whom live in comfort, and could afford to wait!"

Yes, this is the language that these poor people might have been justified in using; instead of which, not a complaint was heard, not a single murmur accused the Minister of unfairness. The people suffered in silence; proud of suffering for the Republic.

Nay, more. Many of them did not hesitate to add to their sufferings, by a generosity which, under the desperate pressure of the times, was really heroic. M. Garnier Pagès received the following letter, which I give here as a specimen of several others of the same

kind that it would be too long to cite, and which by its
very exaggeration, illustrates a salient feature of the
French character :—

"You will want money. Permit a poor operative
who, to use the words of Lamartine, is 'ready to place
at the service of the Republic, heart, head, and breast,'
to be suffered to add the words, 'and all that belongs
to him besides'. All I have in the world is 500
francs in the savings' bank. Be so good as to put me
down the first on your list for the sum of 400
francs, which I hold at your disposal within three
days of its being called for. The country will pardon
me if I keep back 100 francs for my own wants;
but I have been out of work for the last six months." *

These extraordinary bursts of enthusiasm and this
self-denial of the poorer classes, betrayed the minister
of finances into a misconception, for which it is difficult to bring oneself to blame him. He had faith in
the success of a loan, and of a loan, too, on conditions
obviously disadvantageous to the lenders. He could not
conceive that, while in what are called the lower classes
of society, each man was pouring out his substance like
water, the higher ranks should be able to look on
unmoved, when the Government of the Republic was
making every effort to hold back France from the
abyss which had been dug under her by the Monarchy.
For, observe, it was no question now of this or that
form of Government; the subject was France itself;
and when through the lips of the Minister of Finance,

* M. Garnier Pagès gives this letter in his *Episode de la Révolution*,
pp. 171, 172.

she cried out to bankers, to large proprietors, to opulent capitalists, "Bankruptcy is at hand; aid me to escape it: the Monarchy, you may or may not regret, has left us the task of filling up this enormous gulf; help us to fill it." What signified this language, if not this? "The vessel which bears you is foundering, you will, every man of you, be swallowed up with us; help us to save you!"

Patriotism, thank heaven! in France, is not confined to the workshop and the garret. The Republic, as I have already said, had, by its moderation, won over to its cause many an insurgent intelligence; the magnanimity of the people had made converts; and proofs of good will reached us from every class and party.

Unluckily, where loans are concerned, success almost always depends on the wind which blows from the Exchange. Now, all the stock-jobbing princes were leagued against the Republic, and, *coûte que coûte*, had sworn in their heart to destroy it, knowing very well that their reign was over, could a Republican Government but once manage to maintain itself, and to bring forth its natural results. Between them and the Republic, a régime of morality, the combat could be no other than a combat of life and death. To pretend to win them over was an absolute puerility; to count upon their support, a supreme peril. This is what neither the majority of the Government, nor M. Garnier Pagès, were willing to comprehend; so nervous were they at the bare idea of innovation; so completely had they been laid hold of by the fantastic hope of being able to accomplish a Revolution by means of counter-revolutionary elements!

M. Garnier Pagès, therefore, did not hesitate on the 9th of March, 1848, to announce a loan of 100 millions of francs at five per cent. to be taken at par, the price of stock being then at 77. This was asking the capitalists to give the State 100 francs, for what they might, any day, buy at 77. The success of so romantic an appeal to the public spirit of the moneyed classes, would necessarily depend upon the example set by those who give the cue to the financial world. But was it to be expected that they would? The proposed loan turned out a complete failure; at the end of a month, the amount subscribed hardly amounted to 500,000 francs.

On the very day of the subscription list being opened, M. Garnier Pagès got leave from the Provisional Government to alienate the crown diamonds, (the property of the nation, and of which the crown had the usufruct;) the bullion and plate attached to the royal residences—the lands, woods, and forests—making part of the ancient civil list which had now lapsed to the state; and, finally, in addition to this, a part of the national forests, to an amount not exceeding 100 millions of francs.

Though no previous Government had scrupled to touch the public forests, the Provisional Government were exceedingly averse to such a step; first, because they thought it hard to sell national property at a low figure; and next, because there was a serious inconvenience in extending the system of clearing,

which had already disforested the country, changing
the rivers to torrents, and exposing the vallies to
inundations. There was, consequently, an express
understanding that recourse would be had to this
measure only in case of extremity; the preamble of
the decree explained that the measure was not intended for immediate application; * and, in point of
fact, it never was applied.

All this did not fill the public coffers, and the little
money we had in hand "ran off," according to the
strong expression of M. Garnier Pagès, "like water
from an open dam." Every morning the head of the
pay-office, and the central cashier, used to come to the
Minister of Finance, saying, "Monsieur le ministre,
we have not fifteen days' life in us, not twelve, not
ten." † So that, every hour, every minute, was carrying
us a step nearer to death.

And our death, under these circumstances, implied
the death of all!

Among the most inveterate enemies of the Republic,
there were some not insensible to this; and here is
a proof:—

One day at the Luxembourg, I was told M. Delamarre wanted to see me. M. Delamarre was one of
the best known bankers of Paris; the founder, unless
my memory deceives me, of the newspaper *La Patrie*,
a journal of opinions reactionist to excess. What

* *Un épisode de la Révolution*, p. 136. The words of the decree are,
" the Minister of Finance would affect this alienation, *should it appear to
him to be indispensable*."

† *Ibid*. page 111.

could he want of me? I desired him to be shown in; and this was, in substance, what he said to me:

"There is no need, sir, I should apprise you that I am not one of yours, and that the Republic does not command my sympathies? Still I feel, that in the present crisis, it is every man's interest to sustain the Provisional Government. Were it to break down, what would be the result? A universal irruption of anarchy, which I shudder to think of. I have therefore taken the liberty of calling upon you to offer a suggestion, which, as it seems to me, is of the highest importance. The Provisional Government can neither save itself nor others, unless it is able to get money, and, in order to get it, it must apply to those who have it, that is, to the rich. Among my fellow-bankers, there are some who view the matter as I do; others so insane as to be incapable of seeing that the ruin of the Provisional Government, at this moment, would be their own ruin; these must be forcibly saved from destruction, and you only can succeed in effecting this, by bringing to bear upon them that dictatorial power with which the Revolution has invested you."

So that, what M. Delamarre advised was a forced contribution from those of his own class. I thought, and still think, he was sincere. But M. Garnier Pagès, to whom he addressed the same advice, could only see a trap in it, so possessed was he of the desire of gaining over to the Republic, by something that looked very like an excess of gentleness, those who were its declared enemies.

Some decision, however, had to be taken, and what

was it? The voluntary loan had not succeeded; a forced loan was not to our taste; the decree for the sale of a certain portion of public property was, at bottom, nothing more than an expedient for restoring confidence by a grand display of the resources which France had at her disposal in case of extreme need. There was nothing left, therefore, save direct taxation; but whether this were imposed on the indirect taxes which would crush the poorer classes, or on the direct taxes which would affect the most numerous body in France, that of small peasant proprietors, there could be no doubt that it would cause the Republic to be detested by those for whose benefit it had been more especially established.

Consequently, there was no possible way left unless some method could be found of opening up a new path. This was what the Provisional Government was pressed to do from all sides; and, for my part, I did not conceal from my colleagues how contradictory and fatal in my opinion it was to apply ordinary processes to an extraordinary conjuncture. I will mention presently what, according to my views, was the financial policy which ought to have been adopted: but, that it may be justly estimated, I must first state some of the gravest characteristics of the crisis.

On the evening of the 15th of March, M. D'Argout came to the Minister of Finance, accompanied by some of the sub-governors of the Bank. These gentlemen were all in a state of agitation, as was manifest enough from the expression of their faces. M. D'Argout said that there was a great run on the Bank for specie;

that the wickets were absolutely besieged by a highly excited multitude; that the unappeasable anxiety of the holders of notes had reached its height, and that they had penetrated even into the interior passages of the establishment; that the Bank was at the point of not having a single sixpence to give in exchange for its paper. "We have not more," he finished by saying, " than 63 millions of francs in our branches in the departments, whither the panic will soon spread; here we have 59 millions of francs, of which we owe 45 millions to Government, that has urgent need of it, and must have it to pay the army, the national workshops, and other departments of the public service. It is all over with us!" *

In fact, from the 24th of February to the 15th of March, the specie in the Bank had decreased from 140 millions of francs to 59 millions, out of which 45 millions were due to the Government; so that, to meet 264 millions of notes in circulation, and 81 millions of other engagements, the Bank had no more than 63 millions in its provincial branches, and 14 millions *in Paris!*

It may be imagined how completely the majority of the Provisional Government was stupified at this intelligence. Should the bank fall, good-bye to the old financial system of which it was the buttress. And then, who could calculate the immensity of the disaster that must follow? What would become,—when once deprived of the possibility of getting discounts,—of the merchants and manufacturers who were yet upon their

* We are indebted to M. Garnier Pagès for this statement. *Un épisode de la Révolution de* 1848, p. 103.

legs? The winding-up of the Bank,—must it not have been the death blow of credit?

Quite certain it is that to have suffered it to fall, without replacing it by planting by its side an institution of superior credit, would have been a great disaster; but in order to create such an institution, it was necessary to take advantage of the opportunity, and therein lay the salvation of the Revolution.

Here, in a few words, were my ideas on the subject.

If we take the trouble of investigating the causes of commercial crises, and of the disasters they give rise to, we shall find that a very leading one lies in the fact of credit being exclusively supplied by individuals or by establishments such as banks, which are nothing more than a collection of individuals. In fact, when the horizon begins to be overcast, when the premonitory signs of social disturbance make themselves visible, and, above all, when this disturbance exhibits itself by a sudden convulsion, it is quite natural that individual capitalists, trembling at the idea of losing their money, should cut short their discounts. And what happens then? The impossibility of getting discounts brings on stoppages; he who does not receive what is due to him, is compelled to refuse to pay what he owes; failures produce failures; catastrophes are generated by catastrophes. Peril everywhere; ruin threatened on all sides.

When, on the contrary, it is the State that supplies the means of credit, should a crisis occur, then far from having an interest in withholding these means, the State is, on the contrary, interested in imparting to them greater activity, for its special object is not to augment or to save a capital proper to itself, but to remove impediments to the course of business, in order that the levying of taxes should not be hampered ; that the fortune of all should not be jeopardised, and that the blood should not congeal in the veins of the social body. On the morrow of a revolution, is there any one who has less need of eating, drinking, of being clothed—less need, in fact, of living than before ? And does not every man know as well the day after a revolution as the day before, that wherever labour is at an end, there life must soon be at an end too ? Whence then, at such moments, comes the stagnation of business ? From this, that individuals, possessors of credit, take fright and hasten to contract it. In other words, they act and have an interest in acting, under the circumstances, in a way precisely the reverse of that in which the State, were it the arbiter of credit, must of necessity act.

Taking my stand on these principles, the validity of which was but too clearly proved by the spectacle before my eyes, at a moment when everything round the Provisional Government seemed conspiring to destroy confidence, while they alone were doing their very best to sustain it, I wished this critical opportunity should be taken advantage of; not to suppress every establishment of private credit, far from it ; but to create by their side a National establishment of credit, independent of the Treasury, and doing, for the profit of all, precisely what the Bank of France is empowered to do for the profit of a small number of shareholders. In this way, the privilege of coining money by the issue of notes doing the work of specie, would have reverted to the State, which ought never to have deprived itself of it, for the benefit of a company of individuals. For it is surprising that the circulating medium—which is the heart's-blood of trade and commerce, and which, as such, has so essential a relation to the whole public—should be suffered to depend upon private interests.

And when I talk of coining money, I do not exaggerate. What, indeed, is the nature of the operation of banks of issue? Take the Bank of France. A man brings a bill of exchange or other security, realisable at a given date, for which he gets notes, issued by the Bank on the guarantee of these securities, and possessing the faculty of circulating as specie—the consideration to the Bank being what is known as discount.

The issue of bank notes is then, to the letter, the converting into money, or the *monetisation*, of a deposited pledge. Banks of issue make paper money with paper, just to all intents and purposes as gold coin is made with gold. But is this one of those privileges which without inconvenience and without peril can be abandoned to individuals?

This is all the more strange, because if we look into the matter a little closely, we shall find that the enormous profits which are derived from this privilege by those on whom they are conferred, are the recompence, not for services rendered through the agency of their *own credit* only, but chiefly for services rendered by them through the agency of *public credit*.

That it is so, is proved beyond question by the very

mechanism of banks. Everybody must be well aware that the specie in their vaults never completely covers the value of their notes in circulation. Regulating their discounts by the amount of good commercial bills that are brought to them, and not by the quantity of specie at their disposal, they constantly issue more notes than are convertible into cash. Now, these surplus notes produce interest to the bank, and form a considerable part of its profits, though resting on no metallic base whatever. How does this happen? How is it that they are accepted, and circulate as money? It is because the public has confidence in the soundness of that commercial paper which is their warranty. They represent, therefore, abstract public credit, and that only. What reason was there then why the Bank of France should have continued to be a private institution? and why a handful of oligarchs should be permitted to levy an enormous tax on the currency, as the price of a service which society could just as well perform for itself, by organising a National Bank, completely independent of the executive, and subject to the direct control of the legislature?

By this means, not only would society, as a whole, reap the immense profits which are now concentrated in a few hands; but the currency would cease to be the vassal of private speculation, at all times inevitably selfish. The directors of a National Bank being public officers, and having no interest in raising discounts, would rather be inclined to keep them down as much as possible. The consequence would be the lowering of the interest of money in all commercial transactions

—an incalculable advantage to trade, commerce, and agriculture.

But possibly it will be asked, how it could have been practicable to institute a National Bank, in February 1848, when the Provisional Government was in the greatest possible poverty? Where could they have found the amount of specie requisite to form the reserve or cash in hand of the Bank to be created? Such a question takes evidently for granted that a bank cannot exist without a reserve; now, this opinion, generally received though it be, appears to me void of foundation.

What are the reasons which the Bank of France has always put forth to show the necessity for its reserve? Two only: the security given to the holders of the notes in circulation against the eventual losses of the Bank on the one hand; and, on the other, that their notes will be, at all times, convertible into specie.

In the first place, however, the supposed chances of loss are but an imaginary danger put forward to fascinate the eyes of the public. What losses has the Bank of France incurred during the forty years of its existence? None. So far from it, that it has always divided amongst its shareholders profits, not less regular and certain than considerable. The following figures speak for themselves. The shares of the Bank of France at par are worth 1000 francs. Now, on the 1st of February, 1848, they had reached 3190 francs, and, in 1856, they exceeded 4000 francs. Even at the height of the Revolution of February, that is to say, the 1st of March, 1848, they were at 2400 francs, and at the very moment

when, his face pale, his heart beating, M. d'Argout ran
to the Minister of Finance saying, " It is all over with
us ! " the Bank shares (at this moment of its last agony),
were still 1300 francs, that is above par.

In a word, it is undeniable that the Bank of France,
from the first hour of its existence, has been playing
a sure game. Never lending upon paper without three
good and perfectly secure indorsements, and for a term
not exceeding ninety days, it has never run any kind
of risk ; nor do we see why a National Bank should
run any, if subject to the same prudential restraints,
and never lending but on such ample security.

As to the pretending that bank notes owe their
capacity of circulating to the certainty which the
holders have, that when they please they can go to the
Bank and exchange them for gold, nothing can be
more erroneous ; and the proof is that the Bank of
France having been empowered to suspend cash payments, and its notes, as we shall presently see, having
been made a legal tender, this extraordinary step, far
from extinguishing confidence, revived it, and to such a
point, that the public very soon began to prefer notes
to gold ! Nay, they were occasionally at a premium !
Can any fact be more decisive than this ?

In truth, the real guarantee of bank notes, is not
the reserve, it is the whole amount of good commercial
paper, or secure deposits, against which the notes have
been exchanged.

A National Bank, therefore, without a reserve was
possible during the Revolution of 1848.

Only in this case, two conditions must have been

rigorously observed, in order to avoid the depreciation that would be sure to be the consequence of over issue; first, that the National Bank should only issue notes of real value resting upon indisputable security; secondly, that it should be obliged to accept, and withdraw from circulation, the notes returned to it, paying the holders an interest equal to the price of issue. In this way, it is clear that all notes not required would have found their way back again to the Bank, and that no more notes would have remained in circulation than were in due proportion to the amount of commercial operations.

Starting from this point, my plan was as follows:

To institute a National Bank with branches in each Department.

To form a council consisting of persons chosen by municipal bodies, chambers of commerce, and syndics of trade companies, whose duty would be to inquire into the solvency of borrowers, and to offer such local advice as they might think expedient.

To make this Bank independent of the executive, and to place it under the direct control of the legislature.

To make its notes a legal tender, and to base them on any sort of good securities.

To oblige it to receive and to withdraw from circulation such superabundant notes as were no longer required by commercial wants, the holders of these notes being entitled, on returning them to the Bank, to an interest equal to the discount originally paid upon them.

To establish depôts, in which every producer would be allowed to deposit his produce, receiving in exchange a warrant which would constitute a right to the property deposited, capable therefore of serving the purposes of paper-money.

To empower the National Bank to lend money upon these warrants.

To transfer the whole amount of banking profits to a labour fund, having for its object to advance money to the united co-operative associations.

Is it necessary to dwell upon the advantages of this plan?

The National Bank having no reason to keep discounts high, and being able to lend with advantage on the lowest practicable terms, the interest of money required for all commercial operations would have been necessarily lowered; the largest institution of credit in a country being the standard by which all holders of capital and money-lenders are obliged to regulate their transactions.

By the depôts and the transmutations of produce into warrants, a considerable amount of produce, which was in some sort inert, would have acquired a negotiable value and given an impulse to the circulation.

The profits from discounts passing from the hands of a few privileged persons into those of the State, it could have used them for the purpose of enabling the workmen to co-operate, and so make the price of the services rendered to some, subservient to the progressive emancipation of others.

Such a Bank, it is obvious, could have come to the assistance of the Provisional Government, and help it to overcome the crisis.

But these views were summarily disposed of by the fanaticism of routine. M. Garnier Pagès, all whose suggestions were blindly adopted by the majority of the Council, thought of nothing else than the safety of the Bank; and save it he did effectually, by prevailing on the Provisional Government to constitute its notes a legal tender.

Then followed the extraordinary phenomenon I have just mentioned; the notes, after a very slight and almost inappreciable fall, returned to par, and, in a little while, had the preference over coin; while the Bank shares rose immediately from 1300 francs to 1500 francs.

If then M. Garnier Pagès had nothing else in view than how to save an impolitic institution, the keystone of the system supported by all the enemies of the Republic, he could not have acted with more vigour and success. Alas! it was a victory of Pyrrhus. It proved that, amid the ruins of private credit, public credit might preserve the greatest influence; but instead of permitting this influence to operate, by means of a National Bank, through its natural organ, the State, M. Garnier Pagès used it only to reanimate a moneyed oligarchy bent on never allying itself with the Republic.

So little was the convertibility of bank notes a condition indispensable to their circulation, that their existence as legal tender, which began in March, continued till the 6th of August 1850, without in the least affecting their value! What pretence is there then for doubting that this compulsory circulation

could not have been turned to account in favour of a
new, and really Republican institution, and that a
National Bank could not have been established, provisionally to say the least of it, without a reserve?

It has been alleged that the Bank of France was not
without some show of gratitude to the Provisional
Government, since in return for the signal service
which had been rendered it, on the 21st of March, it
lent the Government 50 millions of francs.   That is
true; but what was this sum compared with the wants
of the moment, and in presence of a Republic which
had to be consolidated?   The forests and other National
property of the market value of 800 million francs,
bringing in a revenue of from 30 millions to 35 millions,
were surely a perfectly good and available security on
which a National Bank could without peril have lent to
the State 600 millions of francs in notes, which would
have enabled it to surmount the crisis.   The Bank of
France once safe, was it able to furnish the Government
with the means of avoiding new taxes, a consideration of
the very first importance to the Republic?   No: since
on the very day of its being saved, M. Garnier Pagès
was compelled to obtain leave from the Provisional
Government to impose the fatal, and never to be forgotten tax of 45 centimes, which ruined the Republican Government in the estimation of the peasants.

The dilemma was a terribly difficult one; but where
was the possibility of escaping from it, when once the
majority of the Government had made up their minds
to attempt nothing new?

On March 16th, M. Garnier Pagès called a meeting of

the Council at the Hôtel of the Minister of Finance;
and resting on the precedent set by Napoleon, Louis
XVIII., Louis Philippe, all of whom in succession had
recourse to an increase extraordinary of the land-tax,
he proposed to increase the direct taxes by an additional tax of 45 centimes in every franc, which he
calculated would produce 190 millions of francs.

But what was likely to be the effect of such a
proposal? What clamour was not to be expected from
that immense throng of little peasant proprietors, to
whom that is the best government which asks of them
least, and who never know the State, save in the
person of the tax-gatherer? What expectation was
there that the poor rural population would have any
love for the Republic, thus announcing its existence
by an additional tax upon property? And what arms
would it not put into the hands of the re-actionist
party?

It would have been far better, in spite of all its
inconvenience, to have framed a tax upon revenue,
which, by adopting the English mode of levying it,
might have been divested of those complicated processes that frightened the Minister of Finance, as
likely to cause too much delay, and as being of an
inquisitorial character justly objectionable.

Be this as it may, the additional property-tax once
determined on, it would at least have been expedient,
in order to prevent pressure upon the smaller proprietors, to fix a minimum below which it should not
operate; at the risk of course of making the burden
heavier, if necessary, upon those whose backs were broad

enough to bear it. This limitation, besides being strictly just, would, as an act of policy, have been thoroughly appreciated. The peasants would have clapped their hands with joy; and this alone would have prevented the large proprietors from complaining; while the opposite course, by causing dissatisfaction to the former, gave free play to the murmurs of the latter, and exposed us to the risk of having all the world against us.

Therefore it was, M. Ledru Rollin and myself proposed that a minimum should be clearly fixed by the decree itself. But M. Garnier Pagès opposed this, saying, that the only thing we had to do was to enjoin the tax-gatherers to take into consideration the circumstances of each tax-payer, and to remit either partially, or entirely, the tax, "in the case of all persons whom, in their opinion, had not the means of paying it." On my persisting in my view, he said to me, "You know nothing of the rural districts." Whereupon, old Dupont (de l'Eure), though in the habit of voting with Garnier Pagès, exclaimed with much animation, "But at all events *I* know them, having lived a long while in them; and I know too, if there be one who more than another will be spared in these cases, it will be the rich man, because he has influence, and not the poor man who has none."

In spite of the weight thus thrown into the balance by the remark of this noble-minded and excellent old man, the Minister's proposal passed precisely in the form in which he had framed it.

It was a political fault of the gravest kind, as

the consequences too clearly proved. In vain did
M. Garnier Pagès, on the 18th of March, address a
letter to the Government officers, authorising them
to excuse every one from paying the tax, who was
notoriously not in a position to do so; * in vain did
the same circular require the mayors, assisted by the
tax-collectors, to make out a list of those tax-payers
to whom, after due consideration of their position
and of the *imperious necessities of the treasury*, it
would be possible to let off for either the whole, or a
part of their share of the tax; † these public injunc-
tions, repeated on the 5th of April, again on the 25th
of April, testified the kind intentions of the Minister,
but had the bad effect of leaving at the mercy of local
authorities, that is to say, to chance or caprice, a point
which, from the very first, ought to have been determined with the greatest precision, clearness, and
directness.

What was the result? that these ministerial injunc-
tions were neither faithfully complied with by those
to whom they were addressed, nor probably appreciated
by those they were intended to protect. But the
factions opposed to the Republic, employed with fatal
skill the weapon thus thrust into their hands; their
emissaries scoured the country, inciting the peasants
against the Republic, which had only risen up, they
said, to crush them with taxation; the Royalists set
themselves at work to curse in chorus a tax imposed
for the purpose of filling up the abyss which the

* *Un épisode de la Révolution de* 1848, par M. Garnier Pagès.
† *Ibid.*

monarchy had caused, and of discharging the debts
of Royalty. M. Garnier Pagès, vilified and calumniated
by the very persons whose ruin he had prevented,
became, under the name of "*L'homme aux* 45 *centimes,*" the target for every species of venomous attack.
The mischief which the Provisional Government had
averted, was forgotten; no account was taken of the good
they did, or wished to do; no one chose to remember
that they had abolished the most odious of all taxes,
the tax upon salt, thus giving up, for the relief of the
poor, a revenue of 70 millions a-year. In a word, the
tax of 45 centimes, though levied for the profit of
succeeding governments and by them, was distastrous
only to us and to the Republic.

But what History will say is this: That if the Provisional Government were betrayed by the excessive
timidity of the majority of them, into measures
incompatible with the interests of the Republic they
represented, there was at all events nothing personal,
nothing selfish in their faults. Unlike others, they
did not make use of the money of the people to gorge
the accomplices of a usurpation; to fatten courtiers and
lacqueys; to surround themselves with insolent pomp;
to stimulate stock-jobbing; to inoculate the nation
with a diseased love of gain, by setting it the example
of cupidity. They did not extort from the country
a voracious civil list to be spent, now on the foolery
of a court dress, now on the remuneration of those
base services which Liberty never requires. They did
not swell their revenues with the spoils of the family
of Orléans. They had no need of palaces in the city,

of palaces in the country, of sumptuous equipages, splendid stables, all maintained at the cost of the people; nor were they to be seen eating and drinking, in a few hours, at court festivals, the earnings of thousands of families.

In spite of the impudent calumnies, on which this book will do justice—and which, moreover, have been sometime disproved—I will show by the evidence of the calumniators themselves, that the members of the Provisional Government took no thought of money, save as a provision for the wants of the country; that those of them who were poor, remained poor; that those of them who were rich when they accepted office, were less rich when they left it; and I must do M. Garnier Pagès the justice,—I who more than any one lamented his financial policy—to say, that if his errors proceeded from an unenlightened and excessive fear of all innovation, they proceeded also from an honourable feeling—the desire of fulfilling all engagements entered into, without distinction of friend or foe —and from the firm determination in which we all shared, to save the Republic and France the disgrace of a bankruptcy, which, at that time, was advised by M. Fould, now a minister of Louis Bonaparte.*

* M. Ledru Rollin subsequently charged M. Fould with doing this, from the very tribune of the National Assembly.

CHAPTER XII.

REVOLUTION IN TRAVAIL.

THE Revolution went on its way.

Its ascent to power was signalised in the department of public justice entrusted to M. Crémieux, by acts which manifested profound respect for human dignity, and a sensitive appreciation of the rights of man.

The abrogation of the famous laws of September, against the press; the extension given to the safeguard of the jury; the suppression of the pillory, that inhuman and degrading aggravation of a penal sentence, useless as it affects the hardened culprit, and tending to stifle repentance under the weight of infamy in any heart not yet spoilt beyond redemption; the facilities afforded to the reformation of criminals; the abolition of political oaths, scandalous when broken, and instruments of tyranny when kept inviolable; the lessening of law charges; the abolition of imprisonment for debt; new modes of naturalisation accorded to foreigners; *—such were the acts which did honour to the administration of M. Crémieux.

Among the reforms exacted by republican ideas,

* All these decrees are to be found in the *Moniteur*, the preambles of which explain their purpose and show the feeling which prompted them.

which in this instance as in some others, are in close
conformity with English ideas, the most urgent was
that of the magistracy, composed almost exclusively
of men who, under Louis Philippe, owed their appointment or their promotions solely to the system of
corruption so actively resorted to at that time. Never
had the magistracy exhibited a more servile subjection
to political influence than under Louis Philippe; never
had the administration of justice been so subservient
to party spirit. The principle of irremovability which
obtained in magisterial appointments, and which was
adopted, as was said, to render magistrates independent of the executive, had only served to make their
servility more conspicuous; and it would have been
absurd in a Republic, where everything has to undergo the examination and judgment of the nation,
to admit that a judge was not to be stripped of his
functions, however ill he discharged them. The suppression of this exorbitant immunity was so much
the more necessary, as it was dangerous to place
above all control a body of public functionaries
holding in their hands the lives and fortunes of the
public.

It was wisely done of the Provisional Government
then, to enact a power of revoking the appointments
of magistrates.* It was opening the door to a re-
organisation of the magistracy. But the Minister of
Justice did not avail himself of this power: in the first
place, because it would have required a considerable

---

* *Moniteur*, 18th of April, 1848.

reconstruction, for which there was no time ; and next, because a task of this kind was not suited to M. Crémieux, a learned jurisconsult, a great criminal lawyer, an orator full of grace and vivacity, and certainly one of the most brilliant pleaders of the Paris bar, but a man of extreme benevolence, and of too easy a nature to strike a decisive blow.

Lord Normanby, in his book, has a good deal attacked M. Crémieux, and with invariable injustice. It is false, for instance, that M. Crémieux, on the 24th of February, got himself appointed a member of the Provisional Government by the stealthy insertion of his name in the list. I have already mentioned that Lord Normanby, with inexcusable ignorance, represents M. Crémieux as reading out this list, while every soul in Paris knew that it was read by M. Ledru Rollin.* Consequently, M. Crémieux could not have foisted in his name amongst those of the other persons whose names were then proclaimed. More than this, I have it from M. Ledru Rollin, that M. Crémieux's name was one of those which the bulk of the people in the " Palais Bourbon" received with the most warmth, while under the influence of a lively narrative in which M. Crémieux, already known as a liberal advocate, had been stating how he had helped the fugitive king into his carriage.

In the Council, M. Crémieux sided with the majority; but, being untrammelled by foregone conclusions, and open to conviction, it often happened that he voted with

* See the first chapter of this work.

us; and it can properly be said that he served as a connecting link between the two opinions that divided the Council. A man yielding easily to impulse and warm expression of feeling, he might fail in firmness sometimes, in generosity never.

The spirit of the Revolution insinuated itself where it seemed much more difficult for it to penetrate, that is to say, into the War-Office and Admiralty.

On the 14th of February, one M. Dubourg, who, in 1830, had organised the " *Volontaires de la Charte*," having suggested the expediency of creating a corps to be composed of the combatants of February, M. de Lamartine seized on this idea, and framed it into a decree. Immediately afterwards enlistment lists were opened in the different mayoralties, for the formation of a militia, to be called " *Garde Mobile*," to the number of 20,000 men. The result was, that all the martial children of the faubourgs rushed to the mayoralties, attracted much less by the unusual pay of one franc and a-half, than by love of movement, by military instinct, and the charm of the uniform. Placed under the command of General Duvivier, a man of very ardent and broad intelligence, combining the soldier's courage with the innovator's daring, the Garde Mobile would have constituted a really Republican force, had we had time properly to organise them; but, through a lamentable combination of circumstances, they fell, after the Provisional Government had retired from office, into the hands of the enemies of the Republic, who contrived, as will be presently seen, to turn them into destroyers of their own class and their own cause.

General Subervie having resigned the office of Minister of War,—confided to him in the first instance, but which his great age did not permit him to discharge with sufficient activity,—and his place being offered to General Cavaignac, then Governor of Algeria, M. Arago provisionally filled it. He was already charged with the ministry of Marine. This double burden was not, indeed, too much for so powerful an intellect. Only, the boldness of his political views was not commensurate with his eminent qualities as a man and a *savant*. Whence his hesitation in accomplishing, as a minister of marine, one of those acts which most redounded to the credit of the Provisional Government. Yielding to the importunities of the West Indian planters who were in Paris, he had, on the 26th of February, forwarded a despatch to the Colonial Governors, which had the air of putting off, though for no very long time, the settlement of the abolition question. The arrival in Paris of M. Schœlcher brought the affair to an immediate issue.

M. Schœlcher, now an exile in England,* had then just returned from Senegal, where he had gone to examine into the condition of the slaves, and to pursue the noble investigation which had been the business of his life. Never, perhaps, did any man exhibit so remarkable a combination of the habits of a man of the world, with the austere morality of a philosopher and philanthropist; a passion for art, with the practice of stoical virtue; a sensitive feeling of his own personal

---

* The same who has just published the Life of Handel.

dignity, with a scrupulous appreciation of what is due
to others; a taste for the softer elegancies and refine-
ments of life, with a rigidity of principle which causes
him to shrink from any compromise, however par-
donable or slight. Giving himself entirely up to his
reverence for justice and right, M. Schœlcher was to
France, as respects the blacks, what Wilberforce was
to England. On the breaking out of the Revolution
of February, he was prepared to enter into the
question of emancipation, qualified by his inquiries
and travels, in which he shrank from no expense,
fatigue, or danger. Scarcely arrived in Paris, he runs
to M. Arago, speaks to his feelings, urges, overcomes
him; and, on the 4th of March, appears a decree ap-
pointing a special commission, with instructions to
frame an Act for the emancipation of the slaves. The
object of this Act was thus simply expressed, " Considering that no part of the soil of France can any
longer tolerate slaves on its surface," &c. *

The commission, consisting of MM. Schœlcher,
Perrinon, Gatine, Mestro, and Gaumont, set to work;
and after about four-and-thirty meetings, prepared an
Act for the abolition of slavery, on condition that a
fair indemnity should be paid to the slave-proprietors.

This Act was presented to the Provisional Government, on the 27th of April, and signed by us with an
emotion like that which had affected us when we
abolished capital punishment. It was, under another
form, the consecration of this great principle, the in-

---

* *Moniteur*, 4th March, 1848.

violability of human life. For, not to belong to one-self is to vegetate, not to live.

It is also due to the exertions of M. Schœlcher, that the Provisional Government suppressed flogging in the navy, regarding such a punishment as an insult to human nature, and its suppression as a means of in-spiring the sailor with an increased sense of honour and self-repect.

The interests of the Republic were zealously seconded in the department of Public Instruction and Worship, by M. Carnot, son of that celebrated member of the Committee of Public Safety, who " organised victory." Supported by two superior men, MM. Jean Reynaud, and Edouard Charton, M. Carnot formed a high com-mission of scientific and literary inquiry, for examin-ing such new questions as Republicanism might give rise to; he erected a special school for the instruc-tion of persons seeking employment in public offices; and being thoroughly convinced that the ignorance of the people is the source both of their crimes and wretchedness, he occupied himself with laying the ground-work of a universal and gratuitous system of education.

And yet, strangely enough, it is this man whom the Royalists have attempted to represent to Europe as the systematic enemy of enlightenment, as the apostle of ignorance! And why? Because, like all men of sense, he thought it was given to a very few minds, and those of a high order only, to be able to make laws; that in an assembly of 900 persons, it is absurd to expect we shall find a Lycurgus in each of them; that in such an assembly, smartness, the rage of shining, and pretensions resting on empty talent or superficial acquirements, are more mischievous than useful; and consequently, that sound judgment, a practical acquaintance with the matter which is the subject of legislation, unblemished integrity, and a sincere love of one's kind, are, to speak generally, sufficient grounds for entitling a man to the suffrages of his fellow-citizens. The circular of M. Carnot, or to speak more correctly, the phrase of the circular, which caused so much hubbub among the Royalists, contained two or three words which had not been sufficiently weighed; but, how excessive must have been the bad faith, which could travesty into a panegeric upon ignorance, a passage such as follows, the only one in the circular which was the object of attack!—

"The greatest mistake, against which the rural population must be warned, is to suppose that to be qualified for a representative it is necessary either to have education or fortune. It is obvious that an honest peasant, with good sense and experience, will represent his class infinitely better in the Assembly than a rich and lettered citizen, unacquainted with the habits of country life or swayed by interests different from those of the peasantry. As to fortune, the allowance made to each member would be sufficient for the poorest. We must not forget that, in a great assembly like that which is about to meet, the greatest part of the members must be in the position of jurymen. It is for them to decide—ay, or no—whether the judgment of the *élite*, the pick of the members, be good or bad." *

* Circular to the Head-masters of Schools, *Moniteur*, 7th March, 1848.

The wording of this passage might have been happier, I acknowledge; nor should the word education have been used, without being defined; but could it possibly imply, as the enemies of the Republic did not blush to assert, that the Minister of Public Instruction was the preacher of ignorance? and that according to him, a first condition for making good laws was not knowing how to read? What M. Carnot meant to say was manifestly this, That we should not give refined manners the precedency over practical knowledge, empty college jargon over habits of business, cleverness over good sense, and pounds sterling over patriotism. Now, this was not only very Republican, but very reasonable. Up to this time the people had never been represented; surely it was quite natural that, having obtained the franchise, they should use it to select occasionally one of their own class to represent them. This is precisely what they did, and did well too. By whom, in the Assembly, were their interests supported with greater zeal, more elevated feeling, or greater practical knowledge than by M. Nadaud, a simple mason?

Where M. Carnot committed the mistake was his over scrupulous policy in the education question with respect to the Jesuits, who were in possession of the ground, and maintaining a ruinous competition with private schoolmasters, owing to the clergy's endowment by the State. But how easy was it at that time for the Minister of Public Worship and Instruction to fall into the error? The Church, at that time was so humble, so fawning! Her welcome to the Republic was so fervent! I myself saw, with my own eyes, a procession of 600 priests marching to the Hôtel de Ville, and saluting the Provisional Government with bursts of enthusiasm, almost incredible. I have heard them, too, shouting out their benedictions upon us. Yes, these same priests who, the day after the 2nd of December, went and sprinkled their holy water over perjury and massacre, saying mass in the open air, their feet in blood, I have myself seen, under the Provisional Government, rushing wherever a tree of liberty was to be planted, and, their hands stretched forth, their eyes raised to heaven, imploring God to make the Republic immortal.

I now come to that department which was the most important and the most assailed, the Ministère de l'Intérieur, or Home Department. There M. Ledru Rollin was; and, in many respects, he was excellently suited to the duty he had to discharge, which was that of revolutionary propagandism. A mind quick and penetrating, political energy tempered by frank and engaging manners, great ardour of purpose, integrity, a vehement desire to secure the triumph of the Republic, together with an oratorical talent of the highest order;—such were the qualities which M. Ledru Rollin brought to the accomplishment of his mission; and these qualities were heightened in him by a handsome face, a portly figure, and by I know not what magnetic fluid which seemed, when he spoke, to flow from his gestures.

Assuredly, all this was much, and yet not enough, so exacting were the wants of the moment. With the power of carrying men along with him, the Minister of the Interior should have combined that of restraining them; he should have had that force of character which enables a man to resist the pressure of his partisans, and the solicitations of his friends. But such a force of character could hardly be expected in M. Ledru Rollin, a really artistic nature, confiding, generous, capable of nobly confronting an enemy, but not of offending a friend, and for this very reason, accessible to the influence of those about him, whose antipathies were not always either just or enlightened.

It must also be observed that, to M. Ledru Rollin the Revolution was much more a thing to be recovered than to be continued and developed in a scientific manner. Haunted by the great reminiscences of the past, his ardent imagination panted for the power of transporting it bodily into the future, not allowing for the intellectual progress which has since been made—a progress whose nature he had not sufficiently studied, and which fretted his impatience as though it were an obstacle in his way. It is superfluous to say that those of his friends who had an interest in separating him from the Socialists, made it a point to stimulate this feeling, never talking anything to him but Jacobinism, and missing no opportunity to compare him to Danton.

However this may be, M. Ledru Rollin gave himself up to his duties with a zeal and courage which will be remembered, when the insults hurled at him in libels like that of Lord Normanby shall have been long forgotten. How is it possible for any one who knows M. Ledru Rollin to read, without indignation, the following passage : " Ledru Rollin is a man of no great capacity, and not undoubted moral courage, but a regular mob orator, of *ruined fortune,* who is desirous, as long as he can, to maintain his present power, and quite bold enough to attempt anything, provided he feels himself backed by a multitude."*

If, before hazarding these odious insinuations, his lordship had taken the trouble to make himself master of the facts, as the simplest notions of justice prescribed to him, he would have known that, far from being a man of ruined fortune, M. Ledru Rollin was rich when the Revolution broke out, that he had nothing to gain from it in a purely personal point of view, but, on the contrary, had everything to loose; and that any idea of the derangement which so violent a political crisis might bring down upon his affairs, never induced him to hesitate a single instant. Lord Normanby is a romance writer; but I submit to him that the evidence, or the want of evidence, which is sufficient for a novel, is not sufficient for an historical work. For instance, his lordship describes with the most satisfied air in the world,† but taking good care not to mention his authorities, the following burlesque scene :

" M. Ledru Rollin said to the majority of government, ' Do you know that your popularity is nothing, compared to mine? I have but to open that window, and call upon the people, and you would every one of you be turned into the street. Do you wish me to try ?'

---

* "A Year of Revolution in Paris," vol. i. p. 228.
† *Ibid.* p. 239.

rising and moving towards the window beneath which there were assembled crowds. M. Garnier Pagès, who is a man of great nerve, walked up to him, drew a pistol from his pocket, placed it at Ledru Rollin's breast, and said, 'If you make one step towards the window, it shall be your last!' Ledru Rollin *looked* daggers, paused a moment, and sat down again."

Great must have been the astonishment of M. Garnier Pagès, and of M. Ledru Rollin, the first time these lines met their eyes, if so be they have done his lordship's book the honour of reading it. For myself, having attended the meetings of the Council, while the Provisional Government lasted, with the greatest punctuality, I declare, not only that I never witnessed anything like it, but that neither then nor since have I ever heard a whisper of anything like it having happened; and I can assure Lord Normanby that the members of the Provisional Government, even when their disputes ran highest, never failed in that mutual respect which is usual among gentlemen. As to representing us as bravoes, going to the Council with pistols in our pockets, ready to blow out each other's brains, this is simply ridiculous; and Lord Normanby, in accepting such tittle-tattle, has not perceived, which is rather awkward for a diplomatist, that some one or other has made a dupe of him.

I resume my narrative. In his capacity of Minister of the Interior, it was M. Ledru Rollin's duty to attend to the administration of the departments. He lost no time in despatching commissioners to them; the re-appointment of public officers being of all measures that which was most indispensable and urgent. For what Government ever consented to have its enemies selected as its agents? Would any folly have been comparable with that of suffering the destinies of the Republic to be tossed about in the hands of men known for their hatred to it, and the chief motive for whose promotion, under Louis Philippe, was their notorious devotion to monarchy? Ah! if the Provisional Government can be justly reproached with one thing beyond all others, it is for having, on the contrary, been too much disposed to hold out their hand to hostile parties; for having put too much confidence in the protestations of new converts; for having too easily yielded to a chivalrous desire of winning them over!

In despatching these commissioners, M. Ledru Rollin submitted to a necessity—all the more unavoidable, because, on the first news of the Revolution, nearly all the Préfèts appointed by M. Duchatel, had been turned off by the excited population; others had of their own accord resigned their posts. Was it expedient, then, for the sake of pleasing the royalists, that the Republican Government should leave France without administrative machinery?

As to the selections made, there were no doubt several not of the best; nor is there anything surprising in this, if we reflect that M. Ledru Rollin had to decide precipitately, from one day to the other, often on defective information; and that the absolute necessity of this despatch left no time for necessary inquiries. It was an enormously difficult task to improvise Republican administrators for the whole of France, out of a staff of persons most of them unknown. One man had influence in his department, but his opinions were doubtful; another was a man who could be depended upon, but his influence was limited. Generally speaking, it would have been desirable to assign to each locality such public officers as were known there; but in the confusion following upon a social convulsion so sudden, and in the midst of so many absorbing and such various matters of importance to be attended to, how was it possible to have ready at call the most suitable instruments?

Besides, it is beyond all question, that of the appointments the greater part were good, some excellent; and if a few blunders were made, M. Ledru Rollin corrected them as soon as they were reported to him. Of all the agents chosen by the Minister of the Interior, the one whose appointment gave rise to the most virulent attacks, was a person named Riancourt, sub-commissioner of Havre. Now, what was the amazement of the pious souls who, on this subject, had invoked heaven and earth against M. Ledru Rollin, when it was proved that this Riancourt had been appointed on the recommendation of the Archbishop of Paris! No doubt Archbishop Affre had been deceived with respect to his protégé; but in what respect was M. Ledru Rollin culpable for attending to a recommendation from such a distinguished source?

But these unjust attacks did not stop here. There were some—and Lord Normanby in his book is of the

number *—who found fault bitterly with M. Ledru
Rollin for having, in a circular of instructions to the
commissioners, used the expression, "your powers are
unlimited." The expression was certainly absolute,
too absolute perhaps; but its intention was so satis-
factorily explained in the circular itself as to dissipate
all pretext for an unfair interpretation of it; since,
in speaking of the magistracy opposed, as it was
known to be, to the new order of things, the instructions in question said, "the magistracy depends upon
the Executive only in the manner prescribed by law.† "
Did that signify that the agents of the Executive
should consider themselves placed above the law? If
we go back to the period itself; if we bear in mind the
unsettled state of the departments, and the exigences
of revolution sometimes requiring that power should
do the office of law, it may appear that there was a
certain amount of prudence in addressing the departments in an energetic tone, which, in point of fact,
was used in order to avoid the necessity of having
recourse to measures of severity. For it had reached
the ears of the Provisional Government, that in certain provincial towns there were fanatical royalists
who were calling anarchy to their aid; that functionaries who had been turned off, were in some places
exciting the people against the newly-appointed officials; that several of the commissioners had been driven
away, and others insulted. It was indispensable,

---

* "A Year of Revolution in Paris," vol. i. p. 217.
† *Moniteur*, March 13, 1848.

therefore, while the turmoil was yet at its height, to overawe malevolence, to keep revolt in check, to prevent conflicts, and to give to the representatives of the central power a consciousness of force which would preserve them both from discouragement and inefficiency. But, after all, was there in this so-much-abused circular a single word that could pass for a threat of violence? No! in the instruction given to the commissioners to do what public safety required, it was said: "Thanks to our manners, there is nothing of terror in such a mission." And, indeed, what of terror was there in it? What arbitary acts could in consequence be pointed out? What liberty was assailed? What breach of the law was committed by these formidable "proconsuls with unlimited powers?" What newspapers were there arbitrarily suppressed, as long as the power of the Republic was wielded by the Provisional Government? What homes violated? What wholesale transportations commanded? What victims sent to Lambessa or to Cayenne?

I will hereafter advert to that part of the circular which related to electoral proceedings, and I will prove that there never was a Government which more scrupulously respected the liberty of election; but we are already in a position to judge of the amount of fairness which characterises M. Ledru Rollin's opponents.

In Paris, the power of the Minister of the Interior had a solid support in that of the Prefecture of the Police.

I seem still to have before me the picture which presented itself to my eyes when I first set foot in

the prefecture of police.   What a change !   No longer
that dreary den where, under the preceding regime,
there reigned the silence of death, and where everything breathed suspicion, defiance, and hatred.   The
sombre-looking *sergents de ville* had disappeared, and
there was no fear of elbowing, in passing, any of those
filthy spies out of uniform, with looks as awry as their
souls, who, at the very moment I am writing these
words, are the horror of Paris, the shame of the
civilization placed under their degrading safeguard,
and the dishonour of the government which employs
them.   After February, the prefecture of police no
longer presented that appearance which it had under
Louis Philippe, and was still less like what it is now
under Louis Bonaparte.   It was no longer a cavern,
but a guard-house.   Night had already come on when
I got there : by the light of the torches that were
everywhere stuck about, I perceived numbers of people
coming and going.   The principal court, the staircases
and halls, were filled with rough but honest-looking
men, wearing red woollen neck-cloths, and scarfs of
the same colour and stuff round their waists ; some
were smoking, while others were lying on camp beds;
some too swearing like troopers.   More than one
equivocal word struck my ear.   I do not deny that,
taken altogether, the scene was one very likely to
offend the taste of persons who have never done anything but dangle in drawing-rooms.   But there was
really nothing of a repulsive character in it.   An air of
civic good-nature and heartiness in these red neck-
clothed men softened down their idle swagger and

loose expressions. Their excitement was a hundred times less intimidating than the mute silence of the black phantoms they succeeded; while the endless weapons of every possible kind, which they seemed to take pleasure in displaying, were far from awakening those sanguinary associations which in France always attach to the sword of a *sergent de ville.*

I went up to the office of the secretary-general, having business to transact with the person then in charge of the prefecture; and I found myself in presence of a man whose herculean limbs, bull neck, and gigantic stature, rendered more remarkable by the smallness of the head, disproportioned to the rest of the body, were calculated to produce a feeling akin to fear, but for the confidence at once inspired by the gentleness of his manners, his tone of voice, and a certain air of simple good nature which spread over him from head to foot; this peculiar air, however, vanished somewhat after a first glance; for the half-veiled light of his eyes soon divulged the character of his mind, an extraordinary mixture of pliancy and energy, of eccentric impulses and cautious wariness, of bluntness and finesse. The reader at all acquainted with the personages of this period, will have guessed that I am here speaking of M. Marc Caussidière.

On the 24th of February, at the head of some working-men, who had been fighting on the barricades, he went to the prefecture of police, where, acting under the contingencies of the moment, he took upon himself the responsibility of preserving public order, subject to the future arrangements of the Provisional Government. The short interview I had with him convinced me that he perfectly understood the nature of the task he had undertaken, and that he was well suited to it. Moreover, he was not quite a stranger to me. I had known him when I was connected with the *Reforme* newspaper, and had opportunities of observing the rare zeal and tact he displayed in extending the circulation of that journal. When, shortly before the Revolution, M. Ledru Rollin, Flocon, and myself, went to the banquet of Dijon, he accompanied us; and we had there the opportunity of collecting from his speeches to the people, that he had a sort of untaught eloquence, fantastic, unconnected, full of hap-hazard quotations, and common expressions, but abounding in fire, surprising by unexpected turns, and reaching, in a kind of confused and disorderly way, the end he wanted to arrive at.

There was no reason whatever, therefore, why the minority should not draw well with him, especially as his acts at the prefecture of police bore, from the beginning, the stamp of public utility. He at once addressed himself with zeal and success to the care of the public markets, gave a spur to the sluggishness of official routine, cleared the streets of the obstructions arising from the barricades, attended to the cleanliness and lighting of the city, vigorously revived the police regulations affecting the security and free circulation of the public ways : showed, in fact, an administrative aptness which not even his enemies could dispute, and which subsequently, under critical

circumstances, obtained for him the support of the
bourgeoisie itself.*

Of the forbearance, conciliatory spirit, and even
courtesy, with which he discharged his duties, take
as an illustration the following letter from his pre-
decessor in the prefecture, M. Gabriel Delessert, dated
the 29th of April, 1848.

"Monsieur le Préfêt, I have just learned from my
friends in Paris the kind way in which you have
expressed yourself relative to the short stay that
Madame Delessert was obliged to make at Passy, and
your regrets at her not having applied to you. Permit
me to offer you my thanks, which I do with all the
more pleasure for its affording me an opportunity of
saying how sensible I am of your kind offices in so
obligingly permitting the wearing apparel, horses, and
other objects, belonging to my wife and myself, to be
removed from the prefecture of police. I am happy,
Monsieur le Préfêt, in thus tendering you the expression of my sincere and grateful thanks. Do me the
honour to accept the assurance of my high consideration.

GABRIEL DELESSERT." †

---

* When the Assembly was invaded by the people, May 15, 1848, M.
Caussidière, having been accused of not having sufficiently exerted himself
against the movement, in his capacity of Prefect of Police, resigned, and
immediately appealed to the electors. The result was that the Club of
the Manège of the Chaussée d'Antin, composed of Conservatives, accepted
him as a candidate, and he was elected a representative of the people by
147,000 votes.

† "Mémoires de M. Caussidière."

But all this did not hinder the majority from looking with a suspicious eye on M. Caussidière's presence at the prefecture of police.   MM. Garnier Pagès and Marrast particularly were alarmed at seeing so important an office entrusted to a man who had been so much mixed up with political dissensions, and whose social tendencies were so different from theirs.   Their anxiety was redoubled when informed that M. Caussidière was surrounded by a band of determined men, 2000 in number, who, under the name of the *Guard of the People*, constituted the only organised force existing in Paris.   Various were the attempts made, first to remove him, and then to subordinate his authority to that of the mayoralty of Paris; but the majority of the government met with a resistance in the Council which they did not think it politic to override.   Accordingly, on the 13th of March, on the motion of M. Ledru Rollin, it was resolved not only that M. Caussidière should be officially confirmed in his office, but that the office itself, detached from the mayoralty, should be placed under the jurisdiction of the Minister of the Interior.   Free scope was given to M. Caussidière's action; nor did public order suffer from it.   For he so skilfully made use of his *Montagnards*—it was thus the men with red scarfs of whom I have spoken were designated—in watching over the security of Paris, and keeping a tight hand on all kinds of malefactors, as to be able—to borrow a picturesque expression, which is his own, and which conveys a good idea of his administration,—" to *establish order by means of disorder*."

Among those who accompanied M. Caussidière to

the prefecture of police on the 24th of February, was a pale young man of a feeble frame, named Sobrier, a person of excitable temperament, much intrepidity, inoffensive disposition, disinterested and generous in an extraordinary degree. He had just come into possession of a rich inheritance, and his first care was to appropriate 20,000 francs to the diffusion of republican ideas. There was great talk at the time about an armed and permanent club in an apartment he had hired in No. 16, Rue de Rivoli, which formerly belonged to the civil list. The fact of such a club existing is true, and equally so that the establishment of a garrison in a private house, in the midst of the most tranquil quarter of Paris, was a thing which, in ordinary times, would have been intolerable; even then it was the cause of much complaint. But what was not sufficiently known at the time, and what is still generally unknown, is, that the arms collected in Sobrier's house were furnished by the prefecture of police, without the knowledge of the minority, on the authority of a letter from M. de Lamartine.* Clear proof that M. de Lamartine supposed him incapable of making a bad use of them! And in fact, Sobrier was the most harmless man in the world, and the only mischief his armed club did was to the Republic, by furnishing the royalists with a plausible pretext for attacking it.

We cannot recall the revolutionary incidents of 1848 without mentioning the clubs, meeting daily or weekly, which suddenly sprang up at each point of the

---

* "Mémoires de M. Caussidière," to whom the letter was sent. Vol. ii. p. 177.

capital, and gave vent to an unrestricted expression of free thought by means of free speech.

The two clubs which at this period attracted the most attention and exercised the most influence, were that of the "Société Centrale," directed with much ability by M. Blanqui, and that which M. Barbés had established at the Palais Nationale, under the name of the "Club de la Révolution."

I have heard a great deal of the intellectual powers of M. Blanqui, of his monastic ascetism, of his skill in practising underhand manœuvres, of his capacity of managing popular passions, of the influence he acquires over certain men by his solitary kind of life, by his mode of expressing himself, at once cold and audacious, by his sombre looks and emaciated face. Whether this be a faithful portrait I cannot say ; for, personally, I have no acquaintance with M. Blanqui. When the Revolution broke out I had never seen him but once, and that in passing ; I have never seen him since, and I have never had any relations whatever with him, direct or indirect. Nor have I any better knowledge of what his views were with respect to the organisation of democracy, seeing that he never has, as far as I know, put forward anything precise upon the subject; possibly because he has come to no fixed conclusions about it, or because he is apprehensive of submitting his opinions to the dangerous test of discussion and criticism, or it may have been that he imagined he was making himself greater by looming through a kind of mystery.

As to M. Barbés, whoever has followed the political events which have agitated France for the last thirty

years, must know the part he has played, and in what
degree; while exhibiting the qualities which should
distinguish a public man, he has united in himself
the courage of a cavalier with the devotedness of a
martyr. But they only who have lived on terms of
intimacy with him, know that this man, who never
compromised with injustice, who never bent to force,
who never retreated before danger, who was never
moved in the presence of death, is, in the ordinary
affairs of life, a person of such sweet gentleness of character, and so engaging an intercourse, that it is impossible to approach without loving him. I have
letters of his in my possession which are master-pieces
of grace, sensibility, and style; some of them, in
which he speaks of France humiliated and enslaved,
are of a melancholy so touching, so absolutely irresistible, that they would draw tears from those
who, on the faith of interested calumnies, shudder at
his name.

I question if in the whole of history we can find
an example of self-denial comparable with that furnished by the life of M. Barbés. When first he
devoted himself, soul and body, to the service of the
Republic, which his high intelligence was not satisfied
with regarding merely as a form of government more
or less good, but rather contemplating as a means of
remedying social evils, the sight of which had afflicted
him from his earliest years, M. Barbés had just completed a brilliant education. He was young, handsome,
and rich; he had a cultivated mind, attractive manners,
and might have consequently aspired to occupy a

position in society in conformity with so rare an assemblage of personal advantages. But God had assigned devotedness to him as the part he was to play; and though the possibility of a social renovation was not then to be descried save in the far-distance, he did not hesitate to embrace the cause of those who suffer, resolutely decided to serve it until his latest hour. The struggle in which he embarked against the corrupt government of Louis Philippe I have myself described at length in the "*History of Ten Years.*" Defeated in this struggle, which was not entirely thrown away, since it conduced to the Revolution of February, M. Barbés did not think of defending himself in the presence of the judges before whom he was brought. Averse to everything like stage effect, he, for a long time, maintained an unbroken silence, partly from modesty, partly from disdain, until being pressed by the Chamber of Peers to make some explanation, he replied: "When the Indian savage is overcome, when by the fortune of war he falls into the power of his enemies, he has not recourse to empty words; he resigns himself, and gives his head to the scalping knife." And, the next day, M. Pasquier having been unblushing enough to say that he did right to compare himself to a savage, Barbés replied to him, with calm contempt: "The pitiless savage is not the one who offers his head to be scalped, but the one who scalps."

He was capitally condemned on the false charge, proved to be false, of having, in the affair of the 12th of May, treacherously shot Captain Drouineau while parleying with that officer.* What was really true was, that M. Barbès had taken part in an insurrection; he did not deny it, and this was reason enough for his being condemned. But the calumny I have mentioned, was devised to divert the immense interest excited throughout Paris by the bravery of his conduct; it was however to no purpose. The idea that so noble a head was about to perish on the scaffold filled the capital with sorrow. The workshops were abandoned, the barriers deserted. I was in Paris at that time, July, 1839, and I saw with my own eyes, 3000 students arrive at the Place Vendôme, bareheaded, with crape on their arms; who took the direction of the *Chancellerie*, and went to ask for the pardon of Barbès. Out of respect for this state of public feeling, and also from that aversion to shedding blood, which was one of the virtues of Louis Philippe, the punishment was commuted, and M. Barbès was thrown into the dungeons of the monarchy, from which the Revolution released him. He had passed nine years in prison, when he paid his first visit to the Provisional Government, all the members of which, without a single exception, received him with open arms. Captivity had paled his face, hollowed his cheeks, thinned his hair, and dimmed the fire of his eyes; but his serenity remaining unchanged, was all the more touching.

* This falsehood having found its way into England, I think it my duty to state what actually occurred. The guard under the command of Captain Drouineau being drawn up before the insurgents, the latter, according to a form usual in France on such occasions, invited them to *fraternise*. To this Captain Drouineau replied by an order to fire, on which the insurgents poured in a volley, and he fell.

It is easy to conceive how much popularity must have attached to a club over which he presided. There were to be seen assembled in it a great number of working-men of the Republican party : M. Martin Bernard, an intimate friend of M. Barbès, whose perils and sufferings he had shared ; M. Thoré, who had achieved a distinguished place both amongst journalists and artists ; M. Étienne Arago, a brother of the illustrious *savant* of that name, and M. Emmanuel Arago, his son ; M. Greppo, a Lyonnese workman of great influence, about to become representative of the people; the celebrated M. Proudhon, and finally M. Landolphe, who had taken a prominent part in the political strife of the previous reign, and who, by the nature of his convictions resting on large acquirements, the elevation of his mind, and his indomitable firmness, was naturally summoned to the side of M. Barbès. There, every evening, in the presence of a numerous, attentive, and sympathising audience, were discussed political and social questions of the gravest importance ; there, theoretic views were developed, and expressed sometimes in language very bold, but in general free from asperity, and never taking the form of appeals to violence.

Another Club, much frequented and in the highest degree orderly, was that of the *Amis du Peuple*, which was formed by M. Raspail, in the Salle de la Rue de Montesquieu. The political influence of Raspail, his rhetorical talent, and his great reputation as a physician, and man of science, drew great numbers about him. His club was, in this respect, different from the others, as being rather a place of philosophical and social instruction by one man, than an open arena of discussion. "I had for my audience," he has himself since stated, "my old patients, my devoted pupils, my old companions in the work of self-instruction, welldoing, and suffering." *

Independently of the principal clubs, there were numbers of others, corresponding with every shade of opinion. The Phalansterians flocked to MM. Considerant and Cantagrel, as many of the Communists did to M. Cabet. There were Orleanist clubs, and Legitimist clubs; of the former, take as an instance that over which M. Viennet presided, under the title of "*Republican Club for the Liberty of Elections*," and of the latter, the club of the tenth arrondissement presided over by M. Vatimesnil.

Home policy, foreign policy, taxation, emancipation of working men, the improvement of the condition of poor women, gratuitous national education, the union of peoples,—what questions were there not raised and discussed in these ardent laboratories of public opinion? Oh, how swift was the march of life then! How each man's heart beat quicker! and what swift wings the imagination lent to the mind's conceptions! So intense was the life of society, moved to its very depths, that in a few days the number of the clubs rose to 300; and though immense halls had been placed at the disposal of these popular meetings in various public buildings, yet, from these halls, crammed every night to suffocation, intellectual excitement overflowed into

* Report of the trial of M. Raspail, before the High Court of Bourges, March 5th, 1849.

the streets, spread from man to man, and finally, penetrating into those miserable haunts, where the most noble faculties of man had been hitherto asleep, awakened a powerful and impassioned curiosity.

Add to this, the incessant action of a crowd of new journals, to which the abolition of the stamp-duty had largely contributed ; and the combative character of literature, as represented by such writers as MM. Victor Hugo, Eugène Sue, Felix Pyat, and Madame George Sand.

I need hardly say, that in the midst of this vast *mêlée* of aspirations and feelings, all of which were permitted, without exception, to express and justify themselves, the Provisional Government praised by some, was the object of vehement and repeated attacks from others; if allowance was made for the difficulty of its task in the club of Barbès, it was criticised with ever-increasing severity in the club of Blanqui. If the majority of the council was supported by the *Nationnel*, whose views had undergone no change, and if the minority found an advocate in the *Réforme*, edited by M. Ribeyrolles in the most brilliant manner, how many were the journals that indiscriminately attacked, and even flung their invectives at the whole Provisional Government. Not one of our acts escaped the bitterest scrutiny from M. Émile Girardin, chief editor of the *Presse*. Not a single thing we did which was not cited by M. Proudhon, editor of the *Représentant du Peuple*, as a proof that all governments, be they what they might, ought to be suppressed, and that the only thing which should be left standing was *anarchy*,

or, to use the orthography of Proudhon, *an-archy*.
M. de Lamennais, too, who a little later, came over to
Socialism, opposed it at that time, from not having
sufficiently studied it, and his journal, *Le Peuple Con-
stituant*, waged active war against the Luxembourg.

Thus lashed by every wave of this agitated and roaring
sea, what course did the Provisional Government take?
Were they to be seen, doing what Louis Bonaparte and
his supporters do at this very hour—interdicting discussion, reducing their adversaries to silence, trembling
at the least appearance of criticism, growing pale before
the mere shadow of an allusion, seeking their safety and
force in darkness? No. The Provisional Government
were so convinced of their moral strength, so bold from
the consciousness of their good intentions, and so confiding in the spontaneous support of a free people, that
far from fearing the light—a fear that should be left to
malefactors—they spread their special protection over
the liberty of their most violent enemies. The printing-
house of M. Émile de Girardin having been menaced
by a crowd of people exasperated at the excess to which
he carried his systematic attacks upon the official
agents of the Republic, M. Caussidière at once despatched
his *Montagnards* to keep the crowd in order, and M.
Ledru Rollin went himself to assist personally in preserving unscathed that liberty which M. de Girardin
was so remorsely using at our expense. A fact like
this took place at the Luxembourg. Some delegates having come and told me that the people were
irritated at our persistence in suffering the *Constitutionnel* to pour its venom every morning on the Luxem-

bourg, and that a great number of workmen were assembled at that very moment in the court, intending to go and bring it to account for its calumnies, I instantly went out to them, and turned them from their purpose by words whose extreme vehemence disarmed them.

There survives, moreover, an official and decisive testimony to the confidence of the Provisional Government in the sympathies of the nation. I allude to the Proclamation they published on the 20th of April, concerning the Clubs. It begins with these words: " The Republic lives by discussion and liberty," and finishes thus: " The best safe-guard of liberty, is liberty." *

Let the people of England compare the principles so openly professed by the Provisional Government, with those that are now directing the policy of Louis Bonaparte, and then let them say, if, for Great Britain, an alliance with the Republic would not have been more natural, more reasonable, more certain, than an alliance with the Empire?

After all, the licence given to the Clubs and to the newspapers had, together with some of the drawbacks inseparable from all human things, advantages which will not be lost to the future. The questions under discussion alarmed and irritated egotists of every kind, all who live by abuses; factitious agitation was encouraged; the tendency to innovation sometimes manifested itself under ridiculous forms; there was much declamation; and the allurements offered to public curiosity were not always wholesome or substantial. But pro-

---

* *Moniteur*, 20th April, 1848.

blems of a high interest were proposed, and their solution matured; the attention of the people was keenly aroused on points on which the light of knowledge was cast for the first time; true working ideas sprang up amongst others that were vain and chimerical; in a word, the soil was ploughed in all directions, and seed was thrown into it, which nothing hereafter can destroy, which even at this moment is germinating silently, and which, when the winter shall have passed away, that is, on the morrow of the day when despotism shall have vanished, will yield a harvest whose rich abundance will be the astonishment of Europe.

CHAPTER XIII.

SOLEMN MARCH THROUGH PARIS.

Just born of a popular movement, the Provisional Government had now to define their own position.

Should they regard themselves as dictators appointed by a revolution which had become inevitable, and under no obligation to seek the sanction of universal suffrage, until after having accomplished all the good which the moment required?

Or should they, on the contrary, confine their mission to an immediate convocation of the National Assembly, limiting their action to measures of immediate urgency and administrative acts of secondary importance?

Of these two courses, the latter was unquestionably the more regular and the least dangerous; it placed the disinterestedness of the Provisional Government beyond suspicion; it partially saved us from the reproach of usurpation; it was this which the Council favoured.

For myself, I was of an entirely different opinion, believing that the adoption of the other course would have a most auspicious influence on the destinies of the new Republic.

Not that I, in the least, concealed from myself its

difficulties and perils. For I knew very well that society does not easily permit itself to be carried forward much beyond the present limit of its knowledge and views; that the march of History does not keep pace either with the desires of generous hearts, nor even with the logical development of a sound idea, and that it is within the competence of no one to make it move faster or slower according to his own caprice. Nevertheless, this observation, to be accurate, must not be taken in too absolute a sense; for, after all, circumstances are merely the result of a certain combination of individual efforts; and the action of a few men of character, when they are in a position to apply a great power to the triumph of a great idea, has beyond all doubt its weight in the balance of human affairs.

Therefore, reflecting on the profound ignorance and moral inertness in which the rural districts of France are plunged; the immense resources placed in the hands of the enemies of progress by their exclusive possession of all the means of influence, and of all the avenues to wealth; the infinite germs of impurity deposited in the very foundations of society by half a century of Imperial or Monarchical corruption, and, finally, the numerical superiority of the ignorant peasantry over the enlightened population of the towns, I came to the conclusion that we ought to adjourn the elections to the latest possible moment. I thought that, meanwhile, it was imperatively our duty to take boldly and bravely, at the risk of our heads, the initiative of the vast reforms which had to be accomplished, always, of course, reserving to the National Assembly the right of subsequently affirming or abrogating our work with a sovereign will.

In this way, we should have put time on our side; we should have been able, with all the force which is derived from the possession of power, to act upon the French nation, that nation so sensitive, intelligent, and prompt to obey the impulses coming from authority; we should have thus, as it were, placed a luminous beacon on the summit of society which would have lit it up throughout its whole extent; in a word, by the time that the sovereignty of the people, recognised and proclaimed from the very first, should have been summoned to the ballot-box, they would have completed their education.

This also was Albert's opinion, and nothing was more calculated to confirm me in mine; for Albert, with a rare straight-forwardness, combined a remarkable penetration. Whenever he addressed the Council, it was always to give utterance to just and generous ideas, in language nervous and precise.

What lamentable results would necessarily be the consequences of an opposite course!

The Provisional Government compelled to hurry on its action, and, by hurrying, to compromise it—power urged on by the inherent spirit of the Revolution to accomplish brilliant reforms, and going no farther than crude suggestions—the elections abandoned to the dominion of ancient prejudices and local influences—universal suffrage throwing up, as the necessary consequence of a coalition among the different fractions of the conquered party, an assembly hostile to its own principles — the spirit of reaction encouraged by the ruling power's distrust of itself, and by the temporary character of its functions—the popular leaders, in the very presence of this reaction, prematurely disarming themselves—this is what I foresaw; this is what was but too soon realised.

Yes, I say it without hesitation, it was my wish, from the first hour of the existence of the Provisional Government that we should pitch our duties high and raise our power to a level with our duties. There are, moreover, in the life of a nation, critical opportunities, of which the instinct of real statesmen is sure to avail itself. The creation of a National Bank, the purchase of railways, the *unification* of offices of insurance, the formation of a financial department especially devoted to labour, how many of these things were afterwards denounced as, and really became, impracticable, which, at that time, were easy enough !

It is obvious, therefore, how important was the question of whether the elections should be hurried on or adjourned.

Now, on this point, my opinion was in perfect conformity with that of the people of Paris. Endowed unexpectedly with the right of the franchise — a right to them so novel—the working-classes did not at all understand that they were called upon to extemporise the means of improving their condition.

They had need for reflection on their new position; they asked for time necessary to consult leisurely among themselves as to the qualifications of those who were to be elected.

This desire, though exaggerated in them by the leaders of the clubs, was both legitimate and reasonable. Only in fixing the interval which was to elapse, they committed the mistake of not sufficiently taking into the account the different situation of the provinces from that of Paris. The interval determined upon was about a month; this was too much or too little. The obvious course was either to proceed immediately with the elections, in order to take advantage of the revolutionary impulse of February, or to adjourn them to a period sufficiently remote to give the Provisional Government time to train public opinion to a better appreciation of the true character of republicanism, a larger experience of its vigour, and an accurate estimate of its benefits. But to take a middle course was to give prostrate parties the time to raise their heads, and at the same time to cast away the force which would have been able to restrain them.

Be this as it may, some days before the 17th of March, information reached me at the Luxembourg that the people of Paris were preparing an imposing manifestation, for the double purpose of obtaining the adjournment of the elections (whether of the National Guard, or of the Members of the Constituent Assembly), and the removal of the troops still remaining in Paris.

Now, with both these objects, I completely sympathised. The adjournment of the elections, the question of time apart, I earnestly desired for the reasons already mentioned. As to the removal of the troops, I had been always of opinion that the presence of the army in inland towns, especially

Paris, was one of the most serious perils to which liberty could be exposed. In point of fact, the very day before the revolution of February, I had, as a member of a political society to which I belonged, drawn up a protest against using soldiers for putting down civil disturbances; with the objects of the intended manifestation, therefore, I could not but concur. What, I confess, alarmed me, was the idea of the manifestation itself. I could hardly persuade myself—the prudence of the people has since punished me for my apprehensions, while filling me with joy —I could scarcely believe that more than 150,000 working-men could circulate through Paris without causing the slightest excitement or the least disorder. But what way was there to prevent it? By granting to the people what with justice, according to my view, they demanded; it was to this end that Albert and myself directed our endeavours.

Unfortunately, however, it had got into the heads of our colleagues that the principal object of our warnings was to fetter the deliberations of Government, and to coerce it by menace. In a Council that was one evening held at the Palace of the Petit Luxembourg, and to which M.M. de Courtais and Guinard, Commanders of the National Guard, were summoned, I made a frank communication of all I knew.

The people in a body were to move on the Hôtel de Ville, to obtain the adjournment of the elections; but the question was, could this take place without danger? Up to this time, Paris, the Paris of the Revolution, had been signalised by its attitude of

tranquil majesty and powerful repose; was it not our
duty to see that it should be preserved to the last?
Supposing it were true, that some unknown agitators
intended to take advantage of the vast multitude
once in motion, to cause some disturbance, nothing
would be easier than to foil them. To anticipate
popular wishes is to avoid the risk of being compelled
to obey them. Of course, it would not have become
us to yield to the dictation of these desires, irrespective of their object; for there are circumstances
in which a government, which does not know how to
resist the wishes of the people, betrays them; but though
in certain exigencies it be the duty of men of probity
to place the sovereignty of their own conscience above
that of the sovereignty of the people, why should
they hesitate to yield when the demands are just?
Was it not better, then, to do before the manifestation, in order to ward off its perils, that which
afterwards we should be obliged to do in order to
arrest its course?

The dignity of the Government in this case was
coincident with its prudence. To these arguments
were added others, which a feeling of delicacy induces
me to suppress. That very grave differences of opinion
existed among the members of the Provisional Government is not, at this time of day, to be concealed.
These differences, which, as respects unity of action,
made this government a very defective executive
power, constituted its peculiarity as a government of
transition, whose office it was to watch over the seat
of sovereignty; in point of fact this very diversity of

contradictory elements was well adapted to the protection required, because it tended to keep the different forces of society in equilibrium.

Thus, the antecedents of M. de Lamartine especially qualified him to attract into the paths of progress the most sluggish parts of the nation, while I, through my well-known opinions, was enabled to tranquillise the working class. It was in reference to this I one day said to M. de Lamartine, " We are each of us in this singular position; it is you who are responsible for progress, and I who am responsible for order? "

Hence this variety of elements, bad in settled Government, which implies a concert of opinions, was good in a Provisional Government having to prevent any conflict of views, until the coming of a permanent power. To make a rent in it, would necessarily be to open a breach through which ambitions of every kind, fermenting with avidity and impatience, must have precipitously entered. This was one of the reasons which militated in my mind against the proposed movement. I was apprehensive, after most mature reflection, that it might be used as an instrument to overturn some of my colleagues. It may be conceived, therefore, how much I must have been pained at finding my recommendations rejected by them, from a feeling of suspicion I so little deserved. Deeply wounded, I rose and declared that from that moment I should cease to make one of the Provisional Government. Albert, at the same time, had risen impetuously, and we were in the act of leaving the Council Chamber, when, seized with an anxiety that was honourable to them, our colleagues recalled and retained us. Addressing himself immediately to the Council, M. Ledrù Rollin pointed out with much animation, that there was no necessity for being in a hurry to fix the precise period of the elections; that previous preparations were requisite; that these preparations were not finished; and that information of importance, expected from the provinces, had not yet arrived. This let all of us off easily, and the question was left undecided.

The people, however, still continued to be much excited.

Thanks to the trades' delegates, the Luxembourg being, as it were, a sort of instant echo of the great voice of the faubourgs, I learnt at once that in this excitement there was something of peculiar gravity and import. The suppression of the grenadier companies of the National Guard had given rise on their part to a demonstration as fruitless as it was rash. Paris was greatly disturbed, and my apprehensions vastly increased. It was the trade companies, and not the clubs, which had taken the initiative; I therefore lost no time in calling a meeting at the Luxembourg, on the morning of the 17th, of those workmen whom I knew were in the greatest repute with their comrades. "The movement," they said, "is on foot, and cannot be stopped." I then entreated them to abstain from all inflammatory cries, carefully to keep down their own excitement, in a word, so to manage the demonstration as to convert it into a lasting testimony to the good sense of the people.

This they assured me they would do with such a frank decision of manner, as completely to secure my confidence; and with my mind almost entirely at ease, I returned to my colleagues at the Hôtel de Ville.

The great news of the day had, however, preceded me; but as it was not convenient for my colleagues to confess they were in the wrong in having turned a deaf ear to Albert's warnings and mine, they affected to believe, at all events to say, that all that was meant was a sudden protest on the part of the workmen against the menaces of the grenadier companies; an idle supposition, to which the working men, by their evident organisation, and the very terms of their petition, were about to give the most signal contradiction. We were all of us in anxious expectation of what was coming, when suddenly, at one of the ends of the Place de Grêve, a dark dense mass presented itself.

This was the van of the trades' companies, separated at regular intervals, and preceded by their special banners. They took up their ground in perfect silence, with the order and discipline of an army—a fine and valiant army indeed! but one which, instead of death, brought labour the source of life; and it was with hands unburdened with the weight of swords, and with looks of peace and love, that it came on, deploying its peaceful battalions under the beams of a glorious sun. I was moved to tears, and, recollecting my doubts, I asked pardon of the people in the fullness of my heart.

A momentary cloud, however, passed rapidly over this feeling of joy. The delegates had come up the steps of the Hôtel de Ville, and one of them, citizen Gerard, had read the petition, which, asked in the name of the people of Paris, for the removal of the troops out of the capital, the adjournment of the elections of the National Guard to the 5th of April, and that of the elections for the Assembly to the 31st of May, when I perceived amongst them certain faces unknown to me, with something of menace in their expression. It occurred to me at once, that persons unconnected with the Companies had mixed themselves up with the procession; and that of those who presented themselves as deputed by the multitude some were not really such, or at all events not by virtue of the same title. The object of the Companies was what the petition expressed; but these were evidently men impatient to overthrow, in favour of the views of Ledru Rollin, Flocon, Albert, and myself, the members of the Provisional Government who represented a contrary opinion. What was to be done? The situation was critical; had but a single man been audacious enough to throw open a window, and cry out to the crowd in the square below, "They refuse your demands, they are illusing your delegates," possibly it had been all over with us. Who knows what disasters might not have been the result of a sudden appeal to disappointed hopes and irresistible wrath? What might not have been the consequences of the conflagration? Where would it have stopped? and what frightful responsibility would there not have been heaped upon me by the suspicions which constantly attached to me,—by the intention imputed to me of aspiring to the dictatorship, and by the presence of the delegates of the Luxembourg at the head of the movement. I felt that the peculiarity of my position at this moment made it imperative on me to be the first to break the silence; accordingly, advancing a few steps, I said:

"Citizens, the government of the Republic is founded upon public opinion; of that it will never fail to be mindful. Our force we are well aware is in the people; our will must always be in harmony with theirs. We thank you for the language addressed to us, so full of sympathy and devotedness; the Provisional Government has merited it by its courage, by its firm determination to promote the prosperity of the people by aid of the people, and through their support. The sentiments of order you have expressed, are the consecration of liberty in France; it is requisite that the strength of the people should exhibit itself with an aspect of calmness; for calmness is the majestic expression of strength: the desires you have made known to us shall be the subject of our deliberations. You, citizens, you yourselves will be the last to wish that the government which is your representative, should give way to a menace."

And I wound up by declaring that the matter of the petition should receive our most serious consideration; reserving to ourselves our liberty of judgment, and that unfettered independence which was due to our self-respect.

Thus it was that, at the risk of incurring their anger, I took in hand the cause of those of my colleagues who were most opposed to me. My remarks, as was evident, were very well received by the representatives of the trades; but the ardent men who had mixed themselves up with the workmen, betrayed their discontent by sullen murmurs. I had said that, were it necessary, we should know how to die for the people. Some one in a menacing tone replied, " Be sure of this, too, that the working classes on their side are ready to die for you *as long as, mark it well, you are true to them.*" I then repeated what I had said, " Leave us to *ourselves,* that the world may know the government of the Republic does not deliberate under the influence of threats. They who were but the representatives of privileged classes might be allowed to fear; not so we, because we are your representatives, and to preserve our own dignity is to preserve yours." *

" Not a step will we move from this place without having some answer to carry back to the people," exclaimed some one in a violent tone; but MM. Sobrier and Cabet instantly softened down this imperious exclamation by words full of moderation, good sense, and confiding patriotism.

MM. Ledru Rollin and Lamartine then spoke in succession, the first to call attention to the fact that France consisted not merely of the inhabitants of Paris, but of the whole body of citizens; and that therefore it was necessary, before fixing a day for the elections, to ascertain the feeling of the provinces on the subject; the second, to protest against the anxiety implied in the demand relative to the removal of the troops. " There are no troops in Paris," said he, " except

---

* *Moniteur,* 18th of March, 1848.

perhaps some fifteen hundred or two thousand men, at various posts outside the city, for the protection of the gates of the capital, and the railways; and it is quite false to suppose that the government has thought of bringing any to Paris. It must, indeed, have been mad after what has happened, after the royalty just fallen has witnessed eighty thousand men melting away before the unarmed people of Paris, to think of imposing upon you with a handful of soldiers, full of the same spirit of republicanism, views contrary to your independence. No, we never for a moment thought of it, we are not thinking of it, we never shall. The republic within requires no other defender than the people in arms."

Those who went so far as to desire the overthrow of the Provisional Government were silent, the rest applauded; and the deputation was retiring, when an immense clamour arose from the Place de Grève; the people insisted on seeing the members of the government of the Republic; and we went down in compliance with this desire. But while we were making our way through the closely packed crowd on the steps of the Hôtel de Ville, a man of energetic mien, and whose flashing eyes lit up the extreme paleness of his face, rushed impetuously towards me, and seizing me by the arm, wrathfully exclaimed, "You are then a traitor, even you!" For there were some who imputed it to me as a crime, that I had not availed myself of the opportunity of overthrowing those of my colleagues, on the ruins of whose power I was, according to others, anxious to establish my own.

As I reflected on this injustice which characterises factious passions, a bitter smile played involuntarily upon my lips, and this was the only answer I gave. On our reaching the platform which had been constructed at the Hôtel de Ville, I addressed the Trades' Companies, requesting them to retire in good order.* They replied by a burst of acclamation in compliment to the Provisional Government, and immediately putting themselves in motion, proceeded with a calm solemnity that was truly admirable towards the column of the Bastille, and across the astounded and silent capital. The procession defiled for several hours and it was five o'clock, says the *Moniteur*,* before the last of the one hundred and fifty-thousand men who composed it, passed from before the front of the Hôtel de Ville.

* *Moniteur*, 18th of March, 1848.

CHAPTER XIV.

THE ALARUM.

THE 17th of March had appeared to the Royalists like the revelation of a new world. More alarming to them, even than the rattle of the fusillade, or the roll of cannon through the streets, was that grand silence of the people. In their sleepless nights, they mused on those grave legions issuing from hundreds of fraternal workshops, and again saw them traversing Paris, mute and thoughtful. What a force for Statesmen really imbued with the true spirit of the Revolution. But the lever of Archimedes would be powerless in the hands of men obstinately bent on proving the world immovable. The truth is, the 17th of March had sorely troubled the majority of the Provisional Government, especially M. de Lamartine, and the influence of that day was still, as it were, alive in the Council. There were still seven members on one side, and four on the other; but behind these four the 17th of March brought on the scene a fifth voter—the people! M. Crémieux a man of generous emotions, and of a spirit impressionably sensitive, was, of all the members of the majority in the Council, the only one inclined to make a close alliance with the Revolution. M. Arago, who had been too much removed from politics by his labours in science, drew back aghast at the suddenness and uncertainty of events. M. Dupont (de l'Eure), one of those men whom everybody respects and loves, whether friend or foe, hesitated between the natural apprehensions of old age, and the sympathies of his heart and of his principles. MM. Garnier Pagès and Marrast disguised their uneasiness under an adroit affectation of levity; and as for M. Màrie, his fears were stamped in anxious lines upon his contracted lips, his knitted brow, and his suspicious looks.

With regard to M. de Lamartine, he bore a grudge against the demonstration of the 17th of March, for having been the work of the delegates of the Luxembourg, at whose suggestion that vast, pacific, and powerful army of the working men's companies had displayed itself before the Government. Although he had so prodigally courted and caressed all parties; although he had staked so deeply in order to win the approbation of the clubs as a sort of popular letter of credit on the admiration of the salons; although he had kept up almost uninterrupted relations with Sobrier, and had not even shrunk from contact with Blanqui —nevertheless, he had always betrayed a blind obstinate hostility to the Luxembourg. Must we suppose that he was averse to the official discussion of Socialism, lest it should divert public attention, and that, having chosen the theatrical part of the Revolution, he resented its serious realities? Or was he urged by his fawners to resist a popularity counter to his own? For

my own part, I have always believed that the opposition
with which M. de Lamartine generally honoured me
was perfectly loyal, disinterested, and sincere. Being
a total stranger to the science of Political Economy, he
had conceived a real distrust of doctrines which he had
never studied, and which, besides, his peculiar intellectual organisation was little qualified to apprehend.

Surrounded by selfish flatterers who detested the
bare name of Socialist doctrine, because they understood
it too clearly, he, on the contrary, deemed it dangerous
because he was thoroughly ignorant of its meaning,
and it is more just to pity than to blame him.

Moreover, he was plied with the incense of the
salons. Speculating on his weak point—love of praise
—the enemies of the Republic never ceased repeating
that they looked to him for what they styled the " safety
of society." And he abandoned himself so completely
to this dangerous intoxication of flattery, that it was to
the very persons who, by education, position, and habits,
were most opposed to Republican institutions, he went
to seek the motives and rules of his conduct. Lord
Normanby's book makes it impossible to have any
longer a doubt on this point. What could be more
extraordinary than that a member of the Provisional
Government, a Republican, one of the leaders of a
democratic Revolution, should select as his confidant
and habitual adviser a foreign diplomatist, a member
of the English aristocracy, the ambassador of a country
which had not yet even officially recognised the Republic,
—in one word, a man who, in his book, says : " I told M.
de Lamartine yesterday, that if I were a Frenchman

and a Republican, and I was as little the one as the other, etc. . . . . ! " *

I was not, at that time, aware, as regards the particular steps taken by M. de Lamartine, of all I have since learnt; I did not know, for instance, that he was endeavouring to find in the army and in the provinces the means of overawing Paris, just as the Girondists had done in the first French Revolution; I did not know that, while taking under his protection the fantastic and anomalous military establishment of Sobrier, he despatched secret emissaries to General Negrier, who in the north commanded an army of 29,000 men, † and concerted measures with M. Marrast to change the Hôtel de Ville into a fortress. But what I did see clearly enough was, that the majority of the Council was giving way more and more to groundless prejudices against the people, and was not far from having recourse to bayonets against the daily increasing power of pacific ideas, which it would have been much better to examine.

These tendencies of the majority, known to the public, awakened the spirit of re-action.

A month had now elapsed since the 17th of March. Encouraged by the impassible moderation of the Provisional Government, the vanquished parties were already beginning to count their numbers and to vent their anger audibly. As for the Royalist press, it took advantage of the impunity which it had enjoyed from

* "A Year of Revolution in Paris," vol. i. p. 338.
† "History of the Provisional Government," by M. Elias Regnault, "Chef de Cabinet" of the Minister of the Interior at that time, p. 247.

the first to attack, insult, and calumniate incessantly, and to denounce to the execration of the present and future age, the authority of those very men who, it well knew, were resolved to respect the presence of liberty even in the persons of their calumniators.

On the other hand, the representatives of the working men's corporations were waiting with an increasing but justifiable impatience to see the Government take their sufferings in hand. They reproached a Government born of a Revolution with shrinking from a problem, the solution of which was the be all and the end all of the Revolution itself; and when they turned their eyes to the rural and provincial populations half sunk in darkness, they began to fear that, after all, their hopes and aspirations might be lost in the ballot urns beneath the overwhelming numbers of votes emerging from ignorance, chance, pressure, intimidation, or intrigue. It was felt to be urgent therefore, to sustain and encourage the Provisional Government with unequivocal demonstrations of sympathy, and at the same time to impel them to take a generous initiative, and remind them that among their manifold anxieties, *how to destroy pauperism* ought to hold the first place.

Such was the state of things, when I received a letter from M. Guinard, who was second in command to General Courtais in the National Guard, informing me that the Staff of the National Guard was in process of formation; and that it had been thought expedient to include in it fourteen officers belonging to the working class. All that now remained was to proceed at once to the election of these fourteen officers by their comrades.

It appeared to me that this occurrence afforded a favourable opportunity of proving to the majority of the Council that, in pressing upon them the solution of questions having reference to the improvement of the working classes, I was really the organ of a popular desire, and one which proceeded from a want acutely felt.

It was therefore agreed between the delegates of the Luxembourg and myself, that, after electing the fourteen officers who were to form part of the staff, the workmen should proceed in good order, as on the 17th of March, towards the Hôtel de Ville, to carry to the Provisional Government at once the expression of their wishes, and that of their sympathies—the latter to be testified by a patriotic offering.

This is undeniable; it is proved in the *Moniteur*,[*] on the face of the petition the working men were to present at the Hôtel de Ville. It was as follows :—

"Citizens, the re-action raises its head; calumny, the favourite weapon of unprincipled and dishonourable men, is on all sides assailing with its venemous falsehoods the true friends of the people. It is for us, the men of the Revolution, men of action and devotedness, to declare to the Provisional Government that the people decree the Democratic Republic; that the people desire the abolition of man's servitude to man; that the people desire the organisation of labour by associa-

---

[*] *Moniteur* of the 17th of April, 1848.

tion. ' *Vive la République ! Vive le Gouvernement Provisoire !* ' "

The concluding words which summed up, as it
were, the spirit of the petition—the recommendation
to the working men to assemble unarmed—the associated offering brought by many poor men to the
Commonwealth—the preconcerted measures to prevent
persons alien to the manifestation from attempting, as
on the 17th of March, to alter its character and its
object—all these evidences prove beyond dispute, that
it was very far from the design of the assembled
working men to overthrow a part of the Government.
They simply demanded the organisation of labour on
associative principles; but it was this that the enemies
and the false friends of the Revolution equally feared
and detested.

As far as I was concerned, I acted in all this with
such perfect candour and openness of purpose, that, on
the 14th of April, two days before the manifestation
was to take place, I went to the Council for the express
purpose of informing my colleagues of what was going
on, and apprising them that the operatives were about
to present a petition which would remove every doubt,
on their part, of the moral necessity of attending to
this measure, without which the Republic would be
but an empty word and a fraud. I added that, at all
events, there was nothing to apprehend from this
demonstration; that it would be quite as pacific as that
of the 17th of March; that every precaution was taken
to prevent disorders, and that the pass-word given to
the working men was " Long live the *Provisional*

Government," without distinction of majority or minority.
But, alas! I must say it, these assurances had not the
effect I intended. The idea of a wish emanating from
the people, and expressed in a calm, respectful, and
even sympathising manner, but expressed on behalf of
views which found no favour with them, frightened
MM. de Lamartine, Marrast, and Marie, causing them
more fear than they would have felt at the idea of
an armed attack; and they resolved to leave no stone
unturned to deprive the demonstration of its moral
effect.

The surest way to achieve this, was to make the *bourgeoisie* believe that the intended procession of operatives
was connected with a communist conspiracy, and more
especially with M. Blanqui, to whom the kind of
mystery with which it was his study to envelop himself
imparted the proportions of an enormous scarecrow.

M. Marrast, in consequence, made himself very busy
in circulating the gloomy intelligence throughout the
National Guard, that it was the intention of the operatives to overthrow the Provisional Government on the
16th of April; that the movement had a communist
character, and that the chiefs of the revolt were MM.
Cabet and Blanqui.

If ever fable were absurd, it was this.

In the first place, M. Cabet was a man opposed to
all insurrectionary violence, not only from temperament,
but on principle; nor could there be any misapprehension on this point in Paris, because on the second day
of the Revolution of February he had placarded every
wall in the metropolis with the following proclamation,

which some of my readers it is possible will not peruse
without astonishment, especially such of them as have
been designedly and mendaciously imbued with the
opinion that the Communists were men of violence :—

"Let us rally round the Provisional Government
presided over by Dupont de l'Eure, and which replaces
the odious government so recently stained with the
blood of citizens.

"Let us support this Provisional Government, which
declares itself republican and democratic : which adopts
fraternity, equality, and liberty for its principles, and
the People for its device and watchword : and which
dissolves the Chambers to convoke the National
Assembly, whose office it will be to give to France the
constitution she demands.

"But let us take care ourselves constantly to insist
upon the consequences of these principles.

"Let us demand that all Frenchmen be declared
brethren ; equal in duties and in rights without any
kind of privilege : all members of the National Guard :
all electors and eligible to all the public functions,
without any vile pecuniary conditions.

"Let us demand the natural and imprescriptible
right of association, of meeting, and of discussion :
individual liberty without the arbitrary control of any
man : the liberty of the press without hindrance,
without caution-money, or stamp.

"Let us especially demand the guarantee of all the
rights and all the interests of working-men : the formal
recognition of the right to live working, so that the
father of a family be no more reduced to the terrible

necessity of abandoning his wife and his children to go and die fighting.

" Let us demand the organisation of labour, and the assurance of a fair livelihood by fair work.

" Let us demand the suppression of all taxes on objects of primary necessity.

" Let us demand the abolition of those humiliating, vexatious, and iniquitous contrivances,—the Customs and the *Octroi* (taxes levied on provisions brought into towns).

" Let us demand for the people a system of education, gratuitous, common to all, real and complete.

" Let us demand institutions and guarantees for the happiness of wives and children, so that every man may have a chance of marrying with a prospect of being able to rear up his family in happiness and comfort.

" Faithful to our principles of fraternity, humanity, and moderation, let us always proclaim, and in all places—no vengeance ! no disorder ! no violence ! no oppression towards any person ! but firmness, vigilance, and prudence, that we may obtain justice for all !

" No attack upon property, but unshaken perseverance in requiring all measures consistent with justice for the suppression of pauperism, and especially, as one of these, the democratic policy of gradually abating inequality.

" Let us beware of demanding the immediate application of our communist doctrines. We have never ceased to affirm that we desire their triumph through discussion only, through conviction, through the power

of public opinion, by individual consent, and by the
national will.

"CABET.*

"PARIS, *25th February.*"

So much for the Communist conspiracy. As to the
part so cleverly assigned to M. Blanqui, the better to
frighten the *bourgeoisie,* it is necessary to know that
there never was anything in common between the
delegates of the Luxembourg and M. Blanqui.

As to myself personally, I repeat I never had with
him any kind of relation, either direct or indirect; and
I was the less inclined to make his acquaintance,
because the recent discovery of a document, until
then unknown, had drawn upon him, precisely at that
moment, the suspicions of a considerable portion of the
Republican party, and of that portion amongst which I
reckoned my best friends. The document in question
was a paper addressed to the government of Louis
Philippe, containing a minute disclosure of all that had
occurred in a secret society of which M. Blanqui was
one, together with M. Barbès, Martin-Bernard, Raisan,
Lamieussens, and others. This paper was no sooner
published in the "*Revue Rétrospective,*" by M. Tas-
chereau, into whose hands it had fallen, than an accusing
cry instantly burst out against M. Blanqui. MM.
Barbès, Martin-Bernard, Lamieussens, and Raisan,
declared that, except themselves, M. Blanqui was the
only person who could have knowledge of the facts

* This is extracted from M. Cabet's proclamation, which will be found
in Countess d'Agoult's *Histoire de la Révolution de* 1848, par Daniel Stern,
vol. ii. pp. 409—411.

stated in the document, and the impression left by the
whole of the circumstances upon their minds and
numbers of others, was that he must be the author.
Called upon to explain, M. Blanqui kept out of sight
for a few days, and then published a defence that did
not appear conclusive, and gave rise to a jury of
honour, which was empowered to acquit or condemn
him after due enquiry.

All this took place in the week preceding the 16th of
April, and it is easy to conceive that I, the intimate
friend of M. Barbès, for whom I have as high an esteem
as I ever felt for any man, was not at all disposed to
any acquaintance with one against whom M. Barbès
had brought an accusation still unsifted.

Taken for granted then, that M. Blanqui was inimi-
cally inclined against a part of the Provisional Government, it was surely a singular abuse of public credulity
to mix up his name with the peaceful step which the
operatives were about to take.   I have already remarked
on the strong interest which they, who desired at any
price to   prevent the effect of a petition presented
in favour of the organisation of labour by 100,000
working-men, had in producing a huge confusion of
ideas in the public mind.

A very extraordinary thing is—which no one suspected at the time, and to which I will revert more at
length presently—that, on the 15th of April, the eve
of the very day when the procession was to take place,
M. Blanqui, whom I only knew by name, but who was
everywhere described as my accomplice, as the man
with whom the majority of the Government was soon

to come into collision, as the arch conspirator against whom "M. de Lamartine was *expected to save society,*" had a secret interview—with whom? With me? No. With M. de Lamartine! *

Now, while this was going on, M. Marrast was putting the Hôtel de Ville into a state of defence, as if there were a question of sustaining a siege, giving military instructions to Colonel Rey, and placing at his disposal two battalions of the " *Garde Mobile,*" recently equipped.

This is not all. In the night of the 15th of April, M. Ledru Rollin was beset by a number of persons, at the Ministère de l'Intérieur, who, by dint of talking to him about the supposed projects of M. Blanqui, making use of that person's name as a sort of bugbear, and also by frightening him at the increased ascendency of the Luxembourg, succeeded in impelling him to a step, of which the consequences were much to be regretted, and have, I believe, been deeply regretted by himself since. As minister of the Interior, he exclusively had the right of assembling the National Guard, by ordering the *rappel,* that is, ordering the drums to beat to arms. Deceived by the false rumours with which they had artfully gorged him, he gets up at day-break on the 16th of April, runs to M. de Lamartine to consult with him on the event which was in preparation, and, then, persuaded by the latter, decides on giving orders for the *rappel.*

At this signal, the National Guard rushed out, fully

* The particulars of this interview will be given further on.

armed, to the Hôtel de Ville, and there waited with the intention of forcibly resisting the working men, who, in the meantime, peaceably assembled in the Champ de Mars, thought of nothing but the collection which they were then making amongst themselves, as an offering to the Provisional Government.

It had been arranged that on the 16th of April, a Council at which all the members of the Government should assist, was to be held at the Ministry of Finance, in the Rue Rivoli. To our great surprise, M. de Lamartine was missing. We learned that he had gone on to the Hôtel de Ville, and we thought it our duty to follow him. As we did not go in a body, I walked with my colleague Albert.

What then had happened in the meanwhile? In his *Letter to Ten Departments*, M. de Lamartine relates that, at six in the morning, certain zealous individuals had come to warn him that the Clubs had passed the night in deliberation, and declared themselves *en permanence*; that a Committee of Public Safety had been proclaimed, consisting of a few members of the Provisional Government, nominated without their privity or consent, and of certain agitators whose names were invested at that moment with a sort of power out of doors; that these clubs and their affiliations were about to march at the head of the working men assembled in the Champ de Mars to elect their officers, to lead them to the Hôtel de Ville, and there effect the overthrow of the existing government.*

* *Moniteur* of the 17th of April, 1848.

Strange news, indeed! Here were thousands of working men accused of furnishing an army of conspirators against the Government; and every man of this army had left his musket at home! These factious and violent men who were coming to besiege the Hôtel de Ville, were bringing a patriotic offering in a car! These insurgents who had resolved to overthrow the Government, concluded the petition which they came to submit, with the words *Vive le Gouvernement Provisoire.*

No; it is not true that the working men had been convoked with any design of conspiracy, or that the Government was exposed, on that day, to the slightest risk. What *is* true is, that the counter-revolution which was then hiding everywhere, even in the corridors of the Hôtel de Ville, was interested in transforming a hundred thousand peaceful petitioners into a hundred thousand conspirators, in order to afford a pretext for the violent intervention of the National Guard. At all hazards, it was determined to destroy the impression created by the 17th of March, and, the better to succeed in doing this, what could be more simple than to confront unarmed operatives with an armed force? But for this, the *rappel* must be sounded on some pretext or other. Now, the pretext was no other than the artfully spread rumours of a vast conspiracy, of the creation of a Committee of Public Safety, and of the intended overthrow of the Provisional Government.

The fact is, that after the 16th of April, I made a formal demand that an official inquiry should be in-

stituted into this plot of which so much had been said.
This demand, supported by M. Ledru Rollin, was accorded, and M. Landrin was commissioned to prosecute
the inquiry. We charged him to make a full and
searching inquiry into the pretended plots of these
pretended conspirators. I felt perfectly certain beforehand that the result would be to unmask an intrigue of
the counter-revolutionary party. And the result of the
inquiry was, that the revolutionary conspiracy of the
16th of April proved to be a false alarm, to say nothing
worse.

To tell the whole truth, the pretended panic concealed a real distrust. What was secretly but actually
dreaded was, the ascendancy of the Luxembourg Commission, the moral effect of a second 17th of March,
the spectacle of a demonstration all the more imposing for being a peaceful one, the review, in short,
of the forces of Socialism.

Such is the true meaning of the measures taken by
M. de Lamartine on the morning of the 16th of April,
and which would have been of no significance, had not
M. Ledru Rollin, deluded by false reports, ordered the
rappel to be beaten.

How shall I describe my grief, and that of Albert,
when, on our approach to the Hôtel de Ville, we beheld
the Place de Grève bristling with bayonets, and the
Hotel itself converted into a fortress! Why, we asked
ourselves, all this warlike preparation? Against what
and whom these threatening preparations? Was it
against these poor working-men who were, at that very
moment, bringing to the Government a patriotic offer-

ing, collected from their last centimes? Was it against these unarmed petitioners who, with the cry "*Vive La République!*" on their lips, were coming respectfully to present as sacred and legitimate a demand as ever men made?

A mysterious Committee of Public Safety had been talked of, and Blanqui had been named; but even if it were true that a knot of agitators had conspired to overthrow the majority in the Council, how could they succeed without the aid of the working-men assembled in the Champ de Mars? Now, we knew well that this aid had not so much as been asked for; why then, and against whom, were these warlike preparations?

Gloomy and bitter was the anxiety of Albert and myself as we entered the Hôtel de Ville. It presented a singular spectacle. Distrust was manifest in every face, and vague foreboding. Some were rushing about in wild excitement; others, rooted to the spot and aghast, regarded with a sort of stupor this causeless agitation.

Wading through the ebb and flow of armed men who flooded the staircases and passages, we penetrated into the Council-room, where we found M. de Lamartine engaged in writing. To the observations we addressed to him, he replied, not as he has since supposed, "*with an air of proud and ill-disguised anger,*" * but, on the contrary, with extreme politeness, and that reserve which the character of the two men who addressed him was entitled to produce. For he knew us both well.

* See his History of the French Revolution, vol. ii.

Nor did anything occur on this occasion to justify the boasts of M. de Lamartine to Lord Normanby, as revealed by the latter in the following passage:— "Lamartine recommended silence to M. Louis Blanc, as, if he provoked him to speak, he might find that he knew things which he would wish concealed, and M. Louis Blanc submitted, without reply, to the insinuation." *

Why and to what degree this was impossible, will be presently seen, when we come to explain who the person was who had an interest in concealment!

During that time, unknown persons were going about the city spreading rumours, ingeniously calculated, to create commotion. About mid-day, a man rushed to the Luxembourg, reporting that I had been stabbed at the club de l'Hippodrome; and before he could be questioned, the lying newsmonger had made off. Almost at the same moment, we heard that a messenger on horseback was riding hurriedly through the Faubourg du Temple, with the news that I had been assassinated. The drummers, who were beating the *rappel* in the Faubourg St. Marceau, were telling the same story aloud. A cry passed through the streets, "The Luxembourg is threatened;" and hereupon followed a movement and trepidation which might have led to the greatest disasters. A company of brave students ran to the Luxembourg, to offer their services, and remained on guard there till the Tuesday evening. Presently, the Committee of the Société des

* A Year of Revolution in Paris, vol. i. p. 326.

Droits de l'Homme, sent word that several permanent guards had been established in the eleventh and twelfth *arrondissements,* and that, at the first signal, 3,000 men, armed, would occupy the Court of the Palace.

In another quarter of Paris, in the Champ de Mars, emissaries had secretly received orders to stir up the working-classes, and to turn a peaceful demonstration into a revolt. The *mot d'ordre* was, "Ledru Rollin has been hanged, and Louis Blanc assassinated"*—an execrable provocation to civil war, which might indeed have been only too successful, if, fortunately, the delegates of the Luxembourg had not been on the spot!

The Hôtel de Ville, as I have already described, had been turned into a fortress, and was defended by the National Guard with fixed bayonets. When the trade-companies approached the Place de Grève, in the same order of procession, and with the same peaceful air as on the 17th of March, the National Guard barred their passage, and it was with great difficulty that even their delegates were able to reach the Hôtel de Ville. I was there with my colleagues in the Council-room, when the door was opened, and a voice announced that the delegates of the companies had made their appearance; that they talked of appealing from the insult that had been offered them, to the indignation of the people; and insisted violently on seeing me. I instantly hastened to meet them, followed by one of my colleagues,

---

* *Gazette des Tribunaux* of the 24th of March; "Trial at Bourges;" Declaration of Klein.

M. Crémieux, and we found them certainly in a state of inexpressible indignation. "What!" they exclaimed with vehemence, when they perceived me, "we come here to assure the Government of our sympathy and support; we come without arms to express our wishes; we come preceded by a car, bearing the offering of our last resources to the wants of the Republic; and we are received as conspirators, and we are barred access to the Place de Grève! And to the deputies of the people, the agents of the Mayor of Paris offer nothing but an insulting reception!"

These indignant exclamations were but too well justified; nevertheless, I did my best to calm them with conciliatory words. Attributing to the false rumours that had been spread the motive of these insulting preparations, and of the reception which they so bitterly inveighed against, I made every effort to divert from the Provisional Government a responsibility that might have led to civil war. As the delegates demanded why the working-men were prevented from defiling in procession in front of the Hôtel de Ville, I summoned Colonel Rey, and gave him orders to make every arrangement for facilitating the demonstration. It was necessary to clear a way through the files of the National Guards who lined the Place de Grève; and I recommended Colonel Rey to clear a passage along the front of the Hôtel de Ville. But every legal attempt at conciliation was defeated by the ill-will which was secretly encouraged by the obscure emissaries of the Mayor of Paris, hidden in the crowd. The working-men, *all unarmed*, were obliged to defile between two compact masses of National Guards, *fully armed*, in a long and narrow line, which, moreover, was designedly intercepted every few minutes, in order to deprive it of its naturally imposing effect. As I stood with my colleagues at a window of the Hôtel de Ville, I looked from a distance at thousands of hats raised in the air, thousands of arms waving a salute; but the cries of affectionate enthusiasm and fraternal hopefulness from these working-men scarcely reached our ears, interrupted as they were by a cry of hate, the first which the counter-revolutionary party had raised as yet: "*A bas les Communistes!*"

After the procession had passed, and when the National Guard had almost imperceptibly dispersed, an immense crowd of people invaded the Place de Grève, and took possession of every inch of the square. Let me describe the scene that ensued, in the words of the *Moniteur* :—

"About five o'clock, on a rumour that the lives of certain members of the Provisional Government had been threatened, an immense crowd surrounded the Hôtel de Ville, and demanded loudly to see them. As soon as they caught sight of them at one of the windows, the people testified their joy with loud acclamations. Among the deputations, there was one which had come all the way from the Commune d'Ivry, impelled by the same anxiety. They entered unarmed, and earnestly called for citizen Louis Blanc. On his appearance before them, the deputation greeted his presence with enthusiasm." *

* *Moniteur* of the 17th of April, 1848.

Such was the partial disappointment of those who had fondly calculated on the effect of false alarms. But they had at least succeeded in troubling the demonstration—a sorry attempt indeed, which but for the accident of the *rappel* being beaten by mistake, must have altogether miserably failed.

It was now night. Of all the members of the Government, none continued at the Hôtel de Ville, save my colleague M. Flocon, and myself. On the Place de Grève, a few belated groups only remained of all that tumultuous multitude. Yet the cry, "Death to the Communists," still resounded all the clearer and louder as the crowd diminished; and M. Flocon made a remark to me which threw a gloomy light on the passing events. "Do you see," he said to me, pointing out, as he spoke, about a hundred ill-looking men who stood with their backs against the railing of the Hôtel de Ville, "do you see these men? They have been there since the morning. I have observed them attentively, and I have no doubt at all that they belong to some private police. That green-spectacled individual whom you perceive in the centre of the group, is their chief, and it is at a signal given by him that their cries are uttered."

All of a sudden, we heard a sound of drums. It was a legion of National Guards approaching by torchlight. I went down to the Place with M. Flocon, to see them pass, and I noticed that the individuals ranged against the railing, kept up those shouts of death and hatred, which were to echo throughout Paris. I walked straight up to one of the wretches, and said sharply to him : " Why do these men whose death you cry for, deserve to die ? " He stammered out that he knew nothing about it, that he cried out because he was ordered to do so ; and then disappeared in the crowd. M. Flocon asked a similar question, and (if I am not mistaken), got the same reply.

Such was the first campaign of the counter-revolution against Socialism.

On the following day, the delegates of the Luxembourg, moved by a generous and natural indignation, carried to the Hôtel de Ville the following protest, an historical document of the highest importance.*

" CITIZENS,—

" Our demonstration yesterday, has given rise to counter-revolutionary manœuvres, and to a thousand false reports ; and even, to-day, it is described in certain journals with the most dangerous and absurd commentaries.

" On the other hand, the false rumours which preceded our arrival before the Hôtel de Ville yesterday, occasioned a misunderstanding which it is our duty to explain as clearly as possible.

" We begin by affirming on our honour, that the one sole object of our assembling in the Champ de Mars, to proceed thence to the Hôtel de Ville, was as follows :—

" 1. To elect fourteen from amongst us to form part of the staff of the National Guard.

" 2. To prove that the ideas of organisation of

* *Moniteur* of the 19th of April, 1848.

labour and of association, so courageously upheld by
the men who have devoted themselves to our cause,
are the chief objects of the people; and that, in their
opinion, the Revolution of February would be abortive,
if it did not result in putting an end to the servitude of man to man (*à l'exploitation de l'homme par
l'homme*).

" 3. Finally, to offer to the Provisional Government,
after having expressed our wants, the support of our
patriotism against the reactionists.

"These were our intentions, clearly enough expressed on the banners of our corporations, in the
text of the petition presented by our deputies at the
Hôtel de Ville, and no less unmistakeably evinced by
the unalterable calmness of our attitude, and by the
offering brought by us to the Provisional Government
of the Republic.

" How is it then that the National Guard had received an extraordinary summons to assemble in arms
as on a day of danger? How is it that, before the
arrival of our representatives and friends, citizens
Louis Blanc and Albert, our delegates, encountered
a reception that had all the appearance of hostility ?

" We know the reason, and we will here declare
it :—

"Precisely because they were well aware how calm,
how thoroughly republican and in favour of the popular
Revolution of February, this demonstration of ours was
to be, the reactionists first spread the rumour that we
intended to overthrow the Provisional Government for
the advantage of citizen Blanqui; so as to excite

against us all those who see in the existence of the Provisional Government a guarantee of order and of liberty.

" At the same time, the emissaries of the reaction went hawking about the monstrous calumny that citizens Louis Blanc and Blanqui had encouraged us to sever with violence (*à scinder violemment*) the Provisional Government : a calumny against which we protest with all the strength of our heartfelt indignation.

" Had we been desirous of overthrowing the Provisional Government, we should not have assembled in the Champ de Mars, unarmed ; we should have taken measures to meet, not to the number of 100,000, as we did yesterday, but to the number of 200,000, as we easily might have done.

" Finally, we should not have made amongst us the collection which we carried to the Hôtel de Ville, nor have concluded our petition with these words—' *Vive le Gouvernement Provisoire.*'

" It is well we should declare this in the face of all.

" We deem it right, moreover, to denounce as a proof of the manœuvres employed by certain agents of the reaction, the spreading of a report of an attempt on the life of citizen Louis Blanc—a report spread, without doubt, with the intention of creating disorder; fortunately, however, we knew it at once to be false, and its only effect was to prove to all how intimate and profound is the union, in spite of all the reactionists may say, of the people and of the men in whom the people put their trust.

"We wish it to be well known, therefore, that there was no real cause for alarm, yesterday. The people know their strength, and can afford to be calm. They are ready to defend the Revolution, according to their sense of what it ought to be; under their safeguard, it will not perish.

"We confide this Protest to the Provisional Government, and we pray them to make it public.

"PARIS, 17th April, 1848.

"The Delegates of the Trade-companies,
"LAGARDE, President of the Central Committee,
"DUMOND, GODIN, Vice-presidents,
"A. LEFAURE, Secretary."

Although this vigorous protest amounted to a formal condemnation of the proceedings resorted to by MM. de Lamartine and Marrast, neither of them dared to object to its being officially published, and it appeared in the *Moniteur* of the 19th of April, where any one may find it.

The 16th of April had not completely answered the expectations of the men who had so imprudently sown the seeds of hatred and discord; but the parties vanquished in February had recovered their voice, and were evidently preparing for bolder attempts.

It was, therefore, urgent to repair as much as possible the evil already accomplished, by adopting energetic measures, calculated to act strongly upon public opinion, and to prove that the Revolution was still living, that it had its eye upon its enemies, and that it was determined neither to abdicate nor to yield.

Hence the appearance of several decrees in the *Moniteur* of the 19th April, which were clearly designed to strengthen the action of the Revolution; hence the official warning indicating under what regulations strictly enforced, the right of having the *rappel* beaten was to be placed henceforth, seeing that the unseasonable and irregular beating of the *rappel* " was likely to create trouble in the city, to spread alarm among the public, to injure trade, labour, and industry, and to harass the National Guard uselessly;" and hence, finally, a proclamation which I myself drew up, and which was couched in the following unequivocal terms.

" Convinced that the rights of the human conscience are sacred and inviolable; that among true Republicans, there cannot exist any other contest than discussion, generous and free; that the union of minds is sure to follow close upon the union of hearts; that none but the enemies of the Republic can be interested in spreading distrust, and in provoking dissensions by party denominations which are readily construed into personal enmities;

" The Provisional Government declare that they disapprove, in the most formal manner, of all cries of provocation, of all appeals to discord among citizens, of all attacks upon the independence of peaceful opinions.

" The Government who have inscribed *Fraternity* on the national flag, cannot but be a tutelary and conciliatory authority. The cry they delight to hear, and of which they will be always found ready to give the signal, is a cry of generous victory, a cry of liberty, a cry of hope; it is that saving cry, 'VIVE LA RÉPUBLIQUE !' " *

This proclamation, written by my hand, was signed by all the members of the Provisional Government, and met with no opposition, either from M. de Lamartine or M. Marrast.

The attitude assumed on the morning of the 16th of April by the Provisional Government, astounded the counter-revolutionary factions, and for a few days held them in check ; but, at the sound of that fatal *rappel*, they had risen, and from that time they never ceased to conspire. The result was soon to come ; we know it now too well !

I have already mentioned that, on the eve of the 16th of April, M. de Lamartine had a secret interview with the reputed arch-contriver of plots, M. Blanqui. M. Albert, having become acquainted with the fact, came and told me of it at the Luxembourg. On my expressing my doubts of the possibility of this being true, he proposed to me to go to the Council, engaging to prove it before M. de Lamartine's face. Accordingly, I went with him. As soon as we took our seats, M. Albert, in a plain straightforward way, said to M. de Lamartine : " Sir, you have seen Blanqui." Everybody in the Council looked perfectly astonished. Confused for a moment, but immediately recovering himself, M. de Lamartine smiled, and answered in a light nonchalant way : " Ah ! quite true, I had forgotten to tell you, gentlemen. Well, after all, this Blanqui

* *Moniteur* of the 19th of April.

they make such a terrible fuss about, is really a capital fellow ! "

That there was an interview, and that it took place at this very significant and important date, the 15th of April, will be placed beyond possibility of doubt by the following extract from the evidence tendered at the trial of Blanqui and others before the High Court of Bourges, when accused of having taken part in the attack upon the National Assembly on the 15th of May, 1848.

M. de Lamartine, appearing as a witness, was thus examined by M. Blanqui :

"Is it true that you came to me, as reported by some newspapers, wearing a cuirass, as though I had been a bravo ? "

CITIZEN LAMARTINE.—" I must say that at this time I was not acquainted with Citizen Blanqui. The strong prejudice against him, which, as he has told you, produced its effect a little later, was shared, to a certain extent, by me.   I knew Citizen Blanqui only as a man of remarkable character and intelligence. I happened to be acquainted with Citizen Deflotte, a retired naval officer, who was intimate with Blanqui, and, I believe, a member of his club.   I begged him frankly to tell me without reservation what he thought of Blanqui ; if so fine an intelligence were not weary of bloody revolutions, and of being condemned to be incessantly whirling in the vortex of agitation. Deflotte replied that I was under a serious misapprehension ; that Blanqui was animated by the best feelings, of which I could easily convince myself by an interview with him.

"A few days afterwards, Citizen Blanqui came to see me, and with a smile on his face; I went up to him, and giving him my hand, said in allusion to the absurd reports spread by the newspapers: 'Well! Citizen Blanqui, have you come to assassinate me?' I took him into my study, where we had a conversation that lasted three hours, of the most interesting kind on the part of M. Blanqui. We passed in review every matter of serious import that was then engaging attention.

"I feel it right to say that, upon all these points, property, the family, the necessity for a strong and undivided government, the necessity of concentrating all power in the National Assembly, and of respecting and enforcing respect to the National Assembly, the result of universal suffrage the expression of the popular will, I was happy to hear from Citizen Blanqui sound ideas brilliantly expressed.

"And yet he was not under any constraint whatever; we conversed upon perfectly equal terms. I had on my side moral force; he had on his, the power of public agitation. The result of this conversation was to leave upon me a favourable impression, and to inspire me with just esteem for the intentions and character of Citizen Blanqui."

THE PROCUREUR.—"What was the date of this conversation?"

CITIZEN BLANQUI.—"The 15th of April."

CITIZEN LAMARTINE.—"I think Citizen Blanqui is in error; it was some time before this."

CITIZEN BLANQUI.—"I beg pardon; permit me to

recall a fact to you, which will refresh your recollection. In the course of our conversation, an allusion was made to an article against me which had just appeared in the *Revue Retrospective.*"

CITIZEN LAMARTINE.—" True."

CITIZEN BLANQUI.—" Well, my reply to that was on the 13th of April."

CITIZEN LAMARTINE.—" Yes, but it was not yet printed, which would throw our interview ten or twelve days back."

CITIZEN BLANQUI.—" My reply was not printed, but it was of the reply itself we were speaking.   Here is Flotte, at whose house I was lodging, who, if the jury would be good enough to hear his evidence, can clear up this point."

CITIZEN FLOTTE.—" It was Deflotte who desired me to tell Blanqui that you (Lamartine) would receive him; Blanqui went to your house on the morning of the 15th of April."

CITIZEN LAMARTINE.—" You are mistaken.   Had it been so, I must necessarily have spoken of what was to happen the next day, and must have endeavoured to divert him from having anything to do with it."

CITIZEN BLANQUI.—" Here is General Courtais, who by chance was made aware of this visit, and who can speak to it."

CITIZEN PRESIDENT.—" Speak, General."

CITIZEN COURTAIS.—" It was on the morning of the 15th, at six o'clock, that Blanqui went to Lamartine.   A person, who saw Blanqui enter, mentioned it to me the very same day. The next morning, on my receiving the order to beat to arms, and being told that Blanqui was at the head of the manifestation, I said to Marrast: 'But he was at Lamartine's yesterday!'"

CITIZEN LAMARTINE.—"*I am not mathematically certain of the correctness of what I state,* but my conviction is, that General Courtais is mistaken upon this point, which moreover is of no kind of importance." *

Whether it was of importance or not, the reader, who knows what use was made of M. Blanqui in the demonstration of the 16th of April, may now judge! And he may also judge, if there were a conspiracy, as Lord Normanby intimates on the authority of M. de Lamartine, who the conspirator must be.†

Certain it is that, a few days after the 16th of April, the majority of the Provisional Government (Albert and myself were by chance absent), having despatched an order for Blanqui's arrest to M. Caussidière, the prefect of police, this order, before it could be executed, was rescinded by a counter-order communicated through M. Landrin, attorney-general of the Republic; and the cause of its being rescinded was the "obstinate opposition" made to it by M. de Lamartine.‡

The facts are now under the reader's eyes. It is for him to draw the inference.

---

* Trial at Bourges before the High Court. Proceedings of the 19th of March, 1849.

† "A Year of Revolution in Paris," vol. i. p. 320.

‡ *Mémoires de Caussidière,* vol. ii. p. 51, where this fact and the counter-order will be found.

CHAPTER XV.

CALUMNIES.

AMONGST other fatal results of the 16th of April, was that of so emboldening the re-actionists, that, taking advantage of the unlimited liberty of the press, they converted calumny into a system, and then put this system in practice with unparalleled audacity.

Here is a specimen of the falsehoods with which the *Constitutionnel* crammed its columns :—

" *News of the Court.* A breakfast took place yesterday at the ' Petit Trianon.' There were ladies present. M. Ledru Rollin did the honours. There was a shooting-party at Chantilly ; a stag-hunt and battues in the Park of Apremont."

In answer to this, M. Ledru Rollin wrote the following letter to the *Constitutionnel* :—

" SIR,

" In office, as in opposition, I have always despised the foul personal calumnies of which I have been the object. It is only at such a price that a man can obey the dictates of his conscience. But I cannot overlook those slanders which are aimed at me as a public man, for then it is the honour of the Republic itself that is assailed. The day before yester-

day, you reported me as going out shooting at Ram-
bouillet; yesterday, under the head of *News of the
Court,* you spoke of me as being present at some female
orgies at Trianon, and as going out shooting at
Chantilly. The Court, I am well aware, is the dream
which is constantly haunting you; these dissipations
are those of the people you represent. As far as I am
concerned, you should know that, since the 24th of
February, I have not quitted Paris for a single instant;
that, out of every twenty-four hours, twenty have been
given up to work. If I have not done the people all
the good I could desire, the reasons must be searched
for in any other cause than that of any want of
assiduousness and zeal.

"LEDRU ROLLIN."

But, I repeat, calumny had become a system, and
each day was marked by some new invention. We
shall get an idea of the means employed against the
Provisional Government, from the following letter
addressed, about this time, to *La Réforme* newspaper :—

"CITIZEN,

"I have just been subjected to a singular
inquest. More than twenty persons have, this day,
called upon me to inquire if it were true that Citizen
Ledru Rollin had run up a bill with me of from 23
to 30,000 francs for jewellery. I replied, as the fact
really was, that the Minister of the Interior did not
owe me one farthing. Nevertheless, they went away
shrugging their shoulders, and with an incredulous
look which I could not at all make out. What

possible interest could these gentlemen have in ascertaining whether M. Ledru Rollin owes me anything or not?

"CROCE SPINELLI."

"12, Place de la Bourse."

After the resignation of the Provisional Government, the National Assembly appointed a Commission, consisting of men opposed to the Republic, to investigate its accounts. What was the result? Here it is, in the language of the Commission itself:—

"We unanimously affirm that, after a long and searching inquiry, conducted with the greatest impartiality, we have been unable to find the slightest trace of any irregularity on the part of the Provisional Government, or anything that could suggest the least suspicion of any malversation in administering the public moneys at their disposal." *

And yet, in 1848, the re-actionist papers talked of nothing else but of the immense sums of public money pilfered by the members of the Government, and sent over to England for investment! How is it possible to recall without deep disgust the accusations made by some anonymous libellers against M. Crémieux for having purchased a forest out of his spoliations; and that there was a moment when M. Lamartine, to silence some infamous insinuations, found it necessary to submit to the public a detail of his private affairs, and to introduce, as it were, the passer-by into the privacy

---

* Report, April 14, 1848, of the Commission appointed to examine into the accounts of the Provisional Government.

of his family? If certain people were to be believed, there could be no manner of doubt that M. Marrast, during his two months of office, had amassed an enormous fortune; and these base rumours would perhaps be in circulation even now, had he not replied in a manner, unhappily too decisive, by dying without leaving enough behind to bury him!

It will be anticipated that in this overflow of unjust attacks, the Luxembourg did not escape.

It was with the greatest effrontery asserted, that in assuming the title of *operative*, M. Albert had been tricking the public; that he was in fact a rich manufacturer, a millionnaire! And so pertinaciously did they persist in this falsehood, that M. Albert was obliged to publish the following particulars:—

" Albert, born in Bury (Oise) in 1815, son of a farmer, was apprenticed to one of his uncles, Citizen Ribou, machine maker, Rue Basse-des-Ursins, No. 21. Since which he has been employed by several persons, of whom we may mention Citizen Pecqueur, machine maker, near the Marché Popincourt; Citizen Margox, Rue Ménilmontant, No. 21; and finally, on the eve of the day on which the Republic was proclaimed, Citizen Albert was working as a mechanic in the button-making factory of Citizen Bapterouse, Rue de la Muette, No. 16, where his blouse and working trousers are still to be found."*

* *Moniteur*, May 5, 1848. Mr. Croker has also given currency to the story in England, that this M. Albert was a rich manufacturer, who had taken an important part in the troubles at Lyons, under Louis Philippe, and who was spoken of in my "*History of Ten Years.*" Unluckily for Mr. Croker he has confounded two different persons, who, although bearing the same name, were not in any way connected.

Of course I, too, was swimming in wealth, although I had never reaped from my incessant literary occupations, more than a bare competence. Will it be believed that, in Paris, where it was so easy to ascertain that I possessed neither house nor real property of any kind, the *Lampion* newspaper, from which other more influential journals at that time derived their calumnies, actually announced, that *I had forbidden the porter of my house in the Faubourg St. Germain to let rooms to working men, as I chose to have no other than rich tenants?*

I will not stop here to notice the really detestable way in which my enemies disfigured my views; now ascribing to me things I never had said ; now as studiously suppressing some essential part of what I did say. The principle I had broached, not indeed as capable of immediate application, but as the formula of philosophical truth, which ought one day to become a rule of social actions : " From each according to his faculties—to each according to his wants ; " was everywhere cited with the omission of the first part, that had reference to duty, and without noticing the high and comprehensive definition I had given of the word *wants ;* so that they might accuse me of seeking for the regeneration of society only in the bestial satisfaction of the grossest appetites, and of supposing I meant to elevate the condition of the people by simply fattening them. Now, strange inconsistency ! While some were levelling at me a reproach founded on a falsification, others, on the contrary, were representing me as a mind chimerical to excess, as a builder of castles in the air, as the apostle of a state of moral perfection, and impossible self-denial; because I had said that, in a well-organised society, the interest of each should be, as a consequence of good social institutions, combined with the interest of all!

One of the calumnies launched at the Luxembourg, and with all the more complacency as it tended to make Albert and myself obnoxious to the working men, accused us of being imitators of the luxury of Barras. They talked of our luxurious habits, our delicate refined tastes, our favourite dishes, our select epicurean suppers in those very drawing-rooms which the Lucullus of the Directory had chosen as the scene of his revels.

If ever lie were gross and audacious, this was. For, from the moment of our getting to the Luxembourg, we adopted a very frugal style of living, which would have looked like affectation but for the consideration that the greater part of the working men in communication with us were literally without bread. But the more impudent the imposture, the more did it gratify newspapers, unworthy of being named, to spread and accredit it.

All this excited our pity, nothing else. Why trouble ourselves about an accusation to whose shameful falsehood thousands of eye-witnesses could depose? Had we not made of the Luxembourg a palace of glass? Did not a delegate's card command the *entrée* to us, at any hour of the day and night? Were not the whole people, in the persons of their representatives, daily present at our meals? Besides, there are certain accusations and adversaries, on whom it is a sort of luxury to any honest man they have attacked, to revenge himself by contempt.

Our silence humiliated our detractors, but served them. Disdained by those it assaulted, greedily swallowed and propagated by those whose rancour had need of it, the calumny swept through the departments, where it could meet no contradiction; circulated in Royalist drawing-rooms, and entered into the mud and filth of libels.

But thanks be to Heaven, the triumph of what is unjust and vile, is only momentary. The *Constitutionnel* having one day made allusion to *our luxuriousness,* M. Génevay, then governor of the château of Versailles, and who was comptroller of the Luxembourg under the Provisional Government, wrote the following letter to the editor, which was inserted in that paper, on the 2nd of June, 1848 :—

"Appointed comptroller of the National Palace of the Luxembourg, when this residence was allotted by the Provisional Government to Citizens Louis Blanc and Albert, I think it a matter of honour and duty to protest in the strongest possible manner against a report that has unluckily found its way into various newspapers and other publications. It is pretended that Citizens Louis Blanc and Albert spent enormous sums on their table; this is either a misconception or a calumny. The first month, after much resistance on their part, the table of the two members of the Provisional Government was provided at the rate of six francs a-day each; but, on the second month, Citizens

Albert and Louis Blanc, finding the supply more than strictly necessary, would only sanction an expenditure of *two francs and a-half for their breakfast, and the same sum for their dinner.* The bills and receipts can be furnished at a moment's notice.

" I remain, Sir, &c.,

" A. GÉNEVAY."*

Many of my readers have heard, perhaps, of a pamphlet which appeared at the end of October, 1850, by one M. Tirel, entitled, " *The Republic in the King's Carriages.*" What the author calls the king's carriages were really nothing more than state carriages. Whether these were ever used by my colleagues I do not know, and never inquired. But it seems to me quite natural that, at a time when we reckoned by minutes, and when matters of the highest import made it necessary to go at a moment's notice from one end of Paris to the other, the carriages intended for the highest officers of state should be placed at their disposal, in the performance of their duties. As far as I am concerned, what I have to say on this subject, will be found in the following letter, written from London, 25th of October, 1850, to the Paris newspapers, and which, published by them, remained uncontradicted, no contradiction being possible :—

" SIR,

" In a pamphlet by a Monsieur Tirel, it is said that, while a member of the Provisional Government, I, for

---

* *Constitutionnel* of the 2nd of June, 1848.

the space of forty days, made use of a britska, known as *the colibri*. This is what the author calls *the Republic in the King's Carriages*. The assertion is entirely false. When at the Hôtel de Ville, I never went out except on foot or in a hackney coach. At the Luxembourg, the only carriage I used, when I had need of one, was a carriage attached to the Chamber of Peers, hired from Bryan, Rue Basse du Rempart.

" I have the honour, &c.,

" LOUIS BLANC."

I have mentioned the newspaper called *Le Lampion*. For in this workshop were the calumnies forged, to which the *Constitutionnel*, the *Assemblée Nationale*, and other papers of this kind, gave the support of their influence. Well, on the 31st of August, 1856, M. Charles Bataille published in the *Diogène* a biographical sketch of the actual editor of *Figaro*, the same who edited the *Lampion* in 1848; and this sketch, though otherwise favourable to the subject of it, contains this passage :—

" A raffish little journal was this *Lampion*, edited in a devilish spirit, always on the breach, snappish, worrying, raging-mad in the full sense of the word. Here was invented the famous tale of the *purée d'ananas*, or pine-apple sauce, relished by the members of the Provisional Government; there M. Marrast was made to steal the cradle of the Comte de Paris for the use of M. Marrast's son; there it was discovered that the Duchess of Orleans' finest cashmere served as a table-cloth for M. Louis Blanc, if I remember rightly ; there,

at all times and hours, was kept open a house of reception
for every mischievous suggestion, and every unbridled
invective ; women even, who certainly had nothing
to do with party rage, were not spared by this grossly
licentious policy. . . . . There are in the editor of the
Lampion's repertory two MOTS, of which I would not
certainly be the author for all the wit of Voltaire.
It was in June, 1848. A band of disarmed men was
passing along, escorted by a regiment of the line, and
followed by a carriage filled with the bayonets of the
insurgents. " *There go Père Duchesne's forks,*" * was
his bitter remark, as he saw these unfortunate people
pass. The same night, under the head of *Varieties,*
the *Lampion* contained these lines : " *The following
democratic order was found on the dead body of a
Socialist :* — ' *Good for three ladies of the Faubourg St.
Germain.*' While this ribaldry was being published,
blood was pouring forth in torrents in the four quarters
of Paris ! "

The journalist alluded to replied in the *Figaro*, of
which he is at present the editor, to this explicit and
bitter criticism ; and his reply, which I quote com-
formably to the text, is confined to this :—

" Heaven preserve me from wishing to galvanise into
life the extinct passions of a period, so near and yet so
far from us, in which, victors or vanquished, we have
all sinned in the way of exaggeration. But I must say
that, in the strife of civil war, the most culpable are

---

* Père Duchesne, it will be remembered, was the title of the paper conducted by the too notorious Hebert. The intention was to represent the
insurgents as a species of political cannibals using bayonets for forks.

surely not those who reply to acts of social savagery only with the artillery of witticisms." *

It would require too much space to mention all the murderous slanders which, owing to the unshakeable respect of the Provisional Government for the liberty of the press, found their way in the columns of the *Constitutionnel,* or other papers of this stamp, thence rolling and increasing, like snow-balls, through the whole of Europe.†

I will not dwell any longer on this mournful subject.

But, as I have unsparingly blamed the Provisional Government for what I think was wrong, I shall perhaps be pardoned for stating what I am sure was right.

Whatever opinion may be entertained of the views of which this Government was the representative, and deplorable as may have been the errors into which an extravagant distrust of the new ideas caused some of its members to fall, its passage across the stormy stage of the world will remain an imperishable *souvenir* of honesty of purpose, integrity, love of public good, and self-devotedness. I will not deny that the

---

* *Figaro,* of the 7th of September, 1856.

† The blood rushes to one's cheek, when one thinks that the *historical authorities*—which certain people have relied on, in their attacks upon the members of the Provisional Government, do rely upon to this hour, and will obstinately persist in doing so to-morrow—are creatures such as a Chenu, a Delahodde, a Mirecourt, whose real name is Jacquot, the two first police spies of the vilest stamp, and the third, viler still, if it be possible; a liar by profession, a jobber in calumny, branded and punished by various sentences of the *police correctionelle.*

difference of opinions amongst those who composed it, brought on collisions and misunderstandings which revealed infirmities that are incident to human nature; but still it is my firm conviction, that the Provisional Government, taking its acts as a whole, may challenge comparison with the best that has ever existed. When the clamours of party are silenced, history will say, that never, in the brief space of two months, did any government issue a greater number of decrees favourable to freedom, and stamped with more reverence for human dignity; that never did any government in the midst of an immense conflict of highly excited opinions and unchained passions, display a more even serenity, a prouder courage, a more unflinching confidence in the moral authority of its principles; that never did a government treat its enemies with more magnanimity, show greater horror at the spilling of blood, or more scrupulously abstain from violence of any kind; in a word, that never did a government so marvellously succeed in maintaining its position as long as it thought proper, at the summit of a society disturbed to its very depths, without having recourse to force, without employing courts, soldiers, or police, and without calling to its aid any other power than that of persuasion!

CHAPTER XVI.

THE ELECTIONS.

On the 20th of April, under the name of *La Fête de la Fraternité*, there took place a ceremony, half military and half civic, which strikingly exhibited the moral force possessed by the Republic in Paris.

The object of this festival being the distribution of new flags to the National Guard and the army, some detachments of cavalry and regiments of the line were brought back to Paris.

At seven in the morning, more than two hundred thousand citizens, of the working or middle class, were on foot in uniforms of the National Guard; and the troops of the line, together with the "Garde Mobile," amounted to not less than 100,000 men. The streets were choked with crowds of people. At one of the extremities of the Champs Elysées there had been erected in the form of an amphitheatre, faced with seats, an immense scaffolding resting at one end on the "Arc de Triomphe de l'Étoile." The Provisional Government reached it at about nine o'clock, amid a salute of 21 guns, from a battery at the *Hippodrome*. The members of the government took their place on the first rank, M. Dupont (de l'Eure) seated in the centre. Behind them stood a brilliant staff, magistrates in full dress, and high officers of state. On each side of the scaffolding were two great orchestras, making the air resound with patriotic tunes. Above it, under the arch itself, in a second amphitheatre especially appropriated to them, was a group of ladies elegantly dressed, each holding in her hand a bouquet tied with tricoloured ribbons, who crowned the whole scene as with a garland of flowers.

The colonels of the different corps were ranged in a semicircle at the foot of the scaffolding. At ten o'clock, M. Arago, the standard of the Republic in his hand, rose, and addressing himself to them, said, with a voice expressive at once of emotion and pride:—"Colonels, in the name of the Republic, we take God and men to witness that you swear fidelity to its flag." The colonels replied, raising their swords, "We swear. Long live the Republic!" Then the cannon thundered, blending its roar with revolutionary hymns, and the troops began to defile.

The air was mild, the sky cloudy; but from time to time, a ray of sunshine, escaping through the clouds, threw a glittering light on the moving forest of bayonets which bristled through the whole length of the great avenue of the Champs Elysées. This prodigious mass of armed men marching in good order, though with enthusiasm, the garlands with which the mouths of the cannons were wreathed, the lilacs and hawthorn which waved from the ends of the muskets, the patriotic or joyous songs which almost drowned the beating of the drums, the absence of all constraint, the elect of the people presenting themselves to them with confidence, and the image of war summoned to do homage to that of fraternity, formed a spectacle of grandeur of which no description could convey an adequate idea.

As each legion, detachment, or corps, reached the " Arc de l'Étoile," the colonel or officer in command went up on the platform, where the Members of the Provisional Government, by turns, presented him with a flag, saying, " In the name of God and of the people, swear ever to defend this flag which the Republic confides to you." The officer replied, " I swear. Long live the Republic ! " He then took the flag, returned to his post, gave the order to march; and then the soldiers, detaching the flowers from their muskets, threw them in passing at the feet of the Representatives of the nation, as an act of homage to its sovereignty.

Ah ! it is all very well for Lord Normanby to devote a few hesitating and chilly sentences to this superb burst of feeling on the part of a great people; it is very well for him to pretend that the reception the Provisional Government met with, on reaching the platform, " struck him as very cold ; " it is all very well for him to write, " I should not say from anything I myself saw, that there was much enthusiasm ; " while at the same time he acknowledges, " but I hear that others in different points of the line of march, returned with a more favourable impression." * I affirm, on my side, that never was there, in any

* " A Year of Revolution in Paris," vol. i. p. 335.

country, at any epoch, a burst of feeling exceeding that which, on this memorable day, sent up the shout of "Long live the Republic!" in one spontaneous chorus of 300,000 voices: and, on this subject, the witness I call in refutation of Lord Normanby, is the whole of Paris. What soul was there, in those moments, unhappily too fleeting, that did not melt? What face, that was not pale with emotions of an heroic kind? Party hatred was for an instant forgotten; dislikes and resentments for awhile put aside; petty ambitions and rivalries silenced by mutual shame. It was—I here appeal to the recollection of a whole population—it was, for all, a day of good feeling, of sympathetic meeting, of concord, and of hope.

As was the case with each of my colleagues, I received the oaths of a certain number of the colonels, when giving them the flag; and I declare that I was deeply moved by the enthusiasm with which I heard them publicly utter the sacramental words—" I swear!"

Amongst so many officers, who, in the course of twelve hours, passed before the Provisional Government, one only maintained silence. It was now night; but thousands of torches lit up the scaffolding and the surrounding objects. Of the eleven members of the Provisional Government, who had withdrawn from sheer fatigue, there remained no one but M. Arago and myself. I drew his attention to the officer to whom I have alluded, and inquired his name. The next day, General Bedeau called upon me, and assured me that the officer who had seemed to evince a want of sympathy, was a faithful soldier; that he knew him;

that he would answer for him, and that the Republic would have no truer adherent.

The English who may read these lines, will enquire, perhaps with astonishment, how it happened that Louis Bonaparte, on the 2nd of December, 1851, was able to find tools, and is now able to find supporters in this same army, which, on the 20th of April, 1848, fraternised so warmly with the Parisians, and swore fidelity to the Republic, with so manifest an enthusiasm. The explanation of this fact, so extraordinary to a foreigner, so painful to a Frenchman, is traceable to that which constitutes the essence of every standing army, wherever regular troops are employed in putting down civil disturbances. In France, the army is a vast assemblage of wheels within wheels, all set going by a moving force of some kind. Admirable in war, and animated on the field of battle by the noblest sentiments that thrill the human heart, the soldier in time of peace has, and can have, but one only motive, promotion; but one religion, the hierarchy of grades; but one science, discipline; but one law, obedience. The private soldier being entirely a passive instrument in the hands of the corporal, the corporal in the hands of the serjeant, the serjeant in the hands of the officer, and so on, the only thing which puts the army in motion, either in one direction or the other, is the will of him, whoever he may be, who is at its head. If, on the eve of the coup d'état of December, the Assembly had not committed the inconceivable blunder of putting the army under the command of the President, and had, instead, confided it to General Changarnier, I have a strong moral conviction that, in case of a struggle, General Changarnier would have made the soldiers arrest Louis Bonaparte, just as easily as Louis Bonaparte made them arrest General Changarnier. Whence it follows that, with a standing army in the hands of the executive power, liberty in a country becomes impossible.

This is why I opposed the return of the troops to Paris, foreseeing that, sooner or later, their presence would be fatal. But what was a source of alarm to me, was a source of hope to others. Such, as in their secret thoughts, desired to "bring the people to their senses," made a point of receiving the troops with the most extravagant demonstrations of joy, and omitted nothing that could serve as a pretext for detaining them. Here again, the majority of the Government failed in an accurate view of things. Deceived by the warm reception given to the troops, which, on the part of the enemies of the Republic, was done for a purpose, they played into their hands, without knowing it, by countenancing acts which they ought to have repressed, or, at all events, disavowed; it was thus, that on the 27th of April, disturbances having broken out at Rouen, with respect to the elections, and the officer in command of the troops having ordered his men to charge a number of working people tumultuously assembled — an unarmed crowd partly made up of women, old men, and children, which the National Guard were quite sufficient to disperse,—I could not prevail upon the Council to order a strict inquiry into this lamentable affair. But it was not long, however, before heart-rending tales reached us. We learnt that cannon had been fired in the streets, that the blood of working-men had been spilt out in torrents, without loss of life to a single soldier, so unequal had been the struggle! To make the thing worse, the general in command forwarded a report to us in the style of a bulletin announcing victory, and disfigured by a sort of savage satisfaction. I indignantly required that this officer should be immediately ordered up to Paris, to render an account of his conduct; and, if I remember rightly, M. Ledru Rollin supported me. But I met with so violent an opposition from M. Arago, that, for the first and only time in my life, I regretted the restraint imposed upon me by the respect I felt for him.

The period we had fixed for the termination of our own power was approaching, and the decree calling upon the nation to exercise its right of sovereignty by the choice of an Assembly, was just issued. Never, in any country, was there a more sincerely democratic law than that resulting from the deliberations of the Provisional Government. It provided that all French-men of the age of twenty-one, after six months' resi-dence in the place of election, should be entitled to the franchise; that all Frenchmen should be eligible as candidates; that the votes should be taken by ballot; and that, in order to throw open to the poor man of ability, the avenue to political life, each representative should receive a salary of twenty-five francs a day.* This was universal suffrage in its largest acceptation.

* For the details of the law, see the *Moniteur*.

That it would all at once be attended by satisfactory results, I must say I did not expect. I was but too well aware of the state of ignorance and dependence in which the rural population was vegetating. But I was aware, too, that it is not from the point of view of a momentary interest that we must estimate the importance of the principles which rule society, and that it is the essential property of universal suffrage to become more and more valuable in proportion as the people get enlightened, as their intelligence soars, and their political life is developed. Besides, universal suffrage is based upon the notion of right, and in the bare fact of a solemn recognition of a right, there is something of an immense import. Only, as I before explained, I wished there had been less precipitancy in calling upon the peasants to exercise this right, which I felt they were not yet capable of using to advantage.

My opinion on this point not having prevailed, I signed the decree establishing universal suffrage, as a premature homage tendered to a principle, of which no one more than I acknowledged the truth and desired the triumph.

The elections had been fixed for Easter Sunday, which fell on the 23rd of April. They did accordingly take place throughout France, and with a quietness perfectly remarkable. Not only did they give rise no where, except at Rouen, to any disturbance, but they even assumed in some places the character of a village fête. There were to be seen peasant-electors, forming themselves into a file before the church-door, when mass was over; and from thence, headed by the curate and the mayor, walking in procession, with banners flying and music playing, to the chief town of the district, where the voting was to take place.

There were at Paris some underhand manœuvres that truth will compel me presently to mention, directed against M. Albert and myself; but, excepting these, with which only two members of the Provisional Government had anything to do, nothing that I am aware of occurred, which could be imputed to improper influence.

It is true that in his circular of the 12th of March, M. Ledru Rollin publicly recommended his commissioners to impress upon the electors the necessity of electing Republicans. It is true that his circular contained this phrase: "The country is not yet educated, it is for you to instruct it."* It is true that he sent into the rural districts openly, and with the knowledge of everyone, a certain number of intelligent men commissioned to diffuse the principles of the Revolution. But, in this M. Ledru Rollin only did his duty, and deserves to be highly praised for it. Universal suffrage, operating in the dark, beyond the reach of that influence which knowledge must exercise upon ignorance is nothing better than a miserable farce, a means of making the sovereignty of the people serve for their own oppression.

M. Ledru Rollin would have drawn upon himself the just censure of history, if he had had recourse to the means which we have since seen employed by

* *Moniteur.*

Louis Bonaparte; if he had stifled discussion on the respective merits of candidates, prevented all concert between the electors, interdicted every meeting for election purposes, imposed upon the press the silence of death, and surrounded the ballot-boxes with the engines of constraint—soldiers and gendarmes.

Thank Heaven, nothing of this kind took place under the Provisional Government. They had no fear of broad daylight. Their adversaries, far from being compelled to silence, had every possible liberty of attacking, insulting, even calumniating them. Not satisfied with exasperating against them the discontent caused in the villages by the tax of forty-five centimes, the agents of the vanquished and humbled party abused the gullibility of the peasants to such a point, as to induce them to swallow the most ridiculous fables. It is quite certain, incredible as it may appear, and the fact has not been denied, that in certain sequestered districts, M. Ledru Rollin, under the title of "Duke Rollin," was believed to be a man of most profligate habits, having two mistresses, "La Marie and La Martine;" * whereat the good honest people who had been made to gobble down this ludicrous story, very naturally said, "Oh! one mistress is more than enough; but a couple—it is too bad!"

It will, of course, be understood, that these intrigues could not be played off in towns and large cities.

---

* Mistaking M. Marie and M. de Lamartine for two women, from the first having a woman's Christian name, and the latter suggesting the female name *Martine* with the article *la* before it.   M. Michelet cites this fact, a notorious one in France, as a curious illustration of the manner in which the greater part of the legends of the middle ages originated.

There the republican feeling had, since February, become so predominant, that any candidate not decidedly republican in his views, would have been ignominiously defeated. Hence, in such places, the uniform tone of all the election addresses. I restrict myself to the selection of three as specimens; and these are objects of special curiosity, inasmuch as they emanate from three men who now figure among the first dignitaries of the Empire.

M. Baroche, at this period, wrote to the electors of the department of Chârente Inférieure: "*I am a Republican by reason, by feeling, by conviction. It is not as a* pis-aller, *or as a provisional arrangement that I accept the Republic; but as the only form of government which can assure the greatness and prosperity of France.*"

According to M. Rouher, the Revolution was both *political and social.* Consequently he demanded "*most unrestricted liberty of public meeting, the right to establish clubs, graduated taxation,* * *organised labour: in a word, all for the people and by the people.*"

M. Fialin de Persigny, recently Louis Bonaparte's ambassador in England, thus addressed the electors of the Loire: "*This is not a political Revolution in the act of ending, it is a social Revolution in the act of beginning.*" And thereupon he swore, that "*whatever of courage, intelligence, and resolution, God might be pleased*

---

* By this is meant what in France is called *impôt progressif*, as thus: a man with an income of a hundred pounds having to pay a tax of three pounds; another, with an income of two hundred, would have to pay, not six pounds, but more, and so on in constant progression. Whence it may be inferred how ultra-democratic were M. Rouher's views, during the term of his republicanism.

*to grant him, would be henceforth consecrated to the
abolition of the only slavery that still weighed upon the
people—the* SLAVERY OF POVERTY."*

Any comments upon this would be superfluous.

Here is what happened at Paris.

M. Marrast, in his capacity of Mayor of Paris, was
placed at the very centre of the electoral proceedings.
Completely opposed to Socialism, and trembling least
the progress it had made should be strikingly exhibited
by the result of the Paris elections, he determined to
spare no efforts to undermine those of the Luxembourg, which his peculiar official position was but only
too well calculated to enable him to do, with a certain
measure of success. He was urged on, moreover, by
one of his supporters at the Hôtel de Ville, M. Buchez,
known in France as having mixed up in his writings
the worship of Jacobinism with the worship of the
Pope—a real priest in a lay dress. It was with him
and M. Marie that M. Marrast concerted the plan of a
review of the working-men of the Ateliers Nationaux,
at St. Maur, on the very eve of the day fixed for the
elections in Paris. With what object this was done, I
will leave M. Émile Thomas, whom these gentlemen
chose for their instrument, to explain.

After stating that this plan, suggested by him to MM.
Marrast and Marie, was received by them with the
liveliest satisfaction, such demonstration being calcu-

---

* Those who may be curious to see the kind of language at that time
held by numbers of persons who have since become the heads of the re-
action, or the supporters of tyranny, have only to consult Madame la
Comtesse d'Azault's book, *Sur la Révolution de* 1848, ii. 355, *et seq.*

lated to tell preponderatingly in their favour, M. Émile Thomas continues:

" Consequently, as early as the morning of the 23rd, I had made all my preparations for this review which was to come off in the Manœuvring Ground of Saint Maur, on the 22nd, and to conclude in the evening with a reception of the delegates in the Salle du Palais de la Bourse by the two members of the Provisional Government. On this occasion, in order to indemnify them for the expense of coming from a distance, the working men, besides their day's wages, were to receive the additional sum of fifty centimes." *

However, it seems the effect upon the public mind appeared doubtful ; for, in the course of the day, M. Émile Thomas received from M. Buchez a letter as follows :—

"MAIRIE DE PARIS, 21st *April*, 1848.

"MY DEAR ÉMILE,
        " *La nuit porte conseil.* I have been thinking that a review of the Ateliers Nationaux would look too much like an electoral manœuvre. I have communicated this fear to Marrast and to Reaut. They have thought so, too. . . . .

" Signed, BUCHEZ." †

Thereupon, according to his own account, M. Émile Thomas hastened to the Hôtel de Ville. He represented to M. Buchez the inconvenience of a *countermand,* and remarked to him that " the impression produced was

* *Histoire des Ateliers Nationaux,* par M. Émile Thomas, p. 213.
† *Ibid.*, p. 214.

of little consequence since the object to be attained
would be entirely in favour of moderation and prudence." * In other words, according to M. Émile
Thomas, the end justified the means.

And such, too, was the opinion, we must believe, of
MM. Buchez and Marrast, since M. Émile Thomas,
adds: — " M. Buchez relished my motives, and led
me straight to M. Marrast, who came round entirely to
my views." Consequently, M. Buchez wrote once
more to countermand the countermand.†   After all,
however, the review did not take place. The reasons
whereof, I suppose, M. Émile Thomas was not in a
position to explain, but which I can now unfold.

Being informed of the intentions of the Mairie, I
brought the matter before the Council, and at my
instance it was decided that, if the review of St. Maur
took place, it should be, not in the presence of two
members of the Government only, but in the presence
of the whole Government. As for the extra pay to the
working men, I was not at that moment informed of
that characteristic detail, and it was not mentioned.

However, as the time approached, the project was
abandoned by its authors. For, if all the members of the
government made their appearance, what was to become
of the object indicated by M. Émile Thomas ? How
was a fête, conducted on these terms, to be made to
" give MM. Marrast and Buchez a great preponderance ? " How could it be certain that the scheme would
turn out to the advantage of " moderation and pru-

* *Histoire des Ateliers Nationaux*, par M. Émile Thomas, p. 215.
† *Ibid.*

dence," as these virtues were understood at the Hôtel de Ville?

But I have not yet done with this valuable stock of confessions. For instance, M. Émile Thomas himself has been good enough to inform us, that the Mairie de Paris had a million copies struck off, on rose-coloured paper, of an electoral list, on which the names of MM. Albert, Flocon, Ledru Rollin, and Louis Blanc, did not appear; that it was sent to the district-mayors who could be relied on; and that it was disseminated by M. Barthélémy St. Hilaire.* "We have thought of some omissions to be made," wrote M. Buchez, on the 21st of April, to M. Émile Thomas; "be good enough to see the Minister." And lest the reader should find this phrase somewhat obscure, M. Émile Thomas subjoins these explanations, in his account of their proceedings.

"This note is relative to the composition of the electoral lists. The names of MM. Louis Blanc and Albert had been struck out at first; it was now proposed to do the same with those of MM. Ledru Rollin and Flocon, and their names were also struck out accordingly." †

A fact which might well be doubted, but which is unfortunately too clearly proved, is that M. Émile Thomas did not scruple to employ the funds of the State in furtherance of these disloyal practices. We take the report of M. Ducos on the accounts of the Provisional Government, and we there read:—" It results from the declarations of M. Gariépuy that, some time

* *Histoire des Ateliers Nationaux*, par M. Émile Thomas, p. 216.
† *Ibid.*, p. 214.

before the elections in the month of April, 1848, M. Émile Thomas gave him orders to place thirty-six men of his brigade at the disposal of M. Moutin, who was then President of the *Union des Travailleurs*, for the purpose of assisting him to distribute electoral lists. Some time later, new orders were given that the eight hundred artists (in the *Ateliers Nationaux*) should be employed at the same work, *even if they were to be paid three francs a day each.*" *

To make this intelligible, it must be explained that, amongst the men employed, or properly speaking, *not employed*, although paid, in the National Works, there were a certain number of persons who, having no positive occupation, rejoiced in the name of *artists*.

To extenuate the effect of these confessions, M. Émile Thomas, in his book, seeks to present the electoral manœuvres of his employers as simple reprisals against the Luxembourg. Unfortunately, this assertion in defence of intrigue is disproved by documents whose authority is not to be impeached. The Report of the Commission of Inquiry, drawn up by my enemies, with the avowed object of ruining me, contains a speech of mine which I may appeal to as an authority, since it was not destined to see the light, and is made up of short-hand notes, collected and put together, with complacent ingenuity, by my own accusers.

Let us see, then, what took place at the Luxembourg, when the drawing up of an Electoral List was talked of. I quote the Report above mentioned.

* *Moniteur* of the 26th April, 1849.

A Voice. "You should draw it up yourself."

Louis Blanc. "I cannot do so, because I am a member of the Provisional Government." *

In fact, if there be one man bold enough to pretend that, in any way or degree, directly or indirectly, I caused the exclusion from the electoral list of the Luxembourg of a single one of my colleagues, let that man stand up and assert it! Yet I did interfere, and I will explain how, still *proving* my assertions as I advance.

Invited for the first time to the exercise of its sovereign power, the people appeared earnestly anxious to have the interests of labour represented by working men. Paris had thirty-four representatives to nominate, and it had come to my ears, that, out of this number, the people were prepared to nominate twenty-four or twenty-five working men. This proportion appeared to me excessive, and I explained myself clearly on the point, before the delegates of the Luxembourg.

"You will permit me," I said to them, "to speak to you with frankness. It would be very important to your own interests, that your list should not be composed entirely of working men. Among those who are not working men, there are men, some of whom you know, who, as far as sympathy and feeling go, may be said to be of you; who love you as if they had shared your sufferings; who, although they have not been reduced to the hard necessity of devoting themselves for twelve, thirteen, or fourteen hours a day, to manual labour of a nature to deprive their intelligence of a part

* *Rapport de la Commission de l'Enquête,* vol. i. p. 121.

of its development, have not the less employed their lives in the study of your miseries and your interests; who know them, and are ready to defend them; who desire to do so, and who will. I should propose to you, therefore, to choose, out of the thirty-four names, twenty belonging to the working classes, and fourteen belonging to the category of those who, though not working men, have given pledges to the people." *

The reader will remark that the number proposed by me left room, on the list of the companies, both for my twelve colleagues, and for the ministers who were not members of the Provisional Government, so that I was striving, at this time, to hold the door of the electoral list open even for those who were only thinking of shutting it against myself.

It is true, that on the list of the delegates the names of four members of the Provisional Government only were admitted; namely, Ledru Rollin, Flocon, Albert, and myself. But was this a matter for surprise? Was not the separation of the Council into two groups unequally revolutionary in policy, an open and admitted fact? Was it not natural that the stream of popular preference should flow in the sense of the minority, who were known to represent, in a more special manner, the feelings and the interests of the people? In what degree could I answer for the result of suffrages which were always held sacredly free in my eyes? Had the key of the ballot urn been placed in my hands, I would have thrown it away with

* *Rapport de la Commission de l'Enquête,* vol. i. p. 121.

indignation and disgust. It is the simple truth, which no one has had the audacity to deny, that the delegates of the Luxembourg fixed their choice independently of any personal influence, and after the most serious, searching, and impartial examination of the opinions and titles of each working man's candidate.

The selection was made in the following manner: It was agreed that each trade union should present a candidate; that the candidates should have to present themselves before a commission appointed to examine them; that their replies to the questions put to them should be taken down in short-hand and consigned to a report; that the report should be read before a general meeting, the candidates being present; and that on these *data*, the assembly should select a final list of twenty names to be submitted to popular suffrage. Thus, no concession was made to favour, nor to mere enthusiasm, nor to cliques, nor to any official influence whatsoever.

Three weeks only elapsed between the day of the elections, and the day on which the bases I have described were laid down for the choice of candidates.

It was on the 5th of March, 1848, that the commission for examining the candidates was formed. It was composed of the following citizens:—Viez, delegate of the printers; Six, delegate of the carpet-makers; Bonnefond, delegate of the cooks; Passard, delegate of the brushmakers; Pernot, delegate of the cabinet-makers and joiners; Duchêne, delegate of the compositors.

Where was this commission to sit? No doubt, there

was no lack of room to receive them in the Luxembourg, which had become the Palace of the People. But the delegates would not furnish the counter-revolution with a pretext for suspecting the independence of their choice and calumniating my influence; and as their pride would have suffered too much from the refusal or the grant of a place of meeting at the Hôtel de Ville, they were obliged to look out for two miserable rooms of ten feet square each; and in these were to meet the representatives of that potent army of working men, whose generosity was even then guarding so many deserted palaces! With much grace and courtesy, M. Dumas offered the private lodging which he occupied at the Sorbonne, in his capacity of Professor of Chemistry; it was there that the commission proceeded to business.

A President and a Secretary were nominated; the reports from the different bodies of working men, authenticating the candidates they had proposed, were received, and every candidate was informed by letter of the day and hour when he would be questioned. The principal questions were the following:—

" What do you think of our present Institutions?

" What are your ideas on the subject of Religion? Are you for the liberty of worship? Ought forms of worship to be paid by the State?

" What are your views on the organisation of Labour?

" What reforms do you think should be introduced into the Magistracy?

" How do you understand the organisation of the

Army? What ought to be its office now, and in the future?

"On what bases, in your opinion, ought the system of taxation to rest?

"What is your opinion on the subject of divorce?

"What do you think should be the relations established between France and the different peoples of Europe, especially Germany and Italy?"

The commission sat for eight days. It examined seventy candidates, presented by as many trade companies; and I learned from the short-hand writers who assisted at these grave sittings, that several of the working men displayed in their replies to the interrogatories superior intelligence.

An interesting circumstance marked the close of the labours of the Commission. At its last meeting, one of the officials announced that a man beloved by the people requested an audience. He entered. Although negligent in his attire, his appearance had in it something at once attractive and venerable. His look gentle, penetrating, and thoughtful; his manners simple and noble; his physiognomy sagacious and contemplative; a rich profusion of hair, a fine open face, a head which study had somewhat bent, everything in him inspired respect, but a respect blended with confiding sympathy. "Citizens," he said, "I understand that the working men have done me the honour to place me on their ticket, as a candidate for the Constitutent Assembly. I have thought it my duty to present myself before your Committee, to submit myself to your examination." The workmen looked at one another, both touched and surprised. The man thus addressing them was one of those whose life had been devoted to the promulgation and development of high views. He was well known in France as one of the most vigorous thinkers, and one of the most benevolent teachers of the people. It was M. Pierre Leroux.

On the conclusion of the labours of the commission, the reports were taken to the Luxembourg, and the delegates constituted themselves into a general meeting to draw up a definitive list of candidates.

Of the three sittings employed in this duty, beginning at eight in the morning, the last was prolonged until two hours after midnight. Unwilling to separate before the completion of their work, the delegates took their humble dinner in their bureau. Bread, cheese, and water, such was the banquet of the working men, in that Palace of the Luxembourg, where the hired libellers of the counter-revolution were to lay the scene of their foul calumnious inventions. And as these working men were too proud to owe even a drop of water to anybody, the delegates made a collection among themselves to defray the cost of their modest meal. This collection amounted to forty-two francs; they gave twenty to the waiters in attendance.

Must I here recall the disgraceful acts of the electoral war which was waged against the delegates of the Luxembourg?

On the day of the election, Pernot, delegate of the cabinet-makers, on his return from the Champ de Mars, accompanied by the flag-bearer of his company, perceived several individuals distributing a list which they said was the list of the Luxembourg candidates— it was the list of the Hôtel de Ville! Pernot burst out into contemptuous reproaches at this treachery, which made the people indignant; and it is too certain that, at many points, scenes of this kind were provoked by similar frauds.

Such is the faithful account of the first election which the people of Paris were called upon to make under the authority of this great principle—universal suffrage. For my own part, not only did I put forward no name, but I did not assist at a single electoral discussion, and I carried my scruples so far as even carefully to conceal my sympathies. This is so true, that the list of the Luxembourg did not contain the names which I should most ardently have desired to find there; such as that of M. Pecqueur, for instance, who had supported me, at the Luxembourg, with so much talent and zeal.

Scruples of delicacy are a great impediment, especially in politics. The delegates left entirely to themselves, committed a fault, a very honourable fault doubtless, but one which showed their want of experience in electioneering tactics. Instead of so composing their list of candidates, as to make it acceptable to the fraction of the Republican party which did not go as far as Socialism, they put upon it only the names of socialists of the most decided views, and those of workmen known only to their comrades.

This stiff objection to any kind of compromise had the result naturally to be expected from it; a great number of republicans who would have willingly voted for the working men's list, had it been less exclusive, not only would not support it, but, for the purpose of successfully opposing it, coalesced with Legitimists and Orleanists. Another circumstance, marvellously well adapted to serve the purposes of the Mayor of Paris and his subordinates, was the jealousy skilfully excited between the *Ateliers Nationaux* and the Luxembourg. The first, consisting of workmen who depended for their bread, and that of their families, on the Minister of Public Works, furnished the election ticket of the Hôtel de Ville with a contingent of votes, afterwards bitterly repented by those who gave them, but which were then forced from them, partly by the feeling of their dependence, partly by a spirit of rivalry towards the delegates of the Luxembourg.

The consequence was that the electoral ticket of the Hôtel de Ville, which contained the names of MM. de Lamartine, Arago, Dupont (de l'Eure), Marrast, Marie, Garnier Pagès, Crémieux, and from which my name had been erased, as well as those of MM. Flocon, Albert, and Ledru Rollin, was accepted, on the one hand by that fraction of the working class to which the Minister of Public Works had, as we have seen, given a military organisation; and, on the other, by the coalition of all the old parties with the republicans of the *National's* tint; the ticket of the Luxembourg represented only a party, very united and compact certainly, but for this very reason, less numerous.

I am compelled to add that my opponents, doing

me the painful honour of considering me as a man particularly dangerous, moved mountains to cause my defeat. My "History of Ten Years," my organisation of labour, my constant endeavours to emancipate the working class, had caused me a multitude of implacable enemies. If I could have doubted it before, I must have found it out now. In spite of all this, I was elected by 121,140 votes; M. Albert, against whom the enemies of the Luxembourg were less violent, got 133,041 votes, that is, within 1500 of the number M. Ledru Rollin received. The other members of the Government, with the exception of M. Flocon, had many more votes, and figured at the head of the list of thirty-four successful candidates.

This list, at the bottom of which was the name of M. de Lamennais with 104,871 votes, had, at its top, that of M. de Lamartine with 259,800 votes—an enormous and deceptive number, which misled M. de Lamartine as to the amount of his popularity. It escaped him that the 259,800 electors brought together by a momentary coalition of old parties, and exhibiting sincere convictions side by side with ambition of every sort, many arrière-pensées and hatreds, composed a force much less genuine than the 133,000 votes given to Albert; because in this number there were no less than 100,000 from men sharing the same views, adopting the same programme, and having the same faith—a faith sufficiently profound and inflexible to make them prefer the risk of a defeat to the profit of a compromise.

But the illusion of M. de Lamartine happened to

be as brief as it was blinding. The Legitimists and the Orleanists soon showed that, in voting for him, their sole object had been to use him as an instrument, to be broken to bits when no longer needed.

No one certainly admires more than I do the genius of M. de Lamartine, his integrity, the magnanimity of his bursts of feeling, the splendour of his imagination, made so fascinating by the unparalleled richness of his language. But according to my views, he fell into a fatal mistake, in tracing out the part he had to play, under the influence of this ruling passion of a literary man—to be applauded. With his ear incessantly on the stretch to catch the sound of his name, and always uneasy lest the music, as it were, of his fame should be disturbed, he made it a study to wheedle any one whom he feared. He coveted every variety of homage. He loved to see his image reflected from the surface of every phase of opinion, and, in his handling of parties, he endeavoured to place himself at their point of intersection. With equal ardour was he to be seen courting the approbation of drawing-rooms, and trying to allure that of the clubs; ingratiating himself with Lord Normanby, and making friends with M. Sobrier; offering an embassy to M. de la Rochejaquelin, and looking out for secret interviews with M. Blanqui.

That M. de Lamartine fancied he was in this way contributing to a work of universal reconciliation, is to be inferred from his natural generosity of character. But he would soon have seen how fruitless such an effort was likely to be, depending exclusively on the influence of personal fascination, had he not yielded to an inward motive, of which in all probabilities, he was himself unconscious. So easily do our best feelings conceal imperceptible sophisms, and so skilful is the human heart in deceiving itself!

M. de Lamartine undoubtedly displayed, when in power, eminent qualities. But bravely to espouse the cause of the weak and the oppressed against the strong; to confront, with all the energy of an unconquerable soul, injustice—whether armed with a glaive, or crowned with flowers; to expose oneself, on behalf of everlasting truth, to be misunderstood, slandered, vilified, ridiculed, stung, till the blood comes, by thousands of vipers; to live unmoved amid the hatred of the dishonest; and so to serve our conscience, as not to fear doing battle with the world, for conscience sake, this is what must be done, and what M. de Lamartine did not. Nobly defiant of death, his was the courage of the soldier; trembling before detractors, he had the weakness of the poet. What was deficient in him, was the power of provoking deadly enmities.

And so he had all parties at his feet—for one day. He lay down, believing that France was at his bedside. He went to sleep, in the intoxication of imaginary triumph: he dreamt dictatorship: he awoke—he was alone!

CHAPTER XVII.

INVASION OF THE NATIONAL ASSEMBLY.

THE opening of the National Constituent Assembly, chosen by universal suffrage, took place on the 4th of May, 1848. The mere aspect of the hall intimated the prodigious changes that had occurred in the short interval of two months. People pointed out with a mingled feeling of curiosity and emotion, M. Barbès seated amongst colleagues who had been his judges; Father Lacordaire, in his white dress as a Dominican friar, elbowing M. Coquerel, a Protestant minister; the Voltairian author of "Dieu des bonnes gens," Béranger, in the midst of priests in their cassocks; a Breton wearing the lilac sash of his country, in contrast with groups of representatives in plain black coats; and members of the French Academy seated as legislators between a peasant on one side and a working man on the other.

Nor was the spectacle in the galleries less striking, where the clubs, like the "corps diplomatique," had their seats, and where the eye glanced from the embroidered coat to the uniform of the National Guard, and from the most finished toilette to the *blouse des faubourgs.*

What would be the issue of that assemblage, still indefinite and mysterious, of such divers elements, and of so many conflicting ideas, no man then could say. Would society be confined to the old rut, or be vigorously urged onwards into new paths? The Revolution began at the end of the last century, would it tranquilly pursue its irresistible course; or, once more checked, would it be again compelled to burst its dikes, at the risk of a universal inundation? Such were the ominous questions each spectator asked himself; and certainly it would have exceeded the capacity of human wit at that time to have dived into their depths.

The only thing which seemed certain was, that Republicanism, as a form of government, was henceforth a settled matter. But this did not suffice to the earnest friends of progress. It was less the laying their hands on a political instrument which they had in view, than the future use which might be made of it. Now, the very composition of the Assembly, in spite of its air of novelty, caused them a secret uneasiness. They were alarmed at again seeing in the new chamber the well-known faces they had seen in the old one. With the exception of M. Thiers and some others, they found themselves face to face with the most active supporters of the fallen *régime :* MM. Berryer, Odilon Barrot, Dupin, Remusat, Duvergier de Hauranne, Dufaure, Montalembert. The provinces, it is true, had contributed a large number of republicans. But these in general cared only for Republicanism as a mere political form; and even with these it was a question, whether as a mere political institution, independent of all social consequences, the Republic was sure of a majority, seeing that, out of 900 members there were 130 belonging to the Legitimist party, and 300 to the Orleanist party.

Thus, from the very first day, the enormous fault committed by the Provisional Government in hurrying on the elections, in opposition to my earnest entreaties, made itself manifest. On the 4th of May, it was only necessary to cast one's eyes upon the benches of the *droite*, to comprehend that the elections had transferred political power from Paris to the Provinces, in other words from that part of France which was the most enlightened, to that part that was the least so. This first effort of universal suffrage turned out to be nothing more than the victory of the rural districts, the abodes of ignorance, over a city, the brilliant focus of light. The privileged classes were about to subdue the working classes by means of the peasants—the people by means of the people.

The members of the Provisional Government had agreed to meet at the Chancellerie, Place Vendôme. There Albert and myself found our colleagues assembled on the 4th of May, and it was from thence that we all went to the Assembly. The day was splendid. The 5th Regiment of Lancers, the 2nd of Dragoons, the 11th Light Infantry, the 60th Regiment of the Line, the Republican Guard, and Guard Mobile, lined a part of the Boulevardes, the Place Vendôme, the Rue de la Paix, the Rue de Rivoli, and the approaches to the Legislative Palace. Numerous detachments of National

Guards, who had come up from the country to escort
their Representatives, fraternised with the Legions of the
National Guard of Paris; and an immense crowd
overflowed through all its avenues into the Place de
la Révolution, singing the *Marseillaise.* The members
of the Provisional Government went to what was
formerly the Palais Bourbon, by the Rue de la Paix,
the Boulevard, and the Place de la Concorde. There
was but one opinion as to the reception they met with
on their way. Madame la Comtesse d'Agoult thus
speaks of it :—

" Preceded by the Commander-in-chief of the National Guard with his staff, they marched bare-headed
between two officers with drawn swords, and followed
by all the mayors and sub-mayors of Paris and the
suburbs. Uninterrupted acclamations arising from the
dense crowd through which the procession passed, also
from the windows and roofs of the houses, saluted
these intrepid gentle-hearted men, who, without com-
mitting a single despotic act, without spilling one
drop of blood, without doing violence to one single
liberty, had, under the most trying circumstances,
inaugurated the reign of democracy in France." *

After having given the same details, the author of
another very interesting historical work on the Revolution of 1848 exclaims : " Never did government receive
so splendid an ovation." †

The cannon of the Invalides announced to the
Assembly the arrival of the men, who, all-powerful

---

* *Histoire de la Révolution de* 1848, by Daniel Sterne, ii. 370, 371.
† *Histoire de la Révolution,* 1848, by M. Robin, ii. 260.

the day before, had now come voluntarily and humbly to deposit in the hands of the French people—represented, if not in a satisfactory at least in a regular manner—the dictatorship with which they had been invested by the people of Paris. When the venerable Dupont (de l'Eure) with one arm in M. de Lamartine's, and the other in mine, entered the hall, the whole Assembly rose spontaneously, and uttered the most enthusiastic shouts I ever heard of "Long live the Republic!" The galleries returned them, and when the deep impression produced by this imposing expression of feeling in favour of Republicanism had ceased, M. Dupont (de l'Eure) ascending the tribune, read with a voice betraying great emotion, a short and simple address, which terminated thus : "At length the moment is come for the Provisional Government to deposit in your hands the unlimited power with which the Revolution had invested them. You are yourselves aware whether this dictatorship has been in our hands anything else than a moral power, exerted in the midst of the critical events through which we have just passed. Faithful to our origin and to our personal convictions, we have not hesitated to proclaim the Republic that rose up in February. To-day, we inaugurate the labours of the National Assembly with this cry which must ever be its rallying cry: 'Long live the Republic!'"

Descending from the tribune, M. Dupont (de l' Eure) was led to his seat, where Béranger was waiting for him ; and the two noble old men embraced each other in the midst of general emotion.

Fresh cheers then shook the hall, breaking out again and again during the course of the sitting.

Towards evening, General Courtais, in full uniform as Commander-in-chief of the National Guard, suddenly entered the Hall, announcing that the Place de la Concorde, the bridge leading to the palace, the approaches to it, and the quays, were crowded to excess with vast numbers of people impatient to mingle their acclamations with those of the Representatives. At once, yielding to the influence of the moment, all the members quit their places, and range themselves under the vestibule of the palace, facing the Place de la Concorde. How could we find words capable of faithfully expressing the magnificent and really devotional character of this great scene? It was a soft, bright spring day, and the setting sun was shedding its last rays upon this glorious Place de la Concorde, the most beautiful part of one of the most beautiful cities in the world. The moment the Representatives appeared under the vestibule, the cannon sounded, the flags or banners of the National Guard and of the army waved their salute; the bands of the different regiments began to strike up the *Marseillaise;* and then was to be heard reaching to the skies one of those mighty shouts, which at the Olympic games, as History tells us, made the ravens fall dead into the circus. It was one of those moments, so rare in the life of peoples, when hands are held out to hands, when hearts leap forward to hearts, and men, forgetting their petty dissensions, feel they are members of the same family, and children of the same father—God.

A few days afterwards, the Assembly passed by a nearly unanimous vote, there being only two or three dissentients, the following decree: " The National Constituent Assembly receives from the hands of the Provisional Government the transfer of the powers confided to them. The Provisional Government by the greatness of their services have merited well of the country." *

Thus it was that the Republic was established in France by universal, and, at that moment as I believe, sincere, consent.

But the old monarchical parties, willing enough then to submit to the Republic as a necessity, were not prepared to accept it in its socialist bearing. Now, unfortunately, in this disinclination they happened to be backed by that fraction of the Republican party whose views were merely political, and who, on this occasion, acted like a *corps d'armée*, which, from misconception or any other unlucky cause, should unexpectedly fall upon its own vanguard.

The result of this coalition, in which the Legitimists and the Orleanists cleverly kept themselves, at first, in the back-ground, was to set up everywhere in all offices, *political*, to the exclusion of *social*, Republicans.

Hence the composition of the "Commission Executive," upon which the Assembly appointed MM. Arago, Garnier Pagès, Marie, de Lamartine, and Ledru Rollin. In this manner was a part of the Provisional Government employed under the new order of things. Besides, M. Marrast was left in possession

---

* *Moniteur* of the 8th of May, 1848.

of his office as Mayor of Paris, and M. Crémieux of his, as Minister of Justice. M. Flocon, too, was appointed Minister of Commerce. Of course, the great age of Dupont (de l'Eure) explains why he did not take office. So there were only two members of the late government who were not included in the new arrangements, M. Albert and myself.

The day previous to their announcement, we had resigned our official position at the Luxembourg, and I had taken advantage of the opportunity to intimate my fixed resolution not to take office of any kind until the Constituent Assembly should be succeeded by the Legislative.

Having by this proved that I had no interested motive to serve, and taken away from the Assembly any pretext that might arise out of personal objections to myself, I felt at liberty to insist upon the institution of a public department especially devoted to the labour question, and which, if overlooked, I warned the Assembly, would bring about, not the " Révolution du mépris," as in Louis Philippe's time, but one much more terrible, the " Révolution de la faim ! " *

I did not then myself measure the full force of my own prophecy. Still less accurately was it measured by the Assembly, thanks to unfortunate prejudices both against the cause I advocated and myself—all which I recall "more in sorrow than in anger."

The line the Assembly had drawn, was significant enough, nor did the people misinterpret it. Hence

* *Moniteur*, Séance du 10 Mai, 1848.

the first germs of division between them and the
Assembly. In proportion as the latter deserted, the
former clung to us. Every day making us more and
more the symbols of their wants, they lost no opportunity of giving us proofs of their confidence and
support. The proposal I had made on the 10th having
been passed by, the working classes were not long in
showing the mischievous impression produced upon
them. The Government had appointed a day for a
festival called the "Fête de la Concorde," to commemo-
rate the establishment of the Republic, to which the
working classes were, of course, invited. Whereupon
the acting committee of the delegates of the Luxembourg, without my knowledge, published an address
which was placarded on all the walls of Paris. After
quoting the decree concerning the "Droit au Travail,"
issued by that Provisional Government whose acts
had certainly not been repudiated by the National
Assembly, they said :—

"The promises made on the barricades not having
been accomplished, and the Assembly having refused
on the 10th of May, to form a ministry of Labour and
Progress, we working men, delegates of the Luxembourg, have unanimously decided not to take part in
the Fête, so called, de la Concorde.

"LAGARDE, Président ;

"BESNARD, GODIN, LAVOYE, Vice-Présidents ;

"LEFAURE, DELIT, PETIN, Secrétaires." *

It was when the popular irritation evinced by this

* See *Le Représentant du Peuple*, No. 42.

document was at its height, that rumours spread through Paris of movements in Poland for the recovery of its independence. Sympathy with the sufferings or prosperity of other peoples being a prominent feature of French character,—and, as a Frenchman, I take leave to say, a most honourable one,—the news caused a general excitement, which was fanned into a flame by the action of certain of the clubs.

Such were the circumstances that led to the eventful and melancholy day which, by the invasion of the National Assembly inflicted such mortal wounds on the Republic.

It having been my misfortune to be involved in the consequences, although perfectly unconnected with the cause, and to so sad an extent as to be driven from my country for my alleged participation in acts which I did my best, first to prevent, and then to check; it will be necessary I should give a somewhat minute account of them, though the limits of this work constrain me to confine myself to the part I was called upon to play.

On the 14th of May vague reports reached me, like the rest of the world, that a great number of citizens proposed going the next day to the National Assembly to present a petition in favour of Poland. So far bruit; beyond this, not a syllable did I hear. Of the monstrous project of invading the Assembly and dissolving it, not a whisper. But whatever might have been the object of the demonstration, was there no risk, I asked myself, in the actual fermentation of the public mind, of furnishing opportunities for attempts at disorder, and ultimately putting dangerous weapons into the hands of the reactionist party? This is pre-cisely what there was too much reason to apprehend, especially after the 16th of April. For my part, I certainly feared it; and I can affirm that M. Albert's views coincided with mine. I happened to meet M. Barbès. Communicating to him my apprehensions, he assured me he fully shared them, and expressed himself on the point with considerable warmth. In a demon-stration so susceptible of being perverted by some, and misrepresented by others, he discerned a peril and fore-saw a calamity: he left me, determined to persuade as many of his friends as he might meet with, to have nothing to do with it. As far, then, as to MM. Albert and Barbès being in any way implicated in this plot, I am authorised, by my relations with them, to deny it; a declaration which my conscience, even more than my friendship, prescribes.

On the 15th of May I went as usual to the National Assembly. Certain libellers have not been ashamed to circulate in print, that on the morning of this ill-omened day, I called at the Café Tortoni, and there concerted matters with Blanqui, Barbès, and other chiefs; a detestable fabrication, which I tread upon in passing.

For the purpose of hearing better, I took my seat on the benches of the right, close to the tribune, when suddenly the sound of shouts in the distance announced the approach of the crowd. There was a sudden rush of Representatives into the hall, and cries of "To your places!" I then went to my usual seat on the highest benches of the extreme left. The noise approached nearer and nearer, and the back galleries were presently

filled with men of the people bearing banners. Shortly
afterwards, the doors being burst open by the crowd,
and those in the galleries at the back having come
forward, the body of the Hall was soon completely
filled. Clamours of all sorts contended with one
another, until the tumult grew horrible. In the midst
of this disorder I had nothing to do but follow the
same course as my colleagues, and to remain like them
in my place, a wonder-struck but powerless spectator of
this invasion of a sanctuary which the triumph of
universal suffrage should have for ever rendered as
inviolable as the sovereignty of the people. But it was
not long—there are not wanting numbers of persons
capable of testifying to the perfect accuracy of these
particulars—before I was approached by representatives, ushers, and attendants, coming to inform me that
an immense crowd was pressing into the court close
to the Rue de Bourgogne, calling for me with loud
cries, and which, if I did not show myself to them,
would increase to a dangerous degree the throng that
had already invaded the Assembly. What was to be
done? Ought I not to keep my post in the midst of
the Assembly of which I was a member? And yet not
to go, when my doing so was required as a means of
restoring tranquillity, would not this be to incur a
grave responsibility? For some time I resisted the
entreaties made me; but as they became more and
more urgent, I determined to place myself at the
disposal of the Assembly. I therefore went to the
President's chair, and addressing myself to Citizen
Buchez, who had already been apprised by an usher of

what was going on, I asked him if, in case it were thought useful I should address the people, I should be authorised to do so by the body to which I belonged, and from which I did not wish in any way to separate myself?

Citizen Buchez reminded me, that at a moment when his voice was completely overpowered by the tumult it would be perfectly impossible for him to ascertain the will of the Chamber. "In that case," I replied, "do you, in the name of the Assembly, and in your capacity of Vice-president, authorise me to interfere?" He answered me in an affirmative way, in presence of one of the Vice-presidents Citizen Courbon. His precise answer was: "As President I have no orders to give you; as a man and citizen I urge your going." I insisted upon a less equivocal answer. Thereupon in presence of M. Buchez, who continued silent with an air of acquiescing, M. Courbon, the Vice-president, said to me, "Well, you are officially authorised." It was only therefore to preserve order, and after being thus authorised, that I addressed the crowd. Standing on the secretaries' table, I solicited a moment's silence, which was granted to me, and of which I took advantage—the *Moniteur* will bear me witness—to win over the people to calmness, moderation, and respect for their own sovereignty, personified in an Assembly chosen by universal suffrage.

Nevertheless, the tumult within the Hall continued, while the excitement outside increased every instant. Again, the most anxious appeals were made to me.

With the consent of the President of the Assembly, I went to one of the windows of the court which communicates with the Place de Bourgogne, and mounting on the window-sill, where Albert and Barbès were, I said to the closely-packed multitude, what I thought best adapted to pacify them. I told them in substance, that no one could deny the reasonableness of their desires for a more equitable partition of the fruits of toil, and the gradual extinction of poverty; but that the sacred interests of the working classes would not, they might rest assured of it, be neglected by the Assembly; that the eternal honour of the Republic would be the fact of its having laboured, without ceasing, at realising the right of all to prosperity; that if it were folly to allow our hopes to rise too high on this subject, it was, at all events, one of those sublime follies to which it is very excusable to devote one's existence; that, moreover, a most touching and most noble spectacle was that of a people suspending for a moment the thought of its own sufferings, in order to administer to the sufferings of a friendly people : that it was easy to recognise in this the essentially generous and cosmopolitan genius of France; but that the more the sentiments of the people were deserving of respect, the more indispensable was it they should be expressed in a legal and regular manner.

And I concluded by adjuring the crowd to leave the National Assembly in possession of its fullest liberty of deliberation. This fact was subsequently deposed to by a pupil of St. Cyr, of the name of Lucas, who declared he had heard my entreaties to the people to leave the Assembly, and that the language in which I implored them was so earnest and touching that, in spite of himself, he could not help bursting into tears.* I was withdrawing for the purpose of resuming my seat, when, seized by a number of persons, who had closed in behind me, I was carried across the Salle des Pas Perdus. There was a general wish I should speak again; it was even imperiously required; and a circle being made, I was compelled to get upon a chair, and to make an address. It was then that, speaking of the invincible force of the Revolution of February, and at the same time of the absolute necessity of resting its claims to the admiration of the whole world on moderation and wisdom, as the only means of making it victorious over kings, I pronounced these words, since so cruelly distorted: "This revolution in fact was not one of those which make thrones tremble, but of those which make thrones fall;" and the conclusion, the summary of my discourse, was this exclamation, repeated with enthusiasm by the whole audience: " Vive la République Universelle!"

Almost at the same instant I was hemmed in on every side by robust working men, who lifted me up in order to carry me into the Assembly. In vain did I struggle violently against them; in vain reply at different intervals to the passionate acclamations which resounded on every side of me, the only cry worthy of the people was, "Long live the Republic!" All my resistance was useless. As many as ten times I

* For this deposition, which I quoted in my speech in the Assembly on the 24th of March, see the *Moniteur*.

fell in the midst of the crowd which was pressing me onwards, and as often was I lifted up again by the brawny arms around me; there were some who flung themselves upon me, in order to embrace me; others were crying out: "Take care, or you will stifle him." If to excite such warm sympathies, while resolutely endeavouring to restrain them, and while serving the cause we believe to be the true one, without compromise, without mob-sycophany, without a morbid aim at popularity, be an offence—that offence was mine. Let them convict me of any other, if they can!

It was thus that, in spite of myself, I was carried into the Assembly, athwart the dense mass of its invaders. Those who were present will be able to say, if I did not do everything I could to prevent the coming catastrophe. But of what avail, at such a moment, my personal resistance, and the few words I attempted to make heard in the midst of the clamour? Exhausted with fatigue, and bathed in perspiration, I was pushed on towards the extreme benches of the Hall. There a workman came to me and said: "Your voice is gone, but if you will just write upon a bit of paper that you, for the last time, adjure the crowd to disperse, perhaps I shall be able to read it out loud enough to make myself heard." Taking up a pen, I was hastily writing these words:—"In the name of our country, of the Republican party, of the sovereignty of the people, in the interest of us all, I beseech you to. . . ." When the fatal words, pronounced by a man now known to have been a traitor, were heard: "The National Assembly is dissolved!"

There was now a great rush, which swept me along
with it, into the " Salle des Conferences." My name
was called out in every direction, and I was surrounded
by a dense and very excited crowd, crying out to me to go
to the Hôtel de Ville. I replied, in the deepest dismay,
that to go to the Hôtel de Ville, would be to risk the
spilling of blood. I desired to know where several
of my colleagues were ; of Albert I could hear nothing,
but some one said, that an attempt had been made to
force Barbès to go to the Hôtel de Ville, which he
warmly resisted.* Every one now rushing towards the
doors, I was carried away by the stream, and got out
in such a state of confusion, that I do not know to
this moment, by what outlet and way I reached the
parade ground of the " Invalides."

There I met my brother in company with a painter
and some friends, anxiously looking for me. They
made the most determined efforts to release me. For
I was so hemmed in on all sides that those who
were nearest to me were obliged, by linking arms, to
make a barrier around me against the violence of the
pressure. I took advantage of a moment's halt again
to prevail upon them to disperse. "You are going to
your deaths," I said ; but several of them in a sort of

---

* This I learned afterwards was inaccurate. Although Barbès was
decidedly opposed to the invasion of the Assembly, and had done all he
could to prevent it, still, when he saw that the Representatives had dispersed, that crowds were running through the streets in every direction,
that the terrible cry *aux armes!* was raised everywhere, mingled with the
beating of drums, and that Paris seemed to be in a state of utter confusion,
with great resolution he went to the Hôtel de Ville, for the purpose of
hindering any act that might be prejudicial to the cause of the people.

delirium, pointing to their naked breasts, cried out, they would never dare to injure unarmed men. My brother here exclaimed: "What then! it is him you wish to have killed?" Immediately the crowd opened; a cabriolet happening to pass, it was stopped, and the owner, a wine-merchant, returning to Bercy, was obliged to get out; but on his declaring that he had property of value in his carriage, we all four got into it,—that is the owner, the coachman, my brother, and myself. So completely was I prostrated, that the honest citizen kindly proposed to drive me to one of his friends, where I might refresh myself with a little rest, and took me accordingly to the house of a young man in the quarter of the Ecole de Médecine, where I met the kindest hospitality. I then got home after stopping a few moments to change my linen at a neighbouring bookseller's, Citizen Masson; he was himself absent, but his nephews kindly received me.

To assert, therefore, as a newspaper has dared to do, that I was seen at the Hôtel de Ville, is a falsehood which has never been exceeded in impudence.

Hearing, on arriving at home, that the Assembly had again met, I hurried off instantly to my post.

On reaching the vestibule, I was recognised by some National Guards. They fell upon me in a state of incredible rage. "Impeach him!" said some; "Kill him, and so have done with it!" cried others. Fortunately for me several of their comrades—I mention it with pleasure—defended me with as much warmth as the others had attacked me. General Duvivier protected my life, sword in hand. Among those who

surrounded me, and who succeeded in saving me from
the blind fury of my assailants, I may mention with
gratitude my colleagues La Rochejacquelin, Boulay de
la Meurthe, Wowlowsky, Adlesward, my countryman
Conti, a Representative from Corsica, Citizen Mous-
sette, the artist Gigoux, a lieutenant of the National
Guard, named Féary, a delegate of the Luxembourg.
I have been since informed that M. Arago, true to our
long friendship, had hurried out of the Assembly to
my assistance. I am happy at this opportunity of
here recording my gratitude to him and my other
colleagues.

It is more than probable that without their interference it had been all over with me. My hair was
torn out by handfulls; my coat rent in pieces; some
of the wretches attempted to bayonet me from behind;
and one, unable to reach me in any other way, seized
my right hand, and violently twisted my fingers. When
I got into the Assembly, I was really a heap of rags.
After such treatment, I might, it seems to me, have
expected to receive from every one of my colleagues,
some of those attentions that are suggested by a feeling
of humanity. But such is the cruel effects of misconceptions inevitable in times of revolution, that I encountered from part of the Assembly nothing but the
greatest hostility of feeling. My presence in the
tribune, to which I was summoned by the most imperious of duties, that of testifying in favour of my
unfortunate friends, Albert and Barbès, was the signal
for an outburst of the most violent murmurs.

Can it be true, as several newspapers have stated,

that with these murmurs were mixed up insults such
as a man of spirit cannot brook? I have a right to
deny it, not only because I did not hear them, but
because I afterwards wrote a letter, desiring the
authors of these inserted insults to make themselves
known. Now this letter has never received a reply,
and I have sufficient respect for the Assembly of which
I was one, to believe that it did not contain a single
person capable of descending to an anonymous and
irresponsible insult.

According to the *Moniteur* of the day, permission to
prosecute Albert was given by a *unanimous* vote. There
is no correctness whatever in this assertion.

Such, related with the most perfect and minute
accuracy, is what I did and suffered on the 15th of
May.

As much as I deplore the acts of that day, and much
as I have been injured by them, I think it right, in
justice to the people of Paris, here to protest against
the expressions, "sanguinary vengeance," " desperadoes," "men, only wanting a temporary triumph to select
their victims,"* &c. &c., which were evidently intended
by his lordship to leave upon his readers an impression
of savage ferocity on the part of the actors in that extraordinary scene. If anything is to be wondered at, it
certainly is that in a dense, highly excited, and armed
crowd, no acts of violence or wanton mischief should
have been committed. Can Lord Normanby point out
a single drop of blood spilt, a single personal injury

* "A Year of Revolution in Paris," vol. i. pp. 393—396.

inflicted by "desperadoes," ripe, as he seems to think, for massacre, and that, too, under circumstances when they might have easily gratified their "sanguinary vengeance?" Does he not himself give illustrations of the thoughtful consideration, kindness, courtesy, he and some ladies under his care met from those who chanced to be near him, one of the leaders, at the cost of great trouble, offering to escort Lord Normanby and his party, and making way for them through the crowd, which opened to let them pass?* No doubt his lordship, as a gentleman, returned thanks which, as a historian, he has thought it proper to suppress. But I cannot help regretting, with the *Journal des Débats* in its comments on this very passage, that "he had not a word of kindness to throw to the poor devils that had protected him."

* "A Year of Revolution in Paris," vol. i. p. 398.

CHAPTER XVIII.

It would be difficult to exaggerate the evil consequences of the 14th of May. Then it was that the
monarchical parties began to feel the possibility of
sapping the Republic; then it was that the work of the
re-action really began. The " Commission Executive "
was rapidly undermined. M. Ledru Rollin found
himself the subject of the most virulent attacks in
every Orleanist or Legitimist paper. M. Caussidière
was removed from the prefecture of police, in spite of,
and partly, perhaps, on account of, the protection M.
de Lamartine seemed to bestow upon him. As to
M. de Lamartine himself, who had lost ground amongst
the people by coquetting with the Monarchists, being
now deserted by them, he saw his ascendancy vanished,
as if by magic.

Like these gentlemen, I had not, in the eyes of the
monarchical parties, the serious demerit of being in
office; but mine was the much greater sin of being
still more popular out of power than in it, thanks to
the exclusive policy which had aroused the jealousy
and the apprehensions of the people. It became, therefore, the hope of those who had already conceived the

design of overturning the Republic, in some way or other to dispose of me.

That, after my efforts,—strenuous, known to all, and officially attested by the *Moniteur*,—on behalf of the safety and dignity of the Assembly when invaded, my conduct on that occasion should be seized upon as a pretext for ruining me, might appear incredible, if, in civil dissensions, anything could be incredible.

So little had I at that time fathomed the depths of party hatred, that, in spite of several ominous circumstances, the occurrence of so monstrous a prosecution seemed to me utterly impossible.   On the 31st of May, feeling myself indisposed, I happened to go to the Assembly later than usual; as I entered, I heard my name mentioned by the member who was speaking, M. Piétri, the same person who has lately ceased to be Louis Bonaparte's *Préfet de Police*.   Inquiring of those near me what was going on, I learnt to my great astonishment, that a request had just been made to the Assembly by the two law officers of the Government, MM. Portalis and Landrin, for leave to prosecute me.

Thus, a most important step had been taken against me, without my receiving the slightest notice of it, and I had run the risk of being condemned without being heard.   Carried away by a feeling of indignation which I could not master, I rushed to the tribune. As a man, I had nothing to explain or to excuse; but, as a representative of the people, it was my duty to say, and I did say, that they were precipitating themselves into a path which must lead to sanguinary collisions, to the internecine strife of parties, to the re-establishment of the pain of death, and to civil war. Never shall I forget the violence with which the royalist majority interrupted me, when I spoke of the penalty of death. " Who will restore it? What do you mean? Who will restore it ? "—was the cry which furiously assailed me from all parts of the house. I replied: " The terrible logic of human passions, once let loose." Indeed, this demand for my prosecution was simply a demand for my proscription; and, by a strange coincidence, the day on which it was made, was the anniversary of that memorable 31st of May, 1793, when the proscription of the Girondists gave the signal for the fearful struggles in which the members of the Assembly were seen stained with each other's blood.

Several members rose in succession to give their testimony in my favour. So monstrous was the indictment, that many of my most ardent political opponents took up my defence, amongst whom I have already cited M. Piétri. But the majority of the Assembly would not be persuaded. Eighteen *Commissaires* were appointed to examine whether the demand for leave to prosecute me ought to be admitted. These gentlemen met, accordingly, and, after a warm discussion, in which, I was informed, my cause had been most eloquently and indignantly advocated by MM. Théodore Bac, Dupont (de Bussac), and Freslon, it was decided, by a majority of fifteen to three, that the prosecution should take place.

On the 2nd of June, the report on my case was brought up by M. Jules Favre.

M. Jules Favre is a man of an almost unparalleled talent as orator; he has rendered and can still render great services to the Republic; and, for this reason, I will refrain from uttering any bitter word of complaint as regards the course he thought proper to pursue on that occasion—a course which could not fail to be, in the Republican party, a matter of painful and general astonishment. His conclusion was that the Assembly ought not to interpose a barrier of parliamentary privilege against the claims of justice. Reasonable enough, if there had been even a shadow of pretext for the accusation. But no.

I was accused of having said to the people, on the 15th of May: "I congratulate you on your having conquered the right of petition, which they will never be able henceforth to take away from you." And in a letter addressed to the President of the Assembly, M. Barbès nobly declared that the words attributed to me had been uttered by himself, giving as a proof the account of the *Moniteur*, where, indeed, they were found after his name.

I was suspected of having repaired, on the evening of the 15th of May, to the Hôtel de Ville, with a view to form a new government. And the Mayor of Paris, M. Marrast, one of my bitterest opponents at that period, made a solemn declaration that the result of a minute inquiry was, I had not set my foot there.

In fact, Lord Normanby himself, speaking of these extraordinary proceedings, feels bound to say: " It must be owned that, if the Assembly were to exercise the functions of a grand-jury, nothing could be weaker than the statements in the requisition upon which the indictment was founded." *

This became so manifest that, although the ministers had authorised the demand, all of them with the exception of one only, thought themselves bound, as representatives of the people, to vote against it; and, upon the division, it was rejected by a majority of 369 to 337. †

In consequence of their defeat, MM. Portalis, Landrin, and Jules Favre, gave in their resignation, immediately followed by that of M. Crémieux, Minister of Justice.

One might think the question completely settled. How my opponents contrived to revive it, and under what circumstances, will be seen hereafter.

This was going on just on the eve of a most important event.

Some of the representatives of Paris having been elected also in other places, and two of them, MM. Caussidière and Father Lacordaire, having, from various motives, given in their resignation, eleven candidates were to be elected by the Parisians. The following was the list of the members returned:

Caussidière	. . . .	147,400
Moreau	. . . .	126,889
Goudchaux	. . . .	107,097
Changarnier	. . . .	105,537
Thiers	. . . .	97,394
Pierre Leroux	. . . .	91,375
Victor Hugo	. . . .	86,965

---

* "A Year of Revolution in Paris," vol. i. pp. 436, 437.
† *Moniteur* of the 3rd of June, 1848.

Louis Napoleon Bonaparte . .	84,426
Lagrange	78,682
Boisset	77,247
Proudhon	77,094

Such a result was, in many respects, remarkable. The name of M. Caussidière at the head of the poll showed clearly enough that the feelings of the population of Paris were not in accordance with those by which the Royalists were actuated in the Assembly; and the number, comparatively so considerable, of the Socialist candidates elected, was an unmistakeable indication of the signal progress of the new ideas in Paris. But what, even much more than this, struck both the Government and the leaders of the Assembly, was the unexpected election of Louis Napoleon Bonaparte.

A rumour, skilfully spread by his partisans, that he would not be allowed to take his seat in the Assembly, became a source of agitation. For some days the uncertainty of the decision to be taken on the subject, attracted masses of people towards the legislative palace. Excited groups collected on the Place de la Concorde, and thronged the approaches to the Assembly. They were no doubt, at least to a certain extent, under the influence of a name not less powerful than fatal; but their excitement arose from the idea that an exceptional decree of banishment against Louis Bonaparte was about to be propounded, which appeared to them both an injustice and an infringement of their electoral rights. It is true that the Bonaparte family had been excluded from France by a distinct law, dated 13th of January, 1816; but this law seemed to have been abrogated *de facto*, as two cousins of Louis Bonaparte and the son of Murat were, at that very moment, sitting in the National Assembly.

In this state of things, what ought to have been the policy of the Executive Commission?

It was obvious that, by shutting the doors of the Assembly against Louis Bonaparte, they would create in his favour a new and dangerous influence, independent of his name and in addition to it, as such a course could have no other effect than to procure for him that kind of interest which naturally attaches to a man who is, or is supposed to be, injured. Moreover, thus to single him out as an exception, was to raise him, in the eyes of the nation, to the high position of a rival claimant for the Government of France; to exhibit so marked a fear of him, was to make him formidable. Grant that he would conspire—which I have no doubt he did—it was surely better he should do so in the midst of us, where he could be closely watched, guarded against, foiled, and, if requisite, arrested, than that he should be enabled to cast his nets from a foreign country, with no risk of personal entanglement. Had he got into the Assembly, what then? Without eloquence, without parliamentary experience, without any of those qualifications through which a man acquires a mastery over political assemblies, placed face to face with eminent men in every way superior to him, and constantly subject to be called upon by them for any explanation his acts might suggest, he would have soon dwindled to nothing. Out of the Assembly he must have been surrounded by an *entourage* little likely to recommend him, and exposed to an intercourse with the zealots of his party, whose indiscretions might at any moment have ruined him. On the contrary, being abroad, he was in a position to mature his plans at leisure, and with all required caution; whilst, on the other hand, he had all the benefit of an exile, which in association with his name, was sure to tell on the imagination of the people of France. In the physical world, the farther off a man is, the smaller he appears; but, in the moral world, the farther he is off, the greater he appears. The only danger, then, despite these probabilities of failure, had he been in Paris, lay in the chance that the influence of his name among the peasantry, might throw him up, by means of Universal Suffrage, into the Presidency of the Republic. This, there was a simple and decisive way to prevent. All that was requisite, was to enact in the Constitution about to be framed, that there should be no Presidency chosen by universal suffrage, that is, no executive power utterly independent of the legislative power, derived from the same source, having therefore equal or even superior weight, and often subject, by the very nature of things, to be brought into collision with it.*

---

* So satisfied was I, from the first, of the vicious character of this anarchical organisation, that in a special work on this subject, written at the time and afterwards published as a pamphlet, I thus expressed myself:—

"A society with two heads can exist only at the cost of the most frightful convulsions, and, even so, cannot exist for any great length of time. When power is tossed backwards and forwards between one man and an Assembly, it is absolutely certain that either this Assembly brings

But now arises a much higher question than that of policy. Was this exclusion just? True, Louis Bonaparte had twice come forward as a Pretender— once at Strasbourg, again at Boulogne—but a Pretender against the crown of Louis Philippe, when Royalty existed; whereas he had not only tendered his allegiance to the Republic, but actually offered it his services. As to such a declaration being to all appearance insincere, this was merely a matter of watchfulness, not of punishment; and the Government —more especially a Republican one, was bound in duty to wait for some overt act of conspiracy, and, before punishing, to give him the benefit of a fair trial. I know there are people who think that what are called "reasons of state," may cover any species of policy. Nothing could be more dangerous. To strike at a man not lawfully declared guilty, is to strike at the safety of all, and the blow recoils on humanity at large. For my part, so thoroughly am I convinced of the necessity of undeviating strictness in such matters, that, in my opinion, the slaughter of thousands of men from a mistaken sense of right, is a less calamity than the sacrifice of a single man by an open violation of justice.

Be this as it may, the Executive Commission mistook, as I conceive, both the nature of the danger and that of the prevention. On the 12th of June,

on a 10th of August (the day when Louis XVI. monarchy was overthrown by the Assembly in 1792), or that this man brings on an 18th Brumaire." —*Nouveau Monde*, par Louis Blanc, 1849.

Whether this prophecy has been realised or not, every one knows !

M. de Lamartine went to the Assembly, with the intention of moving that the law excluding the Bonaparte family from France, should be exceptionally applied to Louis Bonaparte. Accordingly, he opened the subject by a long desultory speech, which was received with so much coldness, that he became evidently disconcerted, and, after some time, requested a momentary adjournment of the debate, on the ground of fatigue. In this interval, reports having reached the house of some disturbances amongst the crowds outside, M. de Lamartine rushed again to the tribune, and exclaimed— "A fatal event breaks in upon the speech I had commenced. Several shots have been fired, one at the Commander-in-chief of the National Guard of Paris, another upon an officer of the line, a third has wounded an officer of the National Guard in the breast. . . . . When the audacity of the factious is caught in the act, their hands dyed with the French blood, the law I propose ought to be voted by acclamation."

But it having been, in the meanwhile, ascertained that the reports on which the speaker rested his remarks were inaccurate; that instead of three shots there had been only one; and that the blood shed, was the blood of a National Guard who had accidentally wounded himself; these appeals to the sympathies of the Assembly were not attended with the desired effect. One other reason for this was, that M. de Lamartine had now lost the ear of the Assembly, and found himself under the ban of the same jealousies and dislikes to which I had been exposed.

The next day, the question was to be brought to a conclusion, and I took part in the debate.

Lord Normanby says: "It is understood that all among the lower classes whom Louis Blanc can influence, are in favour of the Bonaparte movement." * His Lordship is entirely mistaken, if he means that the classes alluded to, received any encouragement from me. Not only was I not in favour of what Lord Normanby calls the "Bonaparte movement," but I was most anxious to check it, by removing its cause,— an exclusion, which had an air of injustice, and might lead to a system of political proscriptions.

It was prompted by this feeling that, on the 13th of June, I ascended the tribune; where I stated at length the arguments above-mentiond, against the proscription of Louis Bonaparte: "Don't magnify," said I, "the stature of Pretenders by keeping them at a distance. What we want is, to see them near, that we may take a juster measure of their size." † Having observed that, to make the Republic great, generous, and beneficial to the people, was the surest way to make Pretenders impossible, I added: "What said Louis Bonaparte's uncle? That 'the Republic is like the Sun.' Well! let the emperor's nephew approach the sun of our Republic. I am confident he will disappear in his rays." ‡ And disappear in his rays he certainly would have done, had the Republic, as I warned them, made itself a sun. The

* "A Year of Revolution in Paris," vol. i. p. 466.
† *Moniteur*, Séance du 13 Juin, 1848.
‡ *Ibid.*

grounds on which I supported my views, far from having reference to the interest of any one man whatever, were essential to the cause I had devoted myself to, and such as every true Republican must abide by. A brief extract from my speech will illustrate them :—

" . . . . It is enough for me to say, that, according to my ideas, all laws of exclusion and proscription are laws thoroughly anti-republican. That same logic of Republicanism which does not permit a son to wear a crown, simply because his father has worn it, that same logic also refuses to admit that a son may be punished for the crimes of his father. The logic of Republicanism, which rejects hereditary transmission in the act of exercising power, cannot admit hereditary responsibility in the application of punishments. And this is, as far as I am concerned, why I resolutely voted against the proscription of the D'Orleans family, though I passed ten years of my life in combating their fatal royalty." *

But whilst thus insisting, as the first and greatest of all considerations, upon an unswerving fidelity to justice, I was neither blind nor indifferent to the danger of a possible contingency. Therefore was it I formally moved that the following clause should be inserted in the new constitution about to be framed :

" In the French Republic, founded on the 24th of February, 1848, there shall be no such office as that of President."

M. Ledru Rollin, taking an opposite view of the

---

* *Moniteur*, Séance du 13 Juin, 1848.

question, spoke against the admission of Louis Bonaparte with much animation and eloquence, but in vain.
The decision of the Assembly was, that Louis Bonaparte should be allowed to return to his country, and
to take his seat. Only, the idea I had put forth of
removing the danger of his being ever elected President, by declaring there should be no Presidency,
found very little favour in an Assembly whose majority
saw in a President the shadow of a monarch. M. de
Lamartine, in this particular respect, agreed with the
majority; and, I am sorry to say, even to a considerable
portion of the Republican party it seemed hardly
possible that a Republic could exist without a President.
So much were their minds biassed by the practice of
the United States! So blind were they to the necessity of entirely subordinating the Executive in a Republic that maintains an immense standing army!*

The real danger was there, and not at all in the
admission of Louis Bonaparte as member of the
Assembly. He himself felt so sensibly that his presence in Paris could have no better result for him than
to lower his position, and to lessen his favourable
chances, that he refrained from taking advantage of
the vote of the Assembly, and preferred remaining in

---

* Whether, in France, the evil of a standing army could not be remedied
was not then the question. Right or wrong, a standing army, being generally considered a necessity, could not be discarded as an element of political
calculation.

As to the United States, it must be remarked that there are there three
independent powers, all, it is true, deriving equally from the people, but
by different processes, which peculiarly affect the result; and there is no
standing army.

exile, waiting for the opportunity to present himself as a candidate, were a President of the Republic to be elected.

What was, then, the best way to baffle his expectations? The Assembly had only to declare that there should be no President at all, or, at least, no President chosen by universal suffrage.* Whether I might have succeeded in spreading my opinions upon this most important point, widely enough to make them prevalent, had I been in Paris when the plan of a new Constitution was discussed, is very little probable. But, at all events, I was determined to spare no effort to avert the peril. Unfortunately, whilst I was deprecating the proscription of others, my opponents were at work, preparing everything for my own.

* A President chosen by the Assembly was one of the modes suggested.

CHAPTER XIX.

THE INSURRECTION OF HUNGER!

To reject the remedy is not to save the sufferer. The number of starving or nearly starving men was immense. The institution of the *National Workshops,* such as it had been designed, devoured vast sums of public money in useless labour, sterile and humiliating as being a sort of hypocritical alms-giving, under a flimsy veil. The population in the workshops went on increasing from day to day, and into that bottomless gulf the treasure of the State was recklessly cast. What was to be done?

It occurred to those who had denounced the organisation of labour as a chimera, that there was one way of getting rid of these embarrassing National Workshops. Why not *dissolve* them? Dissolve them, indeed! But to dissolve them without providing an outlet for the menacing turbulence which they contained, without furnishing employment to the legions of men who had been simply kept alive by an expedient —in a word, to dissolve the National Workshops without *falling into Socialism,* which the re-actionists were determined to avoid at any cost, this was a more stupendous act of folly than it had been to organise them; as it was to let loose a hundred thousand famished men, armed to the teeth, and likely to be driven to fury through despair. But alas! the coalesced parties were equally alarmed at the danger and at its only possible cure. Their declaration was, "No more National Workshops, and no Socialism." But what then? The insurrection of June was the reply.

That this fatal result had been clearly foreseen and heartlessly calculated upon, is what I neither can nor will believe. Let our detractors accuse us, in their savage exuberance of hate, of blood-thirstiness and destructive cruelty; it is not for us, as the seekers and servants of true principles, to bandy calumny for calumny, but rather in our bitterest enemies to respect our fellow-creatures. I only make one assertion : *That the Insurrection of June was the consequence of dissolving the National Workshops, without having recourse to Socialism.*

At that moment, the favourite theme of the Re-actionists was this: The people have been deceived by promises which it was impossible to keep. Now, what were these promises which it was impossible to keep? The people had been promised *subsistence by labour.* Was this too much in return for the blood they had shed? for the protection so earnestly accorded by them to their very calumniators? for the devotedness with which these houseless men, who had Paris at their mercy, kept guard at the doors of rich men's palaces? If even promises had been withheld, what, I ask, could have saved our enemies from the famous alternative : "We will live by working, or die fighting." If no

promises were possible to keep, why did not our opponents, who displayed so much courage against our
Utopian follies when there were a hundred thousand
soldiers and a force of artillery in their front, why,
I say, did they not come forward on the tumultuous
Place de Grêve, and tell the people that their confidence was abused, and that, after all their combats,
they could be assured of nothing—not even of subsistence by the sweat of their brow ?

The truth is, that the men who talked of promises
which it was impossible to keep, had exhausted every
effort in preventing them from being kept.

Without again mentioning the obstacles which the
commission of the Luxembourg encountered whenever
it attempted any practical experiment, how was the
writer of these lines received, when, in the sitting of the
Assembly on the 10th of May, he proposed the creation
of a Ministry of Labour; that is to say, a ministry
specially charged with the duty of seeking a remedy
for the distresses of working men, and provided with
resources to alleviate them?   There could be no apprehension of the originator of this motion aspiring to a
return to power.   He had made up his mind, under
any circumstances, to be content with his post of representative; and, in order to cut short objections founded
on odious insinuations, he had declared his resolution
in advance, from the tribune of the Assembly.   Yet,
what happened?   Why, Blues and Whites, with common
accord, cried out, *" No ! no !   No Socialism !"*—But
then it may be civil war—*" No! no ! No Socialism ! "*—
But, simply to drive into the streets the hundred thou-

sand men of the National Workshops, is to drive them
to despair.—" *No! no! No Socialism.*" In vain did
the author of the proposition point out the black cloud
in the horizon; in vain did he utter these prophetic
words: " Before February you were told to beware of
the revolution of contempt. I tell you now to beware
of the revolution of hunger." Warning was useless.
It was determined at all hazards to prevent the realisation of promises which had been declared "impossible
to keep." The idea of dissolving the National Workshops became a fixed determination with the Re-
actionists; and " We must have done with them " was
adopted as a cry.

But *how?* This was the unavoidable question. Will
it be believed that the Director of the National Workshops, M. Émile Thomas himself, was at length obliged
to acknowledge that it was impossible to get out of the
difficulty without bloodshed, except by adopting at
least a part of the doctrines of the Luxembourg—those
very doctrines which he had been appointed by M.
Marie to declaim against and to resist. Lest this conversion should appear too improbable, I will quote text-
ually the precise words of M. Émile Thomas himself:

" I proposed that there should be appointed by
election, in every trade, and in Paris to begin with,
a Syndicate, composed half of masters and half of
workmen; and that there should be nominated a
magisterial syndic as well as a trade manager.
Regularly constituted, these trade syndicates would
have formed beyond the limits of their special
trade, each by a delegation of two members, superior

syndicates (in the building, clothing, or provision trades, &c.). In the same way, these superior syndicates would have composed a council-general of the industrial occupations, subject to the administration of the Ministry of Public Works, or of the Ministry of Commerce.

"Addressing themselves to the urgent question of the day—the general stagnation of business—each of the syndicates would have furnished a provisional tariff for the labour of its branch of trade, taking the hour as the standard measure. Then each syndicate would have delegated its manager to the administration of the special workshops, into which would have been admitted, at half-wages, the men of each trade wanting work. The workshops and manufactories out of work would have furnished immediately, on very easy terms, room and implements.

"In these workshops might have been produced those delicate objects of manufacture, in which the raw material is insignificant as compared with the workmanship; as is the case with the greater part of the Parisian trades. The product of this labour forming a guarantee for the repayment of the advances of the State for the maintenance of the workmen, would have been delivered for exportation, or sold at the ruling prices of the home market; the profits in the latter case being reserved to the syndicates, as a reserve fund of mutual succour. Ranges of buildings would have been constructed, destined for working men, and composed of small furnished houses, of two or three stories only, and inhabited by three or four families.

These buildings would have been furnished with common bakeries, kitchens, and furnaces; and, in short, everything that constitutes the cheapness and advantage of association."*

Now, I ask the reader if the plagiarism be not complete enough? This scheme, which M. Émile Thomas had the intrepidity to call *his plan,* was nothing more and nothing less than a clumsy copy of that very plan proposed at the Luxembourg, which M. Émile Thomas had incessantly denounced.

Special workshops, open to men of each trade wanting work; State security upon the product of the labour for the repayment of the advances made; the collective character given to the employment of the profits; the construction of buildings for working men in association: nothing was omitted! It was all very well for M. Émile Thomas to excuse himself by saying, that "to adopt his plan would not be to fall into the system of M. Louis Blanc," but only "to substitute, *in that order of ideas,* for the direct action of the State, its security or its succour." † Such an evasion as this, was too gross an imposition on the indifference or ignorance of the public. What other action of the State had I ever recommended than its *commandite* and its guarantee? Had M. Émile Thomas been courageous enough to avow his conversion, he would have confessed that his attacks upon the Luxembourg were inconsistent and unjust; that the perils of the situation

* *Histoire des Ateliers Nationaux,* par M. Émile Thomas, pp. 240, 241, 242.
† *Ibid.,* p. 240.

could be averted only by the adoption of the Luxembourg system; that Socialism was not what he had fancied it was before he came to study it; and that it was the only possible means of putting an end to M. Marie's National Workshops, without deluging Paris in blood.

M. Émile Thomas was far from being willing to do this, and down he went to the Hôtel de Ville to develop as his own, the ideas he had been commissioned to calumniate. But MM. Corbin, Bethmont, and Danguy, were not to be deceived. They clearly perceived the origin of the proposed transformation of the National Workshops, and rejected it peremptorily.

M. Marie having been appointed a Member of the Executive Commission, it was upon M. Trélat, as the then Minister of Public Works, that, from and after the 12th of May, devolved the responsibility of deciding the fate of the National Workshops. Never was a more singularly incapable man charged with a more serious task. All that M. Trélat succeeded in doing, was to substitute M. Lalanne for M. Émile Thomas; to form a *Commission of the National Workshops,* whose profound conceptions never saw the light, and whose overt intervention was confined to measures scandalously insignificant; to betray his former friends; to stain his political reputation by an alliance with his old antagonists; and to commit acts of arbitrary power, which recalled to mind the tyranny of the Council of Ten at Venice.

And during this time, the great sore festered and increased. Previous to the dismissal of M. Émile

Thomas, M. Trélat had sent him a decree, which, among other oppressive clauses, contained the following :—

"The unmarried working men, between the ages of eighteen and twenty-five, will be invited to enrol themselves under the banners of the Republic, to complete the different regiments of the army; those who refuse to enlist as volunteers will be immediately removed from the *listes d'embrigadement* of the National Workshops. Masters may call upon as many of their working men (of the National Workshops) as they may declare wanted for the resumption or continuation of their business; those who refuse, will be immediately removed from the general list of the National Workshops."

This monstrous decree was signed:

"For the Ministry of Public Works, by (authorisation) the Secretary-General, BOULAGE."

Thus we find the youngest men called out to make themselves food for powder, and the rest to sell themselves at the price offered for them. True, this was a way to avoid Socialism!

Such was the state of things when the intrigues of the Bonapartist party came to complicate the crisis. Of all the subjects that harassed the Executive Commission, none caused more anxiety than the approaching arrival of M. Louis Bonaparte. Now, the National Workshops were actively tampered with at that moment by Bonapartist agents. Not that their efforts were highly successful; but in that vast mass of *regiments* of workmen, the fears of the Executive Commission and of the political party of the National, discerned an army ready to a pretender's hands. It is certain, however, that the dominant influence set in motion was that of Socialism. This I do not for a moment deny; in spite of all the arts of calumny and corruption that had been industriously employed to sow dissension between the men of the National Workshops, and the delegates of the Luxembourg, yet the moment had arrived when the good sense of the people prevailed, and ranged the entire body, united by one spirit, under one flag. I think it advisable to give the proclamation, which was addressed to the people by the delegates of the Luxembourg, united with those of the National Workshops, in the beginning of June. It will show the sort of influence exercised by the well-abused leaders of the Luxembourg.

" WORKING MEN,

" We, delegates of the workmen at the Luxembourg ; we, delegates of the National Workshops; devoted as we are body and soul to the Republic, for which, like all of you, we have fought : we pray you in the name of that Liberty so dearly bought, in the name of the country regenerated by you, in the names of Fraternity and Equality, neither by word nor act to lend countenance to anarchical cries ; nor to lend your arms and your hearts to encourage the partisans of the throne which you lately burnt.* These unprincipled men would inevitably bring anarchy into the midst of the country, which has need only of liberty and labour.

---

* The royal throne had been taken and actually burnt in the Place de la Bastille.

"No one henceforth can be suffered to claim any other title than the noblest of all, that of citizen.

"No one must resist the true sovereign, the people.

"To attempt it, would be an execrable crime, and whoever should dare it, would be a traitor to Heaven and to his country.

"The re-action is at work and in movement: its numerous emissaries will entice you, Brothers, with irrealisable and senseless dreams; it is sowing gold broadcast: beware! Brothers, beware! wait yet a few days with that calmness which you have already shown, and which is your true strength.

"Hope! for the time is come, the future is ours: do not encourage by your presence manifestations which are only popular in name: have nothing to do with those follies of another time.

"Believe us: listen to us: nothing is possible now in France but the Democratic and Social Republic.

"The history of the last reign is a terrible one; let us not continue it. No more EMPERORS, nor Kings. Nothing but Liberty, Equality, and Fraternity.

"*Vive la République!*

"PIERRE VINCARD, *Président des Délégués du Luxembourg.*

"AUGUSTE BLUM, *Vice-Président.*

"JULLIEN, *Trésorier.*

"LEFAURE, *Sécretaire.*

"BACON, *Président des Délégués des Ateliers Nationaux.*

"EUGENE GARLIN, *Sécrétaire.*

"PETIT-BONNAUD, *Lieutenant.*

"ARDILLON, *Lieutenant.*"

Let us here mention a fact, little known, and which deserves to be published. On the eve of the day on which a Bonapartist demonstration was expected, the President of the Delegates of the Luxembourg was sent for to the Château de Bagatelle, by one of the members of the Executive Commission : by the one who has since declaimed so emphatically against popular manifestations, and who boasts of having, on the 16th of April, saved society, which no man threatened,—by M. de Lamartine, if I must call him by his name. And what, is it supposed, was the object of this singular conference ? The object was, at M. de Lamartine's instigation, to prepare, by means of the delegates of the Luxembourg, against Louis Bonaparte, and in support of the Executive Commission, a second 16th of April. Only, this time M. de Lamartine was to head the manifestation, not to combat it. But the men of the Luxembourg were not the puppets of ambition : they were determined to remain, and they did remain, the servants of the people.

Hours passed on : " We give three months' misery to the Republic," the working men had nobly said, and now the day of payment was past ! On the 22nd of June, the note concerning the enrolment of workmen, the *forced* enrolment (since it was a condition imposed upon starving men), burst in the *Moniteur* like a thunderbolt. At several points, especially on the Place St. Sulpice, working men gathered together simultaneously. The " brigades " sent to Corbeil precipitately abandoned their work, and returned to Paris : the first rumblings of civil war began to be heard. The National Workshops were about to be dissolved *without falling into Socialism.*—But the civil war was at hand!—*No, no! No Socialism!*

How did M. Lalanne, the new director of the National Workshops, the confidential agent of M. Trélat, express himself?

"The chefs d' arrondissement are invited to send each the fiftieth part of their effective strength at three o'clock this afternoon, to the *Manège,* to be ready for departure to-day, to-morrow, and day after to-morrow. I will speak myself to the well-disposed men who present themselves. The Government desires the men to set out. The order of the Government must be executed this very day."

Surely, this was the language of despotism. What destination, what kind or condition of employment, was reserved for the poor proscribed men whom the saviours of society were hurrying away? All this was left in darkness.

At nine o'clock, on the morning of the 22nd of June, M. Pujol, delegated by the working men to the Executive Commission, was admitted with four of his comrades to an interview with M. Marie. He represented that, since the Revolution of February the working men had been subject to arbitrary administration: that they had shed their blood for the attainment of a democratic and social Republic, which would put an end to the tyranny of man over man: that they were resolved to make sacrifices for the maintenance of the public liberties: but that they demanded, above all, the organisation of workshops as a refuge to workmen." "The workmen," broke out M. Marie with violence, " who do not submit to the decree will be sent out of Paris *by force*." Let it be borne in mind that this was the same M. Marie who, during the Provisional Government, said to M. Émile Thomas, " Can you count upon the working men? Spare no money : if need be, you shall be supplied with secret funds. Perhaps the day is not far distant when we must make the workmen descend into the street."

The reply of M. Pujol, as I find it in a journal of the day,* supplied with information by the direct representatives of the working classes, was as follows :

" Citizen Representatives, you insult men invested with a sacred character as delegates of the people; we withdraw with the profound conviction that you neither desire the organisation of labour, nor the prosperity of the French people."

" Your heads have been turned," rejoined M. Marie. " It is the system of M. Louis Blanc. We will have nothing to say to it."

Unfortunately, M. Marie forgot to add what system he proposed to substitute for mine : and, as it had become an imminent necessity to find a substitute for civil war, and as none was found, civil war was declared.

In the evening of the 22nd of June, as soon as the conversation between M. Pujol and M. Marie became known, columns of workmen proceeded from the Panthéon by the light of torches, in a state of great excitement.

* *La Vraie République.*

That nothing could be reasonably expected from a popular rising but lamentable results, seemed obvious from the fact of the Bonapartist faction being busily engaged in fanning the flame. Amongst the agents employed by the Bonapartists, there stood prominent a mason of the name of Lahr. Lahr, a man of uncommon activity and fierce courage, worked under M. Nadaud, a master-mason,—a staunch Republican, afterwards representative of the people. Just on the eve of the insurrection, M. Nadaud, who happened to be directing some important works at the " Place de Panthéon," noticed that Lahr, one of the men he wanted, and whom he knew to be remarkably punctual, was absent. On inquiring what could have become of him, he soon learned that Lahr had, a little before, entered a public-house, at the corner of the Square. M. Nadaud hastened to the place, where he found Lahr surrounded by several workmen, the most of whom were Germans. No sooner had M. Nadaud made his appearance, than Lahr, who was seated drinking, rose instantly, came up to the unexpected visitor, and, presenting him with a glass of wine, exclaimed : " Welcome, old fellow; and now, *à la santé du petit !* " " *Le petit* " was then a familiar expression used by the workmen to designate either Louis Bonaparte or myself. " What and whom do you mean ? " asked M. Nadaud. " I mean," replied Lahr, " that we must drink the health of Louis Bonaparte ; as it is time for us to *set ourselves to work.*" M. Nadaud pushed back with indignation the glass handed to him, saying : " Is this what you call

your business?" and he rushed out.* Well, it was
only three days after, on the 25th of June, that the
murder of General Bréa took place at the Barrière
de Fontainebleau, for which Lahr was sentenced to
death and executed. But who Lahr was, and for
whose sake he had fought, was studiously thrown into
the shade, for the purpose of shuffling off on the
Socialists at large, a murder committed by a Bonapartist, and the only treacherous act, too, connected
with the insurrection of June.

Of the particulars I have just related, I was not
aware at the time; but from many other circumstances
I knew for a certainty that the Bonapartists were on the
watch to turn a civil war to account, and I shuddered at
the mere idea of the people's being deluded into pouring
out their blood in torrents, by men who had nothing
better in view than the gratification of one man's
ambition! Naturally averse as I was to bloodshed
whatever the motive, I had now every reason to
object to any popular agitation; and so little did I
conceal my feelings on the subject from those amongst
the workmen with whom I was then especially in
communication, that the associated tailors at Clichy
took no part in the movement.† But, besides my
being no longer invested with official influence, the

* I have these important details from the best possible authority, M.
Nadaud himself, now a refugee in England, than whom a more honourable
and high-minded man I have never met with in my life.

† During the insurrection of June, the tailors at Clichy remained there,
working as usual. This remarkable fact was stated by me, from the
tribune, on the 25th of August, 1848, and was not contradicted, no contradiction being possible. See the *Moniteur* of the 26th of August, 1848.

jealousies of the ruling power had made it very difficult for me to keep up any regular intercourse with
the whole body of the Parisian workmen.   At all
events, it would have required time successfully to
interfere; and, although there had been for some days
an ominous uneasiness amongst the men employed in
the National Workshops, the insane measures which
swelled their alarms into fury were so suddenly taken
and carried out, that no human power could have
prevented their direful effect.

On the morning of the 23rd of June, I was getting
into a cab with a countryman of mine, named M.
Savelli, who had come to fetch and accompany me to
the Assembly, when some five or six workmen rushed
to the carriage-window, saying : " Friend, a great deal
of excitement prevails in Paris. What is to be done ? "
My heart was breaking. " Is there," I asked, " any
particular place of meeting to which I may repair,
and express what I feel ? " They replied hurriedly,
with much animation : " For God's sake, don't go.
Why should you ? Almost all Paris is in commotion,
from the Barrière Rochechouart on the right bank of
the Seine, to the Panthéon on the left. Where could
you go to ? Only, let us know what you wish us to
convey to such of our comrades as we may chance to
meet with." " Tell them that if they rise in arms,
there is an end of the Republic. Tell them that I
feel acutely how hard their position is, but that, under
the circumstances, fighting would be to make matters
worse. Ambitious men are not wanting, ready to
reap the fruit of any possible tumult. Let the people

be on their guard! Even their success might be fatal to them, whilst their defeat would be death to the Republic." They did not utter a word more, but shaking their heads as if to imply they thought it was too late, warmly grasped my hand, and took their leave.*

All I had now to do was to go to the Assembly, there to endeavour to oppose any inconsiderate or violent measures, come from what quarter they would, which might aggravate or complicate the state of things. This I considered to be my duty, the only course left me: and all my colleagues in the National Assembly, of the Socialist party, had come there prompted by a similar feeling. The fact is, that we had all of us been taken unawares, and were unable, amongst the confused elements which were said to be at work, to discern the real import of the impending insurrection, so extremely rapid was the succession of events! It was not long, however, before its true character developed itself. The Bonapartist and Legitimist factions, which for a moment struggled to direct it in their respective interests, soon perceived that their only chance of abetting the contest, was to strike their own flags and fight under that of the people, which bore these mournful and terribly significant words: BREAD OR LEAD,—DU PAIN OU DU PLOMB!

But, by the time we became completely aware of what the predominant element was, the Assembly had

* A letter from M. Savelli to the President of the Commission of Inquiry will be found in the *Moniteur's* report of the sitting of the 25th of August, 1848.

declared itself *en permanence;* and from that moment, it would have been, of course, impossible for us to stir, without the certainty of being arrested on the threshold.

On Friday, the 23rd, a compact column, which had formed in the Place de la Bastille, fell like an avalanche on the Porte St. Denis, where the first engagement took place. But already, whilst the National Guard were slowly assembling in the aristocratic quarters of the town, the populous streets bristled with barricades.

That was the moment chosen by M. de Falloux to carry to the Tribune of the National Assembly the report which recommended the dissolution of the National Workshops, with the proviso of an indemnity of thirty francs per man! And while M. de Falloux was bringing forward his report, the firing was beginning, the barricades were rising, all Paris was in arms. " I do not think the reading of this report opportune," exclaimed M. Raynal; but the re-actionists insisted that it should be read, and M. de Falloux hastened to comply. Then, in order that the war against Socialism should be general, there began an attack in the Assembly against the execution of railways by the State. Out of doors, the people continued to cry : Du Pain ou du Plomb !

But, as if, to stifle those words of woe, it was not enough to load guns with grape, to set infantry and cavalry in movement, to reinforce the National Guard with troops of the line, and the republican guard with the Garde Mobile,—the aid of calumny was called to their support. In a circular addressed to the munici-

palities of the twelve arrondissements, M. Marrast
dared to represent this insurgent army of hunger
as a horde of brigands in foreign pay. He dared to
write these words, speaking of the chiefs of the insurrection: "It is not only civil war that they would
light up among us, it is PILLAGE that they prepare."

No doubt the parties that wore the legitimist and
imperial liveries had crowded into their ranks, men
ready to instigate disorder in the hope of its abetting
the triumph of their conspiracies; and these men were
in effect the active agents of disorder. But to confound
the instigations of conspirators like these, who scarcely
dared to show their faces or their objects, with the
true cause which was then arming thousands of fellow-
men; to pretend that the barricades were being reared
against the Republic, and that PILLAGE was the object
of men driven to despair, and hurrying to death,—a
more audacious calumny, I say, was never published.
Yet it had the success of audacious calumny. Sincere
Republicans believed that the Republic was in peril:
false Republicans affected to believe that it was
attacked: there was an immense uncertainty, and an
immense confusion. The insurgents continued crying,
as they marched to the combat, DU PAIN OU DU
PLOMB!

Whether the insurrection might not have been prevented from the first—whether barricades need have
been quietly left to boys to construct—whether, in
short, General Cavaignac, by letting the insurrection
pass, reserved to himself the sinister honour of suppressing it,—these are questions for History to solve.

o r the present, I will only state this fact, that, at four o'clock in the afternoon, on the 23rd of June, in the Faubourg St. Marceau, although it was in full insurrection, the circulation was still free, and that it would have been perfectly easy for either the civil or the military authorities to ascertain that many of the barricades were guarded by men incompletely armed, and utterly without ammunition of any kind. I have ample evidence in my possession to produce, when the proper time arrives for doing justice to all.

It is worthy of remark that this insurrection, so general in its causes and in its spirit, assumed at almost every point the character of a local protest. In many districts, the inhabitants reserved to themselves exclusively the guard of their own barricades, rejected the assistance of strangers, and after closing all access to their streets, refused to co-operate in the general attack. After the capture of the Eighth and Ninth Mairies, for instance, when preparations were making for storming the Hôtel de Ville— a very strong position, strongly defended—scarcely a few hundred combatants could be got together at the bottom of the Rue St. Antoine.

Reinforcements were demanded from the Faubourgs, where the barricades could easily have spared numbers of men, but in vain. Not but that among the combatants there were many who knew well that an insurrection which stands still, or does not go forward, is lost ; but that there was a total want of unity of direction, and many of the insurgents were paralysed by the sense of their inferiority in the use of their weapons. Fifty thousand men had taken up arms : how many in that number were utterly unable to use them ! Some, who might have vigorously defended a barricade, were more than inefficient for any other purpose. And whilst in the rich quarters of the town there were thousands of isolated combatants, who were on the look out for a loop-hole to pass over to the insurgents, there was probably a reserve of twenty thousand men in the Faubourgs, whose strength might have changed the fate of the battle.

Another cause of the unwillingness of the combatants to venture far beyond their barricades, was the want of ammunition. The gunpowder was manufactured by the insurgents, and from this fact we may determine their chances of success against regular troops, amply furnished with all the resources of war.

Yet, in spite of the inadequacy of the ammunition for offensive warfare, of the want of chiefs to concentrate their movements, of means to prolong the combat, the indomitable energy of the insurgents was astounding. The regular troops and National Guards fought well, as Frenchmen always fight; but those who were least liable to suspicion of sympathy with the insurgents, confessed that their prodigious resolution and audacity would have sufficed, under an able general, for the conquest of the world !

Besides, thanks to M. Marie, the Ateliers Nationaux had received a military organisation, and had been divided into brigades, squadrons, and companies, comprising the men of the same arrondissement, of the same quarter, of the same street; and, in a war of barricades, in which every man resolved to fight and die at his own door, for the bread of his own household, such an organisation lent a certain *ensemble* to the resistance, although the resistance was a local one.

The movement had continued to spread from point to point, until all Paris was in arms. It was not until Friday evening the Société des Droits de l'Homme was enabled to hold a meeting; and the communications were already interrupted in so many places, that it was impossible to give the sections anything like uniformity of operation. Having at their head men of ardour and decision, the sectionaries of the eighth arrondissement took an active part in the attack of the Place des Vosges. In the offices of the Socialist journals, a poignant uncertainty prevailed amidst the contradictory rumours arriving every moment from the scene of conflict. A list of names for a new Government came from a barricade in the Faubourg St. Marceau, containing the name of M. de Lamartine, together with other names then more dear to the people.

Overwhelming as the forces of the Government appeared, the end was still doubtful. At some points, the desperation of the insurgents was incredibly triumphant. In the Faubourg du Temple, where General Cavaignac had reconnoitred the fortresses, the fight assumed gigantic proportions. At the attack of the barricade Saint Maure, the troops suffered terrible loss, and were repulsed. When the darkness of night enveloped the streets, the insurgents were completely masters of that portion of the city.

Terrible was that night—a night of expectation and grief! On the following morning, the heavy guns began to thunder once more against the Faubourg, without gaining the least advantage over the insurgents, while the troops advanced, retreated, and advanced again, with alternate wrath and discouragement. Until Sunday evening, the blood of countrymen and fellow-citizens was flowing in disastrous rivalry. What was most lamentable of all, was the inexorable fury of the fight between the working-men and the Garde Mobile—between fathers on one side, and sons on the other! Everybody knows now, that when the insurrection began, the Garde Mobile was more disposed to join than to attack the insurgents. But it had been so pertinaciously asserted that the insurrection was against the Republic, that one more terrible misunderstanding was added to the history of civil conflicts.

Let us pass to the Assembly. During all these hours of devastation, the Assembly sat *en permanence,* distracted by alternate hopes and alarms. I was there: and when, at a later moment, I witnessed the defiant boldness of certain men, I could not but remember their fallen looks and their pale cheeks during the uncertainty of the struggle. At intervals, measures of clemency were talked of, with a view to pacification, otherwise only to be effected by the extermination of the Faubourgs. But M. Senart, who, as President of the Assembly, was the official depository of information, took care, hour by hour, to announce solemnly every check sustained by the insurgents, and to conceal the reverses of the troops, so that it appeared impolitic to give quarter to men already vanquished and dispersed. The Minister of Finance, M. Duclerc, was assailed with furious clamour, when he happened to avow that the insurgents had fought with courage. Once, and once only, the whole danger of the situation was laid bare with studied exaggeration. This was when M. Pascal Duprat proposed to declare a state of siege, and to confer the dictatorship upon General Cavaignac. " No dictatorship! " exclaimed M. Larabit, clinging to the tribune, and demanding to be heard in the midst of the uproar. M. Bastide came forward and said: " Make haste; in an hour the Hôtel de Ville will be taken." Thereupon, the state of siege is voted, and the dictatorship placed in the hands of General Cavaignac. In the name of the Republic, the subversion of all republican principles was voted by acclamation.

I do but sketch the dark outline of this disastrous insurrection; but I may add a few details which will be found interesting.

That night passed without any fresh attack by the troops; it was not until the following (Monday) morning, about eight or nine o'clock, that the Faubourg was completely invested. The insurgents beat a retreat, but did not cease to fire until they had expended their last cartridge. At five o'clock in the evening, La Villette was taken : that was the end of the bloody tragedy.

An eye-witness assured me that after that final struggle, a National Guard shot a man for the simple reason that he wore a red comforter round his throat.

I had myself a narrow escape from some of the *party of order*. Going home when the insurrection had just been put down, in company with several of my colleagues, I was set upon by a number of National Guards crying out: *"Here is the contriver of the national workshops. Down with him!"* Not satisfied with *threatening* to kill me, one of them clapped his pistol to my temple; but the weapon, being fortunately struck up by one of my companions, went off in the air. Others rushed upon me with their sabres; and I should have been killed in this cowardly way, had not my fellow-representatives on the spot, and some respectable National Guards come to my defence, and succeeded, after a desperate struggle, in rescuing me from my murderous assailants, by forcing me into the Café Frascati, which I soon after left under the protection of two worthy citizens, M. Bouillon, the lieutenant-colonel of the second legion, and one of my colleagues, M. Dutier. The latter gentleman's tilbury was waiting for him on the boulevard; he put me into it, and we drove to the Assembly. Two shots were fired at me, from behind!

After the victory the reprisals were terrible. Prisoners huddled together in the vaults beneath the terrace, in the garden of the Tuileries, which faces the Seine, were shot at random through the air-holes in the wall: others were shot in masses in the Plaine de Grenelle, in the cemetery of Mont Parnasse, in the quarries of Montmâtre, in the cloister of Saint Benoit, in the court of the Hôtel de Cluny.* Wretched men, whom

---

* See, in the *Peuple* of 12th February, 1849, the *Prologue d'une Révolution ;* also the depositions of the representatives of the people, MM. Mathé and Madet, relative to General Bréa's death. Consult likewise the *Prologue,* &c., by Louis Ménard, where will be found a list of

General Cavaignac in his proclamation of the 23rd of June had addressed in these words — " Come to us, the Republic opens her arms to you"—were dragged before Councils of War to be judged by the men they had fought : and the vanquished, whom General Cavaignac had promised not to treat as victims, were despatched *en masse*, without trial. In short, a horrible and humiliating terror spread over the devastated city for many days. A single episode will complete the picture.

On the 3rd of July a considerable number of prisoners were taken out of the cellars of the École Militaire to be removed to the Prefecture of Police, and thence to the forts. They were bound four and four with cords very tightly drawn. As these poor wretches exhausted by hunger, could hardly drag their limbs along, porringers filled with coarse soup were placed before them. Having their hands tied, they were obliged to lie down on their stomachs, and to drag themselves to the porringers like animals, amidst shouts of laughter from the officers of the escort, who called it " *Socialism in practice.*"—I heard this from one of the unfortunate victims of this punishment, which no Indian savage could ever have invented.

But, for the honour of my country and of human nature, let me hasten to restore to these horrors the purely *individual* character that belongs to them. Thank Heaven, there is no class in France, whatever

vast numbers of witnesses who volunteered their testimony under oath, and were refused, in order to veil the horrors committed by some of the victors.

may be its prejudices, to which such excesses can be imputed, even in the blindness of power and passion. These atrocities were the acts of scoundrels, whom every party would reject, but upon whom, unhappily, the state of siege, the public stupor, the fear and rage of some, the consternation of others, had for the moment conferred an odious authority.

It is also essential to remember that certain journals, —the *Constitutionnel* particularly—had become perfect arsenals of murderous falsehoods. Every morning in their columns were represented, in colours of blood, soldiers of the Garde Mobile with their heads cut off, dragoons with their arms severed at the wrist, corpses of men poisoned by the wine of vivandières. It may be imagined what was the effect at that moment of these infamous calumnies, which were not disproved till long afterwards before the Council of War. History—true history—on the contrary, will say that acts of generosity abounded even where the insurrection left the most deplorable traces. In the trial of a chief of barricade it was deposed to by a quartermaster of artillery, that the insurgents had established in the Rue Saint Maure a sort of prison, in which all who fell into their hands were treated with the greatest humanity, and even the greatest care, whether National Guards, Garde Mobile, or regular troops. According to the deposition of Captain Ribot, in the trial of one of the principal insurgents, it was proved that the latter had saved the lives of two hundred men, whom he might have ordered to be shot. At several other points of the conflict, acts of humanity were exhibited, which party passion might conceal for a time, but which posterity will remember and admire.

Let me now return once more to the *causes*, having related the *effects*. It is in the *causes* that we may read a lesson.

The report of M. Bauchart, produced at a time when the re-action hungered for victims, was a monument of blind and shameless rage. Facts, conversations, and speeches were garbled and distorted; police agents, of that despicable kind always at the service of power, were ready with their revelations. The CONSPIRACY of June was invented! According to these witnesses, there was no doubt but that a vast conspiracy had been formed as long back as March, in which the principal men of the extreme party were concerned, and which, taking its instructions from the Luxembourg, had seduced the Ateliers Nationaux, and organised the insurrection. Yet it may now be asked why, when the numberless reports of the Council of War were in preparation, no attempt was made to throw a light on the causes of that immense uprising? Were the resources of calumny exhausted on the 25th of August? Was it feared lest light, a blood-coloured light, should fall on the brows of certain men? Why was no connection between the various trials established? Why were the trials so carefully circumscribed within the circle of the *material facts* of the insurrection? Why were the men, whose presence at the bar might have cleared up certain questions of moral complicity, sent *untried* to the hulks? Why was a trial obstinately refused to Lagarde, to De Flotte, to Terson, to several accused journalists? Why was Pujol, conspicuous as the bearer of the first remonstrance from the *National Workshops*, and thus more able than any one to throw light on the very beginning of the insurrection, sent to the hulks after a sham examination?

I have explained above how it was that the resistance, although localised, possessed a certain character of *ensemble*, owing to the military organisation given to the National Workshops by M. Marie. But, as it was absolutely necessary to charge Socialism with the responsibility of a plot, how was it contrived? To sustain this charge, the plan of battle prepared by the insurgents, the disposition of their different corps de reserve, the movements of their staff, the order of their attack and defence, were immediately published; leaving it to be supposed that they emanated from the Socialist leaders; and, to give farther countenance to this view, they actually brought up before a Council of War as one of the prime organisers of the insurrection—whom? Dr. Lacambre, a well-known Socialist, who had been prisoner in the Conciergerie since the month of May!*

---

* This reminds me that Lord Normanby represents Barbès as joining the insurgents in June, whilst he was prisoner at Vincennes! It is true that this is not clearly stated in the text, which only says, vol. ii., p. 46: "The colours of the 12th legion (Barbès) appeared on the top of the Barricade," &c. But in the *Index* it is thus expressly affirmed of M. Barbès: "Joins the Insurgents!"

I mention this because the *Index* of Lord Normanby's book is strictly formed throughout upon the principle of stating as occurrences what in the text are mere suppositions or suggestions. Here is another curious instance. The text, vol. i., p. 320, speaking of the 16th of April, says: "The result of M. de Lamartine's secret information, from his own agents, was that a conspiracy was organised to overthrow the Provisional Govern-

I must be permitted to insist, again and again, that the insurrection of June was entirely, absolutely unprepared. It was the sudden, electric, irresistible explosion of a people in despair.

But, having once established the fact that the insurrection was wholly and solely a war of hunger, let us examine what part the spirit of faction may have taken in that war.

In the course of the trial of M. le Comte de Fouchécourt, the witness Guérin declared that, in the month of March, he had seen on the Place de la Bastille, M. de Fouchécourt engaging working men at fifty sous a-day for the Legitimist cause. In the quarter of the Place Vendôme resided a noble personage, whose house was a place of meeting for the emissaries of the Royalist party. During the days immediately preceding the insurrection, there was an unusual movement in that quarter of Gardes Mobiles, of working men—real, or disguised as such—of individuals carrying money to and fro; the neighbourhood was thrown into excitement, and when the subsequent events occurred, the noble personage had scarcely time to seek safety in flight. It need scarcely be added that the authorities made no search. During the insurrection some positions were occupied by Legitimists. At the Marais, they were found in the Rue

ment the next day at the Hôtel de Ville, to appoint a Committee of Public Safety, to consist of MM. Arago, Ledru Rollin, Flocon, Albert and Louis Blanc." But, in the *Index*, each of these names figures in this way : "M. Arago joins the conspiracy to overthrow the Government;" and so with the others. At least M. Arago might have been spared, in this skilful retouching of the text !

St. Louis, the Rue d'Angoulême, and the adjacent streets. M. de Fouchécourt was among those who were taken there. The deposition of the witness Isambert, lieutenant of artillery, states that M. de Fouchécourt replied, on being questioned, that he had commanded a barricade, and had fought for the democratic and social republic. M. Bérard, representative of the people, examined the son of M. de Fouchécourt, who said that he was fighting for the same cause as his father; that it was in appearance for the Red Republic, but in reality for the legitimate monarchy. M. de Fouchécourt, in spite of the efforts of influential men of his party, was condemned to twenty years hard labour. In the Quartier Saint-Jacques, near St. Séverin, a few Legitimists had established a sort of staff, to direct their operations. They distributed medals, bearing the effigy of Henri V., and thousands of these medals were afterwards discovered in a house in the Rue Saint-Jean de Beauvais. That very church of St. Séverin figured at a later date in the trial of the *Légion de St. Hubert:* the pious brotherhoods so carefully organised in every parish in the most populous quarters, were, in reality, nothing but establishments for recruiting mendicity.

Another element, which the insurrection of June brought for a moment into relief, was the Bonaparte element. In the month of June, no one knew anything of M. Louis Bonaparte, except that he was the nephew of his uncle, and author of two famous follies. It would have been easy to have reduced him to insignificance: the Executive Commission, by dint

of fearing him let him live. The discussions to
which his election gave rise in the Assembly brought
him forward: a few foolish people were excited; a
few old soldiers were in agitation; the name of the
Emperor was pronounced, and the song of Beranger
revived.

It is perfectly true, and it is the condemnation of
the enemies of Socialism, that the only real flag of the
combatants of June was the Socialist flag; it is
perfectly true that the explosion of the disease arose
from the violence with which the enemies of the Revolution opposed the remedy; it is perfectly true that the
cry of the revolt was not "*Vive*" some pretender or
other, but "*Du Pain ou du Plomb;*" that the Bonapartists and Legitimists, who had crept behind the
barricades, were obliged to disguise their objects: far
from denying all these facts, they are the very heads
of my accusation against the men who preferred facing
the *lead* to effecting those reforms which would have
given *bread*. Certain it is, however, that in the Faubourg St. Marcel, in the Faubourg Saint-Jaques, at
Montmartre, at Belleville, there were found Bonapartists among the combatants; certain it is that they
were found more especially at Gentilly, at Deux-Mou-
lins, at the Barrière Fontainebleau: in short, in that
district which was the scene of the murder of General
Bréa.

A man who was principally inculpated, and most
severely sentenced for his participation in the affair
of General Bréa, was a conductor of *ponts et chaussées*,
by name Luc.

The following was the deposition of the witness Pierre Menand, a corporal of the Garde Mobile:—

"I went to Luc's lodgings; I found there a musket and a bayonet; I did not find him, but a letter addressed by him to Napoléon, who was at Auteuil." What would the reactionist party have said if this letter had borne the address of Considérant, or Pierre Leroux, or Louis Blanc?

A few words are necessary to explain the motives which brought the provinces down upon Paris in June:—

In June, 1848, the Departments were by no means so far advanced in political ideas as they afterwards became. The Royalists, who had retired from Paris in fear, avenged themselves for their own humiliation by calumniating the Revolution and its authors. The despatches and proclamations in which the Government, in June, represented France as being threatened with pillage and incendiarism, afforded an unexpected confirmation of the falsehoods of the reactionists. The first impulse everywhere was to arm and rush down upon the "*brigands;*" and thousands of volunteers answered to the appeal. They were led to believe that the Republic itself was in danger, and that they were summoned to the rescue. It was under that impression, in fact, that thousands of Republicans flocked to Paris, where their presence was announced by the reactionists as a solemn protest of the provinces against Socialism and the capital.

The people who had thus come up from the provinces naturally inquired who and what these enemies were, who had been so mercilessly hunted down and shot. They examined the smoking ruins: the only incendiarism was the firing of the guns and mortars of the *party of order*. On every deserted barricade they read the following brief code of the insurgents :—

"MORT AUX PILLARDS, MORT AUX VOLEURS."

In vain the *Patrie*, the *Constitutionnel*, and all the organs of the Police repeated their odious inventions of massacres, mutilations, and poisonings: the one great fact that remained, was the barbarous cruelty with which the prisoners were treated when the insurrection was suppressed. Two lamentable occurrences in the insurrection of June have served as an inexhaustible text to the declamations of the reactionist press. These two events are the death of the Archbishop of Paris, and the death of General Bréa.

The death of the Archbishop of Paris was a calamity that cannot be too bitterly deplored, but it was not the result of a crime. If the responsibility of that accident must fall on a party—which Heaven forbid! it would not be on the insurgents, but on what was called the Party of Order. Let me call attention to the following declaration of an eye-witness :—

"I, the undersigned, Vicar-General of the Archbishop of Paris, whom I had the honour to accompany on that mission of peace and charity which he had undertaken, attest, that, as far as it was possible to judge in the midst of a great confusion, he was not struck by those who defended the barricades.

"Signed,   JAQUEMET,*

"(Vicar-General.)"

"*26th June,* 1848."

As to the part which politics may have played in the assassination of General Bréa, it is important to be precise before we listen to odious accusations. It was established on the trial that the general, on arriving at the Barrière Fontainebleau, found the insurgents infuriated at the news of the savage executions at the Pantheon. Those who had introduced him in a spirit of conciliation, soon abandoned him in alarm at the menacing aspect of the mob. The chiefs of the National Guard had deserted their post.

I have already adverted to the Bonapartist letter found in the lodgings of Luc, one of those implicated in General Bréa's murder. Long before the events of June, Lahr, also mentioned above, openly boasted of his devotion to the cause of Louis Napoleon. He mentioned to his neighbours, that when he was a soldier in the artillery, and on guard at the fortress of Ham, M. Louis Napoleon had, on one occasion, given him a piece of twenty francs to buy pipes and tobacco, and that the "nephew of the Emperor" had generously declined to take back the change. During their detention in the forts, several of the prisoners accused of the murder of General Bréa made themselves conspicuous by the exaltation of their

---

* I have the original of this attestation in my possession.

Bonapartist opinions. In truth, those opinions prevailed in the commune of Deux Moulins, as every
election proved. Assuredly, if a political colour is to
be given to that deplorable murder, and for my part I
should be ashamed to do so; it is not on the Socialists
the responsibility must fall.

It would require volumes to pass in review all the
calumnies invented and published, with easy impudence, at a time when the democratic press was arbitrarily suspended. Have we not heard of flags brought to
the National Assembly on which it was pretended that
these words were inscribed—" *Mort aux Propriétaires!*"
Now it is known that these flags had been flying,
since the revolt of April, at the windows of house-
holders who had been generous enough to remit their
rents; they were a complimentary present from the
tenants, and bore this inscription — " *Honneur aux
propriétaires généreux.* In the faubourgs, these flags
were counted by hundreds. The conquerors tore them
down as trophies; and some obscure fabricators of
libels falsified the device they bore.

As to the terrible stories about poisoned balls,
poisoned lint, projectiles intended to produce severe
wounds, &c., ... all these have been officially contradicted by the government itself in a " *communiqué* "
to all the papers of Paris; and also in the *Gazette des
Hôpitaux*, containing official hospital reports, the
latter saying, amongst other refutations: " We think
it is our duty to declare that in no one of the balls
extracted, have we discovered any trace of poison,
and that the wounds themselves presented no symptoms

of having been aggravated by any poisonous matter. . . .
It follows, moreover, from the analysis made by M.
Pelouze, that in no case has any of the liquids supposed to be poisoned justified the suspicions respecting
them." *

I need not say that these disgusting fables have been
entirely exploded in France. But as Lord Normanby
wanted them for his romance, not content with reviving, he has been pleased to discover for them
a respectable authority; and this he does with his
usual infelicity. "I inquired," he says, "of M.
Bastide, whether it was ascertained what amount of
truth there was in the reports of cruelties said to
have been committed by the insurgents. He replied
that there had been *no exaggeration on that point;* "
and his Lordship then goes on with the minute
details of the alleged barbarities. †

Now, on reading this, M. Bastide wrote the following
letter to the *Times :*

" SIR,—Permit me to make use of your columns,
in order to reply to a noble Lord who has been
betrayed by his memory, into supposing he had obtained certain particulars from me, which have doubtless reached him from some other quarter. I have
at heart that it should not be supposed, especially by
the English public, that I had the bad taste to tell

* *Gazette des Hôpitaux,* 14 Juillet, 1848. These official communications render it unnecessary to adduce other testimonies, which exist
without number.
† Vol. ii. p. 79.

such absurd stories to its representative, which would have been a mystification unworthy of his position and mine. Everybody is, at this time of day, aware of how much they may depend upon these worn-out stories of poisoned balls, which, after any disturbance, is a matter of regular gossip. Of course, surgeons usually find pieces of linen and cloth in wounds. These bits that increase the danger, are torn off by the balls from the clothes of the persons wounded, and are not discharged from the musket. It is equally well known that, in the height of summer, dead bodies decompose rapidly, especially when death follows after a period of fatigue and feverish excitement. As far as I am aware, his Lordship is not a chemist; still, I should not have ventured to speak in his presence, without fearing he might think I was laughing at him, of a pump casting sulphuric acid into the faces of assailants. Such a pump would be partially dissolved before it could be made to work. Moreover, it is necessary to imagine insurgents of a very simple nature, who could figure to themselves persons so accommodating as to come within ten or twelve yards for the purpose of being pumped upon. It is certainly not to our Parisian insurgents that I would ascribe such a piece of folly. As to the lint said to be poisoned by some insurgent disguised as a sister of charity, or surgeon, it must be necessary, to pass off this fable on Lord Normanby, to conceal from him that all the wounded, whoever they were, were taken to the same wards, and received the same care, and, consequently, that the insurgent poisoner would have run the risk of applying the fatal substance to his comrade, possibly to himself. But I am ready to acknowledge that I might have made mention of balls tipped with copper points; for though, if I did not see any of these balls in June, I did see some in February, 1848, found in the cartridges that belonged to some of the Municipal Guards of Louis Philippe, who were killed at the Chateau d'Eau of the Palais Royal. It is possible that the insurgents had some of these balls, which they had found upon the *defenders of royalty*. At all events, specimens may be seen at Devisme's, the gunmaker, who no more than the late Louis Philippe, bears the character of a ferocious man." *

About 15,000 citizens were arrested after the events of June; 4,348 were sentenced to transportation without trial, *by a measure of general safety*. For two years, they demanded *to be tried;* all they could get was commissioners sent out to confer capricious pardons, —the liberation of some of them being just as arbitrary as their arrest. With respect to one of the men whom these Commissioners of *Clemency*, as they styled themselves, actually transported to Africa, it is remarkable

* This letter, first published in the French paper *l'Estafette* of the 15th of January, 1858, appeared in French a few days after in the *Times*.

I may as well remark here, that M. de Lamartine and M. Bastide are the only Republicans who have found favour with Lord Normanby, being the only ones whom their official position brought in communication with him. I can assure his Lordship that, had he had a more extensive acquaintance with the members of that party, he would not have treated them as ill as he has done.

that, among the papers forming part of the copy of the evidence of the prosecution, furnished to the prisoner, was found the following description : "*Lagarde, delegate of the Luxembourg, a man of incontestable integrity, of the most peaceful disposition, well informed, generally liked, and, for this reason, very dangerous in the propagation of Socialist ideas !*" *

* See a most touching letter from Lagarde himself, who had been president of the delegates of the Luxembourg, dated "Brest Roadsted aboard the *La Guerrière* hulk," which, addressed to the working-men of Paris, appeared, amongst other papers, in the *Nouveau Monde*, March 15th, 1850.

It is hardly possible to imagine that such a man could have been condemned to ten years hard labour, *without trial*, or that the commutation of his sentence consisted in sending him to a penal colony in Africa ! An incident so monstrous and so revolting to our common humanity, would be regarded in a play or a novel as an outrage on probability. But truth in these matters is often more strange than fiction.

CHAPTER XX.

OSTRACISM.

In the midst of so fearful a state of things, earnest men and true legislators would have directed their first endeavours towards healing the wounds of the country. The reactionists, on the contrary, found a cruel benefit in enlarging and envenoming these wounds. There were in the Assembly certain troublesome individuals whom they were impatient to crush, and with breathless haste, setting aside every scruple, they determined to take advantage of the favourable chances which the excitement of the moment offered to their iniquitous designs. Such was the origin of the famous Commission of Inquiry, instituted by the Assembly to examine into the causes of the insurrection. It must be observed that it was resolved that the events of June should be brought into connexion with those of May, because the counter-revolutionists could not resign themselves to submit to the vote that sheltered me from their vengeance, and because they hoped to induce the Assembly, while under the double dominion of anger and of fear, to recall its previous judgment.

Meanwhile, the reactionary press continued to persecute me with redoubled fury and injustice. The contempt with which the rage of these parasitical lampoons inspired me was so profound, that for a long time I allowed them to enjoy the benefit of my silence. But the *Journal des Debats*, which had maintained a certain degree of dignity and reserve in its opposition to the Provisional Government, having allowed itself to re-echo the falsehoods put forward by my enemies, I addressed to that paper, on the 17th July, 1848, a letter, to which I confidently refer all those who may desire to see from decisively illustrative quotations, how moderate and full of the spirit of conciliation were my speeches at the Luxembourg.

The Commission of Inquiry carried on its proceedings under the presidency of M. Odilon Barrot. Its reporter was one of those subordinate hangers-on of the party of the envious, whom you may at any time put forward without caring about compromising them. His name was Bauchard.

If any one would know to what depths mediocrity can descend in the service of hatred, he need only read the report drawn up by this man.

To involve me in the insurrection of June was impossible, nor was it attempted. But, in order to reach me one way or other, the various stages of the Revolution, the acts of the Provisional Government, the invasion of the Assembly on the 15th of May, and the insurrection of June, were, though utterly unconnected facts, by a monstrous licence, treated as a single event.

But even, with the advantage of this extraordinary expedient, there was no ground for framing any charge against me. For, whatever I might have done or said as a member of the Provisional Government, not only was I obnoxious to no censure, but, in common with my colleagues, I had been declared by a solemn decree of the National Assembly to have *merited well of my country!* * Next, as to the invasion of the Assembly, the majority of this very body had decided that my conduct on the occasion was unimpeachable. †

Now, to give an idea of the length to which political iniquity may go, in times of civil discord, I will briefly state the almost incredible artifices resorted to.

There was a certain man in Paris, of the name of Watrin, who, whilst boasting that he was one of the National Guards who, on the 15th of May, forced their way into the Hôtel de Ville, to arrest the persons supposed to be implicated in invading the Assembly, happened to let fall that he had seen me at the Hôtel de Ville. ‡

In this gossip, the Commission of Inquiry eagerly seized on what seemed to afford an opening for reviving a charge which had already been adjudicated and dismissed.

The value of this man's testimony will be instantly appreciated by the simple statement of the evidence he gave, when called upon as a witness in a court of justice.

* See page 388.
† See page 407.
‡ It must be understood that, after the dissolution of the Assembly had been proclaimed by Huber on the 15th of May, numbers of persons went to the Hôtel de Ville, overpowered the Guards, and entered the Hôtel de Ville, where they took measures to form a new government. The National Guard being moved forward to the place, they were finally arrested.

It was to this effect, that, being on duty as a National Guard at the Hôtel de Ville, on the evening of the 15th of May, immediately after the invasion of the Assembly, and his attention being attracted to a window from which persons were throwing papers, he went up to the room, but that, perceiving he was not followed by any of the National Guards, he contented himself with pulling the door open, crying, " *Long live the National Assembly!* " and then, slamming the door to, went back for assistance; to which he added: " During the short instant that I cast my eyes upon the persons assembled there, there was one only I recognised, or, at least, I THINK I recognised, Louis Blanc. (Hereupon Albert, rising, said: I declare, upon my honour, that Louis Blanc was never in the Hôtel de Ville on the 15th of May.)—He was one of those who were seated. It was the only face that struck me, and for this reason my eye rested upon him a moment." *

Such was Watrin's evidence. His cross-examination was as follows:—

Q. Did you know Louis Blanc before the 15th of May?

Watrin. Not by sight ; but I had once seen him for a while at a little distance.

Q. Are you sure you saw Louis Blanc at the Hôtel de Ville?

Watrin. I think I saw him.

Q. How did you make your way into the room?

* See the report of the trial at Bourges, in the *Représentant du Peuple* of the 15th of March, 1849.

Watrin. I did not get into it. I half-opened the door.

M. Barbès here interrupted the witness, observing, it was impossible he could have got so far, as the sentry at the door would have stopped him; and besides, even had he succeeded in opening that door, he could not have seen persons who were in a back room.

Watrin then continued: " Since my first deposition, several attempts have been made to induce me to modify it, but uselessly. It is true that a person has informed me that there was an *employé* at the Hôtel de Ville *who much resembled Louis Blanc*—(sensation).— *As I could not see very distinctly, it is possible I was mistaken."* *

Such evidence must appear so extremely ridiculous to an Englishman, as the grounds on which a prosecution would principally rely, that I am almost ashamed to introduce it ; but I feel still more so at having to add that it was not only the principal, but absolutely the sole evidence adduced; and that, moreover, it was most positively and incontestably refuted by crowds of witnesses, of all ranks, classes, and opinions, such as MM. Lamartine, Barbès, Marrast,—the latter, one of my bitterest opponents at that period,—all of whom having been, for various reasons, on the spot, concurred in declaring that I was not there, and could not be there without their seeing me. †

* See the report of the trial at Bourges, in the *Représentant du Peuple* of the 15th of March, 1849.

† See the declaration of M. Marrast in the Assembly, in the *Moniteur* of the 4th of June, 1848 ; also M. de Lamartine's evidence as a witness at Bourges, and that of M. Barbès, one of the defendants in that trial.

The public were so scandalised and indignant at the use made by the Commission of Inquiry, of this grotesque and disgraceful testimony of Watrin, that men, entirely unknown to me, then in prison awaiting their trial, in connexion with the events of June, did not hesitate to aggravate their position by avowing their presence at the Hôtel de Ville, on the 15th of May, in order to give the lie to this miserable fabrication, whilst others, in no way implicated or suspected, went so far as to denounce themselves as actors in the affair of May, by voluntarily coming forward as witnesses on behalf of an oppressed man! *

Having thus to make up for the insufficiency of *acts*, the Commission of Inquiry knew of nothing better than to try to adduce *words* against me; and what, in this respect, M. Odilon Barrot, M. Bauchart, and their associates, contrived, is really past comprehension.

My speeches at the Luxembourg had been made as member of the Provisional Government; all of them had been fully and literally published in the *Moniteur :* they were known to all when the Assembly passed the celebrated decree: "The Provisional Government have merited well of their country." Will it be believed that, six months after the issuing of this decree, some of the men who passed it found matter of

---

* The names of those, who so nobly sacrificed their personal safety to the love of truth and hatred of injustice, deserve being recorded; here they are : Pelletier de Lorges, and Thumery. See their letters quoted in my speech to the Assembly on the 25th of August, 1848, *Moniteur* of the 26th.

accusation against me, not in the whole of these speeches, but in seven or eight sentences, garbled and misquoted?

So I was retrospectively denied the liberty of speech, by the very men for whose benefit I had protected freedom, when member of the Government, at the peril of my life! and the few words which I was accused of having let drop, while speaking extempore in the midst of the universal excitement, were not even reproduced fairly!

For the honour of human nature, I should have been glad not to touch upon so deplorable a subject; but I cannot overlook the fact that it has supplied Lord Normanby with an opportunity of calumniating, in my person, the party to which I belong.

Lord Normanby, on the authority of the Commission of Inquiry, gives eight paragraphs, which he calls "extracts from the *unpublished* speeches of Louis Blanc to the delegates of the Luxembourg, received from the official short-hand writer who has taken them down at the time." *

I am afraid Lord Normanby would be very much at a loss to describe the unnamed short-hand writer, who is termed *official*, precisely when brought into play as giving *unofficial* information. Nor do I think his Lordship would find it easy to deduce the grounds on which rests either the veracity or the infallibility of this mysterious personage, with whom I was never confronted.   But let that pass.

* "A Year of Revolution in Paris," vol. ii. p. 145.

Of the eight paragraphs, with which Lord Normanby has thought proper to enrich his narrative, six, more or less garbled, form part of speeches *published* at full length in the *Moniteur*, and two are simply forged.

Had Lord Normanby taken the slightest pains conscientiously to discharge his self-imposed task, he would have seen, by glancing at the *Moniteur*, that the extracts he gives as *unpublished*, belong, although distorted, to speeches which any one may read in that Journal.

For instance, any one may there read this phrase of mine, which I quote in French, to follow the example of Lord Normanby :

" En dépit de tout, l'égalité triomphera, non pas cette égalité étroite et stérile qui consiste dans l'abaissement du niveau général, mais celle qui consiste, au contraire, dans son élévation progressive, indéfinie ; car, suivant une belle parole de Saint-Martin, tous les hommes sont égaux, cela veut dire tous les hommes sont rois."

This was said by me, to show that progress must consist, not in lowering those that are above, but in raising those that are below. It was absolutely the same thought which our national poet Béranger had, before me, expressed in these lively terms : " L'égalité doit consister, non pas à raccourcir les habits, mais à allonger les vestes."

Now, it is curious to see how, by the common trick of some words artfully modified or omitted, this sentence, directed against any blind and narrow feeling of envy on the part of the less fortunate classes of society, has been changed, in M. Bauchart's report first, and then in Lord Normanby's book, into the most fanciful and chimerical promise:—"Mes amis, sachez-le, vous serez non seulement puissants, non seulement riches, vous serez rois. Car tous les hommes sont égaux, tous les hommes sont rois." *

Need I point out the difference?

Again, on the 29th of April, I had said, according to the documentary evidence:—

"Ce que nous voulons, c'est la liberté par la paix, c'est la victoire par le développement de la raison; c'est le triomphe par la modération, par l'essor de l'intelligence, c'est la liberté par l'ordre et par l'amour. Et quand je vous dis ceci, ne croyez pas que je cède à des sentiments pusillanimes. Si jamais la liberté était menacée, vous pouvez en être sûrs, et j'en prends l'engagement devant vous, personne d'entre vous ne pourrait dire qu'il ne m'a pas vu au poste du péril. Seulement, désirons ce qu'il y a de mieux, ce qu'il y a de plus humain; car l'humanité marche, non par vers la guerre mais vers la paix, non par vers l'anarchie mais vers l'ordre, non par vers la haine mais vers la fraternité. Ainsi, sentiments de modera-tion tempérés par une vive résolution de vigilance, sentiments d'ordre, tempérés par la volonté de rester frères, et, s'il le fallait, douloureuse nécessité, nécessité bien comprise de devenir soldats. Maintenant, je ne vous dirai pas que la Révolution, si violemment

* "A Year of Revolution in Paris," vol. ii. p. 146.

attaquée depuis quelques jours par les réactionnaires est en péril. Je ne vous dirai pas qu'il faudra la défendre violemment. En vérité, je n'en crois rien. J'ai une confiance parfaite, inébranlable dans la victoire de l'idée, de la raison, de la justice. Que l'intelligence de tous se forme par le développement de la liberté de la presse, de la liberté de la tribune, de la liberté de l'industrie ; et, j'en suis convaincu, la Révolution triomphera."

That, in this passage, which is so warm an appeal to moderation and concord, a motive should have been found for accusing me of an appeal to violence, seems hardly conceivable. Yet, such has been the case, and the process may be studied in Lord Normanby's book : nothing more was required, to produce the desired impression, than to omit all that precedes, and all that follows this phrase, special care having been taken to underline the last words :—

" Sentiments de modération tempérés par une résolution de vigilance ; sentiments d'ordre, mais tempérés par la volonté de rester frères, et, s'il le fallait, *douloureuse nécessité, nécessité bien comprise de se faire soldats.*" *

For this perversion of my language, I cannot help holding Lord Normanby personally responsible ; as what I now do here, I did at the time, in a speech made in the Assembly for the express purpose of exposing these disgraceful manœuvres—a speech which his lordship tells us he heard himself.† He was,

---

* "A Year of Revolution in Paris," vol. ii. p. 146.
† *Ibid.*, p. 179.

therefore, bound on every principle of honour and equity, to state my reply, using, of course, his right to show its inefficiency, if he could.

As to my having used any phrase intended to pave the way for any future attack on the Assembly, or uttered any denunciation of the existing social system by so violent an epithet as *infamous,* or committed myself to such an empty unexplained form of expression:—"Vive la République qui fera qu'il n'y aura plus de riches et de pauvres;" all this is a fabrication of the parties concerned, and I defy contradiction when I say, that all this is utterly inconsistent with anything I have at any time said or written. What I did say, and what I do say, in common with the most accredited thinkers, is, that the present order of society is *unjust;* that the true source of improvement is to consider poverty as an evil susceptible of being gradually suppressed—which constitutes the very essence of the act of civilisation. And true it is, that to contribute to it with all the energy I am capable of, is an engagement which I made with myself in early life, and to which I am proud enough to think I shall be faithful to my latest hour.

I have now a little matter to settle with Lord Normanby exclusively. After unfairly quoting the perversions of my language, without indicating the complete answer I gave them,—seized I suppose by a noble emulation,—he does a little business in this way on his own account, by perverting even the perversions. Having, at page 146, ascribed to me, on the authority of such a man as M. Bauchart, the phrase, " Le système sur lequel est basée la société est un système infâme," he, in the very next page, proceeds coolly to drop into the same phrase the word "*property*," which enables him to say that it was property I had denounced as a "*système infâme*." And going on from bad to worse, he takes advantage of his own interpolation for charging me with the most ludicrous act of treachery, indeed. Here it is :—

On the 13th of July, M. Proudhon having made in the Assembly a motion inconsistent with my views, supported by a speech in which every one and every thing was attacked, I voted against it, with all the members of the Assembly, except one.

Whereupon, Lord Normanby bursts out, as follows :—

"Verily, Citizen Proudhon might well say, ' Call you this backing your friends ? ' Doubly deep must have been his gratitude for the solitary vote of the less notorious but more faithful Greppo. Changed as the season was the Louis Blanc of August with the Louis Blanc of February ! Was this the result of some late repentance, or merely of recent panic at the consequences of imminent disclosures in the forthcoming report ? " *

How fortunate ! I have just at hand the means of gratifying his lordship's curiosity. The explanation of my motives for opposing M. Proudhon, has been thus given by M. Proudhon himself :—

"Louis Blanc's vote was the most conscientious vote in the Assembly. There is an abyss between

---

* "A Year of Revolution in Paris," vol. ii. p. 147.

us. . . . Socialism, such as I have comprehended it, is just the reverse of the socialism of Louis Blanc. This opposition is a fatal one, and if I particularly dwell upon it, it is by no means for the pleasure of merely contradicting the head of a different school, but because it appears to me necessary to the education of the people." *

What will any man of sense and honesty think of Lord Normanby after this? I should very much like him to explain how he could live so long in Paris without knowing that Proudhon and myself were the most decided adversaries in opinion! Can there be anything more ridiculous than to talk of my deserting one with whom I was never allied, one who has always been my opponent, and who so continues to the present time? And is it not too bad, that a man of Lord Normanby's position should endeavour to decry the character of another, by tacking a blunder to an interpolation? †

---

* *Confessions d'un Révolutionnaire, pour Servir à l'Histoire de la Révolution de Fevrier*, par P. J. Proudhon, p. 54.

† Lord Normanby (vol. ii. p. 180) quotes at length a deposition of M. Trélat, which he acknowledges "received but little credence" from the Assembly, but which, nevertheless, for the purpose of attacking me, I suppose, he introduces, referring to I know not what proposition alleged to have been made by me to M. Émile Thomas, and by him reported to M. Trélat. Had M. Émile Thomas said anything of the kind, it would have been a marvellous piece of impudence, as I never cast eyes upon him; but, when questioned on the subject by the Commission Inquiry, his answer was: "M. Trélat's statement is a falsehood; I never saw M. Louis Blanc in my life." I quoted this contradiction in the very words of M. Émile Thomas, in my speech in the Assembly on the 25th of August, 1848 (see the *Moniteur* of the 26th), which Lord Normanby, who was present, must have heard. Why has he then suppressed all mention of this, leaving the public to suppose that there was really something in

Three representatives of the people, viz., M. Ledru Rollin, M. Caussidière, and myself, were calumniated in the report of the Commission of Inquiry. The first-named of these gentlemen was allowed to defend himself on the very day of the attack; Caussidière and myself were debarred from this right, under the transparent pretext that our defence would come in better after the publication of the documents; and we were thus forced to wait in silence until the false representations in the report had, in the absence of all contradictory discussion, produced the desired effect on public opinion!

In consequence, we remained for several days exposed to all sorts of iniquitous attacks. The report, the product of vulgar spite and of impotent rage, in reality condemned its authors alone, and such was indeed the unanimous opinion of every upright man. But minds previously tainted, received with avidity the poison which had been prepared for them. In truth, there was no lack of commentaries to the text. Reproduced, expanded, enriched with new fallacies, published by various journals, copies of which were struck off to the number of five or six hundred thousand, the odious libel spread through the whole of Europe an accusation which was swelled and prolonged by every echo along the road; and when, indignant at this slow moral death, we asked to be allowed to speak; when we demanded the right in our turn to accuse our accusers, the answer given was, "the copies of the documentary

M. Trélat's deposition, and, consequently, that I was in some way or other in communication with the Director of the National Workshops? Is this fair play?

evidence, which are to be published, are not yet ready," or, "the papers are not yet printed." And during all this while, with the report of the Commission of Inquiry in their hands, they exerted themselves with indefatigable zeal, TO CREATE PUBLIC OPINION!

And notwithstanding all this, truth, on this occasion, supported by evidence, would no doubt have carried the victory, had there not, in the bosom of the Assembly, been formed a league against us, the origin and the character of which it is necessary that I should here determine.

When voting the publication of the report, the Assembly resolved, no doubt inadvertently, that *all* the documentary evidence should likewise be published. But, when this vote was to be carried out, it was found fraught with great peril.

Having never calculated that the minutes of the proceedings of the Commission of Inquiry were to be published, certain important personages had ventured to denounce each other; there had been instances of terrible indiscretions, of fatal confidences. What would therefore be the result, if the veil were to be lifted?

Suits for libel, duels, lifelong animosities, enormous public scandals, civil war within the Assembly, such were the results about to be produced by the publication of the entire minutes. General terror prevailed.

Now, among those who had most reasons to fear a disclosure of this kind, was General Cavaignac himself. His dictatorship, established in the month of June, on the ruins of the Executive Commission, had given rise to strange whisperings in the hall of the *Pas-Perdus,* and these whisperings had been transformed into accusatory evidence, before the Commission of Inquiry. He was represented as having allowed barricades to be constructed, which he might have prevented; as having managed to acquire the sacrilegious honour of drowning in blood an insurrection which might have been averted; as closing his ears to the orders of the Executive Commission; as publicly displaying a contempt for the armed intervention of the National Guard, which was meant to convey a compliment to the regular troops. In a word, he was represented as having conducted himself in such a manner, in the midst of distracted Paris, as to render the overthrow of the Executive Commission inevitable, and his own dictatorship necessary.

These imputations, against which he was protected subsequently, in a famous sitting, partly because of their very enormity, partly because the reactionist party still needed him;—these imputations were put forward by witnesses bearing an official character, by men whose colleague in the Government he had been, and whose colleague he was in the Assembly. Therefore, whether or not the general would have been able to justify himself, his position as dictator would at all events have suffered considerably, had he been placed under the necessity of defending himself against such accusations. This was perfectly understood by his party, and the *National* made prodigious efforts to prevent the publication of the whole of the minutes. But the vote of the Assembly could not be got rid of. There it was, imperious, decisive. There was therefore nothing left for General Cavaignac's party, if it would avoid a debate, the result of which might be fatal, but to draw near to the party represented by the Commission of Inquiry.

On the other hand, the reactionists who had instituted the Inquiry had a manifest interest in so momentous an alliance. If left to depend on their own strength alone, they could not command a majority in the Assembly, and they might run the risk of succumbing to an order of the day and of being removed from the category of judges to that of calumniators. Besides, their plan was to make use of the Republicans of the *National* against the Socialists, *i.e.* of General Cavaignac against M. Caussidière and myself, reserving to themselves the power of destroying the tool after having made use of it.

Out of this community of interests and perils arose the iniquitous pact of which M. Caussidière and I became the victims.

As for M. Ledru Rollin, though accused together with us, he had this advantage over us, that having been a member of the Executive Commission, he was one of those whom General Cavaignac had reason to fear as accuser. It was therefore determined that he should be used gently, and hence that celebrated shake of the hand given to him by the general in the midst of the Assembly, when, for the first time, Ledru Rollin was called upon to defend himself.

It will long be remembered that, on the 25th of April, 1849, M. Baroche ventured to fix the names of the *contumaces* of the 16th of May on gibbets, which the people, in an outburst of admirable and poetic indignation, hastened to cover with flowers. The next day the following paragraph appeared in the journal *La Presse* :—

" In case General Cavaignac passed yesterday across the square of the *Palais de Justice*, at the moment when the sentence which condemns M. Louis Blanc was affixed to a gibbet, General Cavaignac must have felt a pang; for the person who writes these lines, (M. Émile de Girardin) heard General Cavaignac say on the 26th of August :—' As for Louis Blanc, my profound conviction is, that he is not more guilty than I am.' How is it to be explained, that General Cavaignac, entertaining such a conviction a few hours previously, subsequently ascended the tribune and there uttered language of quite a different import ? "

And what answer did General Cavaignac give to this definite assertion of M. Émile de Girardin, to this pressing appeal ? He remained silent.

He was not ignorant, however, that I had been the companion in arms, the fellow-labourer and the friend of his brother; that I had ever evinced towards his mother quite a filial affection ; and that, when called to his eternal home, Godefroy Cavaignac had bequeathed to me his most cherished thoughts. May it not be that to the ardour of an ambition full of anxiety, that to the fear of being a victim in case he did not become sacrificer, was added the spur of some secret resentment ?

At the period of the outbreak of the February revolution, General Cavaignac had long been serving in Algeria. I had, therefore, seen him only two or three times during flying visits to Paris. But he was known to be a Republican; and, besides, I loved him for his brother's sake. It was therefore with heartfelt emotion, that while forming part of the Provisional Government, I joined my influence to that of my two colleagues, Ledru Rollin and Flocon, to raise M. Eugène Cavaignac to the rank of Lieutenant-General, and to elevate his prospects, so suddenly associated with the destinies of the Republic. A Minister of War was to be appointed: the general was proposed, accepted, and informed of the fact by the Provisional Government. Great was our surprise on the receipt of his answer. It was a notification of his refusal in terms of ill-concealed arrogance. He seemed to upbraid us with not having assigned a sufficiently exalted place to the troops in our regard and in our arrangements; the citizen disappeared behind the soldier. The same exclamation, I remember, burst from the lips of all present, an exclamation of astonishment, or rather of indignation. What was the meaning of the assumption of these airs of an independent proconsul? Whence came this audacity of a soldier of fortune towards men, who, after all, had but to give a sign, and the sword would have been broken in his hand? As for the army, far from having held it in little esteem, we had reinstated it in the position whence all its heroic greatness had been derived, by indicating to it, that thenceforward it should know no other enemies than the enemies of France, and by endeavouring to avert from it the possibility of being called upon to wage a terrible and sacrilegious warfare in the streets and lanes of our cities. It was determined that the Provisional Government should express its displeasure to General Cavaignac in an authoritative letter to be drawn up by three of its members, viz., François Arago, Armand Marrast, and myself.

On the day after this resolution had been come to, I went to the Hôtel of the Ministry of the Marine, to meet M. François Arago and M. Marrast. I had already prepared a rough draught of the letter, which I had brought with me, and which I read to my colleagues. In a measured but haughty tone, it gave faithful expression to the sentiments of the Council. The last sentence, the severity of which had been provoked, was as follows :—

" The moment is perhaps not far distant when we may be forced into *a war with Europe : remain in Africa, general, the Government retains you there in the service of the Republic.*"

My draft was approved of by MM. François Arago and Marrast, except that the latter did not think it bitter enough, and in consequence added some words in the margin calculated to render it still more galling to the general. However, these additions of M. Marrast were rejected by the Council, being found to go too far. Thus the letter was sent such as it had been drawn up by me, and was signed by M. Arago in his quality of Minister of War, *ad interim*.

Were the details which I have just narrated, confided to General Cavaignac at a subsequent period ? I know not ; but perhaps in this case there might have been one more inducement to the act of injustice which, I am grieved to say, will always remain a blot on the memory of Eugène Cavaignac.

The ruin of M. Caussidière and myself having been determined, it will easily be understood why it was resolved to bring the matter to a close at one sitting, even though it be prolonged so as to comprise two sunrises. Nothing certainly could have been more unjust, for it was tantamount to depriving us in advance of any chance of a possible change in public opinion as regarded us; it was tantamount to refusing to allow one hour for the working of the moral effect that might be produced by the defence, while a whole week had been allowed for the working of the moral effect produced by the accusation.

The subject was brought before the Assembly on the 25th of August. My first and own impression was not to condescend to defend myself, but to challenge my enemies to do their worst; to answer attacks by attacks, and to show—what was the truth—that I had not come there to clear myself of a crime, but to expiate a defeat. I am now convinced that this impression was the right one. Unfortunately, my best friends in the Assembly, purposely misled by false reports as to the feeling of the majority present, pressed me with the most earnest entreaties, not to throw away the certainty of an important victory for the gratification of my own appreciation of what was due to my cause and to myself.

I therefore consented to accept the position of a defendant, and accordingly took the trouble of tearing to pieces the flimsy report of M. Bauchart, in a long

speech, which, as may be seen by the *Moniteur's* report
of the debate, made a great impression on the minority,
although doubtless "ineffective," as Lord Normanby
says it was, the majority being determined to be diverted
by no argument from their foregone conclusions.*

I seized the opportunity to assert once more, and
justify my doctrines. I showed that all my speeches
at the Luxembourg had been published at length in
the *Moniteur*, and that no other than these had been
uttered by me as a member of the Government. I
showed, moreover, that the reports in the *Moniteur*
were literally exact, with the exception of such few
verbal alterations as it is the practice, in France, for
every speaker to make before his speech is published,
when it is extempore. And this care about words was
all the more imperative, as I was speaking in time of
great excitement, on the spur of the moment, and under
a frightful pressure. But, far from making changes
" which certainly completely altered the sense," † as
Lord Normanby, who was present, is bold enough to
assert, I proved, beyond dispute, just the reverse;
and I earnestly entreat any one who may be interested
in the matter to consult the *Moniteur* of the 25th of
August, 1848, where he will find the fullest confirmation of what I say.

The great change alleged against me by the Com-

---

* At the moment something I said was warmly received on the left of
the house; I remember one of the right rubbing his hands, and saying in
an under tone, "Oh! gabble on as much as you like. It's all up with
you." The expression was considerably coarser in French; but, its
coarseness apart, very well expressed the *parti pris* of the majority.

† "A Year of Revolution in Paris," vol. ii. p. 179.

mission of Inquiry was this.   I had said at the Luxembourg, that in my earliest youth I had taken the *serment d'Annibal* against the existing unjust order of things.   Feeling that the expression used in the heat of the moment might be misconstrued, I substituted for it the equivalent expression, " J'ai pris devant Dieu et devant ma conscience l'engagement," &c. I appeal to any honest man whether this be " certainly completely altering the sense? "   Moreover, how inconceivable that an act of discretion should have been changed into a motive for accusation !

So much for this part of the charge.   As to my presence at the Hôtel de Ville in the evening of the 15th of May, every one knew perfectly well the utter absurdity of the supposition ;   nevertheless, I took the unnecessary trouble of rebutting it in the way with which the reader is already acquainted.

When I finished my speech, which had been interrupted by an hour's adjournment for dinner, the clock struck eleven.   Sinister was the aspect of the immense hall, dimly lit up.   Motionless, silent, full of self-controlled hatred, the proscribers appeared like phantoms.   In the galleries, a sombre curiosity was visible on every face, mingled with pallor caused by fatigue. Had the executioner been near, nothing would have been wanting to make that scene equal to certain other scenes, at the mere remembrance of which, after half a century, men still shudder.

In his turn, M. Caussidière began to speak, opposing to the accusation brought against him, a mass of striking proofs, and, from time to time, breaking out

into happy and energetic sallies. Silence continued,
menacing, implacable.

On a sudden, the President rises, and submits to the
Assembly the demand for leave to prosecute M. Caussidière and myself—a demand which, it will be remembered, this same Assembly, as far as I was concerned,
had already rejected by a solemn vote. In vain did
M. Laurent (de L'Ardèche) raise a protest against the
attempt to mask a *coup d'état* in the guise of a judicial
indictment; in vain did M. Théodore Bac display on
my behalf the power of the most touching and high
eloquence; in vain was the cause of M. Caussidière
warmly advocated by M. Flocon—the votes had been
counted beforehand. The very men to whom we had
held out a helping hand when they lay prostrate at
our feet, now felt strong enough, and were determined
to take vengeance upon us, for the protection we had
bestowed upon them.

But, in reference to me, the decision to be taken
was of a very serious character, as the Assembly could
not condemn me, without renewing a question already
deliberately settled by themselves; without declaring
me guilty, on new evidence, of the same offence of
which they had previously declared me innocent—an
unexampled instance of barefaced injustice. Even
from this did they not shrink.

Must I say that the demand for leave to prosecute
me was supported by General Eugène Cavaignac? I
did not hear him; I would not listen to him. Whilst
he was speaking, all my thoughts were directed to
Godefroy Cavaignac, to whom, when in exile, I had

rendered such services as cannot possibly fade from a good man's memory—Godefroy Cavaignac, the dearest, the most lamented of my friends, who, breathing his last in my arms, whispered : " You have been a second brother to me."

The result was predetermined. The arguments used by ourselves and our supporters to show that there were no grounds for leave to prosecute us, were not met or even considered by any one member of the Assembly. The Procureur-Général, M. Corne, insisted upon the prosecution, and General Cavaignac supported it; but both these gentlemen contented themselves with stating in a general way that leave ought to be granted. Voting then amounted to a mere formality. Ostracism was revived.

During these proceedings, numbers of workmen were thronging the Rue de Lille, awaiting the result with great anxiety; and, although the means of popular resistance had been completely crushed in June, yet the bearing of the people, in reference to the prosecution, was of a nature to create considerable uneasiness.

When the decision of the Assembly was announced, my brother and my friends entreated me to leave Paris, to which I, at first, demurred, from a feeling of indignant pride. On its being urged that my being arrested might give rise to a dangerous excitement amongst the workmen, my own excitement prevented me, for a moment, from acknowledging to myself the full force of the objection. But immediately subduing this involuntary movement of anger, I began to perceive that it was my duty to avoid consequences which might injure others as much as myself. At this instant, a representative belonging to the opposite side, a most noble-minded man, M. d'Aragon, came up to me, and, in a tone of voice which I shall never forget, said: "You do not know me, nor do my opinions agree with yours; but I esteem and love you. If you think me worthy of your confidence, my carriage is at the door. Let us not lose a moment." This was decisive. Unwilling to seem by any show of hesitation to slight so kind an offer, I made up my mind, and followed him. It was daylight when I went out of the Assembly. At M. d'Aragon's house, exhausted as I was, I threw myself on a bed without undressing, and fell fast asleep. Two hours after, I was awakened by my host, who had, with the most delicate foresight and generosity, made the necessary arrangements for my journey.* I got into a cab, accompanied by two friends and reached the railway, leaving behind me a letter for publication, in which I engaged to return to Paris, and to surrender myself for *trial by jury*, the moment I was called upon to do so.

I did not take any precaution to avoid being recognised, and would not have taken any, even had I been sure it was the intention of the Government to

---

* On my getting into the carriage, this excellent man put a pocket-book in my hands containing bank-notes, saying, "You will want something for your journey. Return it when convenient to you."

Alas! hardly had I reached London when I heard of his death, and this sad intelligence clouded the first days of my life as an exile, and caused me a bitter feeling of loneliness and sorrow.

stop me; but it is obvious, from what precedes, that
the Government had nothing better to do than let me
go quietly.*

When in London, I was impatiently waiting for the
payment of a debt due to me, the summons to return
to Paris, to be tried by a jury of my countrymen.
What were my astonishment and indignation, at hearing that, by an *ex post facto* law, there had been
instituted a new and special court, before which I was
summoned to appear, and where I was not to have the
protection of a jury.

In 1818, these species of "Tribunaux d'exception,"
were thus described in a work entitled, *La Justice
Criminelle en France*:—

---

* As a proof how easily I might have been arrested, if such had been
the wish of the Government, and also to show on what depend the likes
and dislikes entertained towards public men, I will mention the following
anecdote:—

On getting into the railway carriage, I found myself amongst several
persons who, not knowing me, were conversing about the event of the day.
One of these, a lady with a remarkably gentle expression of face, having
learned, in answer to an inquiry what had been done in the Assembly, that
leave to prosecute me had been granted, gave vent to her feeling of satisfaction with an emphasis and bitterness singularly at variance with the
mildness of her look. Although deeply wounded, I said not a word. On
arriving at the next station, the rumour of my being in the train having
got abroad, there was a rush of people to the carriage window, some
scowling at me, others warmly giving me their hands. I was now known
to my companions, and when the train moved on again, there was a deep
unbroken silence, whilst it was visible from the lady's face how much she
regretted the unintentional wound she had inflicted upon a fallen man.
At another station, she alighted with her husband, evidently unwilling to
go without speaking to me. She lingered a moment at the carriage door;
and as the train was about to start, she stepped quickly forward, and,
stretching out her hand to me with an expression full of feeling, she said:
"May you be happy!"

" Under whatever form they appear, whatever name you may give them, on whatever pretext you institute them, they must be looked upon as courts of blood. Their only law is the accomplishment of the object for which they have been instituted. Expect from them neither pity, humanity, nor regard for justice. Do not even put trust in the previous character, good as it may have been, of the men who compose them. For, any man base enough to place himself in the position of punishing actions that are crimes only because they displease a despot or a faction, sacrifices his honour, and gives himself up, bound hand and foot, to injustice."

With such words before him, who will possibly believe that the man who thus poured his indignation upon high courts, was M. Berenger, the very man who presided over the high court newly instituted?

Nor was this all. It was at Paris that the acts for which I was so iniquitously rendered answerable, had occurred; but as innumerable witnesses were there to be found, who could place the truth beyond the reach of a doubt, it was at Bourges we were cited to appear, in order that the truth should fall, unassisted and almost unheard.

This being the case, I wrote from London * that, while still ready to redeem my promise to be tried by a fair jury and a lawful court, I utterly refused to appear before a tribunal created three months after the alleged offence, created too for the special purpose

* This my letter, written on the 3rd of March, 1849, will be found in the French papers of the 6th or the 7th.

ef substituting vengeance for justice, and placed precisely where that purpose could be best secured.

Such are the grounds on which I was expelled my
country, and such the grounds on which I am here
an exile in London !

CHAPTER XXI.

PERSONAL INTERCOURSE WITH LOUIS BONAPARTE.

LOUIS BONAPARTE is on a throne; and I am in exile.

To me he was, to a great extent, indebted, when banished, for his return to France; and to him is ascribable that state of things which keeps me from my country.

After his attempt on Boulogne, in August 1840, I was the only man who dared raise a protest against his being tried by an unlawful jurisdiction; and he, once become the President of the Republic, suffered a most iniquitous accusation to be brought against me, not before a jury, but before a sham tribunal.

Whilst lingering at Ham, a poor forlorn prisoner, he entreated me, in a pressing letter, to come and spend a few days with him in his prison, which I did; and when afterwards the vicissitudes of fortune, coupled with the baseness of men, made him an emperor and myself an exile, my utter spoliation was consummated by his own official servants, who were not ashamed to deprive me of a slender sum of about six hundred pounds, which I had earned by many years of literary labour, and which, invested in the public funds, was all my substance.

Could an honest man repent of anything done in strict obedience to the call of conscience, how bitter would be to my heart the remembrance of the prominent share I took, on the 13th of June, 1848, in the decision by which the National Assembly cancelled the proscription of Louis Bonaparte!

But I have no claim to his gratitude on that score, as my conduct was free from all personal considerations. I did what I thought to be just.

"It is understood," says Lord Normanby, writing in June, 1848, "that all among the lower classes whom Louis Blanc can influence are in favour of the *Bonaparte movement.*" *

The sense of this phrase is rather involved. If meant to convey some vague idea that I was foremost in supporting the views of a pretender, the hint would be worse than an error.

The best possible reply I can make to an insinuation of that sort, is the faithful account of all the facts relating to my personal intercourse with Louis Bonaparte, whose present position imparts a particular degree of importance to any such records.

Who does not remember that, after his unsuccessful attempt on Boulogne, Louis Bonaparte was made the laughing-stock of Europe? Strange as the fact may seem now, his failure was hailed all over France with a burst of invective, and attended with marks of universal disgust. There never was, perhaps, such outrageous abuse. His name was by no means a shield

* Vol. i. p. 456.

against the darts flung at him from every corner.   By his very friends he was forsaken.   A paper started at his cost, under the title of " *Le Capitole,*" for the express purpose of advocating his pretensions, joined in the general onset.   The conspirator of Strasburg had been pardoned; if Louis Philippe, a very humane prince, had ordered the conspirator of Boulogne to be shot without any further formality, to no one would the punishment have appeared too harsh.

I was, at that period, the editor of a democratic magazine, entitled " *Revue du Progrès,*" the contributors of which were the most eminent writers of the Republican party, namely, MM. Arago, Michel (de Bouges), De Latouche, Marrast, Godefroy Cavaignac, Lamennais; and in that magazine I had reviewed, just one year before, Louis Bonaparte's book, " *Les Idées Napoléonniennes.*"   As regards the claims laid by the nephew to the imperial succession of the uncle, this article of mine was a very severe one.   It ended with the following words:—

" . . . . Some will tell you, sir, 'The Empire must be restored.'   But it is because the mission of Napoleon was entirely exhausted that he was left to die upon a solitary rock, in the midst of the ocean.   Is it the reign of your uncle, together with war, that you mean to revive?   For that, we need another Europe and a demigod.   Is it the reign of your uncle without war?   It would be despotism without glory; mock lords covered with embroidery, without soldiers covered with scars; courtiers over our heads, without the world at our feet; it would be a great name without a great man, the Empire without the Emperor."

This publication made a very strong impression in Paris.

The next day, at ten o'clock in the evening, as I was returning home, an unknown man came behind me, and, quite unexpectedly, gave me a violent blow with a stick upon the right eye. I fell down covered with blood. Some passers-by took me up and carried me to an apothecary's shop in the Rue de la Paix, where I remained senseless for about an hour. A physician was called in haste, and, at the first glance, declared that there was no ground of hope. The fact is, that I recovered only after a month of cruel sufferings. Although the street was full of people when the blow was levelled at me, my assailant had succeeded in making his escape. The researches of the police were all in vain. The only thing they could ascertain by questioning the neighbours, was that the assailant, who looked a gentleman in disguise, had been noticed standing at my door a long while. Heaven forbid that I should cast upon a whole party the crime of one man! But I have a right to say that an opinion prevailed at the time, and found its way into most of the newspapers, that this cowardly attempt at assassination was the reply of a fanatical Bonapartist to my review of the "Idées Napoléonniennes."

Whether Lord Normanby will find in this record a proof of my adherence to the "Bonaparte movement," I know not. At any rate, such had been my reward, when in August 1840, the conspiracy of Boulogne was baffled, and Louis Bonaparte arrested. As much as any man in the world, I condemned his schemes. Still, I felt indignant at recognising among those who railed at him most furiously, the vilest worshippers of his uncle. I remembered that Malet, when asked by his judges : " *Et vos complices ?* " answered admirably ; " *Vous, si j'avais réussi.*" I had no doubt that, if ever this same Louis Bonaparte happened to get the mastery, many of such as were inveighing against him with so much asperity would be seen crawling at his feet. How true the foreboding, alas ! Moreover, it is my profound conviction that in no case whatever ought the usual rules of justice to be disregarded. I did not hesitate to develope these considerations in an article which appeared in the " *Revue du Progrès,*" on the first of September, 1840. It was like a discordant note in a concert of opprobrious language, and could not fail, on that account, to attract the attention of the public ; it certainly did not escape the attention of Louis Bonaparte.

From the *Château de Ham,* wherein he was imprisoned, by sentence of the Chamber of Peers, he wrote to me the letter above-mentioned, in which he thanked me for not having wantonly insulted a fallen adversary, and expressed, in very affecting terms, a strong desire that I might make it convenient to come to him and stay at Ham for a few days.

He was surrounded, at that time, with the only prestige which a true Republican may be willing to salute : he was unfortunate. His imperial pretensions had, as it were, vanished in the smoke of a wretched adventure. People were looking round for his party; and he, bowed down, tried, condemned, denied by his partisans of that period, railed at by his servants of this day, was doomed to a lonely life in a gloomy fortress, with no other friend to whom he could unburden his heart than his physician Dr. Conneau, and a chemist, named Acar. *Res sacra miser.* With the request of the prisoner, not of the prince, I complied; he procured from the Home-minister a permission for me to enter his prison, and I set off to Ham.

I knew of the Bonapartist party something more than was generally known, owing to my acquaintance with Mrs. Gordon, the real framer of the conspiracy of Strasburg, in which two persons only cut a figure: she and Lieutenant Laity. Mrs. Gordon was a handsome woman, too much addicted to meddling, but warmhearted, naturally eloquent, full of perseverance and courage. I have heard from her own lips that the conspirators of Strasburg wanting an old soldier whose rank and name might tell on the garrison, she hastened to Dijon, where Colonel Vaudrey lived, then in utter ignorance of what was going on, and so powerfully forced upon his hesitating mind the necessity of a prompt determination, that she hurried him away to Strasburg *séance tenante,* without, so to speak, allowing him time to put off his slippers. Her devotion to the memory of Napoleon was heedless and boundless, but she did not make much of the Bonapartist party, which she thought was deficient both in men of intelligence and energy, with the exception of MM. Laity, Aladenise, and Fialin. M. Fialin, who went by the assumed name of *De Persigny*, and who had chosen for his motto these two words *"I serve"*—*Je sers*, was, in Mrs. Gordon's opinion, the pillar of the party. As to Louis Bonaparte, she did not make much of him neither. I remember that one day I asked her in jest whether she loved him. "Well," she said, with a smile, "I love him *politically*. To tell the truth, *Il me fait l'effet d'une femme.*"

These were the things I revolved in my mind, while getting near the end of my journey.

The first person I saw at Ham was M. Acar. The political creed of M. Acar was a most heterogeneous jumble of Bonapartism and Republicanism. No one was more ready than he to dedicate himself to the service of Louis Bonaparte. Yet, he styled himself a Republican, and so he was in his own strange way. He seemed delighted at my arrival.

"Here are," exclaimed he cheerfully, "auxiliary forces, and I hope Louis Bonaparte now will be soon conquered." Then he told me that the prisoner's friends were divided into very different classes; one of which was headed by M. Persigny, and composed of fanatical partisans of the Empire; the other comprising many a sincere Republican, like MM. Frédéric Degeorge, Joly, Peauger, Lieutenant Laity, and himself; that Louis Bonaparte, hauled about by the two contending factions, could not help vacillating; that allowance ought to be made for the difficulty of his position; that his intentions were upright, although they might possibly be perverted, if he were abandoned to the mischievous influence of his *imperialist* advisers, and that it was the duty of us all to prevent such a calamity. I gazed at him in astonishment, as I could hardly imagine that the establishment of the Republic should thus be made the consequence of the adoption by Louis Bonaparte of republican principles.

However, having repaired to the Château, I was ushered into a large, neatly furnished room, where little seemed to be wanting of what is required for domestic comfort. I at once perceived—let this be said to the credit of Louis Philippe—that the prisoner was very kindly treated. He sat in a high-backed arm-chair, between the chimney and a table spread with books and papers. As I entered, he rose, came forward to meet the expected visitor, and shook hands with me with a mingled expression of cordiality and reserve. My impression was that for a moment he thought of assuming a sort of stately countenance; but he was almost instantly sensible of the mistake, did his best to appear easy and free, and we got into conversation. I had never seen him before. Nor was I enabled, at that time, to remark how different he was in his features, his manners, his deportment, from all the other members of Napoleon's family, whom I did not know. But it struck me that there was nothing in him of the Napoleonic type, that he spoke with a rather foreign accent, and that he had less command of language than any man I had ever conversed with.*

As long as the conversation turned on Louis Philippe's policy, we could not but agree. We concurred in

* Immediately after my visit, I took notes of what had passed between us, so as to be sure that my memory would not play me false.

thinking that a system would not last long, which was based upon corrupt practices at home and a permanent humiliation abroad. But when the question arose what the future should be, we began to dissent.

As he professed to be a true democrat, and to acknowledge in full the principle of the sovereignty of the people :

"How is this principle to be carried out, in your opinion ? " I asked.

He answered unhesitatingly : " Through universal suffrage."

"Never was," said I, "universal suffrage more ardently advocated than by myself, as a principle. But the immediate practical results of its operation must be looked to with infinite care. You are certainly aware of the intellectual situation of the peasantry in France. You are aware that most of them abide in ignorance, and that, if we were to compute how many thousands, among the country-people do not even know how to read, the number would be something frightful. Besides, where there is a great inequality of social conditions, an independent vote is hardly to be expected from those who depend entirely on others for their daily bread and the maintenance of their families."

" Do you mean," he interrupted, " that the national will is to be disregarded, and that you have a right, if powerful enough to do so, to impose your political creed, on the strength of your conviction, upon an unwilling majority ? "

" I say nothing of the kind ; but I hold that universal suffrage must not be suffered to be a loaded pistol in the hands of a child. The sovereignty of the people does not imply the intellectual abdication of those capable of giving to their fellow-citizens, either by their speeches and their books, or by their example, an enlightened and generous impulsion. It is the duty as well as the right of all honest men to address themselves to the task of bringing over the majority to them, so as to prevent the people from being foiled at their own weapons."

" So be it."

" Well then, it is not enough for you to acknowledge the sovereignty of the people, and to bow passively to universal suffrage. You must have, as a member of the whole, a clear notion of your intended initiative; you must have, beyond your worship of universal suffrage, a political creed."

Louis Bonaparte looked a little embarrassed; but after a moment's silence : " My creed," said he, " is the Empire. Was it not the Empire that raised the French nation to the summit of greatness and glory? I am convinced that the destiny of the Empire rests on the national will."

" But the Empire involves, I suppose, the hereditary principle?"

" Yes."

" And how is it possible to reconcile the principle of the sovereignty of the people with the hereditary principle? These are contradictory terms. The latter is the negation of the former. The national will may, and it is conformable to the very nature of things that it should, change, whilst any hereditary power is theoretically immutable. It is absurd that the national will of to-day should be called upon to destroy the national will of to-morrow, and that the sovereignty of the people should be forfeited by an act of the sovereignty of the people. The fact of embracing a man in order to strangle him has nothing to do with the acknowledgment of a principle: it would be a downright treachery. A democrat is of necessity opposed to any hereditary form of government whatever. The sovereignty of the people is not, as a principle, to be confined to a given period. How could the present generation be allowed to confiscate the right of all the generations to come? A compact of that sort is in its very essence null and void."

Louis Bonaparte did not insist, as if conscious that he was playing a bad game, and there was a pause. At last, with an evident intention to turn off the conversation, "Well," he continued, " what you have just said may be true; and the main point, after all, is that the government—form it as you like—should be intent on the improvement and the happiness of the people." He then began to speak about the urgency of social reforms, and as I went on expounding my own views on the subject, he seemed to chime in with me from the beginning to the end. In fact, if I had found him greatly at fault in his declaration of opinions, in a merely political point of view, I felt almost amazed at his readiness to adopt those very principles of Socialism which he made use of afterwards to become emperor, by terrifying the ignorant into voting away their liberties. I have still in my possession a copy of his book " *Extinction du*

Pauperisme," which he composed in a strain of *Socialist*
aspirations, and which he gave me, with two flattering
lines written by himself on the first page.

I had leave for a three days' stay. They were spent
in marshalling all the various topics that had reference
either to the general state of affairs or to the particular
situation of the prisoner.

Among the circumstances present to my memory,
there is one which I think worth mentioning, as it
serves to bring out into stronger relief the hard disposition that was evinced by his subsequent conduct.
One afternoon, he was telling me the particulars of his
failure at Boulogne, when on a sudden his voice seemed
to falter; he stopped, struggled a moment to repress
a sob, and burst into tears.

The next day, we went out to take a walk over the
narrow rampart assigned to his melancholy promenade,
which was watched, of course, on all sides by sentinels.
Methinks I see him still, his head reclining, walking
with slow steps, and speaking in a low voice, as if
fearful lest the wind should bear every word he uttered
to the gaoler. The conversation now was about the
" History of the Roman Emperors," as written in a
book which Louis Bonaparte admired very much, on
account of the partiality shown by the author for
those tyrants whom Tacitus branded with everlasting
infamy. In Louis Bonaparte's opinion, Tacitus was in
the wrong, and the modern author in the right. I had
not read the book so warmly praised, but I was not at a
loss to guess the secret reason why Louis Bonaparte
praised it. So I took the opposite side of the question,

in a somewhat excited manner, which called forth on
his part a recommendation I little anticipated. "Pray,
speak low," he whispered, and turning round, he pointed
to a man, who, wrapt up in a cloak, followed at a short
distance, without losing sight of us. Louis Bonaparte
does not remember now certainly, but I do, that he
availed himself of the opportunity to expatiate on the
wretchedness of that policy which needs a dark army of
spies, takes root in the filthiest recesses of human
nature, and glories in the very degradation of its
agents.

My visit drawing near its close, I thought it my
duty to make a last appeal both to his reason and to
his heart; I said to him :—

"Remember the Empire was the Emperor. Can the
Emperor rise again? The march of time has made for
us new conditions of life. The France of our days is
no longer the France of fifty years since. The idea of
labour has outstepped the passion of battles. Other
aspirations and other wants call for other institutions
and other heroes. People have ceased placing their
ambition in blindly putting on a uniform to go to kill
and die. The question is no longer to rule and amaze
men, but to render them good and happy. No, no;
Napoleon, should he rise again, would not repeat himself. Could any one achieve with his name what he,
in our days, could not do with his genius? Were the
Empire to revive, it would only be in the shape of
a bloody meteor. Under the sway of your uncle,
despotism was at least wrapt up in the purple mantle
of military glory, and even this could not so well hide

from the nation the direful skeleton, but she became
horrified. Remember that France let Napoleon fall
because his power had grown too heavy to be borne
any longer. Had he not been abandoned by France,
he would never have met his doom at Waterloo. Remember how he died; remember where he died!
Whether it be absolutely impossible to baptise in
blood a new monarchy, and to maintain it for a time
by surrounding Paris with soldiers, by smuggling spies
everywhere, by gagging the press, by immersing
France in the abject worship of the cash-box, and
by restoring their worn-out liveries to senators and
valets, is more than I will venture to say. But what
would a sceptre be worth, held upon any such conditions? Believe me, there is really nothing acceptable in France but a Republic, provided it be true to
its principle, because the Republic is the only fit
government for a nation in whose mind the revolutionary teaching of half a century has riveted the
principle of equality. The Republic is the necessary
survivor of whatever momentary despotism circumstances may beget. Give up, then, that part of a
Pretender for which you lack a stage. Trust your
disinterestedness with the care of your destiny. Dare
to become and to declare yourself a Republican."

Not only did Louis Bonaparte lend an ear to this
my language, but he seemed impressed by it to a
degree scarcely to be expected. When I took my
leave of him, his eyes were moistened with tears, and
he clasped me in his arms so eagerly that I could not
help being moved. Descending the staircase, I heard

him cry out, with a laugh, as he stood on the landing: "Ah! ah! n'oubliez pas d'embrasser pour moi Madame Gordon," and so we parted.

From the period of my leaving Ham, until Louis Bonaparte's liberation, he occasionally communicated with me through a mutual friend, on matters purely personal, but in a way calculated to give me reason to hope he would come to the manly resolution of declaring himself Republican. This hope may be found expressed in a private letter of mine to him, which, when offering himself as a candidate for the Presidency, he published, without asking my permission, with a view to delude the Parisian workmen into voting for him.

After his escape from Ham, our relations were completely suspended. Nor did I see him when he came over to Paris at the time of the Revolution of February, and made so warm a tender of his services to the Republic, as represented by the Provisional Government.

The Assembly having met, there happened to be, for Paris, eleven vacancies to be filled up, owing to double returns on the occasion of the general election; and Louis Bonaparte came in almost at the bottom of the list, at the head of which figured the name of Marc Caussidière. I have already stated how the Executive Commission was induced to bring in a decree for the maintenance of that law by which the Bonaparte family was not allowed to return to France, whilst I, from a sense of justice, of true policy, and entirely irrespective of any personal leaning, insisted upon all laws of proscription being cancelled.* The result of my interference would have been to baffle his views by putting the Presidency beyond his reach, had my proposition been taken into consideration in all its bearings; but the Assembly having afterwards foolishly written in the Constitution that there should be a President of the Republic, his amazing fortune turned out to be the consequence of his being allowed to return to France, for which thus, by the most strange chain of unexpected circumstances, he was, in fact, greatly indebted to me.

However, he had not yet availed himself of the decree which entitled him to go and take his seat in the National Assembly, when, ostracised myself after having done my best to save from ostracism both the Bonaparte and the Orléans families, I came over to London, where I arrived in the beginning of September.

Louis Bonaparte was still living in England.

Scarcely had I put up at the Brunswick Hotel, Jermyn Street, when a visitor was announced. It was Louis Bonaparte. He came to me in the most friendly manner, expressing how indignant he felt at the iniquitous treatment I had experienced from men, whom I remember he spoke of with anything but kindness.

This considerably embarrassed me. I could not repel the civilities he loaded me with, unless determined to set all propriety at defiance; and, on the other hand, there were public grounds which prompted

* See Chapter XVI.

me to avoid having any connexion with him. That he detected this feeling, which I took no greater pains to conceal than was strictly requisite to keep within the bounds of good breeding, I have every reason to suppose, for he showed himself very anxious to impress me with the idea that he had no other ambition than to serve the Republic; that he was heartily devoted to the cause of the people; and that, on social questions especially, his opinions were, to a great extent, in accordance with my own.

In the first of the celebrated letters of "An Englishman," published in the *Times*, December 20, 1851, I read:—

"If this man's (Louis Bonaparte) reign is destined to continue, even for a brief duration, the world will witness the most heterogeneous jumble of despotism and demagogy, of socialism and corruption, that history has ever chronicled. The bribery of Walpole; the theories of labour of Louis Blanc; the stock-jobbing of the worst days of Louis Philippe; the ferocity of Alva; the deportations of the Czar; the razzias of Algeria, will all meet in one marvellous system of anarchy that will be called Imperial Government."

With all due deference, both to the *Times* of 1851, and to the most eloquent author of the letters of "An Englishman," I am bound to decline the honour conferred upon me, by having my "theories of labour," ranked, in the Imperial programme, between the "bribery of Walpole," and the "stock-jobbing of the worst days of Louis Philippe." To whatever extent the prophecy of "An Englishman" may have been fulfilled,

I trust he will himself confess that his foresight has been at fault, as far as my "theories of labour" are concerned.

Of the many measures the Imperial policy will have to account for, there is one only which can possibly be traced to any views of mine, it is that which refers to the system of direct and national loans, substituted for the ruinous practice of public loans through the medium of private bankers. Long ago, when at the head of a daily paper, the *Bon Sens*, I started the question which led to a public discussion between the celebrated banker, M. Jacques Laffitte and myself, a discussion that was carried on in the columns of the *Bon Sens*, lasted several days, and attracted considerable notice.

But, with this solitary exception, hardly imputable to anything else than a pressing want of money, Louis Bonaparte cannot justly be accused of having made his case worse, by adding the "theories of labour of Louis Blanc," or any other unpardonable sin of the kind, to "the bribery of Walpole, the stock-jobbing of the worst days of Louis Philippe, the ferocity of Alva, the deportations of the Czar, and the razzias of Algeria."*

However this may be, the language held to me by Louis Bonaparte in London, was so far from implying the *Empire*, that, whenever I bring together what I heard then and what I have seen since, the impression produced on my mind is exactly that of a dream.

Yet, even at the time I speak of, I placed no confi-

---

* The *Times* of the 20th of December, 1851.

dence whatever in Louis Bonaparte; nor were any of the circumstances of his sojourn here, of a nature to inspire me with any such feeling.

One day that I had gone to a dinner-party at Richmond, as I was returning home late in the evening—I was then living in Piccadilly—I found the house all in a bustle. The landlady, much excited, ran up to me, saying: "Sir, some serious event has just occurred in Paris, I suppose. How strange!" On my inquiring what all this meant, "A young gentleman," she continued, "called a few minutes ago, asking after you. I answered, of course, that you were not in; but he would not believe me. He looked in a state of extraordinary agitation, insisted upon the absolute necessity of seeing you immediately, and, despite all my remonstrances, rushed up-stairs, in order to ascertain whether you were really out; which done, he seemed, at first, disposed to wait for you; but, on second thoughts, he made up his mind to go, leaving this." I took a card she was holding out to me, on which the following words were hurriedly written: "At whatever hour of the night you may come back, pray come to the Hôtel du Prince de Galles, Leicester Square, without losing a moment. The affair at hand is of paramount importance, and admits of no delay."

Such a kind of invitation, to such a public place, as may well be imagined, seemed to me very singular; and I felt very little inclined to comply with the mysterious request. Still, my curiosity could not fail to be awakened. The situation in France was then quite unsettled. Changes of some sort or other were expected from day to day. Perhaps, a communication of real importance had to be made to me: why not satisfy myself about it? The urgency of the case appeared the more probable, from the fact of its being late at night, and a wild stormy night too. I went.

At the appointed place, there stood in groups some strangers, whose busy gathering struck me at once as something very suspicious. I was immediately ushered into a room on the ground-floor, where I found myself in the presence of two persons, one of whom was an exceedingly young-looking man, and the other Louis Bonaparte. Without allowing me time to express my astonishment, the young man broke out into a desultory speech to the effect, that he had just come from Lille, where he had had a most decisive interview, he said, with some influential members of the Republican party there; that the democratic leaders and the adherents of the Prince—" du Prince "—were playing into each other's hands; in a word, that everything was ready, in France, for the triumph of the people, as represented by the nephew of the Emperor. One may well conceive what I felt. The age of the speaker, the place, the hour, the groups on the threshold of the hotel, and, above all, the nature of the communication made to such a man as I was known to be, all this was so extraordinary, that I would not listen to one word more, that I would not stay one minute longer; and I instantly retired, with a mingled feeling of indignation and amazement. The next day, Louis Bonaparte called upon me; he hastened to say how sorry he was for what had happened; he affirmed that he had absolutely nothing to do with it, having been drawn to the " Hôtel du Prince de Galles," in the same way as myself. But I had seen and heard more than enough to shrink from any further intercourse with him, on whatever ground or pretext. Shortly after, he left for Paris; and, from that moment, he became personally as much a stranger to me as if I had never chanced to meet him.

I can hardly advert to the stay of Louis Bonaparte in this country, without thinking of poor Count d'Orsay, in whom I found so warm a friend, that he could not have shown me more affection, had he been my brother. How far he blinded himself, at least for a while, as regards Louis Bonaparte, what services he rendered him, and in what manner those services were requited, is a matter of public notoriety. But this much I will say, that d'Orsay, with his fine intelligence and his generous heart, was not the man to make what he considered to be the honour and the good of his country, subservient either to his own private interest, or to any motive merely personal. There are in my hands many letters of his which he wrote to me from Paris, and all of them bear testimony to his unreserved disapprobation, both of the policy of Louis Bonaparte, and of the course taken by the parliamentary leaders of the Legislative Assembly. No man, for instance, saw with more indignation and contempt the sending of French soldiers to Rome, there to crush the Roman Republic. Here is a letter he wrote to me on the subject, which I am glad to

publish, as it does honour to him in every respect.   So
thoroughly French it is in its style, that I prefer to
give it in the original :

" Ah, mon cher ami,—Si vous saviez combien je fais
de mauvais sang dans ce sacré pays ! J'ai la France
en moi, et j'ai beau me retourner de tous les cotés,
je ne la vois pas.   Vous vous êtes imaginé que j'allais
gagner ici la gangrène politique, mais je suis vingt fois
plus ici ce que j'étais à Londres.   Oui, je suis de votre
avis en tout ce que vous me dites dans votre lettre.
Mais que vous semble de l'étonnante imbécillité de
l'expédition italienne?   Cette fois-ci, les oies du capitole
riront bien des Gaulois.   La République se faisant le
premier *soldat du pape !*   Je disais à Lamartine que
la Révolution perdait sa virginité par cette intervention.   Enfin, les bétises s'entassent les unes sur les
autres.   Le diable emporte les imbécilles !   Seulement,
il aura diablement à faire !   Au revoir.   Mille amitiés
de ces dames. Et croyez-moi toujours votre affectionné,
                                     " D'Orsay."

CONCLUSION.

— ◆ —

HERE terminates the narrative of the events in which
I was called upon to take part. While retracing my
steps in this rough and thorny path, it has been my
endeavour to refrain from letting my feelings break
out, and speak louder than my reason. If any bitter
word has slipped uncontrolled from my pen, let it
be ascribed to the involuntary revival of my past
emotions; for my heart is, at present, entirely free
from bitterness. Protracted misfortune has inured me
to patient hopes; it has half-healed the long-bleeding
wound of my wrongs. As strongly as ever do I hate
violence and injustice; but having been removed for
so many years from the tempestuous scene of political
conflicts, I have come to form a more placid judgment
of my enemies, and more clearly to discern in their
doings, what is to be imputed to prejudice—to ignorance—to the impulse of the moment—nay, to motives
deemed honourable, owing to the aptness of the human
mind to disguise from itself the true nature of its
promptings.

Moreover, the sufferings I had to go through are as
nothing, compared to those of so many victims of our
civil discords. Nor did the men who treated so

harshly my friends and myself escape a retribution, the fruit of their own acts; the persecutors having been persecuted; the proscribers, proscribed; and those who had trampled upon us, under pretence that "*society ought to be saved*," having been, precisely under the same pretence, trampled upon in their turn.

How this occurred I will briefly state, not from any low feeling of triumphant revenge, but because the fact is pregnant with this solemn instruction, that no party is sure, when violating the eternal laws of justice and liberty, that the time will not come for it to stand in need of their protection.

Amongst the various circumstances which led to Imperial despotism, one must be particularly mentioned as having exercised the most mischievous influence; I mean the establishment of the league known in France as *Rue de Poitiers*. This league of the *Rue de Poitiers*, composed of all the leaders of the reactionist party, like M. de Montalembert, M. Thiers, &c., and respecting which Count d'Orsay once wrote to me from Paris: "*La rue de Poitiers est le vrai choléra de Paris*," opened, at the time of Louis Bonaparte's presidency, a subscription whose object, they said, was to "save society," and by means of which they succeeded in collecting nearly forty thousand pounds.

This enormous sum was avowedly spent to a shilling in printing and circulating every variety of libels against Socialism. In these flying sheets, profusely distributed, and given away in every town, in every village, even to the remotest hamlets, whosoever was guilty of the crime of desiring any amelioration pro-

fitable to the people, was christened "*Communist!*"
and to be *Communist*, in these libels, was to pant
for the equal division of land and an Agrarian law,
although the Communists, on the contrary, supported
the principle of large farms; — it was to advocate
promiscuous concubinage, although the Communists
earnestly defended the principle of marriage;—it was
to aim at the overthrow of religion, although the Communists had laid down as the basis of their social
economy the very moral of the GOSPEL;—it was to
be men of violence and terror, although there were
amongst them some who carried out their peace principles even to excess.* — A doctrine of the Com-

* M. Cabet, for instance, who, from principle, was opposed to any use
of physical force.

As French Socialism has, in this country, been made a "raw head and
bloody bones" affair, which, in the eyes of a certain number of Englishmen, amounts to a sort of justification of the *coup d'état* and its consequences, the following anecdote will do something, I hope, towards
dispelling this absurd and mischievous misapprehension.

I was, one day, discussing with Pierre Leroux, in presence of some of
our common friends, the question of the moral lawfulness of war and
physical resistance to oppression. I expressed the opinion that these were
undoubtedly most deplorable evils, which it should be the greatest task of
humanity to endeavour to suppress, but to which it would be necessary to
have recourse in extreme cases, as long as the causes of oppression and
war were not removed. Whereupon, Pierre Leroux contended that there
were only two doctrines between which thoughtful men, friends of
humanity, had to choose : that of Mahomet, which opposes evil by means
derived, as the use of the sword, from evil itself; and that of Zoroaster,
which opposes evil merely by good. Of these, he said, the latter was his
doctrine, and the only effective one, in the way of real progress. I then
put this case to him : "You think yourself, surely, useful to your
fellow-men by your writings, your ideas, your examples. Well, suppose
you are in a position in which you must lose your life, or defend it against
a murderous attack from some one you believe to be a monster, and whose
very existence you are conscious is a curse to humanity ; what would you

munists was, that all children, after having for a certain number of years, nestled under their mothers' wing, should be admitted to enjoy the benefits of public education, at the expense of society,—a good education bestowed upon all being at least as much a matter of public concern as the maintenance of an army : on that doctrine the lying and monstrous accusation was grafted that the Communists were bent on destroying the family. They had described as the still distant but desirable result of the gradual improvements suggested by science, a social order, in which all the advantages to be derived from the practice of association should be made available, such as common rooms for reception, for recreation, for reading—on the principle actually carried out at the brünnen in Germany, at the thermal establishments in the Pyrenees, in the grand hotels of our cities, in the clubs of London;—but in which, of course, every individual should preserve his independence, his personality, the freedom of his affections, the choice of his friends, his own domestic interior, his own hearth, an inviolable sanctuary. Who could ever have imagined that this would be enough, and more than enough, for a text to the incredibly slanderous state-

---

do ?" He unhesitatingly replied : " It being known that I die for my principle, I should suffer myself to be killed, thoroughly convinced that I should thus serve my cause better than in any other way."—" Then your only means of opposing evil in such a case of self-defence would be . . ." he interrupted : " Martyrdom !"

This is the Socialist leader whom Lord Normanby, speaking of his election as representative of the people for Paris, calls a *" violent demagogue !"*

ment that the Communists had in view I know not what abominable amalgam of confusion.

Unfortunately, this unparalleled system of misrepresentation was promoted by two circumstances: First, by the complexion of the word *Communism*—an expression deplorably selected, as it seemed to imply the idea of promiscuousness, and which was most rashly employed before its precise signification had come to the knowledge of the public; and, secondly, by the power of the traducers, compared with the feeble resources of the traduced. Two or three journals of a very limited circulation, a few books of a very confined publicity, this was all the Communists had to oppose to the most formidable propaganda of falsehood ever organised.

Irresistible, therefore, was the effect of those pamphlets which, issued from the *Rue de Poitiers,* spread all over France like an inundation. Strange enough! The word *Communist,* expressive as it was of a doctrine absolutely and essentially opposed to whatever, nearly or remotely, resembled Agrarianism, was made a synonym of Agrarian law. A powerful PARTI DE PARTAGEUX was *supposed* to exist in the provinces. Many honourable but ill-informed men got sincerely alarmed. Others, clinging to old abuses, were glad to be supplied with a screen for their real and selfish fears. It was given out that the coming elections, in 1852, would be the signal for pillage and murder.

Such gloomy forebodings, however insane, could not fail to secure the energetic support of the *Bourgeoisie* to the reactionists composing the majority of the Legislative Assembly, in their desperate war against all the last vestiges of the Revolution of February; and they availed themselves of the circumstance, not only to destroy universal suffrage, but to disarm the people of Paris; that is, to suppress the very force which, in case of a *coup d'état*, might have effectually protected them. To fill the measure of suicidal blunders, it now only remained to put the army under the direct command of Louis Bonaparte. This being done, there was an end of the parliamentary system. Both the pretext and the means of " *saving society* " had been furnished to the President by the apostles of the great crusade preached, from the *Rue de Poitiers*, against the Socialists. What was the consequence? That Louis Bonaparte hastened to make use of his power to crush those from whom he had received it for other purposes; and that he proceeded to " *save society,*" after his own fashion, by crushing the Assembly, dispersing its members, gagging the press, trampling on a once self-dependent nation, substituting for the fear of unsifted ideas, the much less chimerical fear of the sabre, and creating an unmistakeably real system of permanent terror out of a bugbear!

> " The engineer was hoist with his own petard."

A few words more.

It is now many years since I wrote at the conclusion of my *History of Ten Years* the following lines :—

" God forbid that we should despair of our country. There are nations stiff and inflexible, as it were, who may not inaptly be compared to the heavy cavaliers of the middle ages, cased all in iron; those men were hard to wound through their thick armour, but once brought to the ground, they could not rise again. Very different is France, whose strength is combined with marvellous suppleness, and who seems ever young. What unexampled, indescribable fatigue has she not resisted! From 1789 to 1815 she has gone through fits of intestine wrath, and endured sufferings, and accomplished labours, sufficient to exhaust the most vigorous nation. Well, not only did she not die for all that, but in 1830, after fifteen years of apparent lassitude, her blood was found to have been renovated. And, indeed, France bears within her wherewith to astonish men under various and unforeseen aspects. She is made to live many successive lives, always unexhausted and unconquerable. Why should we be discouraged? The evil springs from an error that may be repaired. Will the *Bourgeoisie* persist in its infatuation? Can it possibly persevere in distrusting as an enemy the people which it is bound to guide and to defend? Those deceive, and are preparing to enslave, the Bourgeoisie, who urge it to this desperate course. It has been made over-afraid of the working-classes, better to be blinded to the sense of its real dangers. They are not so much at its feet as above and around its head. Let it look to this!"

These words contained two prophecies, the one of happy, the other of sinister import; and both of them have been accomplished. In the first place, the Revolution of 1848 came to prove how much of life and energy there still remained in France; and, again, the success of the *coup d'état* of December was a direful demonstration of the perils and the calamities the *Bourgeoisie* was sure to bring upon itself, whenever induced to separate its cause from that of the people. Whilst the working-classes, insulted every day by the so-called *" Saviours of Society,"* robbed of universal suffrage, and baptised *"vile multitude,"* were taught to dread the impending dictatorship of General Changarnier as the most terrible scourge they had to dread, the middle-classes, on their side, shuddered at the looming image of the elections of 1852, and, flying aghast from an imaginary phantom of anarchy, reached the brink of a yawning abyss—the abyss of military despotism.

So was the *coup d'état* of December made, not only possible but easy. There was no need, for its success, of deep calculation, of plans long matured and skilfully framed; there was no need of cleverness: the only thing required was that the man in whose hands all the forces of the State had been foolishly concentrated, should be one of those men who are fettered by no scruple, trammelled by no respect for justice, and determined to shrink, in the attainment of their object, from no kind of violence. Now, thanks to French administrative centralisation, Paris once manacled, France could not fail to be enslaved.

Nor can the maintenance of the Empire to this day be ascribed to the skill of the Imperial *ruler.* It certainly requires a great deal of talent and a high intelligence successfully to govern a mighty nation, despite any such impediments as may be created by the liberty of the press, the fact of every political step being submitted to parliamentary control, the free and public discussion of all the schemes devised, the disclosure of all the blunders committed, and the necessity of observing the laws of the country as well as the principles of justice. But where no such impediments are to be dealt with, the task of governing is one to which the first comer is equal, provided he may have at his disposal a sufficient number of police spies and bayonets. In these cases, brute force supplies the deficiency of genius. Let, therefore, the low-minded worshippers of success kneel down before the Empire; let them call "a great man" him whose greatness consists in the permanent violation of all that is held sacred amongst men; let them, after mistaking might for right, mistake also the power of the sword for that of the mind, and the efficiency of an unopposed will for the triumph of a keen intellect—pitiful as misconceptions of this kind may be, they are hardly to be wondered at, so little are most men capable of forming a sound judgment of anything that glitters:

> "Through tatter'd clothes small vices do appear;
> Robes and furr'd gowns hide all. Plate sin with gold,
> And the strong lance of justice hurtless breaks;
> Arm it in rags, a pigmy's straw does pierce it."

But the time is not far distant, when, the play being over, the actors, stripped of their gilt fripperies, and no longer painted, will appear to all what they really are, and France also will appear what she really is. The increasing terror by which Louis Bonaparte is preyed upon, while spreading it everywhere, and his frantic efforts to prevent France from moving, speaking, whispering, breathing, are decisive proofs that he feels the ground quiver, that he sees it yawn. And who could, indeed, imagine that the genius of France is vanished, that her pulse has ceased to beat, that her lofty aspirations are for ever, or even momentarily, stifled? No. She is forced into silence, but her silence is thoughtful. Beneath the icy surface, the stream flows uninterrupted. The lamp has been for a while put under a bushel, but it continues burning inextinguishable.

THE END.